THE FORMATION OF THE BIBLE

The Formation of the Bible

History of the Sacred Writings of the People of God

BY Georges Auzou PROFESSOR OF SACRED SCRIPTURE AT THE GRAND SEMINAIRE OF ROUEN/PUBLISHED BY B. Herder Book Co. SAINT LOUIS AND LONDON

This book is a translation of *La Tradition Biblique,* by Georges Auzou, published by Editions de l'Orante, Paris, 1957.
The English version is by Josefa Thornton.

IMPRIMATUR:
✠ Joseph Cardinal Ritter
Archbishop of St. Louis
September 13, 1963

15 & 17 South Broadway, St. Louis 2, Missouri
London: 2/3 Doughty Mews, W.C. 1

Library of Congress Catalog Number: 63-22743
Printed in the United States of America
by Vail-Ballou Press, Inc., Binghamton, New York
Designed by Klaus Gemming

INTRODUCTION

Although it will be a difficult task to accomplish, the purpose of this book, which was stated in the preceding volume of this series, is simple: to present a "history of the composition of the biblical writings. This history will establish the position of these writings in relation to one another and above all in their original and living environment, that is, their position in the life which is in fact their most clarifying explanation" (*The Word of God,* p. 11).[1]

The plan of the book is determined by the history itself, whose course will be followed from remote antiquity down to the end of the first Christian century. We must, however, begin with the dawning of Eastern civilizations; they are the soil in which the transmission of the Bible has its distant roots (Jos. 24:2-4; Deut. 26:5) and with which it has remained in contact. When Israel acquires a historical identity, it becomes the center of interest; nevertheless, the countries that surround it and the nations that are its contemporaries continue to constitute the environment in which it lives. Thus, they form part of its history.

We need not be surprised to discover that the books of the Bible, even in their ancient form, did not appear as such in the beginning. A written biblical literature was prepared for from the beginning by a living tradition, from which it sprang and in which it continually took shape. In our account, the history of the men involved and of the writings will be generally interwoven, according as events happened; sometimes, however, especially toward the end, it will be necessary, for convenience and clarity, to speak first of the historical setting and then of the writings. The final writings, those produced at the end of the apostolic era, may appropriately take the place of a conclusion.

In this second stage of our "approaches" to the Bible, the ques-

[1] References to this book will be given hereafter under the simplified form *WG* with the page number.

tion is less one of coming to a conclusion than one of being brought to a beginning of the task. After becoming orientated in this way—cognizant of the development of the sacred literature as a whole, capable at last of placing each of the books of the Bible, at least summarily, in its chronological order and in its original setting—we shall be able to apply ourselves to the study of one or another of these books. May it please God that we can consider many of them! At this third stage a "knowledge of the Bible" is really established.

A historical presentation of the formation of the Bible has been made possible by the many studies which have been carried on for decades. The Ancient Near East and, more particularly, the "biblical environment" are now fairly well known. Moreover, a biblical writing whose text and style have not been studied, whose origins have not been investigated, and whose content and message has not been analyzed no longer exists. Our purpose, that of presenting a comprehensive view which will be useful for beginners, is not, therefore, inspired by temerity, nor does it aim at originality.

Since the appearance of the encyclical *Divino Afflante,*[2] a climate of serenity and of relative security have characterized the field of biblical work, which has resulted in serious and stimulating meditation on the Word of God. Practically unanimous agreement has been reached on many questions, although a certain number have not yet been resolved. Among the solutions proposed, some are only a stage on the way, and sometimes only a hypothesis. Archeology, history, literary studies, and exegesis are always at work.

Our history, then, does not claim to plot a course in so vast and complex a field, nor does it aspire to be decisive or definitive. Most of the positions adopted are those we believe to be common today or on the way to becoming so. They are often fully guaranteed by the authority of the masters and the competence of specialists, as well as by the agreement of these groups with one another. But here again it is appropriate to have a spirit of investigation rather than a desire for decision. From time to time our hesitations will be noticed. Whenever possible, explanations or reasons will be given,

[2] Cf. *WG*, pp. 119-20. The passage of this encyclical which is quoted there condemns attacks and suspicions against "everything new" and proclaims that the great and true liberty of investigation left by the Church to valiant exegetical workers deserves constant rereading and meditation.

but one can easily understand that they can be fully provided and sufficiently detailed only by a special study of each book, and not in this general presentation.

A history such as this is heavily indebted to many authors. To cite all the works used would mean drawing up a bibliography known only to specialists and useless to those to whom this volume wishes to be of service. On the other hand, it may be appropriate either to recommend or simply to indicate the works that will help the less-informed readers to supplement what is said only in a cursory way.[3] These are principally works on history, religions, and civilizations, as well as works on Israel and on early Christianity. Understandably, the time is not yet ripe for citing studies on the individual books of the Bible, although those who wish to have a more complete introduction to each inspired book may have recourse to the fascicles of the Jerusalem Bible (Cerf), which have appeared during the last ten years.

Gratitude could be expressed for each page of the present volume; it is impossible to say to how many scholars and specialists, historians and exegetes, who are usually not mentioned, it is indebted. Nevertheless, it is indebted especially to the masters and students who have brought about, in our times, such a vital biblical renewal. The students of the Grand Séminaire de Rouen are also entitled to a special expression of gratitude; without them, without their encouraging demands and their ardor to know the Word of God, this book would not exist.

[3] One can easily find, for example at the end of most Bibles published in recent years (see also the works indicated in the note on p. 37), geographical maps, either of the Near East or of Palestine, as well as chronological, synoptic, or other tables whose consultation may be useful in the course of the history we are reviewing. We intend, moreover, to bring out a collection of texts, documents, maps, and reference notes which will illustrate this history and so facilitate the knowledge of the Bible.

CONTENTS

INTRODUCTION, V

1 THE ORIGINAL SETTING
One: The Ancient Mesopotamians, 1.
Two: The Egypt of the Ancient and Middle Empires, 11.
Three: The Thought and Language of the Ancient Orient, 19.

2 THE PATRIARCHAL ERA
One: The Land and the Men of Canaan, 33.
Two: The Patriarchs, 41.

3 THE DIVINE COVENANT
One: The Emancipation, 49.
Two: The People God Took for Himself, 57.

4 THE LAND AND THE KINGDOM
One: The Occupation of Canaan, 67.
Two: The King Chosen by God, 76.
Three: Beginnings of a Literature, 84.

5 THE PROPHETIC ERA
One: Beginnings of the Two Kingdoms, 91.
Two: The Ancestral Traditions, 98.
Three: The Prophets, 108.
Four: The Prophetic Word, 116.
Five: Scribes and Singers, 125.

6 THE GREAT TRIBULATION
One: The Lions' Den, 131.
Two: Discovery of a Book, 135.
Three: Witness Torn Asunder, 142.
Four: The Catastrophe, 148.

7 THE REMNANT
One: The Face of the World Changes, 153.
Two: A New Israel, 159.
Three: The Great Torah, 170.

8 THE JUDAIC COMMUNITY
One: Back from Exile, 179.
Two: The Work of Reformation, 186.
Three: The Great Literature of the Poets and Sages, 193.
Four: Israelite Life from the Fourth to the Third Centuries, 204.

9 FACING A NEW WORLD
One: Alexander and the Hellenization of the Orient, 211.
Two: From the Revolt of the Machabees to the Kingdom of Herod, 221.
Three: The Struggle of the Writers, 230.

10 THE CRITICAL ERA
One: The Graeco-Roman World, 245.
Two: Israel in the Roman Empire, 257.
Three: The Jewish Community, 266.
Four: The Faith of Israel, 278.

11 THE NEW COVENANT
One: Jesus, 287.
Two: The Church, 296.
Three: Christian Life, 314.

12 THE MESSAGE OF THE WITNESSES
One: The Evangelical Tradition, 321.
Two: Paul and the Letters to the Communities, 328.
Three: The Gospels, 345.
Four: John and the End of the Apostolic Era, 354.

INDEX, 367

1 The Original Setting

[ONE]

THE ANCIENT MESOPOTAMIANS[1] | Men do not seem to have occupied the marshy regions of the southern valley of the Euphrates and the Tigris much before the fourth millennium.[2] When they came from the mountainous plateaus of the north, as they undoubtedly did, they speedily turned the natural advantages of that humid valley, which was subject to inundation by the two great rivers, to good account by digging canals and building dikes. The intelligent irrigation of the dry plains rapidly transformed Babylonia into orchards, vegetable gardens, and grain fields. This transformation, which was to last for three or four thousand years, provided the setting for a severe and superior human society.

The physical situation gave rise to the political state. The systems of irrigation had to be coordinated, supervised, and constantly maintained. This was a matter of life or death for the whole country, especially because the floods were not predictable as they are in Egypt. Neighbors and villages and cities were forced to unite. Peace and prosperity prevailed during times when the entire network was under the control of a single strong central state.

About the year 4000 B.C. the people were not Semites by race.

[1] For Mesopotamian history and civilization, consult the following: V. Gordon Childe, *New Light on the Ancient East: The Oriental Prelude to European Prehistory* (New York: Appleton Century, 1934); G. Contenau, *Everyday Life in Babylon and Assyria* (London: Arnold, 1954); Samuel N. Kramer, *History Begins at Sumer* (New York: Doubleday Anchor Book, 1959); H. G. May, *et al.*, editors, *Oxford Bible Atlas* (London: Oxford University Press, 1962); H.W.F. Saggs, *The Greatness that was Babylon* (New York: Hawthorne Books, 1962).

[2] It is not necessary to go back to prehistory: the information it provides is too indefinite and much too remote for our purpose. However, the fact must not be overlooked that the Near East and especially Palestine, where important remains of prehistoric man and many stone-age implements of great antiquity have been discovered, are particularly favored regions for the study of the first identifiable stages of human existence on earth.

Their origin, which may have been northern and Asiatic, is unknown. They were the *Sumerians.*

The advanced and superior civilization they had created, which appeared all at once in full flower, was to exert a profound influence. Placid in their manners, the Sumerians were devoted to the practice of agriculture and were organized into a kind of association of cities, each having its monarch.

The Sumerian religion was characterized by the worship of the gods of fertility and of fecundity, by the practice of sacrifice, and by divination. The source of religious traditions we will meet later on can already be seen in the Sumerian cult.

The Sumerian language was the only written language in Mesopotamia for a thousand years. Its written form, now called cuneiform,[3] was in use for three thousand years. The successors of the Sumerians—first the Akkadians and then the Babylonians and the Assyrians—spoke a different language, but they adopted the same writing and did not develop the alphabet. It should be noted that the continuity and stability of cuneiform writing for tens of centuries was due to a solid and highly influential institution in the ancient East: the *scribate.* The scribes, specialized scholars in the knowledge of writing, grammar, and literature, always constituted a powerful body that kept and faithfully preserved the deposit of knowledge and of traditions.

During the third millennium, the Semites who were called "Akkadians," from the name of the capital they had established (Akkad or Agadé), came in waves from the northwest. Originally, perhaps,

[3] The invention of cuneiform writing dates from about 3500-3300 B.C. It was ideographic in origin, that is, it had as its principle a stylized representation of the realities to be expressed: living beings or material objects, and, by derivation or association, the actions, feelings, and ideas evoked. If, unlike the Egyptian, it withdrew rapidly and completely from a representation of visible objects, this fact was due to the materials used; when writing with a hard point on tablets of clay, continuous lines cannot be drawn without blurring them. The reed stylus lends itself especially to the making of small nail- or wedge-shaped strokes, from which cuneiform writing gets its name. The scribe used these characters, arranging them in various ways, and thus composed the conventional signs which corresponded to what he would have drawn. The system, complicated and difficult at first, became simpler as it was perfected. In a few centuries, instead of the some nine hundred signs originally needed, it was possible to get along with about three hundred. Syllabic writing was a later discovery; in it, signs no longer express whole words, but rather various sounds or phonetic units, independently of the meaning.

they came from the southern regions of Arabia. They settled farther upstream than the Sumerians in the fertile valley, and progressively enriched themselves with the Sumerian culture, which, on the whole, was superior to theirs.

Their presence, however, was not conducive to peace, for Lower Mesopotamia was still only a scattering of cities each of which was ambitious to dominate the rest. Historians have acquired the habit of designating as a "dynasty" the period during which this or that city succeeded in maintaining its dominance. Newcomers merely increased, if they did not create, the divisions and the rivalries. Consequently, nothing significant remains of that epoch except the incessant struggles between the cities or small cantons of Sumer and Akkad.

In the meantime, other Semites reached Syria; there, they joined those whom the Greeks were to call "Phoenicians." These were Dravidians who came from the western coast of India.[4] Men of the sea, they had established commercial branches on the Syrian coast. As the centuries passed, they became amalgamated with the Semites, especially the Canaanites.

The Phoenicians are found on the scene as early as 2800 B.C.; Tyre was founded about 2750 B.C. The Phoenician population was remarkably intelligent and active, and admirably equipped for industry and art, as well as for navigation and international trade. Phoenicia was not organized into a state according to the true meaning of the term, but into a kind of confederation of independent cities: the great ports of Tyre, Sidon, Beruta (Beirut), Byblos, Arwad, and Ugarit. Close relations were had, of course, with Egypt, which needed Phoenician wood[5] particularly, and which at that time imposed its tutelage on all of its Mediterranean neighbors.

Not much is known of the *Hellas* of the third millennium. Before 2400 B.C., a Cretan civilization named for Minos, a legendary king, spread through the Cyclades into Cyprus, and even into Egypt. While Crete grew in power and flourished, a coarse but clever group of Indo-Europeans, the Achaeans, came down from the

[4] During the third millennium an extensive civilization had developed in the valley of the Indus, only to disappear with the passing of the same period.

[5] The famous forests, particularly cedar forests, covered the slopes of the Lebanese mountains at that time.

Balkans, about the year 2000 B.C., and overran the Greek peninsula for a long period of time, settling among the pre-Hellenes. A few centuries later, after having learned many things from the Cretans who were so industrious and so refined, they had the audacity to set out to sea to annihilate all that the Minoans had accomplished, destroying Cnossos, the beautiful capital of the island. Then they established the earliest Greek civilization in the Peloponnesus—the Mycenean civilization, which was destroyed by the Dorians in the twelfth century.

In Mesopotamia, Semite superiority was finally established with the hegemony of Akkad and especially the reign of the powerful Sargon the Elder, about the year 2400 B.C. King Sargon, whose rule has become legendary, reigned over the earliest known empire in history; one which extended from the Persian Gulf to the Mediterranean.

At the beginning of the twenty-second century, the region was invaded by the Guti, barbarians who were themselves driven on by Aryan barbarians descending from the north. The destructive and retrogressive domination of the Guti prevailed in Sumer and in Akkad.

A Sumerian named Gudea, however, became the monarch of a great kingdom at Lagash at the beginning of the twenty-first century. Toward the end of the third millenium the Sumerians again became the strong and controlling element, certain "dynasties" or city-states becoming particularly powerful. A notable example was Ur, the homeland of Abraham. Ur, which had a population exceeding half a million, won regional dominance on several occasions. In the twenty-second and twenty-first centuries, before being ruined and brought into subjection, it enjoyed a period of almost imperial splendor and of great economic prosperity, with a style of urban living that was already far advanced.

During the twenty-first and twentieth centuries, the city of Babylon grew; triumphing over its competitors, it attained its apogee in the nineteenth or eighteenth century, under the celebrated Hammurabi, who was simultaneously a great conqueror, an excellent administrator, a distinguished lawgiver,[6] a patron of artists, and a famous builder.

The Hammurabic epoch was more or less contemporaneous with

[6] With regard to his "Code," cf. p. 10, note 15.

that of Abraham.[7] A herdsman of the steppes, with the ways of a Bedouin sheik, he was acquainted with a highly refined world: impressive artistic developments; varied and far-reaching social legislation; an intellectual life rich with great traditions; and a religious life which, though polytheistic, was powerful and serious.

A period of prosperity is not necessarily synonymous with a period of lasting peace. On the contrary, we know that this period experienced internal conflicts and persecutions. An ancient cuneiform tablet states that under one of the monarchs who preceded Hammurabi "there was a great massacre at Ur." [8] Also certain is the fact that Babylon's superiority carried with it the obligation of seeing to it that the other Mesopotamian cities recognized the sovereignty of Marduk, god of Babylon, above their own gods. If this recognition was not freely accepted, it was imposed by force of arms. Furthermore, families and clans who desired to reach quieter regions or to preserve their freedom, departed.

The Babylonia leadership was followed by a period of disorders for the region of the Euphrates, of a kind that were prevalent almost everywhere at that time. The eighteenth and seventeenth centuries were in fact marked by the great Aryan invasions from the north, which shook the whole of the Near East: warlike Hittites on the plateaus of Asia Minor and in Syria; Kassites in Babylonia, where their dynasty prevailed for several centuries, exerting a profound influence; and Horites (Hurrians) in Upper Mesopotamia. Assyria, a vassal of Babylon to the north, attempted to emancipate itself and established a short-lived empire.

Thus, for twenty-five centuries a large and active population, whose *civilization* was highly advanced, lived and developed in Lower Mesopotamia. It was massed in large cities or spread out in their suburbs. The crops of the entirely irrigated region provided support for the country. Clans of cattle raisers either roamed about

[7] A relative uncertainty still exists with regard to the date of Hammurabi's reign; some authorities place it in the twentieth century; others think it came in the following century; and some even put it as late as the seventeenth. Moreover, it is not absolutely certain that Abraham was contemporaneous with his reign (as some suggest, believing that his name was based on the similarity between the name of Hammurabi and that of Amraphel in Gen. 14:1).

[8] Text mentioned in *Le Milieu biblique I,* by C. F. Jean (Geuthner, 1922), p. 25.

or settled down on the outskirts. These men, Amorites or Arameans,[9] came from the neighboring deserts and lived in tents. In the cities, highly developed artisan industries employed many men. The bartering and circulation of goods led to an important commerce. A genuine urbanity of manners was evident in the display, for example, of hospitality and courtesy. In his own way, Abraham bore witness to this (cf. Gen. 18:1-5).

Essentially, science was learned through divine "revelation," although it was also the object of experimental observation. Scientific study was the privilege of a caste, the scribes and priests, and it was handed down carefully by strict traditional methods in the circles of the "initiated." A "scientific" spirit appeared especially in the classifications of plants, animals, diseases, and remedies. Mathematics was comparatively advanced, as calculation tables bear witness; and everyone knows that this was the chosen land of astronomy. The heavens, the world of the divinities, were painstakingly scrutinized. Periodic celestial phenomena, such as eclipses, were known and could be foretold. Still, the true Mesopotamian "sciences" were divination and magic (cf. pp. 29-30).

Art, which the Sumerians early had brought to a high degree of perfection, was primarily religious and decorative. It was much more realistic than that of Egypt (cf. p. 15), but it also appears to have been symbolic and mystical. Their masterpieces were essentially the products of sculpture and architecture, the impressive remnants of which are now arranged as pieces in museums. Studied closely, they never fail to reveal an eagerness for life and something of the profound soul of Mesopotamia.[10]

The governmental system was, naturally, monarchical. It was directly related to the gods, from whom the kings were believed to

[9] Amurru, or the country of the Amorrheans (also called Amorites), was a region of uncertain boundaries situated between the Euphrates and the Mediterranean, and between northern Syria and southern Palestine. Aram designates either Upper Mesopotamia (Arameans of the east), or Syria (Arameans of the west), and refers to a Semitic people related in the first case to the Mesopotamians of the south, and in the second to a people who were a poorly determined nomadic group.

[10] The best way to form a more exact idea of Mesopotamian art and civilization is to visit the section of Oriental antiquities in a great museum; the collection in the Louvre is exceptionally interesting in this respect. Failing this, well-illustrated books on the Ancient Near East, such as the photographic albums of the Louvre itself, may be consulted.

hold their power, if not their birth. Small principalities were followed by kingdoms; as the economic and military life developed, empires were established. An increased and hierarchized bureaucracy assured the practical application of the central authority. The resources of the state were derived from taxation and from the spoils of victory in war. Legislation was made up both of customs and of written laws. Supported by sanctions, the state governed family life, social relations, property, and commerce. Legislation was inspired by a real sense of the meaning of man and of his legitimate requirements.

The ancient Mesopotamians were highly and profoundly religious. Religion held a considerable and essential place in their lives; it was closely linked to their daily behavior, to their every activity, and to all situations. In addition, it was official and hence was constantly being manifested.

The Sumero-Babylonian religion [11] was characterized principally by the worship of the forces of nature and of the sources of life. The most obvious function of the divinities was to govern the motive powers of the world, to assure and to control the fecundity of plants, animals, and men. The sun and the stars, the rain and the storm, the rivers and their floods, were especially in touch with the divinities, as were the animals which were regarded as particularly representative of the mystery of sex, for example, the serpent or the bull. The natural cycle of the seasons gave rhythm to religious life and to its liturgical manifestations.

The religion was excessively polytheistic. Its complexity, its lack of unity, its incoherences (at least to us), and the multiplication of devotions defy all efforts to summarize them. In addition, each city, each country, and each political system had its own doctrine and piety. Usually, the cults were added to one another and became amalgamated. Finally, they acquired a kind of hierarchical or-

[11] This expression is used because the Sumerian and the Babylonian religions were very closely linked in the complex of a historical evolution which it is beyond our purpose to study here; we must content ourselves with only essentials. For a more detailed study, cf. Étienne Drioton, *et al.*, *Religions of the Ancient East*, English trans. by M. B. Loraine (New York: Hawthorne Books, 1959), with selected bibliography; H. W. F. Saggs, *op. cit.*, Chap. 10, "Religion"; *Twentieth Century Encyclopedia*, Vol. CXLI.

ganization. We cannot speak of a theology, but rather of a theogony, that is, a history of gods begetting gods. The most all-powerful and formidable gods were generally astral divinities or patrons of important cities, gods of seasonal phenomena or protectors of the harvests. These divinities were conceived of as being either male or female and as having very human manners, if not indeed inferior to those of men. The naturalism of this religion of the forces of life was evident everywhere.

The Mesopotamian religion, however, must not be judged (nor must any other) solely on its appearances or on the popular beliefs. On the contrary, an attempt must be made to find the essential faith, at least to find the faith of the elite among the believers. The profound content of this faith can be expressed as follows: [12] a sovereign and mysterious Reality dominates men. It is the "Divinity" into which the plurality of the gods merge in some way, or which the gods have by participation; this Divinity has its expression in a supreme Will which is superior to the gods and which is often represented by the "council" or the "assembly" of the gods. The assembly of the gods are themselves multiplied and diversified according to appearances, attributes, and planes of activity; there are divine generations and filiations; a divinity may "be born" of the "word" uttered by a god. The divine word is thus an irresistible force which raises up beings and has the power to overturn the world; it is creative, vivifying, or destructive.[13] One cannot be insistent on stating precisely something that was never clear. At least, however, one should do all one can to be exact and respectful with regard to ancient metaphysics and great religious efforts.

Mesopotamia laid less stress than Egypt on life beyond the grave; they considered it an unhappy life in comparison to present existence. Perhaps the Babylonians had a more lively sense of active involvement in historical time. In any case their more somber outlook on the future life gave to Babylonian thought a profoundly tragic and fertile disquietude.

Perhaps a kind of widespread pessimism always existed in Mesopotamia. Fear was almost everywhere: it disturbed the hearts of

[12] For this, we are indebted to R. Follet, "Les aspects du Divin et des Dieux dans la Mésopotamie antique," in *Rech. Sc. Rel.* (1951), pp. 188-208.

[13] Important texts can be found in the Supplement of *Dictionnaire de la Bible* (Pirot-Robert), in the article "Logos," by Tournay, cols. 429–33.

men and of their kings; it laid hold upon the gods; it spread abroad a terror that men sought to exorcise or to forestall by magic and divination, which were universally prevalent. Babylonian thought may be said never to have found its balance because of a fundamental doubt inherent in it. A still better understanding of this mentality can be obtained by comparing it with that of the Egyptians who were certain that they had gods on earth in the person of their pharaohs, and who were certain also of a survival which they thought they knew in detail down to the means of obtaining it conveniently.

Places of worship were built everywhere. In every large city, an important group of religious edifices was usually enclosed within an area reserved for the sacred service. Particularly notable was the great pointed tower, magnificently decorated, which was called a "ziggurat." [14] This impressive monument, which seems to have been regarded as a place for meeting with the divinity when it came to visit its people in this world below, was admirably suited to the splendors of the official liturgy. In the outer sanctuaries, on the altars, sacrifices of all sorts were offered in superabundance. The year was punctuated with solemn anniversaries and festivities. The ceremonies were carried out according to minute and extremely complicated rituals, which were strictly compulsory. In addition, private piety supported domestic cults and various devotions.

As might be expected, the religious note is dominant in ancient Mesopotamian literature, which ranges from simple commercial bookkeeping notes and the texts of contracts (in which the divinities are invoked) to lofty agricultural hymns, administrative or private correspondence, registry records, and innumerable magic formulas (many texts of incantation and conjuration belong especially to medical magic). The juridical literature has a very great importance; in many cases Sumerian and Babylonian laws lend themselves to

[14] The ziggurat of Babylon was almost 295 ft. bv 295 ft. square and 148 ft. high. It was faced with enameled bricks of a different color for each of its seven steps, and could be ascended by ramps leading to the little temple at the summit. The foundations or the traces of many zuggurats have been found (that of Ur is one of the best preserved, comparatively). These were the "cathedrals" of Mesopotamia, to use the expression of A. Parrot, who has devoted a magnificent study to them: *Ziggurats et Tour de Babel* (A. Michel, 1949); a summary by the same author can be found in *The Tower of Babel* (New York: the Philosophical Library, 1955).

comparison with the legislation later codified in Israel.[15] Furthermore, some kinds of prayers—"lamentations," requests to the gods—invite comparison with the Hebrew psalter; many are poems honoring the gods or expressing grateful praise to them. Finally, certain series of sentences have some analogy with the biblical "proverbs" and the reflections in sapiential literature, which we will encounter later on.

Nevertheless, the most characteristic and the most important Mesopotamian writings are epics with a heroic and mythological theme. These had a great vogue in the Ancient Near East. Current Babylonian mythology habitually made up characters—gods, genii, supermen, and poor men. In them, natural phenomena were personified and historical events were dramatized; or they served to explain existing conditions, notably religious practices. In this manner also, through recitals which were both naïve and fantastic, somewhat heavy but still discerning, the loftiest themes of human meditation were treated: the order of the universe and the conflict of the elements; the government of the world by superior wills; the mystery of life and of fecundity; the mystery of death and the dwelling place of the dead.

Two celebrated works deserve to be mentioned. First, the poem *Enuma Elish,*[16] so-called from its opening words. It may date from the twenty-third to the twentieth century (according to others, it dates from the nineteenth to the sixteenth century). It was composed to the glory of Marduk, a god of Babylon who was exalted above other gods; in practice, his worship was preferred over and to the detriment of other cults and their sanctuaries, which is equivalent to proclaiming the superiority of Babylon over other cities. The biblical interest of this poem lies in its beginning which treats of "origins"; in spite of the mythological entanglement, resemblances between it

[15] The celebrated "Code of Hammurabi," engraved on a magnificent black monolith, can be seen at the Louvre. Besides the comparisons made between its laws and some of the precepts of the Pentateuch, scholars often cite, in connection with the story of Abraham, the Hammurabic prescriptions permitting a man deprived of offspring, because of the sterility of his wife, to have children by his maidservant, and the prescriptions concerning the rights and duties of the persons concerned (cf. Gen. 16:1-6).

[16] That is, "When, from On-High . . ." The text of *Enuma Elish* has been translated by R. Labat, *Le Poème babylonien de la Création* (Maisonneuve, 1935).

and the beginnings of Genesis can be noted.[17] The other document, called *Gilgamesh* after its main character, is an epic which has been found in several versions and which enjoyed wide circulation. The poem was current in Babylonia before the twentieth century. It consists of a collection of epic fragments, whose hero, a legendary king of a Babylonian city and two-thirds a god, in a tragic, but ludicrous manner, goes through adventures in which all the gods become embroiled. The eleventh of the twelve tablets of the poem in its most complete form contains the account of the "Deluge." The resemblances and parallelism between this account and the biblical passage [18] are immediately evident; they will lead to reflection and make it possible for us to understand the way in which a tradition and a Babylonian document were "reused" by the writers of Israel.

This poem is quite a composite of materials woven together, containing as it does elements inserted afterwards. The literature of the Ancient Near East has always possessed works made by compilation, by repetitions, and by additions. Several different editions of both *Enuma Elish,* and of *Gilgamesh* exist. Thus, even in very ancient times, the problems of literary composition and of the transmission of written traditions by several routes had already arisen.

Songs similar to those we have just cited usually had a liturgical object. Thus, on the feast of the New Year at Babylon, a priest of Marduk recited the thousand-odd verses of *Enuma Elish,* standing with hand upraised before the statue of the god. This explains why these literary traditions were transmitted chiefly in sacerdotal circles.

[TWO]

THE EGYPT OF THE ANCIENT AND MIDDLE EMPIRES [1]

Unlike Mesopotamia, an immense basin into which various peoples, especially nordic, poured endlessly, driving out other masses,

[17] Especially to be noted is the fact that the human race was created by a divinity using the blood of a god, which evokes both the "likeness" of Gen. 1:26-27, and the divine "breath" of Gen. 2:7.

[18] Gen. 6-8. Cf. Nancy Sandars, translator, *The Epic of Gilgamesh* (Baltimore: Penguin Books, 1960).

[1] For a quick introduction to ancient Egypt, cf. Cyril Aldred, *The Egyptians*

abruptly and brutally interrupting the periods of normal development, Egypt seems to have followed a continuous course. This was due to her relative independence in relation to the rest of the Near East, to the ethnic permanence of her inhabitants, to their lesser numbers, and especially to the harmonious living conditions created by her fine river with its regular and fertilizing floods. The history of ancient Egypt, therefore, is one of the longest known to human civilization; it can be followed without interruption for more than thirty-five centuries.

Egypt's geographical unity, however, was not perfect. The valley of the Egyptian Nile, a narrow oasis 620 miles in length, was too long and had no natural center. Tension was often evident between Upper Egypt, which was polarized by Thebes, and Lower Egypt, which was commanded by Memphis or by one of the cities of the Delta; it was especially apparent during times of general decline.

At the dawn of the fourth millennium, the country of the Nile was divided and shared among several clans. Regional kingdoms often opposed one another, and rivalry between the north and the south soon arose. The Egyptian kingdom, properly speaking, originated about the end of this millennium as a result of the union of the northern and southern regions. The northern region, however, under the legendary Menes or Narmer, whose royal seat was at Thinis, profited most from the union. The two first "dynasties" are placed in this "archaic period" (3300-2800 B.C.).[2]

The Ancient Empire includes the third to the sixth dynasty (2800-2300 B.C.). Its development was rapid and its ascension impressive. The government was strong because it was centralized,

---

(Glyn Daniel, editor, *Ancient Peoples and Places Series;* New York: Praeger, 1961); James H. Breasted, *A History of Egypt from the Earliest Times to the Persian Conquest* (New York: Scribner's, 1905–59); Pierre Montet, *Everyday Life in Egypt,* English trans. by A. R. Maxwell-Hyslop and Margaret S. Drower (New York: St. Martin's Press, 1958); George Steindorff and Keith C. Seele, *When Egypt Ruled the East* (University of Chicago Press, 1957); John A. Wilson, *The Burden of Egypt, an Interpretation of Ancient Egyptian Culture* (University of Chicago Press, 1951).

Some of the many illustrated art books on Egypt should also be examined; they can provide a clearer idea of ancient Egypt in a shorter time than any other mode of presentation.

[2] Certain Egyptologists are willing to reduce these dates a little. The terms "dynasties" and "empires" were not in use among the ancient Egyptians, but they have become standard expressions in treating the history of Egypt; so also, and with better reason, is the term "period" used.

and the administration was well organized. Memphis [3] became and, for the most part remained, the capital, although the center of gravity of the country tends toward Thebes [4] in the south. The epoch was one of large-scale constructions, of which the pyramids of Cheops, Cephren, and Mycerinos [5] are celebrated witnesses. Important religious buildings began to rise along the great valley which one day would contain many. The clergy held a superior position in society. The mass of the population was occupied in the fields or as laborers on the large works. Apart from these stood the elite or the castes of functionaries, artists, scribes, and rich property owners. Commerce was active all along the river and on land and sea. Expeditions were sent to Nubia. Egyptian influence was strong throughout the whole Near East, neighboring states being more or less vassals. In the twenty-sixth century, Pepi I fought and conquered the Canaanites.

The epoch of political, artistic, and economic grandeur of the Ancient Empire was followed by an "intermediate period" of anarchy and decadence from the seventh to the tenth dynasty (2300-2100 B.C.). This period was marked by a widespread and terrible popular revolution, foreign interference, the establishment of a feudal regime, and the general seizure of territory by the rich property owners.[6]

Everything came to life again under the Middle Empire, which existed from the eleventh to the seventeenth dynasty (2100-1580 B.C.). After the time required for social reorganization and the new strengthening of authority (2100-2000 B.C.), Thebes became dominant as the center of government, religion, and culture in the twelfth dynasty (2000–1785 B.C.). The twelfth dynasty was the dynasty of the Amenemhats and the Sesostrises. The classic epoch

[3] Little remains of Memphis today. It was situated about 18 miles to the south of the site of modern Cairo.

[4] Thebes was about 435 miles above Memphis on the Nile. The ruins of Thebes and its long history are among the most imposing of Egypt. Today, the place is known as Luxor and Karnak. The sites of some temples and a large cemetery can be found on the left bank of the Nile some miles away, and facing Luxor and Karnak.

[5] The pyramids are in Gizeh, a large suburb of modern Cairo, southwest of the city. The pyramids were already seven or eight centuries old in the time of Abraham.

[6] Ancient Egypt never succeeded in developing a social structure other than one favoring a small number of privileged persons.

of Egypt, it gave an important place to the arts and to literature, which flourished greatly. Abraham lived during this era.

The pharaohs of the Theban dynasty, especially Sesostris III (1887-1850 B.C.), built up a strong administration, a system of external defense (fortifications to the south and east), and protectorates in Nubia and in Palestine. In addition, they embarked on fruitful commercial expeditions. Their power, however, was more superficial than external appearances indicated: when the central authority relaxed a little and the foreigner tried his strength, it crumbled.

A second "intermediate period" began with the thirteenth dynasty and continued down to and including the seventeenth dynasty (1785-1580 B.C.). The thirteenth dynasty still exercised sole power over the whole country, although the "Hyksos" were already installed in the eastern Delta. These were mixed populations, mostly Semites, who, undoubtedly, had been displaced by the Aryan invasions that upset the whole of the Near East at the beginning of the second millennium. Their number increased progressively; after establishing their capital, Avaris, in the Delta in 1730 B.C. they conquered the entire country with such savage and terrifying force that the Egyptians would always remember it with horror. Then, they set up a Hyksos monarchy (XV-XVI dynasties).

The Hyksos monarchy, however, did not last for more than a century (1675-1567 B.C.). A nationalist movement for emancipation, originating with Thebes in Upper Egypt, swept down the valley. The Hyksos, defeated by Ahmosis (1580-1558 B.C.), were finally driven out by force of arms. They had, however, proved to Egypt that it could no longer consider itself free from danger next to an Asia which had begun to exhibit its inexhaustible riches of men and of energy.

The career of Joseph, the son of Jacob, in Egypt is thought to have been made possible by the establishment of the Hyksos there, since they were receptive to their Semite kinsmen. The settling of a part of his family in the Delta is explained in the same way.

We are ready to consider certain general aspects of the civilization of ancient Egypt.

One of the ordinary manifestations of this civilization is writing. Egypt was covered with "hieroglyphics" (the designation of Egyptian writing by this term is modern), a form of writing whose discovery was very ancient. Rapidly perfected into an original and stylized form of pictography, it developed, like the cuneiform writings, by departing from ideography and tending toward syllabism. It even arrived at a more advanced separation of phonetic elements, but it did not go so far as to discover [7] or adopt an alphabet; it remained entirely conservative and clung faithfully to the figurative design of the archaic writing.

Writing was not the only evidence that Egypt possessed a genius for stylization. Abundant evidence can be found in the artistic accomplishments which are its glory. If these pictures and sculpture can be called conventional, it is not because the artists lacked skill or because their inspiration was inadequate, but because of that deep logic which does not fear repetition and which represents its subject less according to the photography of the eye than according to the image formed in the mind.[8] Many delightful exceptions, however, can be found. In architecture, Egypt knew how to erect monuments of a grandeur and a beauty that are still striking even as ruins.[9] Everyone has some idea of these structures, as well as of the acres of walls covered with designs in relief (interminable liturgical processions, scenes from the sacerdotal life of the pharaohs, a catalogue of their victories over enemies) and the profusion of statues. Of course, art and religion were connected intimately; the greatest and most beautiful monuments were always temples.

[7] Although in the beginning some kind of alphabet could have been worked out.

[8] The drawings of children has this same rigorous logic which keeps only what is essential, gives proportions according to degrees of value, and enlarges what it considers most important. In spite of this, one cannot deny the taste of the Egyptian, supported by his masters, for a traditionalism in which personal initiative loses its rights. The paintings in the tombs, the familiar statuettes, and many everyday objects or furnishings, on the contrary, are very free and spontaneous, full of realism and charm; but in the eyes of the Egyptians, they never represented true art.

[9] Egypt had excellent material with which to work in the stones from its cliffs or from the mountains towering above the Red Sea, especially its famous Assouan granite and its Nubian sandstone. Mesopotamia would undoubtedly have bequeathed us something more than the foundations of walls and of buildings if it had had anything to build with other than the clay to make bricks, which, even when baked, do not resist bad weather and the passage of time. The great ziggurats, when stripped of their enamel facing, literally dissolved in the rain water of the storms.

From the beginning, the Egyptian religion [10] had a deeply rural character, which it retained; it proceeded from the worship given by peasants who were aware of the manifestations of nature and who expressed their feelings in religious attitude and gesture. Each town or village seems to have had its own god from very ancient times. Furthermore, Egypt always had an astonishing spirit of conservation; hence, the number of divinities quickly increased, because those that acquired pre-eminence did not displace the earlier ones. To understand this multiplicity of gods and the gross forms of worship paid to them,[11] obviously one would have had to be part of the life, because many of its concepts and customs escape us now.

In addition to the local gods, there were cosmic gods, gods of hell, of war, of agriculture, divinized heroes, and sacred animals. The success or the decline of the various cults was related to political or social events. The clergy elaborated theologies which reflected attitudes toward the established power, but which also succeeded in systematizing more or less precisely the traditional inheritance. About 2500 B.C., Ra (or Rê), the sun, became the supreme god, and great sun temples were built everywhere in his honor. Ra was the father of pharaoh, who was thus divinized. This is very important, because the whole edifice of Egyptian thought, as well as its entire social organization, rested on this concept of a king-god. Among the many other cults, the funeral cult of Osiris, god of vegetation, enjoyed a great vogue. About 2000 B.C., pre-eminence belonged to Amon, the god of Thebes, who became Amon-Ra, so that he might be better accepted.

Since religion was mixed with the everyday life of politics, art, and literature, protective or funerary magic grew enormously. Con-

[10] For the religion of ancient Egypt cf. James H. Breasted, *Development of Religion and Thought in Ancient Egypt* (London: Hodder & Stoughton, 1912); J. Cerny, *Ancient Egyptian Religion* (New York: Rinehart, 1952); Étienne Driton, *et al.*, *op. cit.*, pp. 16–59.

[11] The statues or drawings of divinities with hybrid shapes (falcons, cows, hippopotamuses, rams, ibises, cobras, or jackals) have a dreamlike quality about them. Those accustomed to such symbolism, however, must have felt otherwise. A consciousness of animal mystery seems to have been at the basis of the cults. But why this tendency, which seems to have come from something beyond the animals themselves? Their cunning or their maternal tenderness, their courage or their ingenuity, their strength, their cries or their silence—do these not permit comparisons, if not identification, with superior powers, with wisdom from on high, with mysterious activities?

cern for the "future" life also held an important place. Thanks to innumerable murals in cemeteries, we have complete information about the precise beliefs concerning the future life. A great deal of superstition can be seen in these beliefs, but it must be recognized that, as a whole, the doctrine of "eternity" was dominated by a great sense of moral justice and was filled with a kind of spirituality.

What we noticed in Mesopotamia with regard to the heights of doctrine and even of mysticism which are possible to certain religious minds, can be found also, but much more clearly, in Egypt. As early as the Ancient Empire, a belief in the unity of God can be found in expressions which, if rare, often are surprisingly elevated and pure.[12]

More than anywhere else, too, the writings of ancient Egypt were of a religious nature; literature had a sacred character. The epoch we are considering contained genuinely religious pieces: hymns, incantations, "books of the dead";[13] songs and stories; recitals, letters; and juridical and commercial documents.

What was most remarkable, however, and what we must especially take note of from the point of view of the Bible, was a form of literature called "teaching," which is the distant forerunner of the "wisdom" literature of Israel. We know this from certain writings of the third millennium:[14] the "Wisdom for KaGemni" (2900 B.C.); the "Maxims of Ptahotep" (2600 B.C.); the "Wisdom of Ani" (2500 B.C.); and the "Wisdom for Merikara" (2300 B.C.), which was followed by the remarkable "Instructions of Amenemhat" (2000

[12] Besides texts as remarkable and as well known as the hymn to Amon (prototype of Ps. 104), the hymn from the *Papyrus of Leyde,* whose spiritual and theological value is immediately perceptible, can be cited:

> "Unique is Amon, hidden from the gods; his appearance is not known. He is higher than the heavens, deeper than hades; he is too mysterious for his glory to be revealed, too great to be examined, too powerful to be known. One would fall dead with fright on the instant, if one were to pronounce his secret name which none may know." . . . "Hidden-soul is his Name, so mysterious is he." . . . "He possesses eyes and ears, for him whom he loves; he hears the supplications of him who invokes him. He comes from afar in an instant for him who cries to him!" (French translation by Fr. Daumas, in *Etudes Carmélitaines,* June, 1952, pp. 104 and 118.)

[13] These concerned journeys beyond the tomb, describing their stages, judgments that were passed, and "negative" confessions, which justified the recitation of prayers, litanies . . . ; often they cover long lengths of papyrus.

[14] The datings however, should be used with caution, the manuscripts often being several centuries later than the texts themselves.

B.C.). Most of these documents were written as recommendations of a father to his son,[15] in view of the son's education and of his success in administrative service. In other words, they are, as it were, treatises for one who wants to be a good and happy official. A high standard of morality, which teaches submission to the divine will without neglecting personal interests, can be found in the documents; yet, they are eminently practical. The "teachings" are full of a delicate psychology; they have a great sense of human relations and of one's duties toward one's neighbor. They are a mirror of the Egyptian soul, of private and family life, of occupations, positions, and social life. Their literary form usually consists of simple sentences set one after the other, without concern for arrangement or for logical sequence.

The didactic literature may be connected with other forms. A sage like Nefer-Rohu (c. 2000 B.C.) may "utter things past and things to come," which brings us to the domain of "prophecy," in the sense of preaching and of reflection on history. Another literary form puts the events of the past [16] into the future. Although they are only stories, their form will be recalled in connection with certain writings of Israel. It is also interesting to compare the courageous "Warnings of the Sage Ipouver" (perhaps to Pharaoh Pépi I, c. 2400 B.C.) with the frank and free remonstrances of the Hebrew prophets to their kings.

In this rapid survey of two thousand years of Mesopotamian and Egyptian history, it is not possible to take into consideration the small countries and the diverse peoples which also make up the picture of the ancient Near East. Hence, a great danger exists that the extensive international life that prevailed will not be brought out sufficiently. Correspondence and other forms of exchange were a constant feature of international life. Archaeologists and historians are surprised to find traces of these relations, these borrowings from one another, these interminglings of civilizations, almost everywhere.

[15] The father is a king, a great personage, or a private individual; "son" may be taken in the broad sense of subject or disciple (compare Prov. 1, 8, 10, 15, etc.)

[16] Thus, in the *Westcar Papyrus*, the advent of the first kings of the fifth dynasty is "foretold," just as *Papyrus* No. 1116 *of the Hermitage* "announces" the Hyksos and the end of the Middle Empire.

Hieroglyphics and Egyptian art are found from Sinai to the northern part of Syria, and, inversely, the libraries of ancient Egypt contain many cuneiform documents. At Ugarit (Ras-Shamra) in Phoenicia, scribes wrote out tablets in six different languages. In addition, quantities of valuable artifacts (pieces of furniture, jewels, and statuettes) bear witness, when one compares the place of their origin with that of their discovery, to the extent, the facility, and the multiplicity of these exchanges. International trade also took place on the plane of ideas and traditions. It is not surprising that religious poems conceived in the land of Sumer were used on the shores of the Mediterranean or that the voice of the Egyptian psalmists had their echo in the mountains of Palestine. Studies in comparative history are based on the universalism of the Ancient Near East.

Crete, Cyprus, the Phoenician shore, Egypt, Nubia, the Canaanite countries, Syria, the plateaus of Asia Minor, the mountains of Upper Mesopotamia, and the long valley of the Euphrates and the Tigris as far as the Persian Gulf, with India beyond, and the steppes and deserts of Arabia—all these regions had various contact with one another, either by way of commercial and diplomatic relations, or through wars and treaties, the arts, literature, and religion. The interplay of influence was facilitated by the linguistic relationships of a predominantly Semitic environment, principally by the Akkadian language and cuneiform writing whose diffusion seems to have been so widespread.

Mesopotamia, a land of extraordinary vitality, of varied activities, of powerful efforts and of disturbing although enriching restlessness, habitually played the principal role in this ancient oriental universe. The world is deeply indebted to her.

[THREE]

THE THOUGHT AND LANGUAGE OF THE ANCIENT ORIENT | "God is a pure spirit, infinitely perfect, who has created everything and who governs everything": such was the answer to the first question in our childhood catechism, "What is God?" [1] A

[1] Fortunately, there are new ways of speaking of God in catechisms, and it

Babylonian who was taught that the god of his town was the supreme god, above other gods, was told that Marduk "was of magnificent stature, with flashing eyes," that he was "male, begetting from the beginning," that he had "eyes to the number of four, and four ears. . . ."[2]

The history of the world is not left to chance; we believe that it depends on the divine will and foreknowledge. The Babylonian thought the same thing, but not in these abstract terms. He remembered that the tablets on which the fates were written had been in the hands of a monster, Kingu, but Marduk took them from him and held them in his posession forever after.[3]

Instead of saying that the gods are "immortal," the Babylonian said that "they have kept life in their hands."[4] He explained the universal law of death among men by the story of a man who almost acquired immortality, but lost it.[5] Divine protection was promised to the warrior in these terms: "It is I, Ishtar! I will walk before thee and behind thee. Fear naught!"[6]

These few examples show at once that the ancient Orientals expressed themselves and thought in a manner far different from that of modern Occidentals. Their manner of expression and of thought was concrete, or filled with images.

It would be absurd to deny that the ancient Orientals had the intellectual faculty of abstracting, of reaching general concepts, and of arranging ideas. That faculty is inborn in man. The "scientific" spirit we observed in Mesopotamia, elementary though it was, gives evidence of their ability to abstract. The languages themselves and the invention of writing are also sufficient proof. The Sumerian, Akkadian, and Egyptian languages have words for "truth," "goodness," "life," "purity," "sanctity," "evil," "horror," "human" or "hu-

---

may be hoped that an intensification of biblical teaching will result in giving a more personal and striking "knowledge" of the Person of the living God.

[2] Cf. Nah. I, 2-8; biblical texts of this kind are not lacking. To express divine "Providence," see what is said in Deut. 11:12.

[3] What is said here of Marduk is taken from the poem *Enuma Elish.* For the same idea, one can compare Exod. 32:32-33; Ps. 138(139):16.

[4] See how Ps. 89(90):2-3 expresses itself.

[5] This is one of the themes of the poem of *Gilgamesh,* and of course Gen. 2-3 comes to mind at once.

[6] Cf. Isa. 41:4; 44:6; 52:12; 58:8.

manity," and "divine" or "divinity." Such words, however, are rare by comparison with the mass of concrete words used in these languages. Furthermore, perhaps they do not have the precise connotation we attribute to them when we translate them. In any case, they are far from characterizing thought as it constantly manifested itself in the Ancient Near East. That thought did not always present itself in "ideas," nor was it formulated in "concepts." It hardly knew how to translate the reality it grasped, except through representations in the sensible order. The representations, however, were something quite different from the simple projection of a succession of images of the visible world upon the screen of the mind. The Semitic "knowing" was a conscious experience of the existence and of the power of the being known. Unlike a "thinker" who stands apart from the object of his reflection, the Semite was an "actor" solicitous for the beings with whom he must act.[7] It is in connection with these living relationships that he conceived the world he saw, touched, and felt. If he did not "abstract" ideas, it was because he did not withdraw himself from reality. Since he retained only existential and practical images, and since, in addition, he did not reason in a logical manner, starting with general concepts, his mind grasped things by comparing them with data already acquired from his experimental observation. From this, as we have seen,[8] comes the constant use of metaphor and all other forms of comparison.

The realities "conceived" by other intellects in a "spiritual" or "transcendent" way, and expressed in terms which abstract from the material or sensible order,[9] are grasped and uttered in the Semite language as remaining in time and space, resembling the beings of nature and the known activities of man. We must not, however, follow the wrong scent and make the mistake of supposing that the Semite did not know the world of the spirit or the life of the spirit, that he did not attain to realities other than the sensible, or that he had no notion of anything beyond. To avoid such a mistake, one need only note the intensity of his religious life, his extraordinary sense of the "sacred,"[10] which he clearly distinguished from the

[7] Cf. *WG*, pp. 160-61; on "knowing," cf. also *ibid.*, p. 22.

[8] And as a reader of the Bible will constantly note.

[9] Comparatively, that is; one never really thinks without images.

[10] This sense is made up of intuition and of the Semite's impressible nature in the presence of a Reality that is both fascinating and terrible: it is a feeling of its frightening disproportion, its absolute difference from all other known real-

profane. The Near East is contemplative; nowhere have people had greater faith in the "mysterious." Nevertheless, Oriental metaphysics, which is not philosophical but entirely religious, is expressed in living, graphic, imaged representations. This explains the predominance of narratives in its sacred writings: a doctrine is not molded and put into the general formulas of a "credo"; it is told in the form of stories.

The myths are of this kind. Although the subject is a delicate and difficult one, we cannot fail to speak of the myths, because of their importance. A few examples will reveal their characteristic qualities.

Osiris was the god of fertility in Egypt. Annually, according to the rhythm of the Nile floods, he died and was reborn, a symbol of the growth of the crops and of the harvest.

Osiris was also the sovereign of the kingdom of the dead. Formerly, he had been king of Egypt and of the living, but he was dethroned by his brother, Seth. Seth, in his turn, was vanquished by Horus, the son of Osiris, who then became the sovereign god of Egypt, while Osiris continued to reign beyond the tomb. In this way Egyptian thought explained the relationship between this world and the world beyond.

The two brothers, Osiris and Seth, were the sons of Geb, the Earth, and of Nut, the Sky. After the union of Geb and Nut, they were separated by Atum, the Air; in this way the order of the actual universe was established—heaven and earth touched one another at the extremities, while the atmosphere separated them in the middle.[11]

In Syria-Phoenicia, Hadad was the god of storms; his son, Aleyin, was the god of springs and of growth. Aleyin was the enemy of Mot, god of the harvests and of drought; hence, their battles resulted in a putting to death followed by a resurrection. This was manifestly in accordance with the seasons and the agricultural activities they demanded.

---

ities. To express this unique and complex feeling, words of fear and respect are correct, but highly insufficient (R. Otto has analyzed the notion in his fine study on *Le Sacré*, Pavot, 1929).

[11] Representations of this can be seen in bas-reliefs, in the tombs and elsewhere. On the ground a man lies stretched out, and above him, touching him at his head and feet, is arched the figure of a woman (the heavenly bodies and the stars are depicted on the underside of her body); a third person walks on the body of the man and supports the torso of the woman.

A myth closely related to the above, which had an immense success throughout the Mediterranean world, was that of Adonis, the young and beautiful god of love, of life, and of spring, whose death and return to life were celebrated by alternate lamentations and rejoicing. The myth was the heir of a very popular old Sumero-Babylonian myth of Dummuzi or Tammuz,[12] who also died and came back to life annually at the same time as the vegetation.

The myths were, of course, scenically represented at the appropriate seasons of the year. They were ritually acted out in moving dramas which made the spectators vital sharers of the mystery.

The myths concerning the creation–victory and the deluge–salvation expressed especially, indeed, sought to bring to mind, the anguish of man before the overwhelming power of the natural elements. In the drama-poems of Mesopotamia (cf. pp. 10-11), the battles of Marduk and of Tiamat,[13] which involved all the gods of heaven and concerned the whole universe, are so many translations both of natural phenomena and of historical situations.

Gilgamesh is famous because of his search for the "plant of life,"[14] which he discovered at the cost of great difficulties and which, stupidly, he allowed to be stolen from him in the end. In this way, the fate of man, who searched for eternal life but was doomed to death, was explained. The Babylonian hero-king sets out to annihilate Humbaba, the "giant-of-the-cedars," and after dangerous vicissitudes succeeds in cutting off his head. Does this represent the coming of the men of Lower Mesopotamia to Lebanon to fell the trees which did not grow in their country and which they needed? Does it illustrate the struggle of the plain against the mountain? Does it show the rivalry of two cults, that of Shamash and that of Baal, or of two civilizations? Any one of these explanations is plausible; we are far from an understanding of all the myths. Besides, myths, in the course of the many centuries during which they were recited and sung, may have been understood

[12] Mention is made of the lamentations on the death of Tammuz at Jerusalem even in Ezech. 8:14.

[13] This last divinity was a kind of monster who represented the "abyss" of "bitter waters," that is, the hostile ocean. He is the biblical *tehom* (Gen. 1:2), but here he has lost his divine character to become only a creature of God. He is formidable, nonetheless, and can be mastered only by God.

[14] Obviously, one thinks of Gen. 2:9; 3:22.

in different ways. They may have been used in different historical circumstances, and may have acquired several meanings.

A Canaanite poem recounts the desperate struggle of El-Yam, the god of the sea, against Baal, master over the soil. Gold was the stake in their war. Baal succeeded in keeping his sovereignty. In this myth, we see the ceaseless attack of the Mediterranean Sea upon the Syrian coast. Perhaps, however, it deals with the resistance of the Canaanite peasants to the assault of the "peoples-of-the-sea" (Philistines and others; cf. pp. 67-68), formidable invaders against whom, nevertheless, the landsmen knew how to defend their possessions.

These examples suffice for our purposes, but a few further remarks [15] are necessary.

The myths are stories that were told. The characters they are peopled with were not only men, but gods, genii, monsters, and superhuman beings who act in a visible, material world, but in an extraordinary and supranatural way. The stories told—the birth and death of divinities, divine marriages, fantastic adventures, battles between giants—concern both the earth and an unknown universe.

They are also stories beyond time. The myth leaves historical time behind: it is situated beyond that time, in the "beginning," a beginning before which nothing can be grasped because there was nothing but primordial confusion.[16]

Nevertheless, the mythical facts are in some way actual; they are actual precisely because they are not single, dated historical facts. The life of the world is conceived of as a perpetual return or an eternal re-beginning: what was, returns; what took place, occurs again. The nontemporal mythical tales are lived again with the reappearance of natural phenomena: seasonal cycles, cataclysms, wars, and reigns. We saw this in the examples given above.

Thus, the myths concern both the progress of the world and the

[15] Without any thought, however, of presenting the philosophy of the myth. The question is, nevertheless, of the greatest interest and still current in present-day philosophical conjecturing.

[16] Things, not being distinct as yet, could not be "named," as Enuma Elish says, and not being named, they did not exist. Real fairy stories always begin with "Once upon a time," or "At the time when the animals talked": they are trans-historic stories which perpetuate mythism in the popular and childish imagination.

life of men. At first, the men of antiquity [17] did not consider them explanations or answers intended to satisfy the mind; they were primarily solutions for living: they told what must be believed and done, what hopes could be relied upon, to what necessity one had to submit, and what the obligations were that each individual had to meet.[18]

The themes of the myths were both the most elementary and the most profound: the mystery of the government of the world; the uncertainty of the world's dormant energies; the huge and terrible force of water; the surprising and disturbing power of sexuality; the lasting mystery of fecundity, the behavior or the exceptional and enigmatical qualities of certain animals; the attraction of ideal happiness; the formidable enigma of death; the eminence and the power of certain men; the marvelous character of civilization. . . . In this way, the problem of the relationship between man and the universe, of the contradictions and tensions between the unfolding of his own life and rhythms are dealt with in a most striking manner.

Contained in a universe which gives him life, but which also worries him and threatens at every moment to crush him, man has a lively sense of the enormity of reality and of the perpetual danger of rupture. This feeling, which combines amazement with fascination and admiration with terror, is "holy." [19] The myths would be incomprehensible without this instinct for awesome mystery.

That the myths belong essentially to the religious sphere goes without saying. They entered into the religious life and occupied a major place there. Magnificently translated into liturgical rites in which all the people took part, acting in liturgical performances which literally sanctified them, the myths plunged men, so to speak, in "mystery." They brought to life again, in the present, in the heart of each spectator and in the united feelings of the audience, the eternal drama.

Nevertheless, the myths did not satisfy the heart of man, because

[17] It is otherwise for us, who consider them retrospectively and, as it were, from the outside. But is man ever detached entirely from mythism?

[18] The preoccupation of the Semite was not so much to know "what is," as to be directed with regard to "what one must do."

[19] This does not imply the confusing of a feeling of the sacred with a truly religious attitude; one is related to the other, but the religious surpasses the sacred and is, in our opinion, of another order.

they did not really treat his own drama; they were not the history of man, but rather stories of the gods. They told how rival divinities, subject to the basest passions, to suffering, and to death, managed to get out of difficulty in a disordered world which was merely the reflection of a higher disorder. The human ant had to get along as best he could; the gods had no concern for him.

The mentality which fed on myths always tended toward the depths of tragedy and of affliction. To reach such depths was it not necessary first for man to have a sense of his own lowliness, weakness, and dependence? The feeling of being overwhelmed was at the same time a revelation of the vastness that dominated him. From the beginning, his feeling of inferiority and his sensing of the fact that all of these unlimited, incomprehensible powers constituted a divine world, proved to him the appropriateness of his way of understanding. This discovery centered him religiously, and therefore accurately, in the universe.

The ancestors of Israel came from this world of myths and remained close to it for a long time. Echoes of this world can be found in Hebrew literature. We shall see, however, that the genius of Israel freed itself completely from the spirit of the myths. This was due both to the Israelite knowledge of time, which constitutes history, and, primarily, to the revelation of a God who makes a "Covenant" with men, entering into their history.[20]

Nevertheless, the genius of Israel did not prevent the Israelites

[20] The Bible was written outside of the mythic sphere. It has an original inspiration which, as we shall see, renews the whole thought of man. Mythical traditions have been retained in the Bible: think, especially, of the first eleven chapters of Genesis; other traces of them can also be seen (cf. Job 3:8; Ps. 73 [74]:13-14; 88[89]:11; Isa. 27:1; 51:9; the images of apocalyptic literature are of a different order); but they were not accepted without transformation, to such an extent that one can speak of de-mythization (we use the word in its obvious sense, without reference to Bultman) of these ancestral and foreign traditions. Israel was able to accept the subject matter of this inheritance, but gave it quite a different spirit. Furthermore, Israel created no myth; the Bible does not contain one which is properly Hebrew. A certain spirit, new and entirely different, led Israel to break with the psychological and religious customs of its environment, setting it free forever from mythism. It was the "prophetic" spirit, as we shall see, that explained this liberation and this originality. The process took time, of course, and was not accomplished without a struggle: Israel had lived for a long time in the properly mythic religious climate of the Canaanite world we are soon to encounter.

and, therefore, the Bible, from retaining the image of the world which was common to all the ancient peoples of the East.

They considered the earth as the center of the visible universe. It is placed above a mass of water, like a great island on mysterious pilings. From this unfathomable depth come springs, streams, rivers, and lakes. The earth is covered by a very firm, concave ceiling [21] which rests, at its extremities, on high mountains and supports the waters which fall from above through openings in the arch. The planets and the stars travel across the inner surface of the arch; at night, they pass mysteriously beneath the earth.[22] Below ground level is the somber dwelling to which the dead descend. Above the sky, in the heavens, dwell the divinities.

The universe is imagined according to what man can understand of it within the limits of his observations and in relation to himself. According to this relationship he judges the dimensions or proportions of things: they are called large or small, far or near, permanent or impermanent according to their importance to him or according to the consequences that flow from them. The boundaries of the universe are simply the limits of his discoveries.[23] Everything is relative: the master of a small kingdom may regard himself and make others regard him as the sovereign "of all the earth." [24] A narrator may speak of an event "such as one had never seen" (sometimes he will even add: "Such as has never been, nor will ever be again" [Exod. 11:6]). Some beings or situations are believed stable enough to be called "eternal." [25] Here we find an example of the hyperbolic language so common in the Near East

[21] We still say the "firmament" or the "starry vault."

[22] Of course, things were never expressed in this descriptive and general manner. For the Egyptians, the great serpent Apophis, a personification of the shades, attacked Ra, the sun, every evening and triumphed over him until the morning, when their roles were reversed and Ra reappeared victorious. His diurnal and nocturnal circuit was made by a "solar boat," so often represented in Egyptian sanctuaries. The night journey was made in the dwelling of the dead, concrete and detailed knowledge of which was, as we remember, one of the characteristics of Egypt.

[23] Hence, the "islands" in the Second Isaias.

[24] They came from "all provinces" to buy wheat from Joseph (cf. Gen. 41:57) and "from all peoples," with "all the kings of the earth," to hear the wisdom of Solomon (cf. III Kgs. 4:34).

[25] On the meaning of this word, cf. *WG*, pp. 212-13.

(and not elsewhere?), whose "relativity" can be understood easily.[26]

The universe was not conceived of as a machine that runs by itself, something that is "wound up" once and for all. No "natural course" of events exists; rather, superior wills rule everything in the world, so that everything which happens is a sign of these wills. This mentality is as un-"scientific" as possible. We speak of "secondary causes," an expression which would have had no meaning for the ancient Orientals. Rain, drought, children, harvests, flocks, all were sent by the divinity. Disasters and natural phenomenon were due to divine action. The storm, for instance, comes from the gods; often it is a war against men; at least it is a divine "voice," an often terrifying "theophany." [27]

The same is true with regard to the activity of men: the gods direct them. Their great works, in particular, are regarded as due to a special inspiration from above, directed by the divine wills and helped by superior energies. Thus, wars are undertaken and carried to success under the impulsion of a god.[28] Towns and religious buildings cannot be erected without the explicit orders of some divinity. In accordance with this conviction, it is made known that the founder, king, hero, or important figure, received from heaven ready-made, even to the smallest detail,[29] the plan and the description of such and such a city or such and such a temple. The social structure is maintained by laws: legislation, oral or written (but especially written, because it then assumes a hieratic character), cannot be imagined as coming from a source other than the gods, who have dictated its text, if they have not given it already written out.[30] Literature, at least religious literature, and almost all literature is religious, is similarly recognized as coming from sources that are not merely human.

The nature of man is conceived of according to the way it manifests itself and according to the way experience reveals it to be. In a different intellectual climate, a dualist notion will distinguish an

[26] We shall, however, have to reflect on the psychological and theological dimensions of such language in connection with the Deluge in Gen. 6-9.

[27] Cf. Judg. 5:4-5; Hab. 3:4-16; Ps. 17(18):8-16; 28(29):3-9; 96(97):3-5.

[28] The Bible will speak of the "Wars of Yahweh": cf. Exod. 17:16; Num. 21:14; I Sam. 25:28; I Par. 5:22.

[29] Cf. Gen. 6:14-16; Exod. 25:8-9 and the six chapters following.

[30] Cf. Exod. 31:18; 34:28.

"immaterial" soul from the human body. Semitic thought knew only man living in the unity of his existent being. The soul, that which "animates," is his life principle; it is in the "breath" or in the "blood," or, indeed, it is the breath and the blood itself.[31] From this concept comes the whole religious doctrine concerning the blood, and the value of immolations and sprinklings with blood. Death, the decay of the body, seems by that very fact a horror, a chastisement, a mystery. Nevertheless, death is not believed to be an absolute end; indeed, the contrary is true. The Ancient Near East had a profound faith in survival. Any existence worthy of the name, however, and every delight could be thought of only in terms of the present life, with its joys and fulfillment. One must not suppose, however, that the refusal to surrender the values of the present life or of the visible creation implied a disregard for those spiritual goods which we speak of as distinct realities. The simple truth seems to be that the realism of the Ancient Near East, which did not separate spirit and body in man, did not separate them in his destiny either.

The connection between the two worlds, the visible and the invisible, one conceived to the image of the other, was a fundamental conviction in the Ancient Near East; the whole religion came from it. The necessity of worshipping the gods went without saying and was of capital importance. But the relationship between the two worlds had other practical consequences. The gods, who were powerful, intervened in the world below; their enterprises and their actions were unforeseen, but they were not always unforeseeable. Signs exist, which have to be interpreted; suprahuman revelations can be coaxed from above and utilized. Such was the basis of all forms of divination, which was so widespread in the Ancient Near East. Among the practices of this science of prognostication may be cited particularly the observation of the heavenly bodies and the examination of the entrails of animals, especially the liver. Some things could be known by observing the flight of birds,[32] the liquid in goblets,[33] the movement of a magic wand,[34] and the drawing of

[31] Cf., for example: Gen. 7:22; Ps. 103(104):29-30; Job 27:3-5; 34:14-15; in addition, Lev. 17:11-14; Deut. 12:23.

[32] Cf. the omen drawn from the wind in the trees in II Sam. 5:23-24.

[33] Joseph's cup, in Gen. 44:2, 6, had this use.

[34] One thinks at once of the famous rod of Moses: cf. Exod. 4:2, 17; 7:9-12, etc.; cf. also IV Kgs. 4:29.

lots;[35] trial by ordeal[36] was of the same order. Dreams had a considerable importance and were accepted either as reality itself or as a warning.[37]

Divination sought to know; magic claimed to act. Magic rested on the conviction that the gods could in some way be influenced by men, that they could be bound by means known to the initiated. To this end, certain utterances, certain words, were thought to be efficacious, infallible even. Mimicry of action was also employed. For example, to produce rain, a ritual pouring of water upon the earth took place; in order that the soil might be fruitful, it was subjected to a sexual union of a sacred character; to exercise power over a person, his "name" (in the sense of which we shall speak in a moment) was invoked; to injure someone, his likeness in the form of a statuette was bound up and struck, wounded, or destroyed; and so on. This manner of "winning over" the gods, nature, and occult forces—they were all one—these "spells" and "sympathetic magic," were not proper to the Ancient Near East alone, but they formed an integral part of its religion, its official worship, and its everyday life.[38]

The doctrine of names[39] is a result of the same state of mind and comes, in addition, from the concrete manner in which Semitic knowledge is expressed. The language itself was considered identical with what it expressed: the words were the realities they designated; a thing spoken existed, while a thing that had no name did not exist.[40] To pronounce a word not only put a label on a reality or suggested the image of a thing; it brought the content of the word into being, it caused the thing expressed to exist and to act.[41] This

[35] Such seems to have been the use of the *Urim-Turim* contained in the *ephod* (cf. Exod. 25:7; 28:4, 30; Lev. 8:8) in I Sam. 23:9-12 and 30:6-8; cf. *also* Jos. 7:14-18; I Sam. 10:19-21; 14:40-42; Prov. 16, 33.

[36] An example, coming from a very ancient source, is in Num. 5:11-30.

[37] Everyone knows the story of the dreams of Joseph, of the Egyptian officers, and of pharaoh: cf. Gen. 37, 40; 41.

[38] The Torah forbade the Israelites to practice divination and magic; cf. Exod. 22:17; Lev. 20:27; Num. 23:23; Deut. 18:10-14.

[39] The expression is modern, but signifies that a whole doctrine is actually involved.

[40] The Babylonian poem *Enuma Elish* begins thus: "When from On-High the sky was not named and the earth below had no name," which means: when there was neither heaven nor earth.

[41] The genesis of this doctrine can perhaps be seen in the example of the power of an oral command: someone speaks with authority, gives an order in words,

was of particular importance in regard to proper nouns. The "name" of a person was the person himself.[42] To possess the "name" of someone was to "know" and therefore to experience what that person was, to enter into an active relationship with him.[43] A "vocation," which is a "naming" and a "call," means to be set apart for a destiny, the fixing of a destiny, an "ordination." To change one's name, to receive a "new name," signifies a change of orientation in life, a "conversion."

"To say" is always to make.[44] Thus, an "invocation" is thought alike to intervene in the private world of him to whom it is addressed. This creative and operative value of language makes "benedictions" and "maledictions" efficacious. "Benefactions" and "malefactions," that is, benefits and evils, are brought about actually and irrevocably by the use of corresponding expressions.[45] Importance was also attached to riddles, to strange or elliptical sentences, and to plays upon words, because they had practical consequences. Writing shared in the power of words; it materialized words, giving them endless possibilities. From writing came talismans, books of magic, secret parchments, songs, "incantations," dances, drawings, and sculptures.

Numbers were particularly rich in secret meanings and occult powers. Numeral symbolism has become something alien to the modern Western mentality. The Western mind considers numbers nothing more than mere instruments, as simple as they are exact, for measuring and counting. The loss of the secrets of the ancient numerologists, in fact, creates great difficulties in the interpretation of texts containing numbers (cf. *WG*, pp. 175-77).

Since we do not need to make a systematic study of the thought of the ancient peoples of the Near East, but simply wish to awaken our minds to their interior world, and especially to their manner of

and the thing is done; the words, then, have an efficient value; without the spoken word, nothing would be done. Moreover, the order can be transmitted; the word is then "carried," acquiring an existence distinct from that of the one who uttered it; it can even be made permanent by repetition, or fixed by writing; it remains active always.

[42] Biblical examples are many: cf., among others: Deut. 12:5; Ps. 82(83):5; Prov. 10:7; Isa. 40:26; 62:2; Luke 6:22; Acts 4:7, 12; Eph. 1:21; Apoc. 2:17.

[43] Whence the sense of the dialogue in Exod. 3:11-15.

[44] This is why creation can be conceived as the effect of a Word: cf. Gen. 1; Ps. 32(33):9; Jth. 16:14.

[45] Cf., in particular, Gen. 27:35-40.

expressing realities, the considerations we have just voiced concerning the imaged character of their language, mythic thought, and expression, their idea of the universe and of man, and the value of words and numbers, may suffice. The comparisons we have made have shown, if the evidence needed illustration, to what extent the Bible proceeds from the ancient Semitic world and the fact that it cannot be isolated from this vast context.[46] The Bible has a Semitic temperament and heredity. Nevertheless, we have already seen that it has certain irreducible originalities and that it made a definite break from its natural environment. We shall discover these differences and the reason for them.

[46] The study of the Bible itself will contribute greatly to our knowledge of this environment and will accustom us to it gradually.

2 The Patriarchal Era

[ONE]

THE LAND AND THE MEN OF CANAAN | The land of Canaan,[1] which became Palestine, is a strip of ground about 160 miles long from north to south, varying in width from some 25 miles on its northern frontier to about 95 miles on the edge of the southern desert. Its surface is approximately 9,650 square miles, that is, almost the size of Sicily or four of the departments in France. To think of these four zones as parallel to the coast will give a comparatively simple picture of the whole.

To the west lie the coastal plains, whose continuity is broken only by the mountain chain and the point of Carmel. To the north of this cape, which dominates the wide, unique bay of Haifa, is the small but fairly spacious plain of Accko.[2] To the south of Carmel lies a long flat band, which is narrow at the top, but which widens out to 13 or 16 miles. It is called the plain of Sharon as far down as Jaffa; [3] from Jaffa on it is known as the Shephelah. A coastal region, bounded by the ancient terraces and foothills of the central moun-

[1] At this point we will take a geographical look at Palestine, the principal theater of the entire history we are about to study. Palestinian geography is comparatively simple, because the country is not large and, as we shall see, it is composed of contrasting and well-marked zones. A general view will be completed gradually by the study of the Bible itself. Localities (acquire the habit of always identifying them on a map) and diverse characteristics will gradually become memorized, and will facilitate the reading of the Sacred Book.

The reader can complete his knowledge of Palestine with the help of the photographic illustrations contained in numerous works on the country, such as atlases and accounts of travels or pilgrimages (these appear every year). The *Atlas of the Bible*, by L. H. Grollenberg, English trans. by H. H. Rowley and Joyce M. H. Reid (New York: Nelson, 1956), and Grollenberg's *Shorter Atlas of the Bible* (New York: Nelson, 1960) are especially recommended; cf. also, Denis Baly, *The Geography of the Bible* (New York: Harper, 1957); Adrien M. Legendre, *The Cradle of the Bible* (*Catholic Library of Religious Knowledge*, Vol. IX; St. Louis: Herder, 1930); Herbert G. May, *et al.*, editors, *Oxford Bible Atlas* (London: Oxford University Press, 1962).

[2] Or Saint John of Acre.

[3] Close to the present Tel-Aviv.

tains, it is the only one (besides the plain of Jezrael to which we will come in a moment) which permits an easy and rich cultivation.

In the center, a mountainous area forms the most important part of Palestine,[4] one that gives it its characteristic landscapes. In the north, the mountains of Galilee form, as it were, the descending slope of the high mountain chain of Lebanon. They descend toward a large, conspicuous interior plain, called the plain of Jezrael or Esdrelon, which spreads out from the bay of Haifa to the place where the Jordan emerges from the Lake of Gennesareth.[5] The northwest-southeasterly direction thus followed by the plain is caused by the chain of Carmel. To the south of this plain begins a very uneven mass known as the hills of Samaria or the mountains of Ephraim. They end some 32 miles to the north of Jerusalem, although without a definite break between them and the range which follows. The mountains of Juda (or Judea), continue the preceding ones. A break in the chain begins here, becoming very noticeable to the south of Jerusalem and in the desert that joins the Dead Sea. The average height of these three mountain ranges is about 2,600 feet; the highest barely exceed 3,300 feet.[6] From a high position a few other ridges can be distinguished, but for the most part they are merely a group of large hills. The traveler who follows the roads and paths must constantly circle the rather steep slopes of these hills which today are almost completely covered with stones.[7]

The central strip of mountains is bounded on the east by an extraordinary break which is *the* great peculiarity of the physical outline of Palestine: the valley of the Jordan. The Jordan, whose name means "the descending," originates from springs at the foot of Mt. Hermon. It descends from an altitude of 1,847 feet above sea level to one of 682 feet below, at which level it forms the Lake of Gennesareth. The outline of this lake forms an irregular oval 13 miles long by 6.5 miles wide. The Jordan then continues its

[4] Of biblical Palestine, at least.

[5] Also called the Lake of Tiberias.

[6] Jerusalem is 2,460 ft. above the Mediterranean, and the Mount of Olives 2,683 ft.

[7] There were, in ancient times, many trees and forests, and no doubt some cultivation on terraces. The work of restoring the land has now begun; many of the slopes have been planted and will soon produce small wooded areas or fine orchards.

descent from 682 feet below sea level to 1,285 feet below, which is the level of the Dead Sea. Thus, it traverses 62 miles, which it triples by winding through a deep valley, the Ghor. The width of the Ghor varies from three miles to 12 miles and reaches a depth of more than 3,200 feet in relation to the average height of the mountains that border it on either side. At one time the mountains were a single large plateau; then, they were suddenly cut in two by a sinking in of the earth and the valley was formed. The unique Dead Sea, also called the Salt Sea or the Asphaltite Lake, is 46 miles long and averages nine miles in width. Its greatest depth is 1,315 feet,[8] or 2,600 feet below the level of the Mediterranean.[9] The lake is completely enclosed, its water level being maintained by evaporation. It is continually fed at the rate of 200 m. per second by the Jordan and a few wadies and springs, and it is five or six times as salty as other seas. Fish cannot live in the Dead Sea because many chemical substances, principally chlorides, are contained in its waters.

The Transjordanian plateau, which borders the desert on the east, reaches altitudes exceeding 3,280 feet. Viewed from the west it looks like a mountain, because of the sudden break formed by the Ghor and also because of the wadies which cut through it from east to west. Of these, the principal are the Yarmuq, the Jabbok, and the Arnon.[10]

Hence, Palestine is a country of variations; full of contrasts, it is irregular topographically and is broken up into many divisions. It so isolates the groups of humans who are scattered throughout its confines that, if they are to be united, they must will union. Many advantages have been denied Palestine: its coast, obstructed by the sands of the Nile, is unfriendly; few plains are found in the interior; no navigable or fertilizing river can be found at all; the subsoil is not rich,[11] and, with the exception of the oasis of Jericho,

[8] In its southern part, however, the area bounded by the cape of Lishan ("the tongue") which juts out from the eastern shore, the depth is much less.

[9] This is the greatest known continental depression; it forms part of the great Syro-African cleft which, from the Taurus to the Red Sea and the Great Lakes of Africa, cuts through the earth's crust for a length of 3,728 miles.

[10] The biblical names of the Transjordanian regions were, from north to south, Bashan, Gilead, Ammon, and Moab (farther south, Edom).

[11] We are speaking of ancient times, with the means and tools at their disposal.

the "city of the palm trees," the Ghor can hardly be used in any way.

The temperatures are very uneven, their variations are accentuated by the points of origin of the winds and the differences of altitude. Fair winds blow in from the sea, but desert winds, like Khamsin for example, are a trial to men and dry and burn the countryside. Palestine depends for its livelihood solely on agriculture, but since the water supply is very meager,[12] everything depends on the rains. Life is strictly governed by the rhythm of the rains.[13] Continuous rainfall occurs from November to April, especially during January and February; little rain occurs during summer. What little frost or snow there is, occurs only in January.

The biblical expression which calls Palestine "a land flowing with milk and honey" (Exod. 3:8), symbolizes the products of the Palestinian soil, although the inhabitants take the trouble to obtain them. The principal objects of cultivation are cereals (wheat and barley), food plants (lentils, beans, peas, onions, cucumbers, and melons), and fruit trees (mostly olives, figs, and grapes). A few cattle and camels are raised in the South, while the raising of small animals (sheep and black goats) is widely practiced. The terrain and the climate make the donkey, tireless and sure-footed, the ideal mount and beast of burden to be found everywhere. Some deer live in the thickets, woods, and numerous caves.[14] Fish for food are scarcely found anywhere except in the Lake of Gennesareth where they are plentiful.

Except for the maritime plains, the plain of Jezrael, and the area about Jericho, which are fertile and pleasant, the country is rough and exacting, requiring of its inhabitants continual effort and intelligent work (for example, the creation and maintenance

[12] There are many springs, but they are lost in the subsoil.

[13] The author of Deut. 11:10-12, expresses with admirable clarity the "providential" character or the "régime de grâce" of Palestine. Palestine is completely at the mercy of its irregular rains, while in the Egyptian "garden," man does as he pleases with water because it is plentiful (cf. also Deut. 28:12, 23-24; Lev. 26:19-20; III Kgs. 8:35-36). We shall see how great was the Palestinian preoccupation with the rain—and consequently with the winds and storms—and how numerous were the observations concerning it all through the Bible (in the Sapiential literature, read Job 36:27-33; 37:1-22; 38:22-38; Sir 43:1-26). There are also the famous instances of drought (for example, III Kgs. 17-18; Amos 4:7-8; Jer. 14:1-6), which were considered as a divine chastisement, while "rain" was always synonymous with "benediction."

[14] Cf. Gen. 37:20, 33; Exod. 12:29; Jdgs. 14:5-6; I Sam. 17:34-37; IV Kgs. 2:24; Mark 1:13.

of terraces on the many sloping hillsides, and a rational use of water).[15] Courageous and industrious men can live and prosper in Palestine—at least, if war does not ravage a land which is the natural passageway for all foreign invasions.

Palestine is beautiful, with an austere beauty that is never monotonous. Mountains with rounded summits and boldly etched slopes give it a steadfast and noble appearance. A country that has character, it does not make things easy for man, but does remain within his capacities. In the clear air of daytime, its colors are incomparable.

When the Israelites were finally settled in Palestine, they loved it enthusiastically, for they could see that it was God's choice for them.

For a long time, the land of Canaan had neither well-defined borders nor self-rule. Such a status, indeed, it would seldom have in the course of history because of its geography. A corridor between the kingdom of the pharoahs and outer Asia, it was to belong now to one, now to another. At times, the vicissitudes of events provided it with a respite, but in time it bore the stamp of almost the whole world. The region was under Mesopotamian control toward the twenty-seventh century; during the second half of the third millennium, it passed under the control of Egypt and endured domination by that power.

At the beginning of the second millennium, a population made up of various strains inhabited Palestine.[16] Semites from Upper Mesopotamia and the deserts of the East had gradually settled there and become mixed in with the original inhabitants. The Bible often mentions these ancient and diverse ethnic elements.[17] The name

[15] Cf. II Par. 26:10 (the chapter shows that Ozias was concerned also, and primarily, with the safety of the country and its peace).

[16] In connection with Canaan and its inhabitants, some works on Palestinian archaeology may be pointed out. These are easily available and are very important, because they can be used in the study of the entire biblical history: William F. Albright, *Archaeology of Palestine* (Baltimore: Penguin Books, 1954); Willy Corswant, *Dictionary of Life in Bible Times*, English trans. by Arthur Heathcote (Oxford: Hodder & Stoughton, 1960); J. Finegan, *Light from the Ancient Past* (2nd edition; Princeton University Press, 1959).

[17] Cf. the lists (containing usually six names, but no doubt the most traditional are those with "seven" names) in Gen. 15:20 (the most complete); Exod. 3:8, 17; 13:5; 23:23; 33:2; 34:11; Deut. 7:1; 20:17; Jos. 3:10; 9:1; 11:3; 12:8; 24:11; Judg. 3:5; III Kgs. 9:20; I Esd. 9:1; Neh. 9:8. Peoples

"Canaanites," which belonged properly to certain inhabitants of the southern region, was finally generally applied to the other groups as well. The great invasions of the nineteenth to the seventeenth centuries left their imprint on Palestine: the presence of the Hittites [18] from Asia Minor, who made laws and created a kind of feudal regime, has been noted already.

By the time of the Patriarchs, the Canaanites were sufficiently amalgamated to present a common face to the world. "Canaanite civilization" was characterized by the clustering of the inhabitants into small fortified groups, a type of organization facilitated by geographical factors and made necessary in a region too often visited by pillaging bands and armies. These fortresses and principalities,[19] however, were generally rivals in wars with another. For the most part, the life of the people was crude and poor. Although a certain degree of cultural and technical development was reached, due primarily to foreign influences, the Canaanite civilization never became as important as and lacked the originality of the Phoenician civilization. The economic activity in the land of Canaan was enormous.

A language gradually took shape. Written documents, discovered especially in the West, are always in Akkadian cuneiform, proof of the spread of Mesopotamian thought throughout the Near East during the second millennium. Nevertheless, some traces of Semitic dialects with independent forms and alphabetical characteristics exist.[20] The alphabet spread throughout the Syro-Canaanite country and became the basic form of a language which contained the

---

undoubtedly more ancient are mentioned in Gen. 14:5. The Anaqim or "sons of Anac" are met with in Deut. 2:10-12, and especially Jos. 11:21; 14:12-15; 15:8, 13-15; 21:11.

[18] Cf. Gen. 23; Deut. 7:1. The identification of the "sons of Heth" with the Hittites is not, however, admitted by all exegetes; they are more inclined today to think that they were Horites.

[19] Innumerable tiny "kingdoms," such as we shall find mentioned in chapters 10 to 12 of the Book of Joshua.

[20] The alphabet was born the day man succeeded in separating the elements of the phonetic syllable, that is, the consonants and the vowels, especially the consonants which are the framework of words. (Formerly, for this reason, only the consonants were written.) Since these elements are not numerous (22 to 26 consonants are found on the average), the corresponding signs were easy to remember and especially easy to write. The exact historical circumstances of this discovery are not known, although it was one of the most important

various dialects of ethnic groups and places. Hebrew was to come from this Canaanite tongue.

The ideas and the religious customs of the Canaanites were taken from those of the Semitic world as a whole. Individual differences were due to the particular characteristics of the Canaanites —their way of life and the nature of the country.

The divinity had a generic name by which he was known throughout the whole of the Near East: El.[21] The term was used to designate this or that god, one or another aspect of the divinity,[22] but it also designated the supreme divinity or the great god of heaven. Canaan usually preferred to use another generic term for the divinity: Baal. Baal meant "master," he who dominates,[23] the possessor, the lord; he was especially the master of a place.[24] The subdivision of the country into little cantons caused the Canaanites to appoint a baal for each locality, or more precisely they appointed a divine couple, for they scarcely thought of their gods as being celibate. Thus, we find Baal and Astarte[25] together. Nothing, of course, prevented the Canaanites from reverencing and even adopting other divinities.

The mysterious forces of nature were adored in their personifications: divinities of the rain and the fountains, of vegetation and harvests, of war, of virility and maternity.[26] These divinities were

in all history. Everything points to the belief that it took place in Phoenicia, or at least that it was the Phoenicians who perfected the system.

[21] The word may have various longer forms: thus we find in the Bible *Eloah* and especially *Elohim* (plural used as a singular). The word, for the Arabs, has become Allah.

[22] It is often used in combinations to designate places: Babel, "gate of god"; Bethel, "house of god"; Penuel, "face of god," etc. Similar combinations may be found in other languages. Many names of persons are also constructed with El: Samuel, "God hears"; Raphael, "God cures"; Michael, "who is like God?", and others.

[23] "Baal" means also husband, the master of the woman.

[24] Thus Beelphegor, local name of the Moabite Camos (cf. Num. 25: 3-5; Osee 9:10); Baal-Hasor (cf. II Sam. 13:23). Baalbek, "the Lord of the plain," designates the famous city of the *beqaa* in Lebanon to this day. This word has also been used in combination to name persons: Jerobaal (cf. Judg. 6:32; 7:1), Esbaal and Meribbaal (cf. I Par. 8:33-34).

[25] Astarte is the Ishtar of the Babylonians; she was to become Venus for the Graeco-Romans.

[26] Furthermore, a god might be simultaneously both a father and celibate; a goddess both a virgin and prolific.

related to the springs and wells, to the trees and orchards, to sex, and also to the rhythm of the seasons.

Places of worship were carefully chosen and marked out; they were "holy" areas and were barred to all profane contact.[27] A place of worship was usually situated on a summit or an elevation of the ground (whence its name of "high-place") in the shadow of a "green tree" or a sacred grove,[28] and close to a spring. Stones raised up on roughly carved wooden palings adorned the site, whose central or highest part was occupied by an altar.

Certain places of worship, the great high-places, were particularly esteemed by the multitudes, because of some memory attached to them, such as a victory, a pact between clans, or because of the religious manifestations perpetuated there. These were centers of pilgrimage and devotion. Tombs attracted veneration and piety; they were meeting places of families and clans and often were adjacent to the sanctuaries. The funeral rites show that belief in survival after death was common; there was, as it were, a consciousness that the vital energy which animates living beings cannot be lost.

The principal act of religion was, obviously, sacrifice. Sacrifices were of different kinds: the offering of agricultural products; the immolation of various animals; human sacrifice; and, notably, the sacrifice of children.[29] Prayers, magic formulas, and ritual plays aimed especially at assuring the regularity of the seasons, the fertility of the fields, and the fecundity of the flocks and women. "Sacred prostitution" was a form of sacrifice, which had its origin perhaps in the "sacred marriages" solemnized in the great Oriental cults. These ceremonies originated, no doubt, in an attempt to influence nature's power over fecundity. On the high-places close to the sanctuaries, the sacrificial feasts enabled the faithful who par-

[27] A very sharp distinction was made between the "sacred" and that which was not sacred; between the "pure" and the "impure"; it is often found, particularly with regard to food and to marriage (cf. Lev. 11; 13-15.)

[28] Cf. Deut. 12:2; III Kgs. 14:23; IV Kgs. 16:4; 17:10; Jer. 2:20; 3:6; 17:2; Ezech. 6:13; Isa. 57:5.

[29] Archaeologists have found many skeletons of children encased in jars, sacrificed at the dedication of buildings. The Bible provides testimony to the fact that similar practices were introduced into Israel during evil times: cf. IV Kgs. 16:3; 21:6; 23:10; Jer. 7:31; 19:5-6; 32:35. They were formally forbidden and rigorously condemned by the Law: cf. Lev. 18:21; 20:2-5; Deut. 12:31; 18:10 (this is also the meaning of Gen. 22).

ticipated to enter into communion with the divinity and bound the participants into a mutual union. Music and dancing held an important place in the religious gatherings. Mass psychology was easily set in motion and was brought to a fever pitch in these noisy and animated, sensual and bewitching gatherings. The phenomena of delirious exaltation, frenzy, and a contagious ecstasy were given rein to.

Although all the ancient Eastern religions were religions of life and had as their basis the worship of a fruitful Nature, the source of all energies and the quasi-personal reality on which men were dependent in some mysterious way, the religious displays of the Canaanites seem to have been particularly coarse, voluptuous, cruel, and more simple and more brutal than elsewhere. Nevertheless, the religiosity, so spontaneous, so complete, and so frank, of these peasants who were subject to the sovereignty of Mother Earth contains something poignant: it arouses reflection and a certain respect. Their symbols do not seem obscene nor their bloody rituals odious if judged from their point of view, which was not moral, but religious. Their ceremonies were the expressions of a fundamental and unrestrained religious fervor. The evil and the baseness found in them were due precisely to the lack of any moral restraint.[30]

[TWO]

THE PATRIARCHS | The Hebrews of the patriarchal era derived either from Amorite or from a mixed Aramean stock.[1] Their fathers were semi-nomads who had come, perhaps during the twenty-third to the twenty-second centuries, from the borders of the Syro-Arabian desert to dwell in southern Mesopotamia, finding employment there as stock raisers, soldiers, or caravaneers (cf. pp. 5-6).

[30] The Canaanite practices were severly condemned by the Hebrew Law: cf. Exod. 23:24; 34:12-13; Deut. 7:5; 12:2-3; Lev. 16:21-22; 17:2-3; 18:3. The reason is essentially theological: the Baals competed with Yahweh; they were a "snare." This was a serious question, for Israel was always terribly tempted by the gods of Canaan! For the denunciations of the Prophets, cf. p. 63, note 2.

[1] Cf. Deut. 26:5; Jos. 24:2; Ezech. 16:3, for Amorites and Aramaeans; cf. also, p. 6, note 9.

The clan of Terah, the father of Abraham, lived with other similar clans in the country of Ur. Perhaps during the course of the twentieth century, but more probably during the nineteenth, the group emigrated and moved up the valley (cf. Gen. 11:31). We can easily suppose that the reasons for this move were both religious and political, since differences on these two levels usually lead to social conflicts which sometimes result in persecution (cf. p. 5). The Terahites stopped 625 miles to the northwest of Ur, in "Aram-of-the-two-rivers," at Haran. Haran was a branch or daughter city of Ur, both towns being vowed to the worship of the moon god, the patron of nomads and caravaneers.[2] The sons of Abraham retained family connections with Ur, to which they went to find wives (cf. Gen. 24, 28-29); Jacob was to make a long stay there (cf. Gen. 30-31).

The book of Genesis speaks of another migration (cf. 12:1-5), which it recognized as an exceptional call addressed by God to Abraham. Abraham's reply which, in his faith, he gave to God resulted in his "leaving his country." It is probable that Abraham's departure was part of broader events, such as the displacements of populations toward the south, of which various traces have been discovered. Abraham and his followers traversed the Syrian country, crossed the Jordan, and went up by the natural route which forms a link between the Ghor and the mountainous center of Canaan, to Sichem (cf. Gen. 12:6-7). Here the clan later sought to acquire rights. Then, going "from encampment to encampment," they went on to the southern steppes of Palestine (cf. Gen. 12:8-9).

The family of Abraham, which alone held the attention of the biblical authors, afterwards remained nomads in the center and the south of Canaan.[3] In the second generation after Abraham, however, a part of his family settled in the approaches to the delta of the Nile, because of a famine and the remarkable career of one of its members in Egypt (cf. Gen. 37-50). Joseph, the son of shepherds,

[2] Unless it was the migratory clan that took its god to Haran and established his worship there.

[3] Hebron, then called Qiryat-Arba, with its sanctuary of Mambre (cf. Gen. 13:18; 18:1) and burial cave of Macpela (Gen. 23:17-20), became a sort of home point and before long an important place for family pilgrimages. The persistent references to the purchasing of Macpela (cf. Gen. 25:10; 49:29-32; 50:13) is highly significant in view of the claim based on ancestral rights.

upon whom fortune smiled [4] and who became the grand vizier of a pharaoh, either a Semite or one favorable to Semites (Hyksos, no doubt; cf. p. 14), was to establish a large number of Hebrews in the pasture lands of the Egyptian northeast, where they would remain for a long time.

The sources for this history of the Patriarchs are ancient, having been passed down long ago in a certain form: old accounts of clans (cf. Gen. 12:10-20 and 20:1-16 [5]); memories attached to ancient places of worship (cf. Gen. 16:13-14; 31:43-54; 35:20); traditional explanations relating to usages and customs (cf. Gen. 17:9-27; 32:33); relationships, friendships, enmities,[6] fragments of poetry transmitted from generation to generation (cf. Gen. 16:11-12; 24:60; 25:23; 27:27-29, 39-40; the "blessing" of Gen. 49 is composed of elements of which many are very ancient poems or remnants of poems). One of the benefits of modern scientific study and of a better knowledge of the Ancient Near East is that certainties have been established in regard to the antiquity of these sources and the value of their testimony.

Of course, the texts we refer to were put together in comparatively recent times (cf. pp. 101-5); the questions they pose will be approached and clarified when we come to the epoch during which these texts were actually written. Aside from the literary form they received (with which careful reading will quickly make us familiar [7]) we also find in them the ancient traditions.

At present, we are speaking from the viewpoint of the historian,

[4] The Bible says "Yahweh," and we think the same; cf. Gen. 39:2-5, 21-23; 45:7-8; 50:20.

[5] This is one of the many accounts, which must have been told over and over with great pleasure. It has been preserved in Genesis under two forms (cf. also, Gen. 26:1-11); the various sources of these traditions explains the differences of detail in the texts.

[6] Cf. the provocative story in Gen. 19:30-38, which allowed the Israelites to scoff at their Transjordanian cousins whose origin was hardly praiseworthy. Genesis also contains traditions relating to the origin of the Ishmaelites (cf. 16:1-16; 21:9-20), the Edomites (cf. 25:23-34; 27:1-45), and other peoples.

[7] By careful reading, one should acquire the habit of distinguishing between a purely objective notation (for example, Gen. 21:8), a psychological translation (cf. 18:17), a theological explanation (cf. 20:18), an oratorical elaboration (cf. 22:17), a legal text (cf. 17:11-14), a poetic extract (cf. 27:28-29), and a document drawn up by a notary (cf. 23:17-18). These examples are taken at random from the middle of the Book of Genesis.

preparing in this way for the day when a different approach will be used: the search for a Message, the profound understanding of the Scriptures. The life of the Patriarchs as it is found in the Bible is itself a prophetic Saying, which brings us into a history in which we ourselves are involved, a history which judges, reforms, or recreates our own history. The faith and the "justice" of Abraham, the "believer" whose life was rectilinear and yet strangely cut across by the mysterious demands of God; the wandering existence of the complex Jacob, which was a struggle with God but also a communion with him; the wholly "providential" adventures of Joseph—these and many other profound portraits sketched by the sacred text cannot leave a reader of the Bible who does not wish to betray it or a son of the People of God who has received its spirit, indifferent. Nevertheless, before taking up these other aspects (and indeed in order to do so), our first modest inquiry must be content to be merely historical.

One cannot, on the other hand, remain insensitive to the charm of the delightful and oftentimes poignant pictures of pastoral and family life which make up Chapters Twelve to Fifty of Genesis. Pages of incomparable beauty [8] can be found in these chapters, in which are contained true pathos, as well as the wit so characteristic of the free Hebrew spirit whose profound and dramatic religion never interfered with his beguiling simplicity. The whole exhales an air which Israel has always been happy to breathe, that of its "childhood," that of its wandering, independent life. Nomadism, with all its austere implications, was both an ideal and a frequent source of nostalgia for Israel. Furthermore, nomadism was, no doubt, a profound law, governing Israel's concordance with the prophetic destiny God wished for it.

The history of the Patriarchs concerns only a few families. It relates their domestic dramas [9] as well as their contacts with the other inhabitants of the country. The story is a simple one.

These shepherds moved with their animals according to im-

[8] Here, we give no examples, leaving it to the reader to become aware of them.

[9] We will not go into detail until we come to the study of the Book of Genesis itself. These domestic dramas will then be seen to have the importance of a precept and a prophecy, or, to speak in the Bible's terms the value of *torah*.

memorial custom, and according to the natural living conditions of the countrysides they traversed. Living in tents, they were organized according to the simple, and abiding forms of family hierarchy.[10] Generally speaking they maintained good relations with the already established agricultural populations, who were related to them by race. If conflicts sometimes arose, they centered, for example, on shepherd arguments over the water wells (cf. Gen. 13:7; 21:25; 26:15-22). Intermarriages took place (Gen. 25:1, 26:34; 28:9; 34:1-4; 36:1; 38:2). Little by little the shepherds tended to settle down and to engage in cultivation. Although some Jacobites went to seek their fortune in Egypt, it seems probable that others definitively established themselves in Canaan, particularly in the region of Sichem (Gen. 33:18-20; Jos. 24:32).

The importance of the Patriarchs depends more on facts of a religious character than on the passing events and incidents of their lives as keepers of flocks.

Their memory is associated with particular places which, for the most part, already had a sacred character in the eyes of the inhabitants of the country and which remained special sites in the traditions of Israel: Sichem, Bethel, Hebron, Beersheba. The biblical narrators recorded singular events in connection with them. God revealed himself to the Patriarchs, in a mysterious but conclusive way; he "spoke" to them; he announced certain things to them (cf. Gen. 12:1-3; 13:14-17; 15:13-17; 26:23-24; 28:12-15; 35:9-14; 46:1-4).[11] And this God, according to the texts we have, presented himself as unique. Therefore, it seems that the religion of the Patriarchs was no longer a continuation or a derivation of the religions then existing, neither that of their Mesopotamian ancestors nor that of the Canaanite milieu.[12]

Long before Abraham men had arrived at a more or less clear

[10] Many nomads still live this way in the south of Palestine and in Transjordania. The similarity, however, should not be overemphasized.

[11] In order to understand these texts, a more systematic study of Genesis and of biblical Revelation is essential. Formulas such as "Yahweh appeared and said" and the biblical descriptions of "theophanies" do not imply that the existence of the Patriarchs was a tissue of miracles. Cf., in this connection, the discussion of the language of the Bible in *WG*, p. 162 ff.

[12] The scene in Gen. 35:2-3 is highly significant. Furthermore, it certainly seems that Gen. 12:1-3 means that there was a break with the original religious environment. Reread Jos. 24:2-3.

notion of a single God who was the master and providence of the world, the guide and judge of men. We have concluded to this in connection with the Mesopotamian religion, and, especially because of the particularly elevated thoughts of certain Egyptian minds. Consequently, it is possible that the clan of Abraham, in contact with various environments, having come from Babylon, and being acquainted with Egypt, may have acquired this superior notion of the one Lord. Yet the ancient biblical texts do not lead us to think along these lines. Rather, they lead us to believe that we are in the presence of extraordinary facts which are not explicable by natural means. What is certain is that the tradition of a whole people, Israel, recognized one Lord, the Lord of Sinai and of the Prophets, in the God who had "called" Abraham and had "spoken" to their ancestors.

To say that the Patriarchs believed in one God does not place them outside of their actual historical milieu or make advanced theologians of them. Did they think, for example, that their God was universal? The question did not arise in that form for them. Since "their" God was the only valid and efficacious one for them, other gods were practically—and this is the important word—practically nothing (we shall find this reasoning again in the Prophets—that a god who does nothing does not exist). This practical exclusivism and the intensity of the faith it provided an outlet for were enough of a religion for the Patriarchs. In this way, having a faith which is in no way speculative but actually living, many peoples have been monotheists; examples of such a faith, sound but undeveloped, may still be found in fairly homogeneous environments which are more or less closed off from others and which know few beliefs except their own.

Hence, actually, a God conceived simply in ideas was out of the question for them: God was Someone, a Living, Powerful, and Seeing Being (cf. Gen. 16:13; 31:53; 48:15-16; 49:24). One enters into a relationship with him by contacts that are reverential, incomprehensible, and beneficent (cf. Gen. 15:1-17; 16:7-14; 18:17-33; 20:3-7; 22:1-18; 28:10-22; 32:25-31; 46:1-4). The ancient traditions seem to have preserved the name under which Abraham and his descendants, either by preference or by habit, invoked him: "El-Shaddaï" (cf. Gen. 17:1; 28:3; 35:11; 43:14; 48:3; Exod. 6:3). The meaning of this term is not certain but may signify, "God-of-the-Mountains."[13] He is called "their" God, the "God of Abraham, of Isaac, and of Jacob," to show clearly that there were personal relations between the one God and those whom he first "called."

Even though they worshipped a special God, the Israelites did not cease being part of the Ancient Near East. Indeed, they expressed their faith, showed their worship, and lived their religion in the ancient Semitic manner: they prayed and sacrificed near sacred Trees (cf. Gen. 12:6, 8; 21:33; 35:4, 8) and Stones that were elevated above the ground (cf. Gen. 28:18; 31:13, 45-46; 35:14); near precious Wells (cf. Gen. 16:14; 21:31) and cherished Sepulchres (cf. Gen. 23:17; 25:9-10; 35:8; 49:29-32; 50:13). Not everything in the religious heritage from their Aramaean ancestors or in the Babylonian traditions was rejected; many practices in current use by the Palestinian regions could be adopted without betraying the faith that knew how to detach itself from them.

Among these practices, traces of which can easily be found in the Bible,[14] "covenants" must be especially pointed out. An agreement between persons or between groups was always concluded in a religious manner, with rites and oaths. The great rite of the *berith*[15] was a common repast eaten "before God," that is, in a sacred area and by partaking of the victims of the altar. The union thus contracted between the participants was considered conclusive, unbreakable, and sacred (cf. Gen. 26:28-31; 31:44-54). Another rite which established a covenant was union in one and the same blood. Either the participants mingled their own blood in a basin after having cut themselves in several places, or, more often, they were sprinkled with the blood of immolated victims. Since blood was considered to be life itself, it made them partners in a single life.

A covenant between a divinity and one man or a group of men was conceivable.[16] Genesis says that God made a covenant with the

[13] Because of the similarity with the Assyrian *shadu.* Cf. also III Kgs. 20:23, 28.

[14] When Abraham "sets up an altar," for example, and offers sacrifice, he does it in the Canaanite manner.

[15] This is the Hebrew word translated by "Covenant"; in Greak, *diatheke,* that is, "disposition"; in Latin, *testamentum,* that is, "attestation."

[16] A Sumerian text presents the laws of Lagash, about 2400 B.C., as guaranteed

Patriarchs and promised to make a covenant with their posterity (cf. Gen. 15:18; 17:7, 9, 19). Here there is, perhaps, the influence of the great event of the Covenant of Sinai, pictured in these its distant forerunners; but the account here is only influenced, not entirely created. The traditions themselves are old, as is evident from their account of the very ancient rite of Chapter Fifteen. In the case of the "sign of the Covenant" (circumcision), in Chapter Seventeen, the doctrinal and ritual elaboration is obvious (the text is "sacerdotal," from the sixth to the fifth centuries). Circumcision, however, is also a very ancient practice and had a religious significance and value among the Egyptians, where Abraham may have become acquainted with it. Nevertheless, the essential fact of a relation between the Patriarchs and their God, formulated in the terms of a covenant, can be retained. The tradition of Israel would never cease contemplating it.

The divine Covenant promised to the descendants of Abraham was really the foundation stone of the whole edifice of biblical Revelation; or, to rectify this overstatic image, it was the divine decision which created the History of the People of God. Meanwhile, it was necessary to wait: the Covenant had to be one between God and a "people." Before the sons of Jacob could become "the people whom God had chosen for himself" several centuries were needed, after which the events of the Exodus and of Sinai would transpire.

---

by a treaty made between the god and the king of that city (we shall see, however, that this case is not in any way similar to the divine Berith in Israel). There was a temple of Baal-Berith, the "Lord of the Covenant," at Sichem: cf. Judg. 9:4 (cf. 8:33).

3 The Divine Covenant

[ONE]

THE EMANCIPATION | With the triumph of Ahmosis over the Hyksos (cf. p. 14) and the coming of the eighteenth dynasty (1580-1320 B.C.), the period called the "New Empire" began (1580-1200 B.C.). This glorious period was at first an era of conquest in the region of the Upper Nile and, above all, in the Near East. The great Thutmosis III (1504-1450 B.C.) made himself famous by his seventeen expeditions into Syria, Phoenicia, and Mitanni. The army acquired an important position in the state and became a political force. The clergy were also very powerful. Artistic activity continued, and there was a great deal of building, notably in the time of Queen Hatshepsut, who was the regent from 1505 B.C. to 1483 B.C. during the minority of Thutmosis III, her nephew. Under the succeeding pharaohs, an anti-Egyptian coalition took shape in the Mediterranean Orient, once again putting the security of Egypt in jeopardy. On the whole, however, Egypt's cultural grandeur and her military power seemed so overwhelming that the Babylonians, Assyrians, and Hittites thought it prudent to pay tribute to her, considering themselves fortunate to be able to learn from her extraordinary civilization.

The eighteenth dynasty included the celebrated "heretic king," Amenophis IV, a name which he abandoned for that of Akhnaton, "Living image of Aton"; the name itself is both the slogan and the program of his career. Although he was young, he daringly inaugurated a religious revolution, suppressing the cult of all the other Egyptian gods in order to devote himself to one who had no image, but who was called Aton, that is, "Solar Disk." [1] The reli-

[1] Perhaps this was a return to an older and simpler form of the Egyptian religion. Queen Nefertiti seems to have played an important part in the religious revolution attempted by her husband. If the student wishes to read a pleasant, although somewhat idealistic, historical work, he will find it in a small, excellently illustrated volume by Daniel Rops, entitled *The King Drunk with God* (Le Roux, 1951).

gious revolution naturally gave rise to a social revolution, for theology, religious life, the structure of the state, and everyday life, were all wrapped up together. The realization of the number of men who were engaged in serving the sanctuaries and who drew their living from them, can measure the extent of the upheaval. To bring about a more complete break with tradition, Akhnaton created an entirely new capital, Akhetaton, the "Horizon of Aton." [2] Akhnaton's reform directly undermined the cult of Amon at Thebes and overthrew its clergy. But they would know how to get revenge. In reality, the doctrinal and liturgical revolution was foolish, because the Egyptian people were too deeply attached to their gods and their traditional practices. Furthermore, the mystic reformer was a mediocre ruler and, despite its urgency, completely neglected governmental business, notably in regard to Asia. The work of Amenophis IV, which was important from the point of view of the religious history of Antiquity,[3] was carefully undone as soon as he died and had no lasting effects,[4] except that royal prestige was greatly diminished.

The nineteenth dynasty (1320-1200 B.C.) produced some great pharaohs, such as Set I (1318-1298 B.C.) and Rameses II (1298-1232 B.C.). A great deal of building was accomplished, especially under Rameses. Wars were fought, which were not always fortunate, on the shores of Libya and in Upper Syria. In those times, Palestine was traversed constantly by Egyptian armies whose purpose was to

[2] Almost halfway between Memphis and Thebes, Akhetaton is today Tell-el-Amarna. It is well known because of the discovery of its library, containing international archives of unparalleled value. These consist of the correspondence between Amenophis III and Amenophis IV, and the letters between their governors or vassals in Syria and Palestine, the Asiatic kings, notably the petty kings of Canaan who schemed against and denounced one another to the pharaoh. The letters (nearly 400 of them), written in cuneiform on clay tablets, have supplied a great deal of information on the identity of various Eastern countries and on their relations during the first half of the fourteenth century.

[3] The break with tradition is also evident in the field of art. Artists of unforeseen novelties appeared, with original and fanciful works in which realism and a beautiful simplicity, not without overnicety and a certain romanticism, were dominant.

[4] The son-in-law and successor of Amenophis IV (who had only daughters), Tutankhaton, lost no time in leaving Amarna for Thebes and in changing his name to Tutankhamon; this pharaoh, who died at the age of 18 after having reigned for 9 years, has been well known since the discovery of his tomb and the unheard-of treasures it contained.

contain the Hittites, with whom Egypt finally made an alliance, and to oppose the growing power of the Assyrians.

Assyria, whose name derives from the town of Assur but whose capital was Ninive, had already tried its strength five centuries earlier. Now, it was on its way to bringing about the eclipse of Babylon. About 1300 B.C., Assurubalit freed himself from the yoke of Babylon; Adadnirari I later triumphed over the Mitannians to the north and went on to attack Babylon. Under Salmanasar I, the conqueror of the Hittites and the Aramaeans, twelfth-century Assyria became a power with which the world thenceforth would have to reckon.

Following the reign of Rameses II, the power of the pharoahs grew steadily weaker. The history of Egypt still had a long course to run, but it would be a history of a slow decadence. International domination would thereafter belong to the empires taking shape in Mesopotamia, their unification bringing together immense forces. To the misfortune of those who still believed in her, Egypt was to live for a long time on her remarkable reputation. Her time of eclipse, however, had not yet come, and the New Empire still retained its glory.

It must be noted that the various forms of Egyptian literature continued to flourish: narrative prose, stories and novels, memoirs and accounts of adventures; love songs, satiric poetry; state papers, praise of the pharaohs, exaltation of important royal events or services rendered by illustrious personages; mythological poetry, "books of the dead" (cf. p. 17, note 13); religious hymns, psalms; and "wisdom" writings. This literature is not only pleasing, it is often profound. In a later era, Israel would appreciate it, borrow from it, and imitate it.[5] Thus, the influence of Egypt was brought to bear upon Israel from the very beginning.

The descendants of Jacob who came to Egypt in the seventeenth century remained there until the eighteenth, that is, until about the end of the New Empire.[6] Practically nothing is known about their four-century residence, except that the Hebrews increased in num-

[5] Thus, it is possible to compare love poetry with the Canticle of Canticles, songs of disillusionment with Qoheleth, commentaries on social life with the thoughts of Ben Sirach, hymns to Amon and to Aton with psalms addressed to Yahweh. Extracts, delightfully presented, will be found in Gilbert, *Egyptian Poetry* (Brussels, 1943).

[6] Cf. the note on the Chronology of Exodus, pp. 56-57.

ber. If they lived, perhaps not in ghettos but at least close to one another and in groups distinct from the Egyptian population, that was the usual way of ethnic minorities. They could not, however, have remained in contact with a particularly well-developed civilization for such a long time without receiving some imprint from it, from the point of view of ideas and techniques, of customs and of ways of living. They had been witnesses of the religious and political life of Egypt, and of contemporary events.

Nevertheless, the Hebrews were not assimilated; they remained faithful to their origins and to their traditions. They had their own mentality and customs,[7] and they felt that they shared a common destiny. The Delta, moreover, is quite close to Palestine; hence, they maintained relations with their kinsmen who had stayed behind. Besides exchanges of a practical nature, there must have been exchanges in the psychological order as well. Doubtlessly, people came and went individually and in groups.

The narratives pertaining to the departure of the Hebrews from Egypt to Sinai are found in the first part of the book of Exodus.[8] They consist of a discontinuous series of texts, as in Genesis, but with even greater dissimilarity. And, like Genesis, Exodus collects together and puts side by side writings of several epochs, some from the beginning of the royal period, others from the beginning of the postexilic era.[9] The whole Bible bears witness to the fact that the greatest of Israel's traditions are to be found in Exodus. Hence, its accounts are an excellent source of history.

The narratives, of course, were simplified. They were organized in a religious perspective which, with time, became more conscious of the weight of their message. Furthermore, notations which reflect the different epochs in which the texts were prepared, as well as later glosses, can be found in the Book of Exodus. Nevertheless, the notations and glosses give a new dimension and a new value to Exodus, for they testify to the living and successive, organic,

[7] For example, the custom of going into the desert every year to celebrate a religious feast. This was a custom which was to provide support for the demands and the plan of Moses: cf. Exod. 3:18; 5:1-3; 8:24; 10:7-11, 24-26.

[8] The second part, as a whole, is not a narrative. Chapters 20-23 contain "laws" (in the sense to be discussed later), and chapters 25-31 and 35-40 describe the "Tabernacle" and its appurtenances according to views of sacerdotal theology, which take us to a much later time.

[9] For the "Yahwist" and "Elohist" traditions, cf. pp. 98-107; for the "sacerdotal" text, pp. 172-78.

interpretation that Israel gave to its memories down through the centuries. A reader who is unfamiliar with Exodus may be surprised to be promised enrichment just where the unity of the pages of the Bible seems to be taken apart before his eyes. Before long, however, he will discover that a truly critical examination is not only honest but also it enables him to enter into the unveiled depths of a living tradition.

With these remarks as a basis, we can now re-examine and understand the sequence of events.[10]

The Jacobites were few in number on their arrival in Egypt and enjoyed the favor of the pharaohs. A productive people, their behavior allowed them to remain. In time their numbers increased—this very fact making them troublesome to Egypt, because every foreign mass tends to band together. Furthermore, the government had changed and become anti-Semitic.[11]

The account of the oppression (cf. Exod. 1:8-22; 5:6-14) is probably only a summary of a longer history or, perhaps, the recital of its last phases. Repressive measures, forced labor, requisitions, and other vexations [12] tended to strangle and to humiliate a minority that was too large and, if not actually dangerous, certainly troublesome. Oppression, however, was to be the occasion of its liberation.

A man of fiery temper, Moses, under the direction of God, of whom he had had an indescribable and transforming experience in the desert, suddenly became the head of a movement of recovery. Because he had had the advantage of a careful education in high Egyptian circles, he claimed the right to deal with the governmental authorities (cf. Exod. 2-7). But events did not go smoothly.

[10] The study of the Book of Exodus itself will form the subject of the next volume of this series, and will go into greater detail. We shall, therefore, be brief at this time, faithful to our general plan and to our desire to advance gradually. Thus, the postponement until later of the biblical message contained in the Book of Exodus can be understood (cf. our observations on pp. 43-44).

[11] This is the sense of Exod. 1:8. The relation of the history of the Hebrews in Egypt to the presence of the Hyksos in the beginning and their later expulsion is a likely and generally accepted explanation. Nevertheless, it remains hypothetical and the events in question are not linked to this explanation.

[12] Exaggeration should be avoided. The Egyptians had comparatively gentle ways as compared with those of other ancient peoples, such as the Assyrians or, later, the Romans.

When they were recounted later, especially when they were written down (Exod. 7-11), they were seen as a great dramatic contest between the man of God and the powers of Egypt. The facts were not false, and a highly literary stylized scenario brought out the meaning of the facts.[13] It summarized the mounting political and social tensions, the urgent and vehement claims, then the brief relaxation of the governmental constraint which permitted the flight of the malcontents. As for the "plagues" of Egypt,[14] there is no difficulty in thinking that Moses made use, for his purpose, of calamities which the dwellers along the shore of the Nile may have been both witnesses and victims. Nor is there any difficulty in recognizing the possibility of a special intervention by God, inspiring Moses and directing events, as the tradition of Israel did in fact acknowledge.[15]

The drama came to a climax with the Passover. The word signifies the "passage" of God, a divine measure that excepted the Israelites when the scourge fell upon the Egyptians. In the pages which recount the event (cf. Exod. 11-13) narrative texts and ritual or liturgical texts are intermingled (cf. for example Exod. 12:14-22): the story of the "tenth plague"; precepts relating to the rite of the "Paschal Lamb" and to that of the "Unleavened Bread"; the account of the departure itself. This bringing together of various texts is understandable. The "feast" of Passover was celebrated subsequently in a commemorative and symbolic liturgy, a sacramental actualization of the event. Hence, just as in a Missal, historical reminders, prayers, rubrics, and songs are put together to signify truths, and especially facts, in all their dimensions and as their complete explanation, so too with regard to the Bible. The historian is somewhat nonplussed, of course; he lacks precise and detailed nota-

[13] The successive calamities are presented in tableaux with a stereotyped framework. In particular, one will note the leit-motiv: "Let my people go to sacrifice to me" (Exod. 7:16, 26; 8; 16; 9:1, 13; 10:3).

[14] "Plagues" is the accepted term. It is not well chosen, because it refers to misfortunes that fall, literally, that "strike" and "wound"; the Hebrew term can be translated almost exactly by the expression "hard blows."

[15] Remember that for the biblical writers the facts relating to the history of the People of God are never merely "natural." They are initiated and dominated by God, and are the "signs" (*semeia,* as the New Testament was to call the miracles) of his divine action. This sometimes makes it difficult to distinguish between naturally explicable phenomena and truly miraculous facts.

tions about the facts, although the unfolding of these facts as a whole does not escape him.

The "passage of the Red Sea" opened the way to liberty for the Israelites. An exceptional combination of circumstances allowed their escape by a hairbreadth.[16] Consequently, they were conscious of having been "saved," saved by God. This conviction was to grow deeper until it became one of the great "themes" of the Revelation given to Israel. The "Exodus" was to remain the prototype and the promise of all the graces of "salvation"; whenever they felt themselves enslaved, the People of God looked to the one Lord and Savior for their liberation, for the liberty to "serve" their God.[17]

The men and women whom Moses led out of Egypt could not yet be called a "people" or "the people of Israel." Certainly, there were many Israelites among them; but there were also all those who had taken advantage of the opportunity to leave: the dissatisfied and rebellious, men carried along by the discontent and the hope of the Hebrews.[18] During the journey, with the passing of months and years, it is quite possible that the company was augmented by nomads from the peninsula of Sinai, who were pleased at the thought of going up to Canaan. For the moment, the great caravan had to turn its back on Palestine; it had to forego the direct route to the northeast in order to avoid the Egyptian police who formed a military guard all along the isthmus of Suez. Possibly, however, groups of Israelites took the direct route in earlier or, more probably, later times of lesser tension. Some seem to have been settled in the south of Palestine before Joshua. The Book of Exodus has retained only the tradition of those who passed by way of Sinai.[19]

[16] Cf. Exod. 14. The Bible is not responsible for the stories of the prodigy popularized by traditional imagery. The biblical account and an examination of the locality provide information of a less fairylike character. The miracle lay in the simultaneous occurrence of exceptional conditions, as we shall see later in studying the text of Exodus more closely.

[17] Thus, the Sacred History itself was often conceived of as a succession of "exoduses." The Prophets were to speak of the return from the Babylonian exile in terms of an "exodus," especially the Second Isaias.

[18] The Bible does not hesitate to speak of a "mixed multitude" (Num. 11:4; cf. Exod. 12:38).

[19] Although the accounts of the departure from Egypt are highly complex from the literary point of view, composed as they are of "Yahwist," "Elohist," "deuteronomic," and "sacerdotal" texts (these last two forms being easy to classify), it seems that the essential plot is "Elohist"; in other words, it emanated

Note on the Chronology of Exodus

The Bible does not provide precise information concerning the era in which the "departure" of the Hebrews took place, and Egypt has left no reference to the fact (which, indeed, is understandable: the Hebrews were a minority, whom the Egyptians more or less confused with foreign [Asiatic] elements; besides, their story was not one that Egypt would derive any advantage or glory from by commemorating it).

It is possible that the Exodus took place under the eighteenth dynasty: Thutmosis III would then be the builder spoken of in Exod. 1; Amenophis II or Amenophis III the pharaoh of Exod. 5-15. The events with which we are concerned would thus lie in the second half of the fifteenth century. The reasons given in favor of this dating are the following: the expulsion of the Semite Hyksos, having as its sequel the restriction of Asiatics in Egypt and the persecution found in Exod. 1; the correspondence between the apex of power under the eighteenth dynasty and the works to which the Hebrews were subjected; the possibility of an identification between Hatshepsut and "Pharaoh's daughter" in Exod. 2; reprisals of Thutmosis III against Hatshepsut after her death and the flight of Moses to the desert; letter-tablets from El-Amarna (fourteenth century) in which the governors of the vassal cities of Egypt appealed to her against the invasions of Asiatics and notably of the "Habirou," who may have been the "Hebrews" (?) of the time of Joshua and the Judges; alphabetical inscriptions of the fifteenth century (pre-Hebrew ?), at Serabit-el-Hadim in the Sinai massif; collapse of the walls of Jericho dated by archaeologists at the end of the fifteenth century. These arguments are important, but may be susceptible of a different interpretation, and are more a harmonization of facts than positive indications. Some exegetes and scholars, nevertheless, still hold to this dating.

More numerous and more recent are those who adopt a different

---

from centers established in the northern region of Canaan, which gravitated around the tribe of Ephraim and formed part of the kingdom of Samaria. The other traditions, for example those concerning the direct passage to Palestine by certain groups, may have been lost or may not have been preserved. It may also be added that the tribes of the North (or the men who made them up) constituted the majority of the company and so were entitled to represent the whole of Israel.

chronology, called "lower" also, and who place the Exodus in the thirteenth century for reasons which are hard to reject. These reasons, which seem to carry the day because of their convergence, are: the residing of the pharaohs of the nineteenth dynasty in the Delta; the explicit mention of Rameses in Exod. 1:11; the nonexistence before the thirteenth century of the kingdoms of Edom, Moab, and Ammon, which were to bar the way to the Israelites coming from Sinai; the abrupt break and retrogression of civilization in Palestine at the end of the thirteenth century, bearing witness to an invasion; destruction of Canaanite cities like Bethel and Lachish in the second half of the thirteenth century; pursuit and arrest of a group of "Israilou" by Minephtha (or Mernephthah, 1232-1223 B.C.) in the south of Palestine; some thirty years of anarchy in Egypt immediately after the reign of Minephtha, favoring the undertaking of Joshua. Given these conditions, one may prefer the second chronology. The reign of building would then be that of Rameses; the expulsion of the Israelites may have taken place in the long reign of this pharaoh, or more likely in the very weak reign of Minephtha.

Some favor the date 1225 B.C.; others prefer to go back to the middle or even the beginning of the thirteenth century. We hold to a date between 1250 B.C. and 1225 B.C. Thus, the sojourn of the Jacobites in the country of the Nile would have lasted for more than 400 years (which accords with the biblical statements: cf. Gen. 15:13; Exod. 12:40; these, however, should not be taken as absolute mathematical indications).

[TWO]

THE PEOPLE GOD TOOK FOR HIMSELF | Between the Red Sea and the Gulf of Aqaba stands Sinai, the mountainous wall that occupies the southern third of the peninsula of the same name. It consists of a jumble of volcanic rocks, peaks, and lofty summits. A powerful natural sculpture with stately, vigorous lines and covered by marvelously colored rocks, Sinai rises into the pure light and air, a sight of extreme beauty, and at the same time of harsh solitude. It seems to be one of those privileged places where the Creator has let himself be found without an intermediary. Gorges, wadies, and a few plains are deeply enclosed and dominated by the impressive walls of rock. One of these plains was admirably suited for the tents of a fairly large company who made their encampment there.[1]

In this place, at a special hour, something happened that decided the destiny of Israel. An exceptional religious event took place in the imposing setting of the mountain, to the accompaniment of a lightning storm (cf. Exod. 19:16-19; 20:18-21; Deut. 4:11-12, 33, 36; 5:22-26). The Hebrews, like other peoples of the Ancient Near East, heard the Lord in the storm (cf. pp. 27-28). But this cannot be the explanation of the account; the reality far surpassed that. Such is the plain meaning of the account and, originally, the conviction forced upon the witnesses to the event.[2]

Moses and the assembled people received the *revelation of God.* They were certain that God had manifested his presence to them, although he was invisible,[3] and that they had heard his "voice," interpreted by Moses. On this conviction and on the Message received, they based their lives. The Revelation of Sinai was evident in its immediate consequences in the life of the group that had escaped from Egypt. Later, they bequeathed it as the essential in-

[1] This was the plain of Er-Raha, at the foot of the Ras-Safsafé. It is generally accepted as the site of the Hebrew encampment and, in fact, is particularly well marked. The identification, however, has never been established with strict historical proof.

Did the Hebrews make their agreement at a place consecrated to worship? One would be inclined to think so, especially if Moses had led them to the place where he himself had had the vision of the "burning bush" (which appeared as a theophany in the storm, in a sanctuary under the open sky, Moses being surprised not to have been struck by the lightning: cf. Exod. 3:1-6).

[2] We are not afraid to repeat, so that the mind can reflect fully and be entirely settled on this point, a remark already made in connection with the history of the Patriarchs and of the Exodus. The happenings on Sinai are known to us only through the prism of a literature several centuries later than the events themselves. "Tradition" is always our only source of history, and we know full well that it does not present history alone. The circumstances of our information demand a knowledge of how to use it, employing the discernment which is the law of historical science. This is why we refrain from describing or explaining the "theophany" of Exod. 19; it is also why we retain its essential fact, without which the testimonies of tradition would no longer have any meaning or basis.

[3] In this very absence of "appearance," Deuteronomy was to find the basis for the second commandment of the Decalogue: cf. Deut. 4:15-16.

heritance to their descendants. The history of the People of God proceeds entirely from Sinai.[4]

The name of the Lord who had revealed himself was "Yahweh."[5] Quite possibly, this was already the name of a divinity; the important thing, however, was the choice of the name and its use. It became the divine name par excellence for the Hebrews, or, more exactly, the private name for God used among them and by them. The name "Yahweh" seems to express the very impossibility of naming God, drawing attention to his "mystery." It was to be attached, primarily, to the memory of the Exodus and of Sinai; it was to be the permanent reminder of the coming of God and of his Word, and closely connected with the fact of the liberation of Israel.[6]

A connection was to be made also with the past. Yahweh was the "God of Abraham, of Isaac, and of Jacob." Now, however, the affirmation of faith was to be given full scope and was to be made in a clear light: Yahweh is the one God, absolutely exclusive of other gods (cf. Exod. 20:3). This was an essential advance over what we have discovered of monotheism up to the present. Although it is true that certain profoundly religious or exceptionally gifted men had previously been able to arrive at the thought of one unique God (cf. pp. 8-9), they remained rare; never had such a thought become popular and led to the denial of recognized divinities. The religion of Yahweh, on the contrary, was not reserved for a few privileged persons or for superior intellects, but was to be the expression of a whole people. They might be tempted to "return" to idols, but they knew they would be judged precisely by their faith in Yahweh, the One. Israel was to be the witness-people among other men of that faith. Who can say what the world owes to Sinai as a result?

[4] Note, at once, that it is not a question of ideas or of a myth, but actually of an event, placed in historical time and having a historical consequence (cf. pp. 26-27).

[5] Concerning the pronunciation of the four Hebrew consonants corresponding to YHWH, there is no absolute certitude (in the current language they must have been uttered as a single syllable, as certain texts and the "Praise Yahweh" or Allelu-Yah show). A way of pronouncing the divine name and of writing it according to this pronunciation ("Yahweh") came into general use. It is best to adopt this more common way.

[6] How often do we not hear in the Bible: "I am the Lord thy God, who brought thee out of the land of Egypt, out of the house of bondage!"

The people of Moses had the consciousness of not merely being the first beneficiary of the Revelation of Yahweh. They had entered into a rather particular relationship with their Lord; such was the plan that God had made known to them: he wished to enlist himself on the side of the Israelites, to form a partnership with them as a people, and with their descendants, in order to make history. In a word, God made an alliance with Israel, or, according to the classic expression, "Yahweh would be their God and they would be the People of God." [7] Hebrew tradition, in fact, traces the existence of the "chosen people" (cf. Exod. 19:5-6) back to Sinai, and it has kept the memory of the solemn celebration of the Covenant in a rite that uses blood to unite the contracting parties (cf. Exod. 24:5-8). The meaning of this Berith is also an absolute innovation, a revelation properly speaking.

"Ask now of the days of old . . . did any god venture to go and take a nation for himself from the midst of another nation? . . . The Lord set his heart on you and chose you . . . because the Lord loved you. . . . And now, Israel, what does the Lord, your God, ask of you but to fear the Lord, your God, and follow his ways exactly, to love and serve the Lord, your God, with all your heart and all your soul." [8]

The word on which the whole Judeo-Christian Revelation rests was spoken: *to love.* Men could not have invented it; even if anyone had ever thought of it, the idea of such a relationship with divinity would have been rejected. God, then, gave his secret to Israel: he loves men and he wishes to awaken the hearts of men to his most fundamental and yet his most extraordinary law: to love God. The Covenant was an interchange of love, although the initiative and the gift belonged entirely to God.

The Covenant was not merely a historical fact, an Act of God which was to be remembered. It was a permanent state, or rather an activity with God which begins again and again and is continually renewed in the course of generations (cf. Deut. 6:20-24; 29:11-14).

[7] One of the most frequent expressions in the Bible: Yahweh said: "I shall be your God and you shall be my people"; it always signifies the Covenant.

[8] Deut. 4:32, 34; 7:7-8; 10:12. We are perfectly aware of the fact that these texts were written much later (preface to Deuteronomy, composed in the seventh century). The use of the verb "love," proper to these texts, is itself late. We believe, nevertheless, that they should be used to express, in the best possible way, the reality of the Covenant of Sinai and to approach its Mystery.

It was a part of life, the normal, customary, although not natural, relation between Yahweh and his People; a disposition (cf. p. 47, note 15) of love on both sides.[9] The great law of this life for Israel was faith in the divine Covenant.

Love is action and service. Thus, the Covenant was to create an original history (Sacred History or, in precise terms, simply history): God was going to work in this history, concern himself with it in accordance with his pledge; he was going to work for men, and with them, for their "salvation." For he now has need of men and of their effective love: the Covenant is a work in common, a sharing of responsibilities.[10] God invites his People to make history with him from this point on, pursuing his plan of creation and of life. The Revelation of Sinai, which created his People, was also the inauguration of an absolutely new activity in the world.

The Covenant was not slow in inspiring practical attitudes and rules of life. Such was the beginning of the *Torah.* A "torah" is essentially, in its origin, an indication of a line of conduct, given by someone having the mission to do so among his brothers. Concrete and individual cases, contentious or difficult, which required a solution, were the occasion for the formulation of a torah (cf. Deut. 17:8-13; Lev. 24:10-23; Num. 9:6-14; 15:32-36; 27:1-11; the texts are comparatively recent, but the traditions are ancient). The solution imposed in a given case was afterwards considered valid and obligatory in all similar cases; it was expressed in a formula to which reference could be made whenever necessary. Naturally, if the situations or circumstances changed, the formula would have to be revised and adapted, transformed or annulled as required. It might, however, also be preserved as evidence of the spirit and manner of acting from which one ought to draw inspiration in finding new solutions; it would always be valuable as a directive. In biblical terms, it would open and show the "way."

[9] It is a temptation to interpret the word "love" in terms of "conjugal" love, but this should be reserved in connection with the Prophets; it is not certain, however, that one must wait for Osee. Can the esence of the Covenant of Sinai really be formulated outside the sphere of nuptial love? Perhaps the expression "jealous God," which belongs to this language, is ancient.

[10] According to the expressions of A. Néher in his fine study on Amos (Vrin, 1950). A small but profound book on Moses by the same author, in an essentially Jewish perspective, has recently been published (coll. *Maîtres Spirituels,* ed. du Seuil, 1956).

Among the ancient peoples of the Near East, the power of deciding and enacting laws was not thought to come from men alone; the decisions were understood and were to be accepted as an expression of a divine will (cf. p. 28). Thus, the practice of a law, which in Israel was simultaneously and primarily a teaching, was the property of those who had a special relationship to God—the priests. To "consult Yahweh" in the Bible always means to submit one's case to the minister of a sanctuary; the answer was a divine "revelation." Hence, the priests were considered "seers" and, before the word was coined, "prophets" (cf. I Sam. 9:9), that is, men speaking in the name of God. These ideas are found in the archaic period of the history of Israel, either before the time of the royalty or at its beginning, and help us to understand what happened at Sinai.

Moses evidently found it necessary to organize his "multitude" of people. They were a vast horde that had little homogeneity in the beginning and that were often surly.[11] It was necessary to create frames of reference, to regulate social relationships, and to define the requirements of the religious life and its manifestations. The judgments and the decisions of the chief-priest of Sinai were the most ancient "toroth" of Israel. Precisely because of this beginning and the spirit he gave forever to the "Law," Moses is regarded as the first and the greatest lawgiver of the People of God.

His spirit was that of the Covenant. Because of this, there is a radical difference between the Law of Moses and all other laws. The toroth were no longer merely the manifestation of an authority representing God; they were the expressions and fulfillments of the divine Covenant—the words and acts of a Dialogue . . .[12]

Moses had to find helpers who would act as he did, and who would pursue the huge task of leading a people and helping it to live the Covenant. Biblical tradition says that he did find them (cf.

[11] In Exodus and Numbers we read frequent accounts of "murmurings," of recriminations, and even of revolts; cf. especially Exod. 16:2-11; 17:1-17; Num. 11:1-35; 14:1-35; 16:41-42; 20:2-13; these texts contain "doublets" which only give added weight to the tradition (read also, as a poetic echo and prayer, Ps. 78 and 106).

[12] We must continue our history; the time has not yet come to meditate on these fundamental facts of Revelation, which carry such great weight with regard to the mind, the heart, and the life of men. We shall consider that aspect later. It can be understood immediately, however, why Judaism has regarded the Torah as the greatest part of its sacred Writings. The Lord Jesus "summarized" the Law (cf. Matt. 22:37-40) according to the Revelation of Sinai.

Exod. 18:13-26; Num. 11:11-30; Deut. 1:6-18). Life had to continue after Moses; religious instruction, moral direction, social and juridical developments, explanations and decisions could no more stop than could life itself. Those whom the Bible calls the Levites (that is, according to the probable etymology, the persons "attached" to God) were to have a principal and permanent part in this activity which lasted for centuries and which was to have as its final result the great Torah of Israel.

It soon becomes evident, in fact, that a great number of prescriptions which were written in the Pentateuch as if they came from the time of Moses, even as if they were given by Moses himself, presuppose no longer merely the religion of the desert with its necessarily rudimentary forms, but rather the worship of Jerusalem as it was displayed in the finest days of Yahwism. A certain number of biblical descriptions are certainly only recollections or the expression of aspirations that were far from being fulfilled. Such is the case with the detailed descriptions of the Tent-Sanctuary, the sacred object, the ministers of the cult (cf. Exod. 25-31; Num. 28-29; Deut. 14-16; and a large part of Leviticus). These narrations were inspired by the memory of the Temple and of the religious Service of Jerusalem. Similarly, the "camp" in the desert, placed around the "Tabernacle," was conceived in accordance with the ideal of priests who wished to make the postexilic community realize what the holy God wanted from the People consecrated to him (cf. Num. 1-10).

A rather variegated and heavily laden sum of all the "laws" is contained in the Books of Exodus, Leviticus, Numbers, and Deuteronomy. Understandably, when we read these texts we are not always in the thirteenth century and at Sinai. The "Torah" is truly a "collection," and the reader should not forget it. Nor should he forget that it is a collection of traditions, and consequently of things that are often ancient. The biblical Codes retain vestiges of the laws of the Ancient Near East (cf. pp. 9-10). In them are to be found old regulations relating to sacrifices, criminality, "purity," and agricultural feasts; Israel simply inherited these regulations, but subjected them to the amendations of its faith.[13] One cannot be insensitive to

[13] The process of amending would always involve demythization: the agricultural feasts became the celebrations of deeds, filled with historical significance; the spring festival became a remembrance of the Departure from Egypt (Easter), the autumn feast became a commemoration of the Sojourn in the Desert (Succoth or the feast of "Tabernacles").

the archaic flavor of certain texts (cf. Deut. 21:1-9; Lev. 14:2-9, 51-53; Num. 5:11-31; 19:2-22). The Decalogue is more original; there seems to be no doubt that it goes back to Moses.[14] It was the basic charter of the Covenant, expressing in an essential, clear-cut, and surprisingly elevated manner the requirements of the love of God and of life with him.

Moses had to exercise his "legislative" activity [15] chiefly at Cades. The Israelites seem to have remained only a few months in the heart of the mountain. Through the years that followed, hardly anything is known of them except that they stayed for a long time around Cades, the "Holy Place" in the south of Palestine.[16] This was a rather poor but cultivable oasis, surrounded by steppes which could serve as meager pastures. The Israelites lived there partly as nomads and partly as farmers.

Cades was able to serve as a religious center and at the same time as a kind of headquarters. The levites and priests of the following centuries considered themselves to have originated from the men grouped around Moses, ministers of the Sanctuary and officers of that Bedouin society (cf. Exod. 32:25-29; Num. 25:7-13; Deut. 33:8-11). When the great Prophets of the eighth and seventh centuries idyllically evoked the "loves" of Yahweh and his People, they must have been haunted by the ideal of the Desert, thinking no doubt of the time of Cades when this love was still "a child," "in the days of its youth" (cf. Osee 2:16-17; 9:10; 11:1-4; Jer. 2:2-3). Perhaps from these years Israel retained the deepest impressions of its union with the Lord.

This did not prevent the Hebrews from spending a miserable enough time in the desert, however. Besides the habitual grumblings of the wandering multitude, ill-fed and often thirsting, independent

[14] Cf. Exod. 20:2-17; Deut. 5:6-21. Each of the Ten Commandments must originally have been expressed in a brief form, which has remained for the fifth, sixth, seventh, and eighth commandments. The little commentaries with which the others are endowed were added later; moreover, they are not exactly the same in the two traditions.

[15] It should now be well understood that the word "law" has a special and properly biblical meaning: a teaching-and-directive.

[16] Cf. Num. 20:1. Cades is a little less than 62 miles south of Gaza, and about 75 miles southwest of Hebron. There, archaeologists have discovered walls and terraces, and remnants of life earlier than the Exodus and of agriculture.

and in the mood for pillaging, the Book of Numbers reports some tragic mutinies (cf. chaps. 12; 14; 16). The "Forty Years" were interpreted as a punishment of the "rebellious" people (cf. Num. 14:21-35). In reality, however, the people was not ready to leap upon its prey, the "good land" it expected from Yahweh. Penetration was attempted; skirmishes took place between the Hebrews and the Palestinian populations of the south and the southeast (cf. Num. 14:39-45; 20:14-30; 21:1-35). The history relates events up to the arrival of the Hebrews in the plains of Moab, after a difficult journey through the harsh region of Arabah [17] and east of the Dead Sea (cf. Num. 22-25).

Moses died in sight of the land of Canaan, "the promised land" (cf. Deut. 34:1-8).

Tradition cannot exaggerate its debt to this man of God, "the meekest man on the face of the earth," the "servant" whom his faithfulness firmly "established in the house of God" (Num. 12:3, 7), to whom Yahweh "spoke as a man speaks to his friend" and with whom he "knew face to face" (Exod. 33:11; Deut. 34:10). A friend of God, he was no less a man of his People, ready to be rejected with it rather than to forsake its cause (cf. Exod. 32:32). He had liberated this People and had revealed it to itself; he had instructed it in the Knowledge of God; he had opened the paths of its divine History. He was the Mediator of the Covenant.

Until Christ, "no prophet has arisen in Israel like Moses" (Deut. 34:10).

[17] The "Plains of Moab" lie to the northeast of the Dead Sea; the Arabah is the depression that continues it to the gulf of Aqaba.

4 The Land and the Kingdom

[ONE]

THE OCCUPATION OF CANAAN[1] | Before his death, Moses chose Joshua as his successor. The time had come to enter into the coveted land. The men of the desert had become hardened and had learned to unite; having obtained information in advance, they tried their hand in a few raids, and they had spies and relatives in the very heart of the country.

The general situation in the Near East was favorable to their plan. The great powers were not concerned with that side of the world. Babylon, which was declining, kept its distance. The Assyrian had not yet "bathed his sword in the sea" of the West. The Egyptian New Empire, growing weaker, was declining, and its authority was little felt by its little Syro-Palestinian neighbors. A certain crystallization of Aramaean elements was taking place in Syria, but it gave no hint of the danger that would arise in a century or two by a confederation centered around Damascus.

The Canaanites might have succeeded in opposing the invaders if they had formed a political unity of any kind. Their civilization, feudal in style, had some rather splendid characteristics. When the Canaanites were united they represented a real power, as the Israelites were to discover. The conquest of the whole country was to take a long time and would be highly uncertain on several occasions. If the first penetration was a success, it was due largely to a division among Canaanites. By a concerted effort, a few bands of resolute and daring men were able to infiltrate the tiny independent and rival principalities.

The Israelite invasion was not a unique event in that region at the beginning of the twelfth century. At the same time or a little later, the Philistines established themselves in the Shephelah. These

[1] The history of this period and of the following one, up to the death of Solomon, has been written with great care by Desnoyers in his *History of the Hebrew People*, 3 vol. (Picard, 1922 and 1930).

"Pelishti" [2] were adventurers of Cretan origin; they were part of the peoples whom the Dorians, coming from Aegea (cf. pp. 3-4), had overthrown and driven out, and whom the Egyptians called the "Peoples of the Sea." They had tried to descend into the Delta, but Rameses III (1198-1166 B.C.) had driven them back. Some disembarked on the neighboring shore; this was the origin of the Philistine colony. In time, it would be necessary to reckon with these highly gifted men, who were well organized (in a confederation of towns), and equipped like the soldiers of the Iliad.[3] In their attempt to expand they would become the greatest enemies of Israel.

Other groups cast covetous glances on Canaan and if they could not appropriate it for themselves, they planned at least to raid and to bleed the territory. Among these groups were the Ammonites, who were more or less settled in central Transjordania; the Moabites, who were on the plateaus overlooking the Dead Sea; and the Edomites, Amalekites, and Madianites, who dwelt or wandered on the southern fringes.

The history of the conquest is told in the Book of Joshua. Among the texts gathered together in this book are some very ancient ones, earlier than the eleventh century, or, in other words, the first set form near enough in time to the events narrated.[4] The essential part of Chapters Two to Ten are judged to have been written down at the beginning of the tenth century, giving almost definitive form to the traditions which had been in the process of transmission for one hundred or one hundred and fifty years. The rest of the book is composed of "deuteronomic" fragments of the seventh century, or rather of a general revision by the hand of a "deuteronomic" author.[5] This literary clarification makes it possible to grasp the properly historical data of the book, the style of which is "prophetic" (cf. *WG*, p. 181 f.), through the use in the works of stylized traditions.

[2] They gave their name to "Palestine," which is one of the ironies of history.

[3] This was the time of the celebrated Trojan War (1180 B.C.) sung by Homer. The description in I Sam. 17:5-7 is of Greek armor.

[4] There are notations which are "from the period" (for example, Jos. 6:25). It may be admitted that this form was first set orally, as is the case of the oral traditions generally found at the dawn of any historical literature.

[5] A person who has read Deuteronomy immediately feels that he has come upon pages of it again when he encounters discourses like those of Joshua 1 or 23.

The stages of the invasion are not described in the style of a campaign journal, of course, or in the manner of a military report. No dates are given, and there is uncertainty concerning the duration and the chronological sequence of the events.[6] The Israelite units sometimes acted as a whole, but more often they operated as independent bodies. Joshua had a great part in the overall enterprise, but he cannot always be found in the role of commander; at times he seems to have served as an arbiter between groups which would not always have reached an understanding without him. Some events took place without him, or even after him. Nevertheless, the tradition of Israel has always recognized him as first in importance, and has given his name to the first volume of the "earlier Prophets." Just as Moses became the man in whom the Exodus, Sinai, and the Law were epitomized, so Joshua has become the one who introduced Israel into the Promised Land.[7]

The Israelite maneuvers are easy to grasp as a whole. As a preliminary step, the pasture lands which lie to the east of the Jordan were occupied with little difficulty.[8] After the crossing of the river not far from Jericho, and the capture of that town by means which depended more on cunning than on strategy (cf. Jos. 2-6), the armed bands made several forays into the mountain, falling back each time to Galgal, their "bridgehead."[9] Then they gained a footing in the rough terrain of the central region (cf. Jos. 7), where conditions were more favorable to them. The Canaanites could not recover the advantage except on level ground where their cavalry and their chariots were of use. At Sichem, where the arrival seems to have been made without striking a blow, a great Covenant with

[6] Reread Jos. 1-12 and 22-24. Chapters 13-21, containing topographical details, which are invaluable for a knowledge of biblical Palestine and are a kind of "prophetic geography" whose statements, in relation to history, range from indications of the establishment of Israelite groups in certain regions as early as the time of the conquest to precise delineations of tribal boundaries, such as they were set later on or such as they may have been wanted.

[7] The prologue to the book draws the parallel clearly: cf. Jos. 1:5, 17. Cf. also the parallels between the crossing through the Red Sea and the crossing of the Jordan: cf. Jos. 4:21-24.

[8] Cf. Num. 32; Jos. 13; 22. In spite of the occupation by two and one-half Israelite tribes, this region was never, properly speaking, Palestinian. The "Promised Land" was bounded on the east by the Jordan.

[9] Situated in the Ghor, between the Jordan and Jericho, three miles to the south-east of the site of the ancient city. Cf. Jos. 4:19; 9:5; 10:6, 43.

Yahweh, the importance of which for the rest of the history cannot be minimized, was celebrated (cf. Jos. 8:30-35; 24:1-28; Deut. 11:26-32; 27:2-26). No doubt, the meeting of the invaders with the Hebrews who had been settled in the country for a very long time was celebrated at the same time. Canaanite reactions, which were usually kept under control by ambushes and surprise maneuvers, are mentioned in the south (cf. Jos. 10) and in the north (cf. Jos. 11).

Due in part to enthusiasm, the Book of Joshua presents the Israelite invasion as a quickly successful conquest. Ignoring the failures and the enormous effort that remained if the Israelites intended some day to make themselves truly the masters of the country, was an encouraging way to look at things. The wars of Israel were the wars of Yahweh marching at the head of his People (cf. Exod. 15:3-7; 17:16; Num. 10:35; Deut. 33:26-29; Judg. 5:23; I Sam. 18:17; II Sam. 5:24), and his People was never so united as when it was at war. A great religious vision can be seen in this viewpoint.

Another point of view, no less religious but considering a different aspect, is found in the Book of Judges. The documentation of Judges is organized to show the nonfulfillment of the work undertaken and the resultant dangers. At the same time it denounces the infidelity of the Israelites to Yahweh as the underlying cause of this state of affairs and thus teaches an essential lesson.

Like the Book of Joshua, Judges has a long literary history. Accounts of the exploits of heroes who had made themselves famous before the institution of the monarchy no doubt had been circulated among the tribes at an early date. A written compilation of these traditions seems first to have been made in the eleventh and tenth centuries.[10] Writers of the royal period later worked over the anecdotes in order to draw instruction from them. The work of the deuteronomic editors in the seventh century, to whom we owe the book as it is, completed this historical and didactic creation by framing the collection and each of its sections into stereotyped and significant formulas.[11]

[10] It is thought that one tradition concerning the "judges" of the north and another concerning those of the south can be distinguished. The history of Samuel, that is, a part of I Sam. 1-15, would have belonged to the same ensemble at first.

[11] The "deuteronomic" intentions are very evident in chapter 2. The reader will discover them easily for himself, almost always at the beginning and at

A summary of the situation as it emerges from this source of the tradition is the following (cf. Judg. 1): some twenty or thirty years after the assault on Jericho, the Israelites, in addition to being partially established in Transjordania, were well entrenched in the mountainous region. The Canaanites, however, continued to defend themselves successfully in almost all their strongholds; they held the fertile regions, and often forced the newcomers to enter into practical agreements with them. A new and important improvement in the situation for the Israelites began with their victory, on the plain this time, over Sisara in the valley of Jezrael (cf. Judg. 4).

The danger for the Israelites was that they would break up and become lost. Scattered now in isolated groups, and usually materially inferior to the people who had been settled in the country for a long time, they were exposed to the influences of the Canaanite environment. No doubt they were faithful to Yahweh, but their fidelity was moderated by pagan customs, by "baalizing" tendencies. The highly moral religion of Moses, which forbade graven images, seemed quite severe. Besides, Yahweh was the "God of armies on the march" (Yahweh Sebaoth), the Lord of nomads and soldiers, the Sovereign of an untilled and rugged Sinai; could he also be a specialist in agricultural questions? The Canaanites had divinities for their sowings and their reapings. Was this not to their advantage? Having become farmers, ought not the Israelites show some regard for these protectors of the earth, at the same time keeping all their reverence for Yahweh, from whom other services were to be asked? People who were rather disappointed, and uncouth, under the powerful grip of their surroundings, might well think in this way; besides, all peoples have a secret paganism in their hearts.[12] Great weight must also be given to the marriages or chance unions with the Canaanite women.[13] The instincts of the Israelites

the end of the stories of the principal Judges. The most typical piece is certainly the highly schematic history of Othoniel: cf. Judg. 3:7-11.

[12] If a complete view of the situation can be had by reading the story of Gedeon: cf. Judg. 6:25-32. Moreover, Gedeon's end is highly questionable from a religious point of view (cf. Judg. 8:22-32). The story of Michas and his Levite is also quite revealing: cf. Judg. 17:1-13.

[13] The religion of these women was also embraced to some extent (cf. Deut. 7:3-4; Judg. 3:5-6). The chance unions seem to have been easy and widespread (cf. the story of Samson: Judg. 13-16). And what a temptation might not be presented, in actuality, by prostitution, which was carried on, precisely in virtue of religious principles, "on every hill and under every green tree."

were too much in sympathy with a pulsating religion of physical life.

Their attachment to the soil also carried the danger of making them forget their origins and of dissolving the historical consciousness of their unity. Blood ties, territorial organizations, regional groups centered round the towns, could not be substituted for a historical consciousness. As a matter of fact, the substitution took place, but not very quickly or completely. Israel remained, in spite of everything, an ethnic community. The feeling for family relationships cannot disappear easily in an Oriental people. Documents show that an explicit will to unity characterized the Israelites even in these difficult times. The "Twelve" tribes seem to have quickly formed themselves into a federation which had representatives and delegates in general assemblies.[14] Probably there was even a kind of permanent "council" for the tribes of the north who lived in the mountains of Ephraim and another for the tribes of the south, having at its head the tribe of Judah. The "assembly of Israel" (plenary) must have been held yearly. During the course of its religious ceremonies and deliberations, the people renewed the "Covenant" with Yahweh and the one among themselves; decisions were taken and "toroth" established. Elements of these are preserved in the Bible.

Hence, Yahweh remained the God of the Israelites. He had his high places. To the sanctuaries already set by tradition, by the Patriarchs, and by divine meetings, others were added like Gilgal, Shiloh, Mizpah, Qiriathyarim, Nob, and Gabaon. Shiloh occupied a place apart and had become a central place of pilgrimage, because the Ark of the Covenant had been set up there (cf. Jos. 18:1; 19:51; 21:1; 22:9, 12; I Sam. 1:3; 4:3).

The religion of Yahweh entered quite naturally into the sphere of Canaanite religious customs,[15] those which the Prophets were later to call "abominations." But noble thoughts and a pure piety could be found in the hearts of the faithful and of the pilgrims.[16] Moreover, the priests of the religious centers did the best they could according to their knowledge and ability as representatives or witnesses of a more or less developed religious mentality. We are of

[14] This organization and these gatherings have been justly compared with the Greek *amphictyonies,* the religious leagues and political associations of ancient Hellenic society.

[15] An indication of this can be seen in the fact, among others, that the god of the covenant of Sichem was a "Baal": cf. Judg. 8:33; 9:4, 46.

[16] What could be more suggestive of this than the scenes in I Sam. 1-2?

the opinion that through them the essential teachings of Yahwism were maintained. Furthermore, the numerous particular traditions concerning the Levites, woven together by the "deuteronomist" and "sacerdotal" writers, cannot be deprived of their origin or their ancient foundation. These men "set apart," deprived of property, living on public charity, teaching their brethren history and the acts of God, pointing out to them the consequences of the election of Israel and of the divine Covenant, represented better than any others the deep stream that linked Sinai to Jerusalem, Moses to David. The importance given to them by the Bible was not without justification.

Perhaps the rough hewed and uncompromising religion of the desert also had its witnesses reduced to a special class, the Nazirites, an institution which seems to have had several forms in the course of the centuries. They were the pioneers of an ascetic and community life that would develop later on in Israel.[17] In any case, there were "seers" (I Sam. 9:9), "inspired" men; but by what "spirit" they were inspired, we do not always know, although the spirit of Yahweh was certainly not ruled out.[18] There were "prophetic" manifestations, accompanied by states of physical excitement, but in which true spiritual values undoubtedly sought to break forth from the elementary psychological disturbance (cf. I Sam. 10:5-10; 19:20-24).

This period is called the time of the "Judges." The Judges were picturesque heroes rising up in this or that canton to remedy, by fortuitous means, some disastrous situation. They doled out "justice," that is, "saved" their brethren,[19] or some among them at least, by giving back to them the taste for independence and self-assertion, for racial unity, and for a union of their powers. Besides the professional warriors,[20] unexpected leaders appeared who were ani-

[17] Concerning the Nazarate, cf. Num. 6:1-21; Judg. 13:5-14; I Sam. 1:11, 28.

[18] The "seizing" of the spirit may be the sensation of physical energy which laid hold on a Jephtha or a Samson (cf. Judg. 11:29; 14:19; 15:14), just as well as the superior wisdom bestowed on Samuel (cf. I Sam. 3:19-21); the case of Gedeon partakes of both forms (cf. Judg. 6:14, 34).

[19] The very word, "savior," or "liberator," designates a particular person (cf. Judg. 3:9, 15).

[20] The *gibborim*, that is, the strong, the daring elements of a voluntary legion or of a somewhat aristocratic chivalry, which was formed in imitation of the Canaanite warriors and which would constitute the framework of future regular armies (cf. Judg. 5:23; I Sam. 23).

mated with sudden zeal. They won small local victories which, added together, created a feeling of conquest and of encouragement. Tradition preserved an exalted memory of them.[21] Their history is made up of anecdotes, but its historical truth is all the more certain because of them.[22]

This history shows that there was much to endure and to struggle for, because of nomads plundering the harvests, ill-disposed neighbors, and the Philistines who grew ever more aggressive. The times were hard and troubled; the atmosphere was penetrated by superstitions. One might say it was a kind of early medievalism, anarchichal and barbarous,[23] nonconforming and unrestrained, but not without generosity and with a kind of disfigured joviality[24] and plenty of faith, although, indeed, it was an elementary faith. The Israelite way of life became more and more agricultural; Israel attached herself to the land.

For this reason, the Laws which are found collected in the Code called the "Covenant Code"[25] are thought to belong to this era. Some exegetes would date them as far back as the last years of Moses, in the time of Cades. The concrete situation they presuppose, however, seems rather to be that of a people which had become sedentary and agricultural.

These former nomads did not deny their past; they sang of it in narrative or epic *poems*. In their world of endless words, improvisers were not lacking. While they rested in the evenings or after the heat of the day, and on days of festival or rejoicing, they told of adventures and exploits; they glorified personages and events. Thus, their memories became a lasting inheritance, acquiring a form which was to be perpetuated. A part of the Pentateuch and the essential substance of the Books of Joshua and of Judges come from that time, or at least they passed through that oral transmission before being collected and definitively fixed. Indeed, collections of traditions are known to have been made at an early time; such were

[21] We can compare our stories of legendary heroes.

[22] At this point reread Judg. 3-16.

[23] The acme of what is to be read will be found narrated in the appendices to the book of Judges: cf. Judg. 17-22.

[24] Everyone knows the coarse farces of Samson.

[25] Cf. Exod. 20:22-23; 19. It would be well to reread this Code (cf. 22:20-26; 23:1-9).

the "Book of the Wars of the Lord" and the "Book of the Just" (cf. Num. 21:14; Jos. 10:13; II Sam. 1:18). They have not been preserved, but, before the monarchy was established, they must have gathered fragments together, some of which are found in the books of the Bible.

The pages of the Pentateuch are studded with small poetic pieces that are obviously archaic: benedictions or maledictions, supplications or thanksgivings, calls to arms or notices of victory (cf. Gen. 4:23-24; Exod. 15:21; 17:16; Num. 6:24-26; 10:35-36; 21:17, 27-30). They were recited and undoubtedly already had received definitive form a century or two after the entry into Canaan.

It is especially fitting to mention the first great evidence of ancient Hebrew poetry, the vibrant and magnificent "Canticle of Debora" (Judg. 5). Composed immediately after the events of which it is still the breathless and passionate echo, the canticle is an evocation, at once savage and eminently lyrical, of the greatest military engagement of the time. It is composed of appeals, proclamations, and epigrams which distribute praise or blame to the Israelite tribes according to the attitude they took toward the events. The great poem rather incorrectly called the "Blessing of Jacob" (Gen. 49) is somewhat similar in style; it is, in its definitive form, later than the song of Debora, that is, it undoubtedly dates from the beginning of the monarchy, but it contains older elements and even vestiges of patriarchal traditions. It supplies information about the characteristics and the geographical situation of the Israelite tribes that settled in Canaan.

As everywhere, but especially in the Near East, bons mots, *maxims*, riddles, short satires, lapidary counsels were current among the people of Israel.[26] In them we find the dawn of a "wisdom" literature which, in a few centuries, would enjoy a great development. Among these, although under a more developed form, the very ancient and remarkable fable of Joatham must be cited (cf. Judg. 9:7-15).

Finally, we must point out a kind of "credo" or solemn declaration on the ancestral faith which probably already had a place in liturgical actions. There is good reason to think that fragments like Deut. 6:20-24; 26:5-9; Jos. 24:2-13, even if they were given a literary

[26] Examples: Gen. 10:9; Judg. 14:12-18; I Sam. 10:12; 19:24; 15:22-23; 18:7; 21:12; 29:5; II Sam. 5:8.

revision later, existed before the Davidic monarchy. The peculiarly historical character of the content of these ritual formulas of piety should be noted. Even in ancient times the religion of Israel was based on facts, on a positive Revelation.

In the preservation and transmission of all these traditions, the part played by the priests attached to the sanctuaries and to the places of pilgrimage was certainly great. The traditions connected with the sacred places, explaining their origin and practices, obviously must have been given a privileged place.

Thanks, then, to the officiating priests of the religion, to the itinerant singers, and to the good graces of the people themselves, the threads which, in two or three hundred years, writers would piously gather up to form the first history of the People of God, were woven together more and more tightly.

[TWO]

THE KING CHOSEN BY GOD | The period of the Judges seems to have lasted nearly a century and a half. It came to an end in the first half of the eleventh century with Samuel the priest-prophet,[1] the last of the "liberators" who tended little by little to become rulers.[2]

Things could not continue the way they were going. The miseries of anarchy and fratricidal conflicts, never-ending guerilla warfare with the Canaanites and, above all, the presence of the Philistines, who were no longer merely a threat but who exerted a tyrannical pressure, awakened the realization that order was urgently needed, that there must be a unifying and stable political regime. One might even say that the Philistines had been raised up providentially just to incite the Israelites to make common cause; to mobilize them against the factors of disunion and sloth; in short, to save them and arm them for a long history. The desire for unity finally came to be clearly formulated among them. They wanted, like other peo-

[1] Attempts at personal government with Gedeon and Abimelech (cf. Judg. 8:22-27; 9:1-56).

[2] For the history of Samuel, read I Sam. 1-7. The composition of these chapters is similar to that of the Book of Judges (cf. p. 70).

ples, to have a king at their head. But were they like other peoples? Their last "judge" put this question to them.

Indeed, Samuel did have to struggle at the crossroads found in every great crisis; this, at least, is the sense of the biblical account taken as a whole (cf. I Sam. 8-12). In reality, his account is made up of pieces that echo divergent and noncontemporaneous tendencies. Such richness of documentation is always welcome.[3] The most ancient current of ideas (cf. I Sam. 9; 10:1-16; 11) is favorable to the monarchy, recognizing it as a gift of God and a benefit; it is in agreement with the requirements of history; it is in the logic of events. This was what Samuel may have thought when he chose the first king, Saul.

The other current of ideas (cf. I Sam. 8; 10:17-24; 12) is, on the contrary, antimonarchical. Perhaps it had asserted itself as early as the time of Samuel, and perhaps he was personally persuaded that Israel ought not to have a king. However, the words attributed to the harsh Prophet, the manner in which he is made to proclaim not only the risks but also the real and precise misdeeds of the new regime, show such a clear sense of the severities and abuses for which the autocracy of Solomon was later reproached that one cannot fail to see in them the grievances of a time which had already suffered from them (compare I Sam. 8:11-18 with III Kgs. 5:2-8; 9:15-23; 12:4; cf. also Deut. 17:14-20). The second current, inspired by the reflections of Prophets, considered the setting up of a monarchy a theological deviation. Was not Yahweh the only king of Israel (cf. I Sam. 8:7; 12:12)?

Another lesson is evident. The last "judge," who was a Prophet, created the first king by virtue of divine inspiration. The Israelite kingdom, therefore, was given to understand that it was subordinate to prophecy, which depends solely on God. The royal power would not be able to fetter the free speech of the "men of the Spirit"; on the contrary, the Prophets would always hold that they had the right to judge and to censure the kings, and even, if necessary, to make and unmake them.[4]

[3] We have already had occasion to notice this. The plurality of the traditions corresponds, in fact, to the very diversity of the ways of life; it is always a piece of good fortune to find them non-"harmonized" in our complex Bible.

[4] Cf. I Sam. 8:22; 10:1; 13:14; 15:11, 23, 28; 16:1-14; III Kgs. 11:29-39; 16:1-7; 21:17-24; IV Kgs. 1:4, 17; 9:1-13; 11:4-19.

The monarchical experiment made under Saul was mediocre and ended in failure. Among the reasons the Bible gives for its failure is the drama of God's Chosen People torn between certain religious requirements and the necessity of making a practical response to emergencies (cf. I Sam. 13-15). Another reason was the misfortune of having a king who lacked a balanced temperament (cf. I Sam. 16:14). Considering concretely the position of this farmer-king (cf. I Sam. 11:5), whose elevation sanctioned the triumph of the high-strung tribe of Benjamin, one sees that the other tribes were far from accepting the new chief, especially those of the south: Juda immediately rallied to the side of another claimant coming from Bethlehem.

Saul will be remembered as a clumsy, rough, unsuitable, but loyal man. Israel will always respect the unhappy mystery of its first king.[5]

In order to triumph over tribal self-interest and rivalries, Israel needed a person capable of thrusting himself on all, and also of pleasing all.

David, a successful adventurer, pious and intelligent, was such a man. Strong and clever, gifted with charm and originality, he was a prince after the heart of the people. None was so greatly loved. His type, somewhat idealized, of course, by tradition, has remained that of the perfect king and the perfect "servant of Yahweh."

In the beginning, at the time of his struggles with Saul, who was out of his mind (cf. I Sam. 16-31; II Sam. 1), he had known what it was to take the hills. Before Saul met defeat at Gelboe, the banished David had proved himself a valiant warrior, a clever spy, and an excellent politician. Having won a great deal of sympathy for himself, when Saul died he was acclaimed king by his fellow citizens of the south (cf. II Sam. 2:1-4). The tribes of the north, not much inclined to union, distrustful, and at grips with the Philistines, waited several years before declaring themselves (cf. II Sam. 2:5-32; 3-4). It was impossible, however, to resist the ascendancy of this hero or to neglect the advantage of having such a leader. Hence, unity was established at the hands of this providential man (cf. II Sam. 5:1-5).

[5] This, indeed, is the meaning of the silence of all later tradition in regard to Saul.

The principal business, which had to be taken care of immediately, was the liberation of the territory. David and his military companies fought so well against the Philistines that, within a few years, all difficulty from that quarter was definitively eliminated. David was even considered to have a certain authority over the towns of the Shephelah.[6] One by one, Aramaeans, Ammonites, and Moabites had to recognize the superiority of Israelite arms (cf. II Sam. 8:1-14; 10:1-19; 12:26-31). Meanwhile, the last Canaanite citadels of the interior were subdued and incorporated. An independent kingdom was born. David was the creator of the Israelite State.

He gave Israel a completely new capital, which he chose [7] very intelligently, and which will be famous forever. He made it an important religious center by having the Ark of the Covenant solemnly installed there (cf. II Sam. 6). Jerusalem, the city of David, became the city of God. The ancient centers of pilgrimage, the high-places dear to popular piety, did not disappear all at once; nevertheless, the sanctuary of Sion was thenceforth to hold a pre-eminent place. Political unification, as well as the power of attraction possessed by the government administration, brought to the royal city a great religious development. A true clergy was established [8] there and a liturgy, properly so-called, was developed. This liturgy expressed, more purely than did provincial cults, the incomparable religion whose seed had, since Sinai, lain in the hearts of the Chosen People.

[6] Cf. II Sam. 5:17-25; 21:15-22. The Philistines did not disappear as if by magic, but, beginning with the tenth century, they no longer had a national identity and little by little they let themselves be assimilated or become lost in the mass of various ethnic elements in the country.

[7] This was his personal conquest, the citadel of the Jebusites having up to that time resisted all the Israelite attacks (cf. Jos. 15:63; Judg. 1:21; II Sam. 5:6-9). It was situated between Juda and Benjamin, between the tribes of the south and those of the north, about 13 miles south of Ephraim, which could be considered as the center of culture and influence at that time. It was admirably placed on a sort of spur defended by deep valleys; this hill is today to the southeast of the present city and outside its walls, which extend from Ophel, adjacent to the esplanade of the Temple, to Siloe, at the crossing of the valleys of the Cedron, the Tyropaeum, and the Gehenna.

[8] Less rapidly, of course, and less pretentiously than the reading of the Book of Paralipomenon, outside of its proper perspective, would lead us to believe (cf. I Par. 23-29).

The reign of David is to be placed about the year 1000 B.C. One generation had sufficed for Israel to pass from oppressive insignificance into a number of free and strong states.[9]

Israel had, however, weaknesses. A work completed with such rapidity lacked depth and maturity. Fraternal divisions would not disappear suddenly. The cohesion of the kingdom was due to the personal prestige of David and was in danger of lasting only as long as that prestige endured. This was evident when the king was challenged and disputed by another clever and seductive personality, his own son Absalom, who almost succeeded in dethroning his father (cf. II Sam. 13-19). It became still more evident when another revolt broke out in the central region and the north, under circumstances which were a true prelude to the division of 933 B.C. (cf. II Sam. 20).

Clever tactics, however, succeeded in transmitting the kingdom of David intact into the hands of one of his sons (cf. III Kgs. 1).

There is something deceptive about the solemn personage of Solomon. In vain did this son of David become a little pharaoh, surrounding himself with marvelous pomp, not even forgetting Yahweh in the rather ostentatious prayer given him or in the woodwork and gold lavished in order to raise a temple to God which would be not less splendid than his own palace.[10] Despite all this, the impression he leaves is not completely reassuring; one could say that he was not fully within the axis of Israel's destiny. He was not a soldier, nor was he a friend to his people. Consequently, the traits of the valorous David are not to be looked for in his son.

Nevertheless, the People of God are indebted to Solomon for having gilded the insignia of the Davidic kingdom. Without concealing the things that tarnished his glory, tradition has recognized Israel's debt to him. Solomon was, in fact, able, with great intel-

[9] There is no question, of course, of comparing this principality, scarcely as large as Normandy, with the enormous neighbors who flanked it.

[10] Was it not, after all, merely his "royal chapel"? Is it certain that this building was really in the thoughts expressed to David by a Prophet of the Lord of the Hebrews, who had no "dwelling" (II Sam. 7:6)? True Yahwism, however, even that of the intransigent Prophets, would know the way to make it a religious center and to accord it a major place in the divine economy of Salvation. God always knows how to recover history and there is no deviation which cannot be reoriented according to his Plan.

ligence, to take advantage of the state of affairs left by David and, although he scarcely increased the acquisitions that had already been made, he did exploit and improve them. The great lord was a man of affairs.

Important works date from his reign: the improvement and extension of the city of David; the building of the temple whose memory will never fade; an administrative organization along grand lines, such as the institution of fiscal districts; and the entrance of Israel into international diplomacy and foreign trade. As examples of this opening up to the world abroad we can cite the marriage of the king to Pharaoh's daughter, the commercial alliance with Tyre, state and trade exchanges with Arabia, the creation of a merchant fleet (cf. III Kgs. 4-10).

The epoch of Solomon was both brilliant and peaceful,[11] although a certain Razon, established at Damascus as early as the reign of David and grouping under his authority Aramaean populations of southern Syria, lived as a declared enemy of Solomon and prepared the most serious disturbances for Israel (cf. III Kgs. 11:23-25).

Such a reign was certain to bring about many changes in the social, cultural, and religious order. The Israelite civilization, which at first was like the Canaanite type, through the abandonment of nomadism and adaptation to farming, was now to adopt Phoenician ways. The reasons for this were the possession and organization of the coastal regions of the country and especially the fact that the Israelites would thenceforth devote themselves to commerce. The development of cities, the creation of an aristocracy and of a bureaucracy, the advent of new riches and, correlatively, of a proletarian minority which soon became the object of oppression—all this took place at the expense of the ancient structure. Based on the profound unity of the rural clan, this structure was now daringly liquidated by the new regime at the expense of ethnic and religious bonds which held together, not very apparently perhaps but actually, the members of the ancient groups.

Social crisis, religious crisis. Was Yahwism, which was served by the monarchy and also made use of by it, not to become hardened in

[11] With help from the etymology of the king's name (*shalom* means "peace"), Solomon was to remain the symbol of peace.

formalism as it became an "official" religion and established itself in administrative centers? Was it not in danger of copying the pagan cults to such an extent that it would end by allying itself with them? This was indeed the case in the times of certain kings, not only at Samaria but also at Jerusalem, beginning with Solomon himself (cf. III Kgs. 11:1-8; 3:3). The prosperity of Israel threatened to compromise it as gravely as had its condition of inferiority a hundred years earlier. The situation would become critical enough to call forth a succession of champions of the Spirit, true and intrepid heralds of Yahweh.

The Israelite unity brought about by David did not survive Solomon, who died in 933 B.C. The stupid arrogance of his son Roboam soon led the Israelites of the north, who found their leader in Jeroboam, to separate from Jerusalem. They formed the kingdom of Israel, distinct from and a rival of the kingdom now called Juda.

We have already caught a glimpse of the profound causes for the rupture. A fundamental cause was a tension and even discord that was as ancient as the conquest of the country. It may have had its starting point as early as the Exodus itself, if not during the patriarchal period (cf. pp. 45, 52-53). In any case, two movements were evident, one centering around Juda, the other around Ephraim. A tribe which was assuming increasing importance, Ephraim's name became synonymous with the kingdom of the north. David had cleverly created his capital in an intermediate zone, but Jerusalem was, nevertheless, southern and represented especially Juda, the tribe of David himself. Although this king, magnanimous and beloved by all, had rallied to himself both sympathy and approbation, the same could not be said of his successor, the first national despot. Now, Israel, however, always would have a free spirit. The men of the south soon began suffering from Judean favoritism (cf. III Kgs. 4:7-19). Solomon was expansive, his works and his pomp were ruining the country, and the people had to endure taxes, forced labor, and requisitions (cf. III Kgs. 5:7-8, 27-32; 11:28; 12:4). Finally, from the religious point of view, the importance suddenly given to the Temple of Jerusalem was premature: a convenience and a glory for the south, the Temple was a difficulty for the rest of the country and represented an attempt to supplant or to stifle the other sacred places.

Unity, therefore, lasted only three-quarters of a century; [12] a state of separation seemed more in keeping with the natural tendencies. Ought the People of God to rise above these differences within the common fraternal union? An affirmative reply to this question would not be spoken for several centuries. For the moment, they were convinced that God himself ratified the split, taking charge of the two kingdoms.[13]

The political division was necessarily accompanied by a separation on the plane of worship. The sanctuaries of Bethel and of Dan [14] were the northern equivalent of Jerusalem and its temple. In principle, everyone remained faithful to Yahweh, but orthodoxy was challenged and put in a minority more than ever by the cult of Baalism, the true beneficiary of the separation.

Jerusalem, however, lost neither its prestige nor its real supremacy; it had no competitor until later, when Samaria was created. In building his fine palace and the great Temple of Yahweh, at Jerusalem, at the cost of enormous labor, Solomon made of the royal town the first great Israelite city. There he could display all the pomp of an Eastern court and invite monarchs to formal receptions with great effect. The clergy of Jerusalem, moreover, knew how to make the Temple a worthy dwelling of God; they knew how to attract pious throngs to it, how to establish a liturgy of great style and one

[12] Insofar as it is prudent to take the indications of II Sam. 5:4-5 and III Kgs. 11:42 as mathematically precise.

[13] Cf. III Kgs. 11:29-39; 14:7-8. It does not, therefore, seem accurate to contest the legitimacy of the northern kingdom, as is often done. Can one speak of a religious schism? Jerusalem was not at that time, either in principle or in fact, the sole place of worship recognized by all the Israelites. Jeroboam was not culpable for having drawn the faithful of Yahweh to Dan and to Bethel, but he was guilty of having made images of Yahweh, forbidden by the Law of Moses, and of having, by that means, led the people into idolatry. The "sin of Jeroboam" constantly deplored in the Book of Kings was certainly infidelity; an infidelity with which Juda was to be similarly reproached when idolatry was practiced there. But there was no question of a "schism," denounced as such, before the end of the northern kingdom. Who will say that Elias, the Prophet of that kingdom and the sacrificer of Mount Carmel, was a schismatic? or the Prophet Osee? Amos, although he was Judean and vehemently outspoken against Israel (cf. Amos 7:11), never thought of accusing it of schism (cf. Amos 2:6-16). Cf. also IV Kgs. 9:3, 6, 12: the "anointed" king, the "messias" of God, might occupy, on the authority of the Lord himself, the throne of the kingdom of Israel.

[14] The golden bulls of these two sanctuaries represented Yahweh under the symbol of strength and of fecundity.

that was truly Israelite,[15] and how to conduct the rites, the sacrifices, and the ceremonials of the feasts. It is easy to understand that these priests acquired, little by little, a value and an authority which set them above the officiating clergy of the provincial sanctuaries.

In addition, Jerusalem was thenceforth to shelter a whole world of functionaries: military chiefs and soldiers, administrative officers and diplomats, men responsible for finance and justice, and overseers of public works and the various state enterprises.[16] The king likewise needed men about him who were the regular interpreters of Yahweh; hence, Prophets are found in the retinues of David and of Solomon, and their institution was to be lasting.[17]

We must point out particularly the men who handled brushes and reed-pens, those who knew how to put things in writing on tablets or on papyrus. These "writers" or "scribes," established no doubt in a kind of hierarchy (cf. p. 2), could take care of diplomacy and bookkeeping as well as compose songs for the liturgy, draw up laws, and make progress along the various paths of literary art.

[THREE]

BEGINNINGS OF A LITERATURE | When they settled in Canaan, the Hebrews were not long in adopting the language of the country. They retained, naturally, something of the ancestral Aramaean and gave to their new tongue the mark of their own mentality. Probably they also accentuated its development. Thus, the Canaanite language became Hebrew, a Hebrew that was spoken

[15] This means the adaptation, the "Yahwization," of practices and ceremonies which might be "standard" in the Near East—which in turn means the very significant innovations of a radically original religion, founded on a historical Revelation.

[16] There was even the launching of a fleet in the Gulf of Aqabah (cf. III Kgs. 9:26-29), but with seamen who were Phoenicians. The Hebrews were never to be sailors. Perhaps, however, some of them were Danites (cf. Judg. 5:17).

[17] The royal courts of Egypt and especially of Babylonia always had such "prophets." There is no clear information concerning the duties of this office in Israel; it was liable, one may suppose, to falsification by adulation, complacency, laxity, or selfish calculations. What can be more instructive than reading III Kgs. 22?

at first, and in various dialects.[1] When it soon became necessary to write it, Hebrew, which had developed within the Syro-Phoenician sphere, became alphabetic. Writing was executed in characters which were later modified little by little.[2] The "golden age" of the Hebrew language was the eighth century, the century in which the stories of Elias and Eliseus, of Amos, and of Isaias, were written out. In the tenth century, the evolution toward "classic Hebrew" was already far advanced, as witness the documents of which we are about to speak.

The establishment of a monarchy, which transformed the country and made a nation of Israel, produced consequences in the literary field. The governmental administration soon found itself obliged to possess and to supply official documents: letters, statutes, lists, accounts. Hence, the archives to which the biblical writers were later to have recourse began to be established.

Soon something better was produced. There was a consciousness of having lived through a great era with David, the exact memory of which ought not to be lost. Besides, young nations like the stories of celebrated personages in biographical form. Thus, the need of having a national history which would at the same time be a history of David soon made itself felt in Israel. The man who wrote it, during the reign of Solomon, was neither a cold chronicler nor a fawning courtier, nor, on the other hand, a hard pamphleteer. He loved his king and wrote because of his love, but without letting himself be blinded and without losing the liberty of frankness.[3] This man, whose name we do not know, was wrapped up intimately enough with the events to be remarkably well informed about them.

[1] According to the regions; the difference was especially noticeable between the southerners and the northerners. Remember the anecdote in Judg. 12:6.

[2] The writing before the Exile is called "palaeo-Hebrew." The "squared" writing we know is the "nea-Hebrew" of the third or the second century before the Christian era, which is also sometimes called Phoenician Hebrew as a reminder of the origin of this script. Concerning its archaic state little is known because of the scarcity of archaeological evidences. In relation to the characteristics of the Hebrew language, cf. *WG*, pp. 162-64.

[3] How different from the official documents of the other countries of that time; Israel did not know the despotism which made the annals of Assyria-Babylonia and Egypt no more than either dull or emphatic personal vindications of kings, and pompous listings with no relation to actual life. The political regime in Israel was always liberal enough to allow criticism, often ironical, and the inspiration of subtle minds to have free play.

A simple storyteller, but with a delicate and penetrating mind; one who excelled in painting characters, in analyzing interior feelings, in bringing scenes to life, but with respect for facts and with a sense of the complexity of real life: such was the man who wrote out the precious *Memoirs of David* which, for the most part, have gone into the composition of the two Books of Samuel.[4]

To this history of David were added the cycle of narratives relating to Samuel, taken no doubt from a collection dealing with the Judges (cf. p. 70, note 10), and the cycle about Saul, in which we have identified a later current (cf. p. 77). The whole work was taken up again in the great history of the deuteronomists at the end of the royal era. We are exceptionally fortunate in possessing, almost in its original words, a first great text, which can be dated from the years 960-950 B.C. and which is a pure masterpiece of ancient historical literature.[5]

Traditionally connected with the name of David is a literary collection which was to hold a special and important place in the Scriptures of Israel: the Psalms.

Poetry, which appears early in the age of every people, was already ancient at that time among the Israelites. Beyond all doubt the psalm form is ancient; it is quite possible that the biblical Psalter contains songs earlier than the royal era. Hebrew tradition, however, has made David its first great poet. Undoubtedly, no one will ever know exactly which compositions are his; and only rarely have they been transmitted without being remodeled or retouched.[6] Loans, however, are made only to the rich; thus, while recognizing the true literary place of the "Davidic" poems, credit must be given to the strong tradition which gave to Saul's musician the title of "singer of the songs of Israel" (cf. II Sam. 23:1; cf. also I Sam.

[4] II Sam. 9-20 and III Kgs. 1-2 constitute a homogeneous and original entity. I Sam. 17-31 and II Sam. 1-8 are of a less simple and sometimes reworked definitive composition (thus II Sam. 7), but contain ancient traditions, even if they are not completely by the first author.

[5] This shows how little myth there was in biblical literature from the very beginning.

[6] The Psalms "of David" are rather "to David," that is, dedicated to the Davidic King, either David himself or one of his successors. It was also found appropriate, at a later date, to establish a historical link between a particular psalm and certain events in the life of David (cf. Ps. 3; 7; 18; 34; 51; 52; 54; 56; 57; 59; 60).

16:14-30; 18:10). In somewhat the way Moses was the first "author" of the Torah (cf. pp. 63-64), David was the initiator of the Psalter. Just as Moses did for the Law, David opened this new literary channel.

Gradually, with time, chiefly in the sphere of the liturgy, which was both the beneficiary and the promoter of this inspiration, a vast collection of religious songs was formed. They have a certain similarity to the hymns and prayers of Mesopotamian and Egyptian religious literature. In its use of this form, however, Israel was not greatly dependent: it was able to create, and the psalms manifest its spirit, its genius, and its original inspiration in an incomparable manner.

A biographer, whose work is contained in the Book of Kings, was found also for David's son, Solomon. As we have it today, in two books, it contains primarily the story of Solomon (cf. III Kgs. 1-11); the cycles of Elias and Eliseus (cf. III Kgs. 17-22; IV Kgs. 1-13); and biographical sketches, generally short, on the kings of Juda and of Israel, written from a deuteronomic viewpoint (as we shall see) with the help of royal annals which were referred to constantly (cf. III Kgs. 12-16; IV Kgs. 14-25—with few exceptions). In its present state, the Book dates from the beginning of the sixth century.

The Chronicle of Solomon [7] was composed simultaneously with his reign, and thus constitutes a special event in literary history. It is, nevertheless, as pompous as its subject, and much less alive than the memoirs of David. Making the most of the undeniable natural gifts of the king and his religious dispositions, the chronicle insists on the "glory" which, even during his life, made him legendary. Still, it does not hide the weaknesses and perils of a reign which was a political failure.

David sang. Solomon was a "wise man," the "crowned scribe." In fact, a literary activity, which was to know later a rich development, is attached to his name: the composition of "wisdom writings" (cf. III Kgs. 4:29-34; 5:9-14). In such a composite book like the Book of Proverbs, it is impossible to know which are the authentic "proverbs" of Solomon; there may be a certain number in the oldest sections

[7] Cf. III Kgs. 3-5 and 9-11. The first two chapters of the book are to be attached to the story of David in II Sam.; chapters 6-7 are of sacerdotal origin; chapter 8 is deuteronomic.

of the collection (cf. Prov. 10-22; 25-29). As in the case of David the "psalmist," proverbs were attributed to Solomon only because he already was in the field of wisdom.

Of course, the axiomatic form had been practiced for a long time in Israel (cf. p. 75). In its biblical form, sapiential literature savors strongly of an exotic origin; it owes much to Egypt, which had specialized for centuries in this form, and to the Egyptian scribes who recorded maxims on "how-to-live-happily" (cf. pp. 17-18). Egyptianism was the snobism of the era of Solomon and was to remain such at the court of the kings of Juda. A tradition was therefore created, which scribes were to preserve in the Egyptian style.

It remained to be seen whether the somewhat scanty morality for honest townsfolk and perfect functionaries, which began making itself at home in Jerusalem from the tenth century on, would remain on such a worldly level or whether, on the contrary, entering into the spiritual current of a different nature which was at work in Israel, it would provide a road by which to attain to less tranquil spheres perhaps, but otherwise profound and near to God, the supreme and living Wisdom.

From early times, Israel possessed an astonishing spiritual maturity, and, like leaven, a power of transforming common values, which prevented it from simply copying or borrowing. This was done with regard to its idea of royalty.

We have seen that the question of royalty had been from the beginning, or had soon become, a serious and difficult one. The People of God could not have a king in exactly the same way as other nations (cf. pp. 76-77). Once established, the monarchy was placed in a characteristically Israelite perspective. It was rethought out in relation to a Yahwism whose theology was becoming more and more profound. Undoubtedly, many comparisons could be made with the conceptions current in other countries. The king was the sacerdotal representative of and the person responsible for his people before God. In the dimensions of the revealed Covenant and of the hope of salvation, however, the royal function was capable of being promoted to another level and to quite a different meaning.

The success of the monarchy with David had struck the minds of the public, while, at the same time, the person of David himself had impressed his people profoundly. They soon began to dream of a new monarchy of the same kind, and of a new David. His successors were disappointing; as time passed the concept of the perfect king became idealized. The prophecy made to David by Nathan (cf. II Sam. 7), although perhaps worked over later on, is the first landmark of the special course taken by a waiting Israel.

The king was ritually consecrated by an anointing with oil; the word "anointed," which is called "mashiah" in Hebrew (in Greek "christos"—the same etymology as "chrism," holy oil for anointings), has become "messias" in our language. Messianism, according to our way of speaking, is a profound movement of hope founded on a perfect king to come, one who is patterned after David. This aspiration, of course, would make itself felt in the course of time. We shall see it appear in Hebrew literature, in the words of the Prophets especially, and in the psalms (many of the psalms were to express praise, thanksgiving, desires, and prayers for a king who would reign in Juda or in Israel; a day would come when these songs would be addressed to an ideal king, to the expected Messias, especially when there was no longer a king and when little by little the people found themselves obliged to go beyond the limits of purely human hope).

The idea of such a Messias would take some centuries to develop. It was, therefore, not applied to the first "son of David," Solomon. However, in spite of his faults, he had seemed great and glorious to Israel. A magnificent king, he had been the builder of the House of God, the Prince of Peace, the one who had received the divine gift of wisdom in an extraordinary way. Thus, Solomon supplemented the figure of the "son of David" whom the people would some day look for with longing.

The preservation of the family of David on the throne of Jerusalem, while the kings of the north were usually usurpers who did not succeed in establishing a lasting natural succession, could be regarded as a proof of the divine election of the Judean dynasty. Unhappy experiences and sufferings of every kind were to contribute greatly to impressing on the heart of Israel its waiting for a perfect king, the salvation of his People.

5 The Prophetic Era

[ONE]

BEGINNINGS OF THE TWO KINGDOMS | The division of the Israelites on the day following Solomon's death (cf. pp. 82-83) resulted in the weakening of the two new kingdoms. The fifty years that followed were difficult for both; to make matters worse they regarded each other as hostile brothers (cf. III Kgs. 15:7, 16-17).

Israel did not succeed in attaining political balance; in the course of this half century, three of its five kings were assassinated by competitors who seized the crown (cf. III Kgs. 15:28; 16:10, 18; II Par. 13:1-18). Convinced of the superiority of its forces over Juda, the northern kingdom often made war upon the southern.

Juda had already suffered an attack from Egypt. Sheshonk, pharaoh from 947 B.C. to 925 B.C., pillaged southern Palestine about the year 928 B.C. (cf. III Kgs. 14:25-26). To defend itself on the north from Israel's encroachments, Juda appealed to Damascus; this, however, was an unfortunate and disastrous move from the political point of view (cf. III Kgs. 15:18-22).

In the first part of the ninth century, the frontiers of Juda began to suffer from the Aramaean power, whose ambitions and exploits it was highly imprudent to encourage. Up to that time, the Aramaeans, who were numerous but unstable and lacking in unity, had been more or less settled in Syria for four or five centuries, but had not constituted a force capable of lasting predominance. Things were different after the tenth century (cf. p. 81); a few Aramaean kingdoms were established between Mesopotamia and the Mediterranean. For three centuries, Damascus in particular was genuinely strong and enterprising, and either imposed its sovereignty on the Palestinian kingdoms or made war on them. Damascus was even able to resist Assyria and to stir up successive coalitions against that country.

The eleventh and tenth centuries were a time of weakness for the land of Nineve. Assyria had made a name for itself as early as the thirteenth century (cf. p. 51) and it had recently established the beginnings of an authority with Tiglath-Pileser I (1115-1093 B.C.), who had reached the Mediterranean and waged a victorious campaign in Syria, Phoenicia, and Palestine (the biblical texts say nothing about it). But this was only a transitory assertion of power, and Assyria was forgotten again for a while.

In Palestine, after some decades of crisis (930-880 B.C.), each of the two kingdoms, the north especially, found itself fairly solidly established. They knew genuine prosperity and a comparatively brilliant civilization, with kings of the stature of Josaphat (872-850 B.C.) in Juda, and Amri (885-874 B.C.) and Achab (874-850 B.C.) in Israel. Amri founded Samaria, which his son Achab continued to build and to improve. The creation of this magnificent capital, which was admirably situated, can be compared to the foundation of Jerusalem by David, and was evidence of great power.[1]

A reconciliation, which was symbolized by a marriage, took place between the two kingdoms. Josaphat united his son Joram to the daughter of Achab, Athalia (cf. IV Kgs. 8:26). The two kings even made a common expedition against Ben-Hadad II, king of Damascus, whose yoke Achab succeeded in shaking off to some extent (cf. III Kgs. 20) and whose claims he opposed in Transjordania. Achab, however, was killed in the expedition, which ended in failure (cf. III Kgs. 22).

The king of Israel had previously been confronted by a new and formidable danger: the reawakening of Assyria under Assurnasirpal (884-859 B.C.). His successor, Salmanasar III (854-824 B.C.), marched toward the sea. Ben-Hadad II organized a confederation, in which Achab was forced to take part, to offer resistance. The battle of Karkar in 854 B.C., was, however, only a half-success for the Assyrians. Damascus was later besieged, in 841 B.C. and in

[1] For the reigns of Josaphat, Amri, and Achab, cf. III Kgs. 16:23-24; 20; 22; II Par. 17-20. For the creation of Samaria in 870 B.C., cf. in particular III Kgs. 16:24 and 22:39. This town was situated on a large and beautiful hill, surrounded by valleys which separated it from the mountains that circled it like a crown. It was about eight miles, as the crow flies, from Sichem, which was the first capital of the northern kingdom but which was soon replaced by Tirza, the capital abandoned by Amri.

838 B.C., but it held out. Adadnirari III (805-782 B.C.) would continue the struggle against Damascus. How long would the conflict last?

Obviously Assyria's ascending curve inaugurated by Assur was triumphant. Its system of government was absolute; its method of waging war terrible. The brutal and cruel army destroyed and burned everything in its path, torturing and massacring without pity.[2] It was to be the terror of the whole Near East. Good sense suggested that this formidable power should at least be taken into account.

The Palestinians preferred to close their eyes to the problem. They either relied on problematical help from an Egypt whose few attempts at recovery had not arrested its decline, or they entered into an anti-Assyrian league, also usually set up or maintained by Egypt, which brought on the danger more often than it removed it. The Prophets always blamed Palestine for this ostrich-like policy, which brought it to the eve of disaster twenty times before the fatal blow was struck.

We have scarcely glanced at Egypt since the Exodus and the reigns of Rameses II and of Minephtha (cf. pp. 51, 56-57). Its history was only one of decadence, and can be summarized briefly for the period extending from the thirteenth to the eighth century.

In an atmosphere of anarchy, the nineteenth dynasty had come to an end under pharaohs who were usurpers and who had no prestige.[3] During the twentieth dynasty (1204-1100 B.C.), which extended from Rameses III to Rameses XII, except for the reign of the former (cf. p. 68), disorganization increased and the economic position of the country became precarious. As in the archaic period, Egypt was cut into two regions. The center of one of these regions was in the Delta; the center of the other was at Thebes. Herihor, the high priest of Amon, founded the twenty-first dynasty (1100-947 B.C.). His successors were insignificant, and disorder was everywhere; under these difficult conditions the unity of the kingdom could not be re-established. From the heart of the army, composed

[2] The Assyrian bas-reliefs, on view in the British Museum and the Louvre, show, among other cruelties, scenes of empalement and flaying alive.

[3] This favored the undertakings of the Israelites and of the Philistines in Canaan, Egypt having lost her suzerainty over that country (p. 67).

of Libyans, came the twenty-second dynasty (947-740 B.C.). Its first pharaoh was the Shehonk I who attacked Roboam (cf. p. 91). A rival power was found at Thebes, where princesses carried out the duties of the sovereign office; the temple of Amon was in complete decadence and was falling into ruins. The twenty-second dynasty more or less paralleled the twenty-third, twenty-fourth, and twenty-fifth; during this time divisions and anarchy continued. With the exception of the last pharaohs, Shabataka (701-690 B.C.) and Taharqa (690-664 B.C.), who, as we shall see, favored the Palestinian revolts, under Ezechias and under Manasses, the pharaohs no longer even considered opposing the claims of Assyria over the Mediterranean regions. Like Jerusalem itself, Egypt escaped destruction by the Assyrians by no more than a hairbreadth.

Thereafter it found safety only by summoning Ionians and Carians, whom it employed as mercenaries, to its side. The greatness of the twenty-sixth dynasty (663-525 B.C.), and also the beginning of the Greek influence, was due to this policy.

Hellas was, in fact, about to assume its historical position.[4] It will be remembered (cf. pp. 3-4) that following the Achaian dawn of the fifteenth to the eleventh centuries an eclipse took place with the Dorian invasion. The peninsula withdrew into itself. In the course of the three following centuries, Greek civilization again soared forward. Social development was evident: the clans began to make up cities, the royal regime gave way to an oligarchical form of government, and a propertied middle class, which was active and determined, finally made a place for itself between the common people and the landed aristocracy. This was the beginning of a social balance, which the Egyptians, for example, would never have made successful. Furthermore, self-interest gradually gave way before the Greek consciousness of the ties that bound them together. The great Greek city of the time was Sparta. A prosperous and

[4] There can be no question of giving a bibliography, which would be extensive, on Greece. For those who think themselves insufficiently informed from the historical point of view, cf. J. B. Bury and R. Meiggs, *A History of Greece to the Death of Alexander the Great* (New York: Macmillan, 1951); R. M. Cook, *The Greeks until Alexander* (New York: Praeger, 1962); Cyrus H. Gordon, *Before the Bible: The Common Background of Greek and Hebrew Civilizations* (New York: Harper, 1963); N. G. L. Hammond, *A History of Greece to 322 B.C.* (Oxford University Press, 1959); Emile Mireaux, *Daily Life in the Time of Homer* (New York: Macmillan, 1959).

happy city, it had acquired military glory, and had made artistic and literary achievements. The eighth to the seventh centuries was a period of expansion and prodigious colonial effort. Greeks were to establish themselves on the Euxine and all along the shores of Asia Minor, in Crete, in the delta of the Nile and in Cyrenaica, in southern Italy and in Provençal Gaul. The Hellenic influence did not, however, make itself felt in the interior of the Near East; the Palestinians, in particular, would remain practically ignorant of it for several centuries.

In the countries bordering the Mediterranean, Greek influence was in perpetual competition with the enterprising and bold activities of Phoenicia. Tyre, which was to resist the terrible assaults of the Assyrians and the Babylonians, had also established branches of its maritime enterprises everywhere, notably at Carthage. The Phoenician and Greek powers thus shared control over important places on the sea, which was to have fortunate economic results.

In the Italian peninsula, the Ligurians, the Umbrians, the Siculi, the Oscae, the Latins, and the Etruscans had mingled for several centuries. The Etruscans, who had come from Asia Minor, were a great people.[5] They were dominant in Latium and in southern Italy during the course of the eighth to the sixth centuries. The legendary foundation of Rome is dated 754 B.C.; it was, in the beginning and for two and one-half centuries, governed by "kings." During this time it had a dramatic local history. Much time would still be needed before it would make a name for itself in the world at large.

These few glimpses of the world of that time [6] will pinpoint the history of Palestine and give it balance. The country with which we are concerned was always a small one. Nevertheless, the kingdom of the Davidians and of the Amrides apparently had now attained a comparatively favorable position.

Economically, things were going well. Life was, therefore, easy, at least for the privileged and the unscrupulous. There was an air

[5] Their art, greatly influenced by the Near East, is held in high respect due to the studies that have been made of it and that have made it known to the public at large.

[6] We can consider only a part of world history. Consequently, we will pass over facts that are not connected closely enough with our biblical history or did not effect it. Thus, nothing will be said concerning central and eastern Asia, or concerning India and China, whose history began at this time.

of opulence and unconcern, of luxury and libertinism, which made the oppression of the poor and every other kind of injustice all the more scandalous.[7]

The people of Moses and of David was on the road to becoming completely secular. Men no longer feared dealing with foreigners —Egyptians, Syrians,[8] Phoenicians.[9] Besides trading in merchandise and women, the divinities proscribed by the law and the faith were being added to those the Canaanites had succeeded in preserving. The *cult of Baalism* was widespread and flourishing.[10] Since the people did not yet want to abandon Yahweh officially,[11] all sorts of compromises were adopted. But inspiration was profoundly transformed. Every true believer—and they were rare (cf. III Kgs. 19·10, 18)—felt that a break had been made with the simple past, with the original tradition, and with the spirit of the Mosaic Covenant by which the sons of Abraham had come to know that they were the people with whom God had entered into a personal and special relationship for the carrying out of a great Plan in history.

The first man to set himself clearly in opposition to this destructive tide was a moving Prophet whose words were on fire, Elias the Thesbite (cf. III Kgs. 17-19, 21; IV Kgs. 1-2). In the midst of general slackness, Elias completely reaffirmed Moses and the austere grandeur of the religion of the desert. Nothing is known of him except his action, and of that only isolated acts, which were brief but sensational. Tradition was to see in Elias a kind of contemplative hermit. One cannot deny, in any case, that he met with his God in solitude; [12] and he did not leave this solitude except to utter his blunt exhortations (cf. III Kgs. 17.1; 18:8, 18-19; 21:19;

[7] Accounts of the social conditions of that day can be found not only in the traces that can be gleaned from the Book of Kings and in the recriminations of the Earlier Prophets, but also in the findings of archaeology, which bear ample witness to the material situation.

[8] Israel had businessmen in the souks of Damascus: cf. III Kgs. 20:34.

[9] Achab married Jezabel, daughter of Ittobaal, king of Sidon: cf. III Kgs. 16:31; their daughter, Athalia, was married to Joram of Juda.

[10] Sufficient information can be had by reading the notice concerning Achab in III Kgs. 16:29-33.

[11] In the northern kingdom, with Achab and Jezabel, the apostasy was practically consummated.

[12] Even if we had no more than the marvelous chapter 19 of III Kgs., which recalls the great hours of the life of Moses: cf. Exod. 33:18-23; 34:1-9.

IV Kgs. 1:3-4). He attacked with savage energy the profane civilization spread around him; he knew that this way of life, which was becoming common and which was extolled by the leading social circles, was in absolute contradiction to the idea of fidelity to the One Yahweh; the hour for a decisive choice, all or nothing, had come (cf. III Kgs. 18:21). The most celebrated and representative phase of Elias' mission was his resistance to Jezabel, the pagan wife of Achab, whom she had seduced. She was furious at the intransigence of the terrible prophet.[13] Nevertheless, at the same time he fought against idolatry, Elias also undertook the defense of the weak (cf. III Kgs. 17:7-24; 21). Thus, prophetism found its twofold form of action in Elias.

Elias' disciple, Eliseus, continued the work of the Prophet, although his personality was different. He was less violent and more politic. He was closer to the archaic or, if one may say so, the natural type of Prophet.[14] He was in the midst of the people and of things; he was not unwilling to live like everyone else. He was seen among the "sons of Prophets,"[15] whose groups he encouraged. He was in contact with kings and with leaders, not only of Juda and of Israel, but also of foreign lands (cf. IV Kgs. 3:12; 5:1-19; 8:7-15). And above all, as a disciple of Elias, he traveled throughout the land to reawaken the ancient and genuine soul of Israel.

The narratives of Elias and Eliseus are found in the two Books of Kings (cf. p. 87), but they were not influenced by the "deuteronom-

[13] Elias, in the famous incident on Carmel, had had the representatives of the cults of Baal and Astarte, protected by Jezabel, massacred en masse (cf. III Kgs. 18:16-40; 19:2).

[14] He lived in "prophetic" circles (cf. note 4, below); he had himself prepared for "inspiration" by music (cf. IV Kgs. 3:15), and made use of a kind of magic wand (cf. IV Kgs. 4:29).

[15] Cf. IV Kgs. 2:3, 7, 15; 4:1, 38; 6:1; 9:1. These men were Prophets from choice and from their state of life. They lived in a kind of confraternity, an ancient form of religious life in Israel, different from that of the Rechabites (cf. IV Kgs. 10:15; Jer. 35:6-10), who preferred to withdraw absolutely from the common social life. The "sons of the Prophets" (that is, disciples of Prophets and Prophets themselves) were certainly more highly developed from the religious point of view than the inspired men of the eleventh century (cf. p. 73). They had a center at Galgal, not far from the mouth of the Jordan and the Dead Sea (in the region where John the Baptist was to exercise his prophetic ministry and where, some miles away, the Essenes of the last century before Christianity were to have their community).

ism" which inspired the theme of the entire work.[16] Derived from a mixture of sources, these pages, written no doubt about the year 800 B.C., that is, some fifty years after the events related—the "cycle of Elias" being written first and the "cycle of Eliseus" afterwards—preserved in all their freshness the traditions concerning the two Prophets which had begun to circulate rapidly. These beautiful pages bear witness to the maturity of the Hebrew language and to a style that had attained perfection. Moreover, the stories contained, born of the powerful impression the two men made on their contemporaries, are representative of a militant Yahwism, of a vigorous and implacable struggle to be waged thenceforth against Baalism, and of a perfectly clear conception of the one true Lord and of his adversaries. Narratives like these contributed greatly to the spread of prophetism.

Eliseus was the contemporary of four or five kings in Israel and in Juda: in Israel, Ochozias (853-852 B.C.), Joram (852-843 B.C.), Jehu (843-816 B.C.), Joachaz (816-800 B.C.), and Joas (800-785 B.C.); in Juda, Joram (850-843 B.C.), Ochozias (843 B.C.), Athalia (843-837 B.C.), Joas (837-798 B.C.), Amasias (798-790 B.C.). A complex and troublesome period, its history should be reread in the Bible (IV Kgs. 8-14). The history of the northern kingdom was especially marked by the bloody revolution of Jehu, the absolute and savage foe of Baalism, and the violent partisan of Yahweh, who seems to have confused religious reform and affairs of state. The great event in the kingdom of Juda was the overthrow of Queen Athalia by the sacerdotal movement.

[TWO]

THE ANCESTRAL TRADITIONS | Before the histories of Elias and of Eliseus were written, another literary work, which was much more important by virtue of its size and of its plan, was begun a century earlier. It was to rank among the most precious writings in the collection of the Sacred Scriptures.

[16] It is evident that the sacrifice of Elias on Carmel, for instance, is quite contrary to the deuteronomic thesis on the unicity of place of worship (cf. Deut. 12).

The work was born of the need for having a history, the history of the People of God. Israel, in its most faithful members at least, had never forgotten what the Lord had done for it. The pressure of the surrounding paganism certainly increased its consciousness of his aid. Now, it realized that it had a memorable past, marked by the interventions of Yahweh. For this reason it was not "like other" nations. Israel's distinctive identity, its faith, its religion, its law, its individual behavior, all came from its history, from an experience which it regarded as exceptional and which it was sure it would not have had at all without God.

Israel had cherished and preserved its memories. Oral tradition —popular, sacerdotal, or official; poetic, liturgical, or juridical—had already given these memories more or less established forms. Since the use of writing spread with the development of civilization, it is also highly probable that Israel already possessed narrative, poetic, ritual, or legislative texts (cf. pp. 74-76). Furthermore, the history of the beginnings of the kingdom had been composed in a very successful form (cf. pp. 85-87). The next thing to be done was to go back further in time, as far back as possible, to the very beginning of the history of the People of God if that were possible. Traditions were available which extended back beyond the period of the Judges and of Joshua, to the great days of the Exodus and of Sinai and, further still, to the time of the Patriarchs. Even the origins of Abraham were known, although these traditions were more intermingled with diverse elements and, as it were, lost in the darkness of time, which made their use difficult.

Someone, whose name is unknown, made the effort, although the literary undertaking may have been divided among several writers or carried on in common in some learned and religious circle. Unhindered by this inconvenient anonymity, biblical scholars have come to designate the "author" as the "Yahwist," to distinguish him from another "author" who is not directly known either and who carried out in parallel fashion, and almost at the same time, a work of the same kind and of similar amplitude; he is called the "Elohist." The first author usually called God "Yahweh"; the second used the term "Elohim" (cf. *WG*, p. 37). A table of the "J" and "E" texts will be found as a note at the end of this section, with some of the reasons on which the distinction between them is based.

In both cases, certain lasting characteristics and the power of the overall conception suggest that the writings were produced by two men of genius. However, the complexity of the composition of each work and the richness of documentation indicate that other writers also worked on them. The other writers were probably a group or a succession of narrators who took up the work one after another. Israel will give us many other examples of literary works completed by generations that took up and rounded out an original text.

The Yahwist and the Elohist did not come from the same place and were not quite contemporary. The Yahwist text seems to have been composed in Juda, at Jerusalem no doubt, and dates from between 850 B.C. and 750 B.C.[1] The Elohist text was written in the northern kingdom, at Samaria, or, more probably, in the religious climate of a sanctuary such as Bethel, undoubtedly during the course of the eighth century.[2] The separation of the kingdoms kept the two literary currents distinct.

However, we do not know them in their separate state. By referring to the table of Yahwist and Elohist texts (cf. pp. 105-6), one can see immediately that we have to deal with fragments or short sequences, "J" or "E" by turns, which are also mingled with other texts. This situation, knowledge of which is often disconcerting to those unaccustomed to it but which is very valuable for study, must be explained.

When the northern kingdom disappeared in 722 B.C., forcing its religious and learned circles to withdraw to Jerusalem, the Elohist text or texts were taken there. A pious and intelligent concern for the traditions was found at Jerusalem. No doubt, two observations were soon made. First, the isolated Yahwist and Elohist texts seemed incomplete; and second, they contained passages that were almost identical. Therefore, the plan of making a single history was conceived. The procedure by which it was done seems to have been very simple. Since the general framework was the same in each,

[1] Some recent exegetes go so far as to make the work begin in the time of Solomon.

[2] The question has been asked: Is the point of departure of the "Elohist" traditions not the old sanctuary of Shiloh (cf. p. 72), which had been dispossessed of the Ark by Jerusalem (cf. II Sam. 6), and whose priests having been disestablished by Solomon (cf. I Sam. 2:27-36; 3:11-14; III Kgs. 2:27), may have regrouped themselves in the north? There are exegetes who think that the Elohist is earlier than the eighth century.

it was necessary only to choose one of the texts, eliminate the duplicate passages, and compose a continuous history by putting together the sections or bits retained from each of the texts. Although it deprived us, no doubt, of a part of each version, there is every reason to believe that this patient work was well done. What complicates the search for the original texts still further is the fact that later, after the Exile, another work was introduced into the already double framework: the text called "sacerdotal" (which we shall meet again on pp. 172-78). The definitive arrangement of the texts, which is one of remarkable scope, is due to this work.

The combination of all of these literary elements is possessed now under the form of the Books of Genesis, Exodus, and Numbers (except for a few additions or reworkings). Due to the patient work of two centuries of exegesis (cf. *WG*, pp. 115-24), today we are able to understand these books better, and to recognize almost completely each of the "traditions."

We have already had occasion to observe, in connection with the old traditions of Israel (cf. pp. 43-44, 63-64), that many archaic elements have been perpetuated, and often under a very ancient form. The Yahwist and the Elohist texts, which are collections of traditions, generally reproduce their sources with a naïve fidelity. This often makes it necessary to distinguish, as we have frequently done, between the time of the preparation or the final revision of a text and the possible antiquity of the traditional content it establishes. How many narratives and "toroth" we have met, and legitimately used, whose sources are indeed earlier than the ninth to the eighth centuries, but which can be read only in the Yahwist and Elohist texts! Furthermore, the antiquity of the sources explains the many similarities and common ideas of the two documents. In each, the same traditional source has been drawn upon. Thus, the individual characteristics of each depend essentially on the personality of the authors or on the peculiarities of different literary environments.

To the Yahwist are due the following principal fragments: the accounts of the "earthly Paradise," of the Flood, and of the Tower of Babel; the greater part of the traditions relating to Abraham, Isaac, and Jacob; a substantial number of passages in the first half of the Book of Exodus, and a dozen chapters of the Book of Numbers, in which the Yahwist texts are intermixed with the Elohist texts. Even if the work was originally longer and more complete, the whole formed by the fragments that have been preserved seems a great historical sequence, going from the beginning of human history to the formation of the Israelite people as the "People of God" at Sinai.

The Yahwist is a true storyteller of the people; he is simple and direct, intuitive and practical, patient and grave, but one who often wears an amused smile and who writes with delightful irony, which is picturesque and moving by turns, with rare psychological delicacy, and with quite remarkable dramatic talent. He shows concern over the explanation of the names of characters and places, of the origin of groups, and of a certain number of sanctuaries (those in southern Palestine particularly). These preoccupations, however, do not keep him from treating the most profound problems concerning the difficult condition of man and his relations with God. A sense of God, whom he makes seem startlingly present,[3] and a sense of man, whose heart and ways he knows, give the Yahwist surprising penetration. It would be difficult to deny him a knowledge of truth beyond the common measure.[4]

He is famous for having written, in part,[5] the first chapters of Genesis. His documentation was not personal to him. He utilized traditions of distant origin—Babylonian myths,[6] ancient folklore—but he did so according to his faith, in the perspective of the religion of Moses and its requirements. In addition, he takes into account the religious conditions of the environment in which he lives: the temptations of the corrupting Baalism, which threaten the purity of Yahwism; and the idolatrous practices of the fertility cults [7] on the high places of Canaan, which are so attractive to the Israelites. Demythicized, the ancient legends serve to denounce the lack of fidelity to Yahweh on the plane of faith and of morals; they teach

[3] By that very human manner of speaking of God which, in a somewhat barbarous term, is called "anthropomorphism" (cf. *WG*, pp. 219-20).

[4] If it can be said that he only transmits the ideas current in his environment, then we must recognize in Israel itself an exceptional approach to noble truths.

[5] Another part is to the credit of the postexilic "sacerdotal" literature—precisely that part which is omitted from the enumeration on pp. 105-6.

[6] Geographical indications, mythic themes, literary borrowings even (from the poem of Gilgamesh, for the Flood) make this statement obvious for Gen. 1-11.

[7] Under the symbol of the serpent; the archaeological discoveries bear ample witness to the fact.

men the true relationship God wishes to have with them, and what his "judgment" is—the punishment of evil, and the hope and promise of "salvation." These eleven chapters are, moreover, visibly organized and orientated to serve as a preface to the true purpose of the Yahwist. The ethnic selections, presented with simplicity, lead to Abraham, with whom Sacred History, properly speaking, begins.

The patriarchal and Mosaic history is, then, the true work of the Yahwist. Its sources are usually Hebrew, and consist of the traditions of families, clans, sanctuaries, and regions: songs and stories which the common memory preserved in "oral style," helped along by poetry and music, which were always important in ancient ages, and kept alive also by virtue of the fidelity of the religious liturgies and of piety. Another source lay in the *toroth* which had become traditional, and which were no doubt already grouped in collections, or in more or less extensive codes.

In transcribing and in organizing the traditions he preserved, the Yahwist was the first to create a great religious history, namely, one which considered the grace of God for sinful men, and the faithfulness of God in the contingencies of history, revealing his plan of salvation for the people he had chosen for himself. A text like Gen. 12:1-3 would be enough to make the Yahwist one of the most important messengers of biblical Revelation. He is, in short, the first whose vision was powerful enough to embrace and to dominate centuries of history; the first, as a result, to show with vigor that "sense of history" which seems to have been the property of Israelite prophecy. Of course, one does not feel in him the severe indictment and the constant need for "self-criticism" which were soon to be a dominant note in the voice of the prophets. Even though he is less tragic than they, the Yahwist is in some sense their precursor; probably he would not have written if he had not had, to a slight extent, as they were to have to an intense one, the presentiment of a crisis and the will to save, along with the traditions that expressed them, the essential values of the Revelation given to the Fathers and to Moses.

The Elohist is also an accomplished storyteller. To him we owe especially: three important passages on the history of Abraham; a large part of the story of Joseph; many of the accounts relating to the departure from Egypt and to the events of Sinai (cf. p. 55, note 19); the Decalogue and the Covenant Code (pp. 64-74); the account of the episode of the Golden Calf; the mutiny of Mary and Aaron told in the Book of Numbers; and a large part of the story of Balaam. He does not go back as far in time as the Yahwist writer and records nothing about the "origins," but he does carry his history down to the eve of the entry into Canaan. Although he draws from the ancestral stock of Hebrew traditions apparently used by the Yahwist, he uses, in addition, his own documentation: he is especially well-informed in regard to matters relating to Egypt; and he utilizes and integrates a body of "toroth." The concern of his accounts is generally centered on the sanctuaries of southern Palestine. He is the one who relates the wandering in the desert of Sinai.

The Elohist writes in a less personal and lively manner than the Yahwist. His work is, moreover, more "learned"; it seeks for precision in names, dates, and in the details of the laws. Nevertheless, it is not without its admirable pages, for example, Gen. 22 and 45; Exod. 2:1-15.

The Lord God is less boldly humanized by the Elohist than Yahweh is in the northern tradition, and is more enveloped in mystery. To express the divine "appearances," the Elohist prefers to evoke dreams. He has, on the other hand, a great sense of the divine "providence" which guides events; he shows this, for instance, in the history of Joseph. Less spontaneous than the Yahwist, the writer (in the sense referred to above) has deeper religious reflections and is in some ways more properly a theologian. Thus, to him we owe the tradition concerning the archaic rite of the Covenant found in Gen. 15, the extraordinary meditation of Gen. 22; the account of the revelation of the divine name in Exod. 3, of the great "theophany" and the celebration of the Covenant in Exod. 19 and 24, and of the drama of the "Golden Calf" in Exod. 32. With Exod. 33, this contemplator of the mysteries of God invites us to the summits of mysticism. We are very close to the great prophets. In addition, the Elohist has collected poems of such importance as the Canticle found in Exod. 15 and the Benediction found in Deut. 33. Finally, he has written down formulations of law that are as fundamental as the Decalogue, and as archaic, and at the same time as purely Hebrew in vein, as the Covenant Code (cf. Exod. 20-23).

The Elohist is the first to have given Abraham and Moses the name of "Prophets" (cf. Gen. 20:7; Num. 12:6-8). Without going any deeper than the Yahwist did into the battle against Baalism (cf., however, Gen. 35:1-8; Exod. 20:3-5; 22:19; 23:13), he is marked by the same very clear "prophetic" tendency which was beginning to assert itself so strongly in Israel, and which secured for us this second great vision of the past of the People of God.

With the Yahwist and the Elohist each working in his own field, a great work, which would influence considerably the religious thought of Israel and, in consequence, its literature, came into existence. The distinctively Israelite idea of history found expression; in fact, it found the history of the world, for Israel was well situated with regard to other nations.

We cannot restrain our admiration for the anonymous writers whose stature enabled them to look upon the whole diverse and confused national inheritance of their people, as well as what they knew of other countries, in the pure light of their faith and in a unique perspective. This perspective was both providential and universal; it knew how to distinguish the important personalities of the ancestral history, to eliminate the mythic spirit, to make evident key events, and everywhere, in every act, to manifest the will and the power of God, and the sense of his Plan.

THE "J" AND "E" TEXTS IN THE PENTATEUCH

The following table may surprise inexperienced readers. If they refer to the biblical text, they will find that the task of criticism has resulted in an extreme fragmentation. At the same time, however, they will come to see that this work has been accomplished with exceptional care. If there is not too much insistence on precision in details, which are sometimes partly conjectural, one can accept the results with confidence. They make it possible to restore the texts to their historical setting and to read them according to their own genius, which is one of the first conditions for acquiring a knowledge of them.

THE YAHWIST TEXT

Gen. 2:4*b*-25; 3; 4; 5:29; 6:1-8; 7:1-5, 7-10, 12, 16*b*-17, 22-23; 8:2*b*-3*a*, 6-12, 13*b*, 20-22; 9:18-27; 10:8-19, 21, 24-30; 11:1-9, 28-30;

12:1-4*a*, 6-20; 13:1-5, 7-11*a*, 12*b*-18; 15 mixes with E; 16:1*b*-2, 4-14; 18; 19:1-28, 30-38; 21:1*a*, 2*a*, 33; 22:15-18, 20-24; 24; 25:1-6, 11*b*, 18, 21-26*a*, 27-34; 26:1-33; 27:1-45; 26:10, 13-16, 19; 29:2-14, 31-35; 30:3*b*-5, 7, 9-16, 24-43; 31:1, 3, 46, 48-50; 32:3-13*a*, 22, 24-32; 33:1-17; 34:2*b*-3, 5, 7, 11-12, 19, 25-26, 30-31; 35:14, 21-22*a;* 37:3-4, 12-13, 14*b*, 18*b*, 21, 23*a*, 25-27, 28*b*, 31*a*, 32*b*-33, 35; 38; 39; 40:3*b*, 5*b*, 15*b;* 42:2, 4*b*-7, 27-28, 38; 43:1-13, 15-23*a*, 24-34; 44; 45 mixes with E; 46:28-34; 47:1-6, 13-27*a*, 29-31; 49:1*b*-28*a;* 50:1-11, 14. Exod. 1:6, 8-12; 2:16-23*a;* 3:2-4*a*, 5, 7-8, 16-20; 4:1-16, 19-20*a*, 22-31; 5; 6:1; 7:14-18, 23, 25-29; 8:4-11*a*, 16-28; 9:1-7, 13-21, 23*b*-34; 10:1-7, 13*b*-19, 28-29; 11:4-8; 12:21-27, 29-30; 13:3-16, 21-22; 14:5-7, 10-14, 19-20, 21*b*, 24-25, 27*b*, 30-31; 15:22-27; 16:4-5, 15, 19-21, 29-30; 17:1*b*, 2, 7; 19, 20-25; 20, 22-26; 24:1-2, 9-11; 32:9-14; 34:1-28. Num. (with E) cf. infra. Deut. 34:1*b*-4.

THE ELOHIST TEXT

Gen. 15 mixes with J; 20; 21:6-32, 34; 22:1-14, 19; 28:11-12, 17-18, 20-22; 29:1, 15-23, 25-28, 30; 30:1-3*a*, 6, 8, 17-23; 31:2, 4-18*a*, 19-45, 51-55; 32:1-2, 13*b*-21, 23; 33:18*b*-20; 35:1-8, 16-20; 37:2*b*, 5-11, 14*a*, 15-18*a*, 19-20, 22, 23*b*-24, 28*a*, 28*c*-30, 31*b*-32*a*, 34, 36; 40:1-3*a*, 4-5*a*, 6-15*a*, 16-23; 41; 42:1, 3-4*a*, 8-26, 29-37; 43:14, 23*b;* 45 with J; 46:1-5*a;* 47:12; 48:1-2, 8-22; 50:15-26. Exod. 1:15-22; 2:1-15; 3:1, 4*b*, 6, 9-15, 21-22; 4:17-18, 20*b*-21; 7:20*b*-21*a*, 24; 9:22-23*a*, 35; 10:8-13*a*, 20-27; 11:1-3; 12:31-36, 37*b*-39; 13:17-19; 15:1-21; 17:3-6, 8-16; 18; 19:2*b*-19; 20:1-21; 21; 22; 23; 24:3-8, 12-15*a*, 18*b;* 31:18*b;* 32:1-8, 15-35; 33. Num. (with J) 10:29-36; 11; 12; 13:17-33 (+P); 14 (+P); 16:1-34 (+P); 20:1-9, 12-35; 22; 23; 24; 25:1-5; 32:1-17, 20-27, 34-42. Deut. 10:10, 6-7; 27:5-7*a;* 31:14-15, 23; 33; 34:5-6.

How have scholars succeeded in distinguishing "traditions" so intermingled? It is difficult to give the uninitiated an understanding of critical methods. They suppose an exact knowledge of the original texts, precise and complete information about the whole of biblical literature, the ability to make very detailed analyses and many comparisons, and also extensive information in the fields of ancient history, archaeology, languages, literatures, and religions. Here, we will content ourselves with pointing out the criteria of discernment which are the easiest to discover.

The frequently discontinuous character of the texts is immediately perceptible. If the titles and subtitles that have been added by translators are ignored, the abrupt breaks can be still more easily noted. Compare, for example: Gen. 2:4 with 2:5; 4:26 with 5:1; 5:32 with 6:1; 10:32 with 11:1; 11:9 with 11:10; 11:32 with 12:1; and others. See also Exod. 6:8-14; 20; 17-18; 23:19-20; Num. 10:28; 11:3.

Some passages are needless duplicates. Examples of these "doublets" are: Gen. 12:10-20 and 20:1-18; 28:10-19 and 35:9-13; Exod. 3-4 and 6-7; 12:1-3 and 12:43-49; 22:28-29 and 34:19-20. Differences in detail, found when the two "traditions" report the same fact or the same law, may help to characterize them.

Consideration of the vocabulary and of the style also facilitates the classification of the texts. Each "source" (J, E, D, P; we shall meet these last two later on) has its own words and modes of expression. Thus, "Yahweh" and "Elohim" (from which come the names given to the traditions), "Amorite" and "Canaanite," "male and female" and "man and woman," "Sinai" and "Horeb," "Jacob" and "Israel," and others are not used without reason. The style may be more archaic or more developed, popular or technical. Even in translation, it is not difficult to see that Gen. 2:4-4:25 makes up a whole in the same vein, which is found again in Gen. 9:18-27 and 11:1-9, and often thereafter; the same thing can be seen (and this time it uses the "sacerdotal" text or P) for Gen. 1:1-2, 4; 9:1-17; 17; etc.

The question is one of a convergence of signs. An immense, complex work, it was not carried out lightly or rapidly. The results are not all equally definitive; some texts cannot be labeled without doubts and hesitations. Furthermore, the critics have carried their study to the point of trying to distinguish several "Yahwists," and several "Elohists" (J^1, J^2, J^3, and E^1, E^2, and E^3), etc. Refinements of this kind are obviously more and more fragile; for that very reason the approval of specialists is less unanimous. For the frequent conclusions, those of which we make use of, however, the agreement of the exegetes is amply sufficient to insure freedom from doubt and to prevail in all serious study of the Pentateuch.

[THREE]

THE PROPHETS

The first half of the eighth century is a high point in the history of Palestine. The period is marked by the full development of the northern kingdom under Jeroboam II (785-745 B.C.) and by the great and prosperous reign of Azarias (Ozias) (790-739 B.C.) in Juda.[1]

The material condition of the country was as good as could be desired, at least if one consider appearances alone. The people could feel that the frontiers were safe, both from a disabled Egypt, from Assyria, which had not yet gained control of the Mediterranean regions,[2] and also from the Aramaeans, who were in trouble with their neighbors.

The government was solidly established in both kingdoms: the administration was working well, and business prospered for those who managed it. Traders, some of whom were not afraid to engage in speculation and who turned everything into money, even slaves, formed a new and important group in the society of Palestine. When Solomon began economic relations with his neighbors, especially the Phoenicians, it was solely for the benefit of the royal domain; but two centuries later the great office-holders of the country had learned how to become rich for their own advantage. The result was what always happens in similar circumstances. Those who had property had the means of acquiring more, to the detriment of the little people who were soon burdened with debts and were obliged to sell their goods, their fields, and their means of livelihood, hiring themselves out for poorly paid tasks.

Hence, the well-to-do were happy, and profiteers lived hand-

[1] The short texts in IV Kgs. 14:23-29 and 15:1-6 are far from giving an account of the greatness of these two reigns, which can be known from other sources (notably from the prophecies of Amos and of Osee). The reading of these two prophets also enables us to present a brief sketch of the society of Palestine at this time. We cannot give many references to the texts; they would be incessant. We simply invite the reader to read again each of the prophetic collections, which are short.

[2] There was, in addition, a kind of eclipse between the reign of Adadnirari III (cf. pp. 92-93) and the reign of Tiglath-Pileser III, whom we shall soon see making his appearance.

somely. The poor, on the other hand, had to endure, in silence and in suffering, all the abuses and evasions of human law, and all the challenges of the holy Law. How far distant this was from the simple, almost equalitarian, happy society of the premonarchical period! To this corrupt and insolent display, an ostentatious religion lent a deceitful façade. For religion was practiced in the belief that as far as God was concerned this was also the way to obtain tranquility.

Then, suddenly, Yahweh roared (cf. Amos 1:2).

From the south of Judea, torn away from his everyday tasks by the irresistible inspiration of God, who wished to express himself through him (cf. Amos 7:14-15), Amos, a just and simple countryman, with a great and courageous heart, came to deliver incendiary speeches [3] on the threshold of the sanctuary of Bethel. We are in the years 760-750 B.C.

Like Elias of old, he rose like a flash of lightning in the midst of a brilliant but contemptible world. His words were firm, rigorous, and sometimes cutting. He proclaimed "justice" and "judgment." Men must live as God would have them (cf. Amos 5:4, 6, 14, 15); otherwise, the terrible "day" of Yahweh the purifier would come.[4] These utterances contain trenchant formulas, words which will remain forever. The perfection attained by a single stroke of this new style is absolutely amazing.[5] Amos, of course, was not the first to speak in this way. However personal his words may be, they form part of a tradition; they enter into a movement of prophetic inspiration that was evident already. But that which had been ripening for a long time broke forth with a strange force in the preaching of the unexpected Prophet from Teqoa.

In less than twenty-five years, just after Amos had made alarming pronouncements concerning the descendants of Jeroboam II and the destiny of his kingdom (cf. Amos 7:11), Samaria saw a

[3] Seven times in the first two chapters, Yahweh repeats: "I shall send fire . . ."

[4] Cf. Amos 5:18; cf. also 2:16; 8:9, 13; 9:11 (in the plural: 4:2; 8:11; 9:13). The expression voiced by Amos was to become classic in prophetic oracles. So, too, was the idea of the "remnant" (cf. Amos 3:12; 5:15; 9:8), which the other Prophets were to pick up—especially, before long, Isaias. Amos was a great innovator.

[5] With the exception of the prose passage of 7:10-17, the little book is remarkably composed, with an intricate structure of strophes and refrains, in language that is admirably strong.

succession of six kings, four of whom came to power by the assassination of their predecessors (cf. IV Kgs. 15). This governmental anarchy was aggravated by an unintelligent policy which relied on Egypt, close by but weak, whereas it was Assyria, considered far distant, which was formidable. Tiglath-Pileser III (745-727 B.C.) was ready to show what Assyria was capable of by imposing, on the grounds of protection against Damascus, a fairly heavy tribute on the Syro-Palestinian principalities. Manahem submitted (cf. IV Kgs. 15:19-20). Regardless, economic conditions in Israel remained prosperous on the whole. The spiritual and moral decline was accentuated, however, by impiety and by social and institutional defects of all kinds.

Shortly after Amos, another Prophet was sent to Israel; Osee, a northern Israelite, spoke between the years 750-725 B.C.

Although he was emotional and profoundly sensitive, Osee was truly a chosen spirit. For this very reason, he was doomed to an unhappy fate. He too knew how to speak of justice; and he had to speak of it when idolatry, misconduct, and crime were widespread, and when the men in authority, priests and kings, hastened toward ruin. But the emotionalism, which his vigorous declarations do not conceal, torments the Prophet. Words of the most terrible severity are mingled with accents of the most profound tenderness.

He formulates in upsetting terms, which reflect his intimate experience (Osee had to love a woman who was faithless to him: cf. Osee 1-3), the love of God for his people, the Alliance of Yahweh and Israel. It is a great nuptial mystery, traversed by the drama of Israel's shameless betrayal and by the misfortunes of separation from Yahweh.[6] The Days of his Wrath will come; in order to live again, it will be necessary to undergo destruction. For although the divine love is exacting and terribly "jealous," it rises above every-

[6] To think of the Covenant between God and his people in terms of marriage was in accordance with the Revelation given on Sinai (cf. p. 61, note 9). It was for Osee, whose private life itself was revealed as having a symbolic value, to give expression to it for the first time and in the most poignant manner. Is it merely an image? Rather, only a union of this kind can be perfect (St. Paul, who was to present its final formulation, suggests sufficiently that human marriage is a participation in the union of God with his people: cf. Eph. 5:22-33). Such a love of God for men makes history dramatic. We will not yet allow ourselves to meditate on this mystery, the most profound in the Bible, but from now on we know the heart of God and we will not again be able to forget what he has confided to us about himself.

thing; it is tirelessly faithful; it never ceases to invite conversion, and it always pardons with mercy. By this time men knew how God loves.

Never had anyone spoken in this way. The religious beliefs of Israel were at their peak. The Spirit of Yahweh was communicating itself abundantly. And, while Osee addressed the Ephraimites, the turn of the Judeans and of Jerusalem, which saw the rise of its greatest Prophet, came.

In the year 739 B.C., Yahweh manifested his "holiness" in the Temple by revealing himself to Isaias. The mission he enjoined upon Isaias was to threaten a hardened people, while still retaining their confidence in the salvation that comes from God (cf. Isa. 6:1-13).

He whom the Lord had chosen this time lived in the city and was an aristocrat by birth. He had been given a complete education and was endowed with great culture. Noble of character, he would be able to speak on an equal footing with the most important personalities of Jerusalem, without being any the less an advocate of the humblest folk (cf. Isa. 3:14, 15; 10:2; 11:4; 14:30, 32; 29:19; 32:7). He would be inflexible in denouncing vice and injustice, in defending the common people and the oppressed, and in recalling to the entire world what life means according to God. He too is opposed to all that is deceitful and empty. Like Amos, Osee, and his own contemporary Micheas, he severely criticizes the pretense of the present hypocritical state of religion, at the same time preaching social justice and charity among all.[7]

The mighty power of his thought can embrace the most lofty questions; he has a superior sense of the public good and true political genius. We shall see that his depth of perception comes from faith, which dominates and surpasses all politics. He has, above all, an intensely religious soul. His perception of the "Holy" God is incomparable and conditions his entire message (cf. Isa. 2:10-21; 5:16; 6:3-5; 8:13; 12:4-6; 29:23; 30:30; 33:21).

Since he was from Jerusalem, Isaias did not cease to share what

[7] Isaias must have been born about 765 B.C. His first utterances are read in the first five chapters of the collection that bears his name (Isa. 2:1-5 is, however, problematical; this passage is found as such in Mich. 4:1-4). The admirable first chapter should especially be reread; the "Song of the Vineyard" (Isa. 5:1-7) is also very famous.

seemed to him the tragic life of his people. In the name of God, he pledged himself wholeheartedly when the hour of the most terrible dangers arrived.

While the Urarteans held Tiglath-Pileser to northern Assyria, a confederation was formed against him. The confederation assembled at Rasin in Damascus, and consisted of the kings of Gaza, Samaria, Sidon and Tyre, and Arabia, with the support of Egypt. Achaz of Juda (735-720 B.C.) refused to enter the league. The men of Damascus and of Samaria, wishing to force his hand or at least to punish him, made war on him, even threatening Jerusalem (the war is known as the "Syro-Ephraimite War" of 735-734 B.C.). Isaias, who scorned all help that did not come from Yahweh, declared that faith was enough; beginning with the king, he asked the men of Jerusalem to remain tranquil. Achaz, however, was skeptical; he thought it prudent to call Assyria to his assistance, in return for a large sum of money. Tiglath-Pileser, who now had some spare time, wanted nothing more than to intervene. He used this opportunity profitably, making a great military circuit throughout the whole Syro-Palestinian region, and bringing almost everything under his dominion. Damascus was besieged, taken, and chastised by severe destruction (732 B.C.). Its inhabitants were deported and the region transformed into an Assyrian province. Samaria saved itself only by getting a new ruler, Osee, who was in the pay of the Great King. Achaz, a victim of the "liberation," was one of those who had to pay tribute. All Jerusalem saw the extent to which he had to carry his servility toward the all-powerful monarch (cf. IV Kgs. 16; Isa. 7-8). Such was his recompense for refusing to trust in God alone and in the word of his Prophet.

The disappointments Isaias suffered from men could never turn to despair in a man who really had faith and whom God enlightened. A dam raises the level of the waters behind it. Isaias even profited by the circumstances to make known his revelations concerning "Emmanuel," "God-with-us." This was the name of a mysterious son of David whose perfection and divine sublimity would never be realized in any of the kings who would occupy the throne of Juda. Nevertheless, he was an ideal who would gradually raise the gaze of men toward a "Son of David," a "Messias," one who would not be limited by the ordinary measure of other kings, but who would be a gift of God to the people of the Covenant (cf. Isa. 4:2; 7:14; 9:1-6; 11:1-5; 16:5).[8]

The situation in Palestine was to be simplified, rapidly and tragically, by the disappearance of the northern kingdom.

On the death of Tiglath-Pileser (727 B.C.), King Osee, giving in to the political faction favorable to Egypt, stopped sending his annual payment to Assyria. Salmanasar V (727-723 B.C.) had him seized and imprisoned; then, he undertook the siege of Samaria (725 B.C.). The siege was prolonged because the Assyrian army wanted to make Tyre surrender at the same time, a project in which it was unsuccessful. Salmanasar died in the meantime. But his successor, Sargon II,[9] took Samaria, demolished it (722 B.C.), deported its inhabitants to Media, and replaced them by strangers. Obviously, the loss of Samaria was bad from the religious point of view.[10] Afterwards, the region was, like Syria, no more than a colony annexed to the empire. Thus, the "proud" kingdom of Samaria came to an end, as foretold by Amos, Osee, and Isaias.[11]

The disappearance of its sister kingdom deprived the principality of Juda of its protective rampart against invasion from the north. But the lesson was not learned. The perversion of religion and

[8] Isa. 7-11 constitutes what is generally called the "Book of Emmanuel." Who is Emmanuel, and what is the exact sense of Isa. 7:14? The question is difficult, and one that is constantly debated. Recent exegetes would see in it threatening words, because of the context of chapters 7 and 8, and the name "God-with-us" as cruelly ironical (the child would be born of Achaz and a temple servant, which would be extraordinary, since women of this kind did not have children; Prov. 30:19 is cited). On this assumption, the passage would not relate to the "Messias" of chapters 9 and 11. We prefer, however, to see in Emmanuel the royal and legitimate child of the house of David.

In the prophecy of Isa. 7:14 and in the prophecy of Nathan in II Sam. 7, the birth of Ezechias, like that of Solomon, can be seen as a first realization and pledge of the fulfillment of a prophecy which, in conformity with the Davidic dynasty, can go far beyond that stage and later be understood of the Messias to come. However, it is not possible to exclude utterly the hypothesis according to which the child announced would be one of the sons of Isaias himself, whose names are "signs and presages" (Isa. 8:1-4, 8, 10, 18).

[9] Sargon II (723-705 B.C.) was the creator of the Assyrian "Versailles," the famous and ephemeral imperial residence of Khorsabad, 10 miles from Nineve.

[10] In IV Kgs. 17, a meditation on the end of the northern kingdom, the "deuteronomic" style is readily perceptible (beginning with v. 7).

[11] For example, cf. Amos 3:11-12; 5:1-3; 7:11, 17; Osee 1:4; 7:8-12; 8:8-10; Isa. 28:1-4.

morals increased; completely pagan cults with the worst practices, such as the sacrifice of infants, were officially installed at Jerusalem (cf. IV Kgs. 16; II Par. 28).

Nevertheless, Isaias continued his ministry of preaching; he disquieted guilty consciences, denounced sinfulness, insisted on faith, and revealed the horizons of history.[12]

Fortunately, the son of Achaz made up for his father. The reign of the pious Ezechias (720-692? B.C.) was characterized by great effort in the sphere of politics and of military tactics.[13] More important still was the energetic religious reform he inaugurated. Reform was urgently needed, and the influence of prophets like Isaias and Micheas certainly contributed a great deal to it (cf. IV Kgs. 18:3-6; II Par. 29-31).[14] The House of God once more saw the worship of Yahweh alone celebrated with solemnity. A campaign was organized throughout the country to systematically suppress every vestige of idolatry. Twenty-five years of peace, of great prosperity, and of great works followed.

In the meantime, Egyptian propaganda reached out insidiously and finally succeeded in once more compromising men. Ezechias entered into an anti-Assyrian coalition which regrouped all the little Syrian and Mediterranean states. The coalition was subsidized by pharaoh (cf. p. 94) and encouraged by the revolt, in 721 B.C., of the Babylonian Merodach-Baladan, who succeeded in recreating an independent Babylonia for a few years.[15]

Assur took to the road again for a grand tour of reprisals. After having defeated Egypt and put down the rebels in the south of Palestine, the army of Sennacherib (705-681 B.C.) camped under

[12] Begun before the fall of Samaria, the prophecies which form chapters 28-32 were continued in the following years. So, too, with the "oracles against the nations" which go from 14:24 to the end of chapter 23. Especially to be noticed are Isa. 28:16; 29:19; 30:15, 18; 31:1-3.

[13] Particularly to be noted is the construction of the famous subterranean canal, which brought water from the fountain of Gihon, in the valley of the Cedron, to the reservoirs of Siloe: cf. IV Kgs. 20:20. Thus, the water no longer came in from outside the city, a wise precaution in case of siege.

[14] The chronicler is to be understood according to his point of view. He takes advantage of the historical facts relating to the reform of Ezechias to put emphasis, a levitical and postexilic emphasis, on the requirements of worship.

[15] The embassy of Merodach-Baladan to the king of Juda, like the illness of Ezechias, occurred before the siege of Jerusalem by Sennacherib, in spite of the order of chapters 18-20 of IV Kgs. The same inversion should be made for Isa. 36-37 and 38-39.

the walls of Jerusalem. Jerusalem would not yield in spite of the threatening demands for surrender (701 B.C.). From the human point of view, however, the city's situation was desperate. But Isaias was there, and he demanded, as he had thirty years earlier, with extreme firmness, that not a soul should give way. This time they listened to him; unexpectedly, the enemy broke camp, and the Holy City was saved (cf. IV Kgs. 18:13-31; 19:1-36; Isa. 36-37).[16]

Such was the faith preached by the great Prophet of Jerusalem: salvation comes from God (cf. Isa. 7:9; 8:17; 10:20; 12:2; 22:10-11; 28:16; 30:15; 31:1). The siege of Jerusalem would not be his only problem: the People of God would be subject to other dangers; they would not be spared crises and catastrophes. Misfortune is a punishment which should purify and lead to conversion; God wishes to save men on the ruins of their pride and of their sins (cf. Isa. 2:6-22). If betrayals and apostasies were enormous, so was the slaughter. God always keeps a "remnant" for himself, however, even though it be a minority weak in appearance and "poor" (cf. p. 122). From this humble remnant will arise a new people and a perfect King, the Savior, "God-with-us."

Isaias is always lofty and heroic. His thought contributed in an exceptional manner to the endowing of Israel with a pure and demanding theology. In the collection of his words declarations can be found upon which ages to come will never cease to meditate: the "holiness" of God; the humility and sincerity of a truly religious attitude; faith; and the Messias. Everything he says is uttered in magnificent language, the most beautiful ever spoken in Israel. He uses new and pleasing images; his style is lofty in character, sober, limpid, and powerful.

Isaias spoke during the course of some forty years. Those of his sayings which have been collected and preserved make up, in a rather disordered way, the greater part of the first half of the book that bears his name.[17]

He had disciples; other Prophets were to inherit his spirit and prolong his activity. Hence, following a practice which became

[16] Two accounts of the same fact are mixed in these passages. The "angel of Yahweh" of IV Kgs. 19:35 is an exceptional circumstance in the hands of God, no doubt consisting in an epidemic that ravaged the Assyrian camp and forced the army to leave the scene.

[17] Except 2:1-5; 13:1-14, 23; 19:18-25; 21:1-10; 23:15-18; 24-27; 34-35. We shall meet these passages again.

common in Israel, with the passage of time the work of Isaias was augmented, receiving numerous additions, especially in the century of the Babylonian Exile.

Micheas, the author of a small group of wise sayings which have many affinities with the collection of Isaias, addressed the Word of Yahweh to his compatriots as early as the time of Joatham,[18] and on into the time that followed the fall of Samaria. He defended those in humble circumstances (cf. Mich. 2:2; 3:2-3, 11), and denounced public shortcomings (cf. Mich. 3:1-12). A man from the country, he was as courageous as Amos and as discerning as Isaias. He revealed the "justices" of Yahweh in events, realizing that the difficult but exceptional destiny of Israel runs through and affects the whole course of history. He was also able to show in a storm-filled sky the rays of the pure light of the marvelous goodness of Yahweh; he leads us to discern a renewal, a restoration of the People of God under the leadership of the "son of David," "Prince of Peace" (cf. Mich. 4:6-13; 5:1-5).[19] Although Micheas is not an initiator, yet prophetic teaching was clearly expressed by him. In summing up Amos, Osee, and Isaias, he was able to express in an imperishable formula (cf. Mich. 6:8) the program of the true life according to God.

[FOUR]

THE PROPHETIC WORD | The Prophets of the eighth century and those who were to follow in the course of the next three or four centuries of the People of God [1] had a full and clear conscious-

[18] Who reigned alone from 739 B.C. to 735 B.C., but who had already exercised the royal functions for about 12 years in the place of his father, who had become a leper (cf. IV Kgs. 15:15, 33).

[19] Mich. 2:12-13; 4:1-5; 7:8-20 seem not to be by Micheas, but to have been added during the time of the Exile or even later.

[1] We will present a bibliography for each prophet only when we come to study each one individually. Concerning prophecy in general, the following works may be consulted: J. Chaine, *God's Heralds: A Guide to the Prophets of Israel*, English trans. by Brendan McGrath, O.S.B. (New York: Wagner, 1955); Bruce Vawter, C.M., *The Conscience of Israel: Pre-Exilic Prophets and Prophecy* (New York: Sheed & Ward, 1961); a non-Catholic work which covers

ness of their divine mission. Their ministry had, in addition, acquired certain fundamental and specific characteristics. Because of them, a new literature, which was to occupy an important place in the Bible, finally appeared. These facts now require some consideration.

Understood according to a rather general acceptation, prophetism was not a novelty in the period under study, nor was it, in this sense, properly Israelite. In ancient societies,[2] there were always men who had the reputation of possessing a knowledge superior to that normally obtainable. The manner in which they manifested their gift or their art was, moreover, very diverse, from that of the professional diviner, who was often a practitioner of the science of omens which was so widespread in the Ancient Near East (cf. p. 29), to that of the "inspired" person, who acted in a rather surprising manner.

As soon as Israel became a people, it also had its specialists in "seeing"; they behaved like seers of other countries, but within the limits of revealed Yahwism.[3] This archaic type of seer is represented by two kinds of men: those whom people visited in order to "consult Yahweh" (cf. Gen. 25:22; Exod. 33:7; Judg. 18:5; 20:18; I Sam. 14:37; 22:10; 23:2; 30:7-8; II Sam. 2:1), who exercised the office of medium and who were usually priests; and those who dedicated themselves to a freer or more extemporaneous prophetism, such as those we find in the history of Saul (cf. I Sam. 10:5-13; 19:20-24), who were generally subject to the phenomena of elevation, frenzy, or ecstasy, and who lived or wandered about in groups (cf. p. 73).

We find these groups again, but apparently in a more developed state (cf. p. 97, note 15), under the name of "sons of Prophets,"

the matter thoroughly is Johannes Lindblom, *Prophecy in Ancient Israel* (Oxford: Blackwell, 1962).

At this stage in our study, the reader should inform himself concerning history, both the history of Israel and international history, with the help of the works already cited and primarily with the help of the Bible.

[2] These reflections might start from a still more general observation. Is there not a fundamental prophetism which is inherent in human nature itself, from the mere fact that man grasps and expresses the meaning of things? Language is an interpretation. Poetry is a divining instinct and a power of evocation. In the same way, the arts enable us to cross the threshold of simple sensible experience.

[3] Moses, the inspired inaugurator of Yahwism, was eminently a Prophet in the deepest meaning of the word. For that very reason, however, he cannot be classed purely and simply among the seers of the ancient common type.

around Eliseus (cf. III Kgs. 20:35; IV Kgs. 2:3, 15; 4:1, 38; 5:22; 6:1; 9:1; Amos 7:14). As early as the creation of the kingdom, however, Prophets of a very different kind had already appeared in Israel; they represented themselves as having been sent by Yahweh. The names of some of them are known: Samuel, Gad, Nathan, Ahias, Semeias, Jehu, Micheas, Holda, Hanani, Eliezer (cf. I Sam. 3:20-21; 9:6; 22:5; II Sam. 7:2-4; 12:1; 24:11; III Kgs. 1:22; 11:29; 12:22; 16:1; 22:8; IV Kgs. 22:14; II Par. 16:7; 19:2; 20:37); some have remained anonymous, and are called simply "men of God" (cf. I Sam. 2:27; III Kgs. 13:1; 20:28); it may be supposed that there were others of whom the texts do not speak. Among these seers or Prophets (this name has developed: cf. I Sam. 9:9), some practiced an official prophetism before the kings; others arose as unforeseen messengers of divine communications.

Thus, we can agree on a precise, a superior conception, clear and essential, of prophetism, that prophetism which characterized Israel and which is peculiarly biblical. To prophesy was to speak in the name of God to the People of God.[4]

The Prophets whom we have just mentioned from biblical sources, like Elias and Eliseus, who are known from the accounts in the Book of Kings (cf. pp. 96-98), did not write anything, at least as far as is known. Consequently, the Prophets whose words have been preserved in writing are distinguished from the other and pointed out in a still more special manner. They are often called the Writing Prophets; more commonly still, they are the ones who are called, without any other qualification, "the Prophets" of the Bible; their work constitutes one of the major sections of the Holy Book. Beginning with Amos and ending with Second Zacharias, there are seventeen of them,[5] extending from the eighth to the fourth

[4] "Prophets," in Greek, comes from *pro-phanai,* "to speak for someone," "to speak in the place and name of someone." The Prophets are not, then, necessarily or primarily "foretellers" or "predictors," they are preachers. The Hebrew word *nabi* (plural: *nebiim*) is of a more obscure, uncertain etymology, but the way it is used certainly indicates its meaning which is well translated by the Greek word. To clarify this meaning, cf. Exod. 4:16; 7:1-2; Deut. 18:18; II Sam. 23:1-2; Isa. 51:16; Jer. 1:9; 15:19.

[5] We do not count the anonymous authors of small sections or isolated prophecies, such as Isa. 13-14 or 24-27, for example, or Daniel or Baruch, whom we will place elsewhere. But we do count the Second and Third "Isaias" and a Second "Zacharias" (cf. *WG,* pp. 193-96, where the chronological list will be found).

century. They are an extraordinary, brilliant, and unique group of men in the history of the world.

The Prophets, then, are essentially the messengers, the interpreters, the spokesmen of God. They are characterized by an expression which they repeat constantly: "Thus sayeth Yahweh." They are preachers who say that their statements are the Word of God and that they have been sent for the precise purpose of making the Word known to their people.

How were they recognized? Why were they listened to and believed in? For "false prophets" were never lacking. These were of two kinds: the prophets of a religion other than Yahwism—prophets of Baal, of idols, of foreign gods (cf. III Kgs. 18:19-40; IV Kgs. 3:13; Jer. 2:8; 23:13); and prophets who claimed to speak in the name of Yahweh but who do not seem to have received a mandate from him and who spoke "according to their own heart" (cf. Isa. 9:14; Mich. 3:5, 11; Jer. 5:13, 31; 6:13; 14:14; 23:14, 16-18; 27:9-15; 28:8-9; 29:31; Ezech. 13:1-10; 17-23; 22:28). The Prophets who claimed to have been sent expressly by God had to struggle incessantly against the pretenders, the visionaries, or simply the politicians and courtiers of easy and complacent speech (cf. in particular III Kgs. 22 and Jer. 26). A sure instinct seems to have enabled the Israelites, or at least the best or the most faithful among them, always to recognize those whom Yahweh had really sent. The testimony of their personal lives and their faith was, moreover, decisive enough. In addition, the theology of prophetism (cf. Deut. 18:15-22) was not slow in noting that the realization of predictions made by a Prophet, within a short time, was ordinarily a good criterion of judgment and guaranteed the authenticity of his other utterances (cf. I Sam. 2:34; 10:2-9; II Sam. 12:10-15; III Kgs. 13:3-5; 14:10-18; IV Kgs. 19:29; 20:10-11; Isa. 7:14-20; Jer. 28:16-17; Amos 7:17). The Prophet himself was so sure of being called by God (cf. Amos 7:15; Isa. 6:9; Jer. 1:5-10; Ezech. 2:3; 3:10-11) that sometimes he even undertook the task reluctantly, against his will, and complained of it (cf. Amos 3:8; Jer. 20:7-8; Ezech. 3:14).

Furthermore, his mission was a difficult and thankless one. It was all the more so because he often went against the tide of general opinion; he had to resist the pressure of the powerful and the slackness of their sycophants. Hence, he could not expect immediate success, but rather resistance, isolation, and even persecution.

The Prophets, as we have seen, were men of action,[6] enlisted in their times from contemporary life. They addressed themselves to men living under definite conditions. What they said found support or occasion in concrete circumstances, and hinged on actual situations and events.[7] Theirs was the exact opposite of the mysticism of escape. They conversed with men, or more exactly, by their mediation they carried out the conversation of God with his people. If the tone of the Prophet is habitually that of a man absolutely certain he is transmitting a superior message, if his assertions seem for that reason excessively intransigent and his language extraordinarily strong,[8] he remains, nonetheless, constantly accessible to men and to their problems. But, he is firm and intrepid in the faith, a faith not shared equally by those to whom he speaks. His involvement in the web of events does not obscure his view; he knows that in spite of appearances God is never kept in check.

God raised up the great Prophets when things were beginning to go badly, when society was becoming profoundly corrupt, when the leaders and guides failed in their task, and when the masses of the people were entering onto the path of their destruction. The prophetic era corresponded to a period of infidelity and crisis. This explains why the Prophets often appear as censors of the people's conduct, using such harsh words and such violent vituperation.[9] They uncover and denounce evils and the causes of evil; they assign

[6] Unlike those men who are satisfied to bear witness by their manner of life, such as the members of the "Rechabite" movement (cf. Jer. 35).

[7] Amos 4:6-11 comments on a series of public calamities; Osee 1-3 is inspired by the conjugal drama of the Prophet; Isa. 7 and 36-37 are preachings on faith because of the siege of Jerusalem. Among the manifestations of this bond between the prophetic word and a real and living environment, are the symbolic actions performed by the Prophets in public, where they "act out" in surprising pantomime and striking scenes their actual announcements: cf. Isa. 20:1-10; Jer. 13:1-11; 18:1-12; 19:1-13; 27-28; 32:6-44; Ezech. 4-5; 12:3-13; 37:16-28.

[8] *To express* is to select and to show. Because of the general lack of attention and because of the hardening of hearts, *to express* was often to be exclusive and to exaggerate: for deaf ears, using intemperate language. Because of the truths they wished to propagate and the circumstances under which they worked, one should not be surprised at the lack of rhythm which characterizes their language. Hyperbole, with them, was not a simple rhetorical figure; it was the normal form for important declarations concerning God, men, history, and salvation.

[9] This is why it is absolutely indispensable to return them to their historical setting, and consequently to know that setting, even in some of its details.

individual and collective responsibility; and they point out every evasion of the law. They undertake courageously and indefatigably the defense of minorities and of the downtrodden; they are not slow to consider the poor man as the friend of God, the man to whom salvation is especially promised.

If the Prophets proclaim God's demands or announce his severities, it is because Israel is the People of God, and a profound fidelity to its Lord should correspond to its special vocation as the God-bearer (cf. Amos 3:2; Osee 11:1-4; Isa. 1:2-4; 5:1-7; Jer. 2:2-3, 12-13, 21; Ezech. 16). The constant reference, explicit or implicit, of the prophetic preaching is the Covenant between Yahweh and Israel, an act of special benevolence on the part of God, an arrangement which places Israel before God and with him, a way of life whose norms were the holy Torah, which established fraternal relations between the members of the holy people. The revelation of Sinai was plumbed to the depths by the Prophets; it was a marriage of love (cf. Osee 1-3; Jer. 2-3; 31; Ezech. 16; Isa. 54; 62). For this reason, the Prophets were able, in the name of God's "jealousy," to speak of treason and of perjury, of adultery and of prostitution, as readily when religious worship became false as when they were in the presence of social injustices. But they also have the secret of using speech of infinite tenderness, of making the overwhelming appeals which God has them address to the "faithless," and of constantly proposing conversion, pardon, and the renewed Covenant.

The Prophets saw things so exactly in different historical conditions because their vision of history was entire, one which looked backward and, consequently, forward. They understood the past in relation to the Election of Israel, and they revealed the significance of events in the Plan of God. This was what later caused the Books of Joshua, Judges, Samuel, and Kings to be ranked among the "Earlier Prophets" (cf. *WG*, pp. 190-91). It is in this sense that we have been able to say that the Yahwist and the Elohist shared in the gift of prophecy (cf. pp. 103-5). Israel's ancient "confessions of faith" were undoubtedly the oldest sketches of this manner of speaking of history (cf. pp. 75-76). Hence, we come back to Moses, whose genius, enlightened by God, must have been the first to conceive of the exceptional destiny allotted to his people. Now, with the masters of thought whom God inspired, this kind of vision and explanation of history was affirmed with such force and such clarity that the Prophets of the eighth century are commonly recognized as the actual creators of this notion of history.[10]

Actual problems, which preoccupied the Prophets more than any other kind, were finally thought of only as part of the great historical channel. A new conception of prophetism was proper to Israel: the understanding of a time whose course is unique and irreversible (cf. *WG*, pp. 159-60); the sense of the dramatic progress of history, the certainty of a tending toward an end; the value of a "sign" of events; the perception of the stages and of the crises that mark the maturation of history, of the moments which divide its development, and of the "days" which are always approaching to announce the "pangs" of a new "birth" (cf. *WG*, pp. 159-60). From this superior point of view, the People of God were taught where they were going.

"Watchman, what of the night?" The Prophets were the watchmen charged with giving warnings (cf. Isa. 21:6-12; cf. also Osee 9:8; Mich. 7:4; Hab. 2:1; Jer. 6:17; Ezech. 3:17; Isa. 52:8; 62:6). Their gaze into the future was given perfect focus by the certainty of salvation, that is, by the liberty, happiness, and peace given and assured by God. Certainly salvation could not be achieved without catastrophes and severe destructions, because there things were considered necessary purifications. Perhaps only a small "remnant" will remain, surviving by grace, but converted to God (cf. Isa. 1:9; 4:3; 7:3; 10:20-22; 11:11-12, 16; 17:6; 28:5; 37:4, 32; Mich. 2:12; 4:7; 5:6-7; 7:18; Soph. 2:9; 3:13; Jer. 23:3; 31:7; Isa. 46:3; 65:8; 66:19; Agg. 1:12; Zach. 8:6, 11, 12; Joel 3:5).

The movement of this history, guided by God, toward an era in which the Plan of Salvation will be accomplished through an Elect of God who will have exceptional prerogatives was a conviction which became Messianism (cf. p. 89). Messianism began with the prophecy of Nathan (cf. II Sam. 7) and with the promises made to the offspring of David. The Prophets would never cease announcing this "Anointed One," this perfect "Servant of Yahweh," "God-with-us," Prince of Peace, Savior of his People, Light of the Gentiles (cf. Amos 9:11; Osee 2:2; 3:5; Isa. 4, 2; 9:3-6; 11:1-5; Mich. 5:1-4;

[10] Herodotus (fifth century) can only be called the "father of history" if, on the one hand, one forgets the Prophets who preceded him, and if, on the other, one calls history not that which proceeds from an orientated and coherent vision, but merely a simple reporting or a panorama of events.

Jer. 23:5; 33:15; Ezech. 34:23-24; Isa. 42:1-9; 49:1-7; 50:4-9; 52:13-53:12; 55:3-4; Zach. 9:9-10); it is one of the great invariables in their messages.

We can already see that their message will undergo constant elaboration, becoming more profound and more precise. When new situations arise, the Prophets will assume new attitudes, bringing up to date ancient findings, making declarations appropriate to the times. Thus, prophetic language evolved during the second half of the royal period and still more after the Exile. The great events that were to change the face of things, such as invasions, treaties, and deportations, were to have their repercussions in the preaching of the men of God. The progressive discovery of the outside world, relations with the "nations," and the contemplation of their diverse destinies, were also to open the mind of Israel to problems, and were to inspire the Prophets with more and more profound ideas concerning the vast drama of history.

We have anticipated to some extent by considering these aspects of the prophetic movement and of revelation as a whole, but the anticipation was necessary to prepare us for the appearance of the collections of oracles.

From the point of view of literary form, these usually appear as poems. They have all the characteristics of Hebrew poetry (cf. *WG*, p. 169). Poetry, then, is in harmony with the requirements of prophetic inspiration.[11] We may ask whether these poems sprang into being directly and were reproduced in writing just as they were, or whether they were the result of literary composition, that is, whether they began with words which did not at first have the same literary form. The truth of the matter is somewhat complex. It may be that the Prophets sometimes improvised poems which

[11] Poetry corresponds to the essential rhythms that scan the profundities of life. Now, the Prophet is a hypersensitive man, vibrating in unison with the whole of life. Poetic knowledge is a more profound existential and intuitive penetration than rational conception. This is what prophetic knowledge seems to be. The poetry of words, sounds, accents, rhythms, and assonances is enchanting; it is a power which invites man to go beyond the mundane. The Prophet used it spontaneously to direct man to God and to bring them to the borders of mystery. The poetic form is the most impressive to the hearing and it makes the deepest imprint on the mind. The Prophets wished to impress minds (compare them with the many great poets of universal history).

could be immediately committed to memory; more often, no doubt, the compilation was made at some other time, apart from the actual event and apart from preaching. The Prophets who preceded the Exile do not seem to have been writers themselves (cf. however, Isa. 8:1; 30:8); their words were probably preserved [12] by disciples or in prophetic circles, and recorded more or less quickly on papyrus or parchment. Beginning with Jeremias, we already find writing which is really dictation (cf. Jer. 36). After the Exile, the prophecies were more often written. The second part of the collection of Isaias (chaps. 40-66), for example, is primarily a literary composition.

All sorts of literary forms are found in the prophetic collections: narratives, dialogues, allegories, parables, maxims, prayers, psalms, hymns, and letters. The tone is by turns one of appeal, blame, exhortation, supplication, counsel, and promise. The oracles of the Prophets, texts originally spoken or intended to be spoken, are usually written in "oral style," that is, in a direct, animated language filled with emotion, a style whose development is entirely psychological, born of the Prophet's own life and marked by it. The language, then, reflects the particular conditions of the prophetic proclamation, the origins and character of the inspired speaker, his temperament, culture, and tastes. Men as different as the rustic Amos, the artistocrat Isaias, and the priest Ezechiel were called to prophetism; they were, furthermore, more or less gifted in expressing themselves. The Hebrew language itself developed. It attained perfection in the eighth century, but declined after the Exile, losing both vigor and beauty. Hence, a great diversity can be found in prophetic literature.

The writings of the Prophets were first known and circulated in fairly short fragments on rolls or folios in small collections or booklets. These, sometimes unfinished, sometimes mutilated or divided, were subsequently collected in a manner which is not very well known. An "edition" of this kind resulted in a partially artificial presentation and a certain lack of coherence. This is especially noticeable in Osee, Isaias, Jeremias, and Ezechiel. Many of their sayings have been misplaced; separated from their initial sources or from an explanatory context, their real historical position is difficult to recognize. Additions and glosses further complicate the work, but

[12] More than a hundred years after Micheas, men existed who were able to repeat from memory some of his prophecies (cf. Jer. 26:18 and Mich. 3:12).

the results are extremely enriching, because they make us present, period by period, at the different stages of prophetic reflection. Deep research, new interpretations and viewpoints are so many indications of an astonishing unrest in the People of God, for which they were indebted to their Prophets.

[FIVE]

SCRIBES AND SINGERS

The fall of Samaria in 722 B.C., bringing to an end the existence of the northern kingdom of Israel, increased the religious importance of Jerusalem. Among the men whom the Assyrian army had not deported, those most attached to Yahweh, to the traditions, and to the Torah, must have returned to the Holy City and the territory of Juda. Such was the case with a certain number of priests and scholars.

Thus, the work to which we now give the name of "Elohist" (cf. pp. 99-100) could be put together. Nor were the writers of Jerusalem slow in joining this work to its parallel work, the "Yahwist."

Another work, which was to appear only after a century, may well have been begun in the time of Ezechias in similar circles of writers. The writer must also have begun with the ancient traditions, which had been preserved until then in the kingdom of the north.[1] The subject matter consisted of the old "laws," witnesses of Israel's past, and of customs that had been transmitted, with certain adaptations, down through the centuries. Toward the end of the eighth century, at Jerusalem, qualified men were not lacking, especially among the clergy, to take care of the precious traditions and to begin the work of collating them. The work of collation was the origin of the book which was to become Deuteronomy. The disappearance of the northern sanctuaries, competitors of the Temple of Sion, could only encourage and confirm the sense of a new need of one sanctuary for all the Israelites, to the exclusion of any other cult. It cannot be stated with certainty that the law of Deut. 12

[1] We will adopt the explanation for the composition of Deuteronomy commonly accepted among recent authors: cf. Salo W. Baron, *A Social and Religious History of the Jews* (2nd edition; Columbia University Press, 1952); Giuseppe Ricciotti, *The History of Israel,* English trans. by Clement Della Penta and Richard T. A. Murphy (Milwaukee: Bruce, 1955).

was drawn up at this period, although it is probable.[2] The law was already part of the spirit of the religious reform undertaken by Ezechias for the whole country.[3]

The archives of Samaria had also been brought to Jerusalem. We shall find frequent mention of them, as well as of the archives of Jerusalem, in the Book of Kings.[4] Records of kings and of events were consigned to writing; the documents were brought up to date periodically[5] by the functionaries of the official chancellery (such as those named in IV Kgs. 18:18). What would we know about the four centuries of the monarchy without these records? We shall see how they were put to use by the author of the Book of Kings and by its chronicler.

We meet the scribes or "sages" in the same governmental and learned environment. The Book of Proverbs calls them "the men of Ezechias" and points out that we are indebted to them for having "transcribed the proverbs of Solomon" (cf. Prov. 25:1).[6] They did not merely collect; no doubt we owe more to them, as well as to their colleagues throughout the whole royal epoch, than to Solomon himself (cf. pp. 87-88).

Scribes in the Egyptian tradition (cf. pp. 17-18), these "servants of the king" formed part of the administrative framework and were upholders of authority; furthermore, they advocated its just exercise, when it was ordered to the common good. Next to the lawyers,

[2] To some degree, for the text is certainly not from one source.

[3] Cf. II Par. 29-30 (cf. in particular, 29:5-10 and 30:1). Of course, the spirit, the manner, and the ideas of the chronicler himself are found in these texts. About the year 300 B.C., he undertook to write anew the royal history, in order to reveal the hierocratic character of David's kingdom (the only one with which he was concerned), profiting by the opportunity to make ample observations on the worship, the sacred ministers, and the liturgy. Traditions (preserved in frequently cited Annals) were gathered up in this way, not all of which are found in the Book of Kings.

[4] Fifteen times for Juda, seventeen times for Israel,—using the formula which so often closes an abridgement of royal biography: "Is this not written in the book of the Annals of the Kingdom of . . . ?"

[5] There is proof of this with regards to Elath, on the gulf of Aqaba, reconquered by the Edomites about 850 B.C. (cf. IV Kgs. 8:22: "up to this day"), retaken by Juda about 790 B.C. (cf. Kgs. 14:22), and restored to the Edomites about 735 B.C. (cf. IV Kgs. 16:6: "up to this day").

[6] The text says: "Here again . . . ." It indicates not only the collection that follows (cf. Prov. 25-29), but also other sayings, such as those that form chapters 10-22. Between the two collections, there are other "words of wise men," which are not attributed to Solomon.

who were expert in sacred matters, and the priests, who were born defenders of the traditions and of liturgical worship; next to the Prophets, who used bold and unpredictable speech and who scattered the tempests of God over the world to keep it alert and aroused, were the scribes, men of good family and of good sense. Although they held a high place in society, they were well informed about every situation. Their ears were kept open to their contemporaries, even to the most humble; hence, they were the prudent and solid teachers of an Israel which had been, until recently, uncouth and harsh.

They wrote in a literary form which the word "proverb" translates somewhat inaccurately, or at least only partially. The Hebrew term *mashal* (in the plural *meshalim*) is the name for a wide variety of expressions of thought and of manner of speech. The two extremes of this form seem to be, on the one hand, the short, sententious, or provocative saying, tailored to the taste of the popular spirit, and on the other hand, a learned and developed form of the maxim, of the "thought," of satire, or, in general, of teaching. To this second kind of *meshalim* belong the great sapiential writings of the postexilic period. The Book of Proverbs, however, is still only a collection of short independent sentences.[7] Reading them, one discovers that primarily their wisdom is realistic, but not very venturesome; some would even say that they are limited and highly selfish. Certainly, these wise men were not carried away by the sublime vehemence that animated the Prophets. Nevertheless, they had the same faith; and, if they were more calm, if their ambitions seem more modest, their purpose, which was to bring the People of God into harmony with God, was the same. These discerning observers, these precise and reserved moralists lived through the same hard times, in an Isaian climate,[8] so to speak, and in the same place as the fiery spokesmen of Yahweh. All of these men, priests, Prophets, and scribes, knew one another; they met with and talked to one another in Jerusalem; they were friends and companions in arms for a single cause, the cause of God, and the cause of the friends of God, the "poor." The "inspired scribes" differed from the

[7] This book contains nothing but *meshalim*, but it is not the only book of the Bible, outside the sapiential literature, that does contain them. They appear notably in the most archaic literature of Israel (cf. p. 75). They are found also in the prophetic collections and, to a great extent, in the Psalms.

[8] Compare the ideas found in Prov. 21, 22, 31, with Isaias.

others only in that they did not feel the vocation to contemplate and to proclaim history. Conscious of the concrete situation and desirous of remedying it within present conditions, of doing what could be done rather than of aiming too high or of permitting illusions or dreams, they gave advice that was immediately practical and that, if applied, would constitute reform and the beginning of renewal.

Their concern for learning from experience, their moderation, their sense of sincerity and fidelity, of respect for others and for integrity, and the tender benevolence they never ceased to advocate, make of their counsels admirable invitations to self-examination and amendment. They made powerful contributions to the forming of Israel's conscience and of the spirit God wished it to have.[9]

Faith in the justice of God, as it is found in the Proverbs, always expresses itself somewhat in the following way: to do good is to be happy (the "way of the just"); to commit sin leads to misfortune (the "way of the transgressor"). Perhaps some day men would see things less simply, for actual existence poses problems that cannot all be resolved in this way. Nevertheless, the doctrine as it stands is a fundamental and solid basis for morality. It contains an underlying optimism which, in fact, seems to be one of the marks of the soul God fashioned for his people. This optimism would help Israel to be steadfast during hours of great crisis. Reversed, the formula would provide explanations which would at least, fit the times: if happiness disappeared, it was because people no longer practiced justice. Punishment appeared as the consequence of sin; and the consciousness of sin, in a "contrite and humble heart, is the first act of "conversion." The teaching of the Prophets was the same.

We will find this firm and simple morality taking shape among the representatives of the school of thought called "deuteronomist."

The same kind of thinking is not lacking in another kind of literature, a literature which we have not discussed since we met it during the Davidic period (cf. p. 86), but which had not ceased to develop throughout the course of the royal period.

From the dawn of its history, Israel had had a liking and a gift for song. It had an ardent and epic soul; its religious spirit found expression in hymns, praises, and supplications. With the passing of

[9] If the reader wishes to find quickly some of these "pearls" of the book of Proverbs, consult the citations given in *WG*, p. 198.

time, through experience and trials, Israel's heart became more profound. The best songs, no doubt, were the work of those with a deep faith, of pious and fervent inspired souls, of priests, and of prophets (some are found precisely in the collections of oracles). But of the Psalms we know, that is, of those preserved by tradition, which are the most ancient?

Nothing is more difficult than to date poems which either have not, or no longer have, very precise connections with historical events,[10] which may have been rewritten or completed in another era, and which ordinary and liturgical use have combined to detach from particular circumstances. It seems that some of the psalms, such as Ps. 110 or the second part of Ps. 24, go back to the time of David himself. Psalm 29 (Yahweh thundering) is very ancient. Others were composed during the royal period, although exact sources cannot be given. The time of Ezechias, that of the first great prophets, was certainly very favorable to the development of sacred poetry; the same is true of the period of Josias (last third of the seventh century; we will come to it in the pages that follow), in which great prophets appear once more (Jeremias is, so to speak, spontaneously a psalmist), and in which the worship at Jerusalem was restored to honor.[11]

The religious soul of the Chosen People expressed itself in these songs. They exalt the Lord Yahweh: Ps. 8; 29; 89 (vv. 1-19); 104. They celebrate the great deeds of history: Ps. 18; 46; 47; 60; 68; 76; 78; 80. They magnify the Holy City or the king commissioned and blessed by God: Ps. 2; 20; 21; 48; 72. They reveal the piety of the priests and of the faithful: Ps. 42-43; 61; 63; 81; 84. They supply the choral repertory of the ceremonies of the Temple and of the processions: Ps. 24 (vv. 7-10); 46; 48; 69. The liturgy is the cause of many canticles, prayers, and hymns, which have been preserved because of it. Through the liturgy, indeed, they have come down to us; and we continue to sing them and to pray them, amazed at their freshness, their vigor, and their perpetual timeliness. Through the psalms we come to realize that we are the selfsame People of God.

[10] The titles were often added later; cf. p. 86, note 6.

[11] The psalms cited in the paragraph that follows are thought to be a product of the royal era, on the basis of serious critical studies. A rigorously sure position, however, cannot be taken nor any absolute assertions made in regard to this dating.

6 The Great Tribulation

[ONE]

THE LIONS' DEN [1] | Nineve was so named by Nahum (cf. Nah. 2:12), not merely because of the famous wild animal hunts of its kings, but also because of their fearful armies which were the terror of the whole world of that day. Once returned from their incessant expeditions of torture and of massacre, they dragged after them in chains all those who would not bow before the "power of Assur, of Ishtar, and of the other great gods." They paraded these thousands of new slaves, which they had promised to the great public works, along the triumphal ways of the enormous capital. Then they piled up the riches, pillaged throughout the world, in the temples and in the giant palaces which were constantly being built behind the shelter of the tremendous ramparts dominating the Tigris. And at the gates of the ramparts they stacked the heads of the conquered.

At the beginning of the seventh century, therefore, two policies did not exist in the Near East. No one was dispensed from being a vassal of the great king, nor from paying him homage and tribute. Jerusalem had escaped destruction by Sennacherib (cf. pp. 114-15) only by a hairbreadth. The same was not true of Babylon, although it was strong in other ways. In 689 B.C., Babylon paid for the attempt at liberation in which Merodach-Baladan had involved it by being subjected to severe pillage and to the most savage demolition. Sennacherib was assassinated (cf. IV Kgs. 19:7, 37). His son Asarhaddon (681-668 B.C.) rebuilt Babylon, but he was an all-powerful

[1] Before continuing the biblical history, we must review the events relating to Assyria and to international politics in the seventh century, both in order to understand the end of the kingdom of Juda and because of the prophetic oracles connected with the events in question. A little book, readable as well as learned, may be recommended here: André Parrot, *Nineveh and the Old Testament,* English trans. by B. E. Hooke (New York: Philosophical Library, 1955).

monarch, a man of savage energy, who showed neither kindness nor weakness toward anyone.

Nevertheless, was there not a presentiment that the universally detested Assyrian colossus, might indeed crumble? National feelings were beginning to awaken in the Mediterranean regions. Asarhaddon kept these regions in line through his emissaries, his soldiers, his taxcollectors, and when necessary, by convoking assemblies at Nineve and by imprisoning kings.[2] Evidently, the revolts were almost always instigated by Egypt, that crumbling and divided Egypt which Taharqa (690-664 B.C.), pharaoh of the "Ethiopian dynasty,"[3] was trying to dominate. In 671 B.C., Asarhaddon decided to attack Egypt directly; he took Memphis, then the Delta, and put Thebes in great jeopardy.

As he had decided, at his death, his succession was divided between his two sons: Assurbanipal at Nineve, and Shamashumukim at Babylon. Asarhaddon's decision was a dangerous one, because of the age-old rivalry between the two capitals. In fact, Shamashumukim did rise up against his brother and instigated a coalition with Elam, Asia Minor, the Aramaeans, and Egypt. Assurbanipal hurled his brutal forces against Babylon, besieged it (651-648 B.C.) and took it. Shamashumukim died in the flames, and was replaced by Kandalanu, who gave proof of docility, at least in the beginning. The Assyrian army then pushed on into Elam, which it completely ruined.

Taharqa profited by Asarhaddon's death in that he was able to resume power over Egypt. Assurbanipal took up the conflict again (666 B.C.), however, and this time seized the territory of the Nile as far up as Thebes. When the capital of Upper Egypt, which had been famous for two thousand years, because of the wonders amassed there by many pharaohs, fell, the effect on the whole world was profound. Fifty years later, Nahum used it as an example of the most extraordinary destruction (cf. Nah. 3:8-20). A third Assyrian campaign (664 B.C.) drove the successor of Taharqa, Tentamon, as far as Nubia. Truly, Egypt was no more than "a broken reed" (cf. IV Kgs. 18:21); the prophecy of Isaias was fulfilled (cf. Isa. 20).

[2] Manasses had a temporary experience of this: cf. II Par. 33:11-20.

[3] The twenty-fifth (751-656 B.C.). The twenty-second (950-730 B.C.), twenty-third (817-730 B.C.), twenty-fourth (730-715 B.C.), and twenty-fifth dynasties were partly parallel, because the country was divided (cf. pp. 93-94).

Nevertheless, thanks to the twenty-sixth dynasty (663-525 B.C.), the land of the pharaohs would know another era of greatness, although it would be a relative greatness, one owed in large part to the Greek mercenaries it employed. The Greeks were now constantly colonizing the Delta and the Asiatic coast. Psammeticus (663–609 B.C.), the founder of the twenty-sixth dynasty, succeeded in driving out the Assyrians after nearly ten years of conflict. With remarkable diplomacy and, evidently, with help from the Greeks, he reforged an Egyptian unity of sorts, and re-established its military power both on land and sea.

Nineve was still at the height of its power. In addition, it was headed by the greatest, perhaps, of its great kings: Assurbanipal (668-631 B.C.).[4] He was not only an invincible warrior who hunted lions as a change from subduing men and for exercise,[5] he was also a highly cultivated prince, artistic, lettered,[6] and, like his grandfather and his father, a remarkable and tireless builder.[7]

His sons and successors, Assuretililani (631-628 B.C.), Sinshumulishir (627 B.C.), and Sinsharishkun (627-612 B.C.), were not nearly of the same stature. Even Kandalanu was able to oppose them. Then, an unknown,[8] Nabopolassar (625-604 B.C.), proclaimed the independence of Babylon and founded a dynasty.[9] World control was about to change hands. Every quarter of the world was growing restless. The Medes, established to the south of the Caspian Sea, had been preparing to descend for some time. During the

[4] Since the beginning of the publication of the *Babylonian Chronicles* in 1956 and the recent studies relating to them, the date of Assurbanipal's death has had to be moved back from 626 B.C. to 631 B.C. (cf. Parrot, *op. cit.*, pp. 58-59).

[5] The wounded horses, lions, and lionesses of the bas-reliefs of Assurbanipal, which are preserved in the British Museum, are among the great masterpieces of art.

[6] Assurbanipal's library yielded thousands of tablets engraved in cuneiform when excavations were carried out at Nineve. The seven tablets of Enuma Elish and the twelve tablets of Gilgamesh were found there (cf. pp. 10-11).

[7] Nineve must have had a considerable number of artists. It is thought that the decoration of Khorsabad (cf. p. 113, note 9) alone included at least 16,500 square feet of bas-reliefs.

[8] "Son of no one," that is, not succeeding his father.

[9] The dynasty currently called "neo-Babylonian," the first being that of the nineteenth to the seventeenth centuries (cf. pp. 4-5). In connection with Babylon, and especially the neo-Babylonian era, cf. André Parrot, *Babylon and the Old Testament*, English trans. by B. E. Hooke (New York: Philosophical Library, 1956).

final quarter of the century, the Scythians, barbarian hordes who had come from the Crimea by way of the Caucasus in the wake of the Cimmerians, would come in from Asia Minor. More than once, they would cause terror among the various countries of the Near East. Allies of Nineve, they saved it once from a Median invasion led by Cyaxaras.

In 616 B.C., the Babylonians began their advance and waged a campaign in the Middle-Euphrates, which Nineve had dominated up to that time. If they were forced to withdraw, it was because the Assyrians received help which history could not have foreseen a few years before: the help of an Egyptian army! Psammeticus seems to have concluded that the danger now lay in a different direction; hence, he formed an alliance with Assyria. But just at that time, the soldiers of Cyaxaras reappeared (614 B.C.); they swept away the fortresses which were the "gates" and the "bars" of Nineve (cf. Nah. 3:12-13); Tarbis, three miles from Nineve; and Assur, a powerful citadel. Nevertheless, in 613 B.C., the Assyrians succeeded in repulsing a new Babylonian expedition in the Middle-Euphrates.

The year 612 B.C. marked the end of Nineve. Babylonians, Medes, and Scythians had formed an alliance. They joined efforts in a general attack, and after several weeks of battle the city was taken (July-August). The whole world rang with cries of relief and of joy. We shall hear those that came from Palestine.

Sinsharishkun had been slain.[10] Nineve was thoroughly sacked and demolished with extreme savagery. Still, an Assyrian contingent succeeded in escaping toward the west. When it halted at Haran, it had a new king at its head, Assuruballit. Two years later, Babylonians and Medes drove him farther to the west, to Carchemish on the Euphrates. Nekao, the successor of Psammeticus, thinking no doubt that Egypt would again act as arbiter in Asia, went up to help Assuruballit. Josias, the king of Juda and the reformer whom we shall presently see at work, also lost his head and thought he could bar the way to the pharaoh. He was slain at Megiddo in 608 B.C. (IV Kgs. 23:29-30). Nabopolassar had willed the command to his son Nabucodonosor.[11] The Egyptians were completely crushed

[10] His name, changed to Sardanapal, and his death in the heart of his capital and in the midst of his fabulous riches, have passed into legend.

[11] This is the current form of his name. He was called Nabukudurriusur, that is, "Nabu protects my boundary"; in the Hebrew of the Bible, he is called Nebuchadnezzar (as certain translations transcribe it).

at Carchemish (605 B.C.) and the Babylonians descended on Syria, Phoenicia, and Palestine, where they seized both goods and people. Fortunately for Egypt, Nabucodonosor was suddenly forced to halt his advance and return in haste to Babylon (August, 605 B.C.), because his father had died. Nabucodonosor's reign (605-562 B.C.), one of the most powerful of all, had begun.

[TWO]

DISCOVERY OF A BOOK | The history of Israel developed against the background of the history of the seventh century, which we have just reviewed, and in connection with it.

The lesson learned by Ezechias in 701 B.C. had brought him back to his initial wisdom. Never again would he depart from that attitude of unconditional docility to the events directed by Yahweh. Isaias had always proclaimed faith to be the only worthwhile attitude. Thus, having ceased to plot against the Assyrian monster, the son of Achaz ended his days in peace.

Did the kingdom of Juda's servile condition as a tributary and its obligatory obeisance to Assyria explain its great religious misfortunes in the years that followed? Political dependence would involve, obviously, complacency and compromise. In any case, Juda had never before sunk so low. Manasses' reign of more than half a century (691-638 B.C.) [1] was an unfortunate one, because he swept away all the reforms carried out by his father. He did "what was evil in the sight of Yahweh" to such an extent that Juda and its capital sank into polytheism and practiced idolatries worse than those known by the Canaanites. The picture presented in IV Kgs. 21:1-16 is as explicit and as deplorable as any that could be imagined.

Naturally enough, a depraved and offensive regime of this kind could not bear reminder of the past and of Israel's true vocation. Nor could it endure the judgment which God unfailingly pronounced through the mouths of his envoys. Manasses seems to have silenced the Prophets, or simply to have suppressed them: for

[1] It is true that the date at which the reign of Ezechias came to an end and that of Manasses began is not exactly known. Perhaps the date ought to be reduced a few years.

sixty or seventy years after Isaias,[2] the People of God no longer heard the Word of God. Religious persecution may also explain the disappearance of documents that had come from the northern kingdom. Gathered together after 722 B.C. at Jerusalem, they had a certain relation to the religious reform of Ezechias (cf. p. 125). But vigilant and pious men, priests no doubt, knowing the risks these documents ran, had carefully hidden them in the hope of better days to come.

Amon (cf. IV Kgs. 21:19-26) was not as impious as his father only because he lacked the time. He was assassinated at the end of a year's reign (638 B.C.), leaving the power to an infant.

Not much is known about the youth of Josias (638-608 B.C.). Nevertheless, there is every reason to believe that a reaction had already begun to set in. As early as 630 B.C., the priests and Prophets who surrounded him inaugurated an energetic campaign against idolatry and the laxity of public morals. The foreshadowing of Assyria's decline gave men a greater sense of freedom to act on the national plane. Other threats, however, began to appear on the horizon: Nordic barbarians were unleashed on the Near East, taking part before long in the destruction of Nineve.

Sophonias, an heir of Isaias' thought, needed nothing more before beginning, in the years 630-625 B.C., vehemently to proclaim the imminence of the "Day of Yahweh," a day of destruction and of a salutary but terrible justice (cf. Soph. 1). Men heard prophetic words that were in full possession of themselves, that were expressed clearly, briefly, and with great vigor.

Sophonias prepared the way for Jeremias. If, like his predecessors, he denounced the religious and social causes of the evil which God was about to punish in his people and in other peoples, he also plumbs the depths of man and of his intentions, primarily man's refusal of God and his preference for himself (cf. Soph. 2:1-3, 8). But what is new is the manner in which Sophonias speaks of the "poor" (in Hebrew, *anawim*) and of the People of God as a people of the "poor." He does not mean merely the poverty which had increased in the country during these difficult days. For the Prophet, "poverty" (*anawah*) is a condition which will enable the People

[2] Isaias, according to the ancient Jewish tradition (which has passed into the Roman martyrology), is to be counted among the victims of Manasses' religious persecution.

of God to become itself again, to abandon itself to God alone, and to be pleasing in his eyes. This poor people, "humble and indigent," will be the saved "Remnant" whose joy will be overflowing, for in them will be their Lord (cf. Soph. 3:11-20).

About this same time the union of the Yahwist and the Elohist traditions seems to have been worked out (cf. pp. 100-101); the hand of the "deuteronomic" writers was beginning to make itself felt in this task.

Josias, several years before, had undertaken the religious and moral reform of his kingdom by a return to complete Yahwism (cf. II Par. 34:1-7, which corresponds to IV Kgs. 23:4-14). The people helped by contributing money (cf. IV Kgs. 22:4). Josias had the task of restoring the Temple. Then, suddenly one day in the year 621 B.C., the news came of the discovery, in a secret place in the Temple, of the "book of the Torah" or "book of the Covenant." When the text was read to the authorities, they were alarmed, because it showed that their present efforts still fell short of Yahweh's requirements (cf. IV Kgs. 22:8-13).

At once, thanks to the concerted action of the king, the priests of Jerusalem, and the Prophets, the reform of Josias conducted a full offensive. The Temple was solemnly purified and a real evangelizing "mission," which was both enthusiastic and rigorous, was methodically organized throughout the country. Of course, success could only be partial; to accomplish the program that had been laid out, the help of events would be needed, particularly the tragic Exile. Efforts were made, however, to suppress the places of worship which had been contaminated by idolatry. The ministers of provincial sanctuaries were asked to abandon their duties, and were offered secondary positions in the Temple at Jerusalem as compensation.[3]

The "law" which had been found was ancient enough to be authoritative and could make use of the name of Moses.[4] At the same time, it was new enough to authorize changes as important as the reduction of all the places of worship in Israel to one.[5] The

[3] Here arises the difficult question (to be treated elsewhere) concerning the composition of the clergy of Jerusalem before and after the reform of Josias: What is meant by "priests" and what by "levites"?

[4] Comparison between v. 23 and v. 24 of IV Kgs. 23; cf. II Par. 34:14.

[5] Legitimate up to that time, by virtue of Exod. 20:24, and as history proves.

only book that fulfills these conditions is Deuteronomy.[6] It was in the very nature of "torah" to provide answers, in the spirit and according to the requirements of the Covenant, to the problems posed by new historical circumstances.

The priest Helcias certainly had not found the Deuteronomy we know. The book in question consisted of those elements of the torah that proceeded from more or less ancient traditions, which had been hidden in the time of Manasses. They are found today in Chapters 12-26 of the book (the "Proto-Deuteronomy," as it is called by the critics). Their discovery led to their publication; they were recopied in various books, which were united later to give us the text we now possess.[7] Then, a preface (corresponding to Chapters 5-11) and a conclusion (Chapters 27-28, except 28:47-68, which belongs to the Exile) were composed.

In order to give a report of the improvements made over the ancient toroth by Deuteronomy, it is enough to make a few comparisons. Not only did it include a certain number of new laws (some of which may have been ancient but not yet collected) which were not in the preceding codes,[8] but many ancient prescriptions were rewritten according to a distinctive formula, one that was cordial in tone, that clarified additions, and that assigned motivations [9] to make the reason for certain requirements understandable. The broad style, wordy but clear, slightly monotonous but with a great inspiration, warm and persuasive, the style of an orator and of a master of "wisdom," is such an exception in the Bible that one can easily recognize it, even in translation and even when "deuteronomic" fragments are encountered outside Deuteronomy (cf. p. 68, note 5).

The entire book is constructed as if it were an address by Moses speaking to the people of Sinai. The authors, then, were convinced that they had captured the spirit of the great prophet-legislator, that they were presenting traditions that went back to him, and that they were perpetuating his work. Using new terms and writing

[6] In the opinion of almost all the critics.

[7] This is what authorizes specialists to distinguish texts by D^1, D^2, and D^3.

[8] Cf. Deut. 12:1-27; 15:2-11; 17:8-20; 21; 22:5-8, 13-21; 24:1-5, 16; 25:1-12, 17-19 (certain of these laws, not collected in the other codes, are, however, very ancient).

[9] Compare Deut. 15:12-18 with Exod. 21:2-6; Deut. 22:1-4 with Exod. 23:4-5; Deut. 24:7 with Exod. 21:16; Deut. 24:17-18 with Exod. 22:20-21.

for new times, they proposed the ancient Covenant for meditation, making of it the foundation of a spiritual renewal, of a profound transformation of life.

Truly, these writers understood the analogy, or rather the continuity, which existed between the Israel of the desert and the Judean kingdom of the seventh century. The people were the same; always tempted and seriously faithless, sinful and rebellious, they were the ones whom God chastised, whom he tried severely, but to whom he always promised his pardon, and whose complete annihilation he would never permit (cf. Deut. 6:10-15; 8:2-20; 9:3-7; 13:4; 28:9-10). The sufferings and setbacks, the humiliations and dangers which threatened the little Palestinian kingdom from all sides were, as in the time of the "Judges," punishments and warnings. The Lord of the Covenant called his people to "conversion," to abandonment of idols, to change their "ways," to the "circumcision of the heart" (cf. Deut. 10:12-22; 30:2-10). God wanted the heart of his people, because he loved them.

Citing Deuteronomy, we were not afraid to anticipate and to say God's love in connection with the Covenant of Sinai. In fact, the Covenant presupposed the love of Yahweh for his people (cf. pp. 60-61 and notes 8 and 9). Actually, however, his love had never been explicitly declared; the word had not been spoken. The revelation was reserved for the deuteronomic writers. They spoke of the love of God for his People as it had never before been spoken of: a personal love; benevolent; a love that is freely given and takes the initiative; patient and merciful; irrevocably faithful (cf. Deut. 7:6-13), but also a "jealous," that is, an exacting love. Israel had to cling to this God who loved it, with faith and hope. Above all, Israel in obedience, gave proof of true love, which is wisdom and life, by obedience to the Commandments (cf. Deut. 6:4-9, 24-25; 7:12-13; 11:13-25; 12:28; 13:5; 30:15-20). God also desired mutual love between men as brothers, and he wanted them to prove their love in actions (cf. Deut. 23:20-21; 24:14; 25:1-3).

Thus, Deuteronomy was able to give Israel a sense of its wonderful and tragic election. Although Deuteronomy spoke with a clarity unknown heretofore, and in the affective language of Osee and Jeremias, yet it did not conceal the divine requirements or the punishments promised to infidelity.

Of course, some precepts of the new code seem to be inspired by generous dreams rather than by a realistic view of the situation. To consider Israel as a completely fraternal community in the midst of which dwelt the One whom it was necessary to love by loving one another (cf. Deut. 15:1-18; 22:1-8; 24:10-22) was more an ideal than a practical program. Nevertheless, such entreaties could not remain entirely vain. Although, in order to make Israel "hear his voice," it was necessary for Yahweh to speak more forcibly concerning the events of a terrible "Day," still there had previously been Israelites to "love God with all their heart, with all their mind, and with all their strength" (cf. Deut. 6:5), "following his ways exactly and holding fast to him" (Deut. 11:22). The Lord was already preparing for himself a "Remnant" which would be faithful to him. Deuteronomy undoubtedly would bear upon the future.

In the literary environment in which this great work was carried out, the history of Israel seemed to be eminently rich in teachings. The writers had in hand documents concerning the past, such as the Memoirs about David and Solomon and the narratives of Elias and Eliseus. They could supplement these documents with the help of official archives and thus could easily write a complete history of the kingdoms of Juda and of Israel. The more ancient narratives, which were also more fragmentary and more popular, dealing with the conquest of Canaan and with the times that preceded the monarchy enabled them to link this history to that of Moses. The whole was recast according to the then accepted conception of the Covenant and of its requirements and benefits, and in terms of "benedictions" and "maledictions." Thus, the four books so precisely called the "Earlier Prophets" were composed.

In its very first page, the book of *Joshua* reveals its connections with Deuteronomy.[10] Gathering together very ancient narratives (cf. p. 68), this history of the entrance of the Hebrews into Palestine became a brilliant and inspiring example of fidelity to the Torah. If the "gift" of the Holy Land was received by valiant hands (Jos. 1:6, 11; 23:3-5; comp. Deut. 1:8, 20-21; 2:24; 31:6, 23), it was because Joshua and his men had observed the conditions of the Covenant. The composition of the book explains why it has retained a genuinely epic tone and why, in addition, the events are greatly simplified in it.

[10] We have already mentioned the deuteronomism of Jos. 1 and 23 (cf. p. 68, note 5). Compare also Jos. 8:30-35 with Deut. 11:26-32 and 27:1-26.

The Book of Judges is even more typically deuteronomic (cf. p. 70, note 11). The correlation between evil conduct and misfortune, conversion and prosperity, is set down with rigorous simplicity. The editorial formulas enshrine anecdotes of popular tradition which in themselves have no general significance. They are clearly revelatory of the intentions of the final editors and give the whole book its value as a message. Additions were to be made later on along the same line (e.g., Judg. 19-21). The book was not finished, apparently, until the fifth century.

A repetition of the history of David (cf. pp. 85-86), already written, was sufficient, essentially, for making up the Book of Samuel (cf. I and II Sam.). The life of David, ideal king, strikingly illustrated the effects of fidelity to Yahweh. In prefacing it with the history of Samuel and of Saul (cf. pp. 76-77), the deuteronomic writers did not fail to use the opportunity to reaffirm the principles that were so dear to them (reread, notably, I Sam. 12:14-25).

Their masterpiece, however, was certainly the Book of Kgs. (cf. III Kings and IV Kings), composed during the period between the reform of Josias and the fall of Jerusalem.[11] Sources for the book were, on the one hand, the Acts of Solomon (cf. p. 87) and the Geste of Elias and Eliseus (cf. pp. 97-98), and on the other, the royal Annals of Juda and the royal Annals of Israel (cf. pp. 125-26), as well as various documents coming from learned, sacerdotal, or prophetic circles.

Apart from the reigns of David, of Solomon, and of a few religious reformers such as Jehu, Ezechias, and Josias, successive reigns are presented only as brief sketches, and follow formulas that are almost always alike. Each king is judged by comparison with David or with Jeroboam, and according to whether he was faithful to Yahweh in destroying idolatrous symbols or whether he had "done evil before Yahweh" by retaining the worship of Baal. The purpose of the Book of Kings, then, was to examine the conscience of the People of God, primarily in the person of its representatives. Four centuries of effort and of greatness, but also of lamentable failings and misfortunes, thus illustrated and fully justified the thesis of the seventh century theologians.[12]

[11] Not counting a few alterations and additions made after 586 B.C. and in view of the ruin of Jerusalem; cf. for example, III Kgs. 9:6-8; IV Kgs. 25.

[12] The Book of Kings is filled with deuteronomisms: cf. III Kgs. 2:2-4;

The seventh century, or more precisely the reign of Josias, was not to end without the priests, in the same environment in which, no doubt, the principal part of the deuteronomic code had been restated, again collecting and rearranging the traditional laws. This was the beginning of a literature which was to be called "sacerdotal," and which was to develop especially during the time of the Exile. Its most representative book would be Leviticus, which has unquestionable similarities to Deuteronomy (e.g., cf. Lev. 18-20), and bears witness in its own way to the change that was taking place in the religious history of Israel.

[THREE]

WITNESS TORN ASUNDER | Deuteronomy stands at the junction of the three great powers of inspiration, which have fashioned and built the soul of Israel: the Mosaic Tradition; Prophecy; and Wisdom. Undoubtedly, this is the reason why Deuteronomy so manifestly exceeds the historical limits of the time of its composition. In addition, it represents the inclinations of the men with whom God makes history.

Let us consider the little people, first of all. In the new Torah, one feels at the same time both the reaction of the oppressed, who were supported by the Prophets against the governing classes (the clan primarily responsible for all the misfortunes that had come to pass, and that spirit of the "poor," which was to become characteristic of the people whom God was fashioning for himself.

The clergy had played an important part in a reform movement about the year 620 B.C. The priests had received much deserved reproaches, and after the abominations of Manasses, which had disgusted and revolted them, they were ready to support all of Josias' efforts. Although the reform was advantageous to the priests of Jerusalem, because it suppressed provincial competition, it remains

8:23-61; IV Kgs. 17:13-23, 34-41; 21:9-16; compare III Kgs. 5:17-19 with Deut. 12:8-11; III Kgs. 14:21-24 with Deut. 12:2-5, 29-31; IV Kgs. 14:6 with Deut. 24:26. Note that if the importance of the Temple of Jerusalem is affirmed in practice, in conformity with Deut. 12, still the sources of history are not changed, as the story of Elias (offering sacrifice on Mt. Carmel) testifies. Cf. also note 13, p. 83.

true, nevertheless, that it was accomplished by them in the best spirit of prophecy.

The Prophets of Yahweh had reappeared,[1] resuming their task of admonishing, and of awakening courage and hope. They were the echoes of a God who was rigorous but amazingly benevolent and faithful. One seems always to be reading their ideas in Deuteronomy. Their attitude had evolved parallel to the cult of Yahweh. The Prophets of the eighth century cried out strongly against the soulless formalism of a religion that had become wholly external; [2] they could, and indeed were bound to make their complaints known as long as genuine, Yahwist rites and sacrifices existed and as long as the people clung to them, even if their hearts were elsewhere. In the following century, the pratices of the revealed religion were threatened with disappearance, and with being supplanted by foreign cults. Thus, it was necessary to confront another danger, to save what was about to be lost, by infusing a renewed spirit into it, and by making the prophetic ideal the soul of the rites and ceremonies. For this reason, the new Torah combined liturgical laws with moral and social precepts.

It had been asked whether Jeremias, the great Prophet of that time, was a member of the "editorial board" of Deuteronomy, so evident are the similarities in thought and expression between Deuteronomy and the one which bears the name of the Prophet. No doubt, the men who spoke and wrote during that period breathed the same air, had the same inclinations, and used the same language. More probably still, Jeremias, because of his voluntarily spontaneously acquired deuteronomic ideas, strongly influenced the editions that have come down to us.

Jeremias had been called to prophecy five years before the celebrated discovery of the manuscript in the Temple (cf. Jer. 1:4-19), and he was thrilled by this news which would hasten the reform. He had worked for reform in his preaching (cf. Jer. 11:1-14, a text filled with deuteronomic expressions).

At the age of twenty, this descendant of an ancient sacerdotal family which was relegated to a village in the environs of the Holy

[1] Opinion of the prophetess Holda in connection with the discovery of the Law (cf. IV Kgs. 22:14-20). Sophonias and Jeremias had already begun to prophecy.

[2] Cf. Amos 5:21-22; Osee 6:6; 8:13; Isa. 1:11-15; Mich. 6:6.

City,[3] was already exhorting Jerusalem and the Judeans to conversion. He did so in terms which, from all evidence, were reminiscent of the Prophet Osee—the appeal to the Covenant, to a return to the Lord of the Covenant and to the necessity of "conjugal love" between Yahweh and his people. One cannot reread these pages from his youth (cf. Jer. 2-6, with a few exceptions) without being moved.

Of course, as a writer he cannot be classed with Amos or Isaias. His style, reminiscent of that found in Deuteronomy, and therefore rather tedious, is that of an orator, but of an orator whose emotional power is much less the result of his natural gift of expression than of the consciousness of the burdens which weigh upon him. His complete sincerity keeps him from fully developing his images, although they are very numerous and original, and are taken from nature and from life. He is a great poet. However, can anyone merely dwell on the literary form in reading this Prophet who, rather than a text, is a living experience?

The emotivity of this passionate man is immediately evident. He is as sensitive to God as to men, as timid and fearful as he is fearless, intrepid, and obstinate, as much drawn by the silence of a completely interior life as he is anxious about his responsibility to all men and his duty to speak out. He loves his country and his brethren tenderly, even though they are abandoning God; but above all he loves God, who condemns his brethren and who has charged him with announcing the punishment. His mission was one of perpetual contradiction, dooming to cruel solitude a heart which craved affection. How could he not have been literally torn apart?

His complaints and his violent accusations enable us to reconstruct the corruption of the world in which he lived; religious deceptions and evils of every kind, which he had to combat; the habitual incongruity of his words. The words which he spoke, moreover, were spoken only with reluctance, because Yahweh obliged him to speak. He groaned over them and cried out his suffering (cf. Jer. 4:19; 11:18-12:2; 15:10-21; 20:7-18). Although he had a personal attachment to the sacred traditions of his people, he had to fore-

[3] Anatoth, a village three miles northeast of Jerusalem. The family is thought to have descended from the priest Abiathar (removed by Solomon: cf. III Kgs. 2:26-27), who was himself a descendant of Heli of Silo (cf. I Sam. 1-4).

tell a ruin that would seem to annihilate the past and even the sacrosanct Temple, presumptuously regarded by the people as an infallible buffer against destruction (cf. Jer. 7:1-8:3). Naturally inclined toward life, toward peace and joy, the poor prophet received the mandate to predict wars, defeat, destruction, and uprooting (cf. Jer. 4; 6:8-9; 12-13). Hence, a vicious vacuum was created around him. Against his will and against the tide of the times, Jeremias had to prophecy in this way for half a century, up to the end of the tragedy through which he so sorrowfully lived.

God did not ask him to perform only a thankless task. After the reform of Josias, Jeremias, convinced of its happy results, in enthusiastic poems, again reminiscent of Osee (cf. Osee 14), sang of the conversion of the ancient Palestinian kingdom of the north in pictures that were moving, ideal, and encouraging (cf. Jer. 30-31:22; also 3:6-13). This was the beginning of Jeremias' "Book of Consolation," to which would be added some other Jeremian texts composed in his worst hours.

At the close of the century, both national and international events moved quickly onward. The era was an extraordinary one; the whole world was on the march and was changing rapidly. Jeremias was to experience it all within himself: he heard God speak, terribly, of that history which would avenge his betrayal and which would finally bring his people to salutary reflections. Nevertheless, no echo of Assyria's destruction is found in what has been left to us of Jeremias.

Assyria's downfall, forms the main theme of the little collection of another Prophet, Nahum. In the weeks that saw the fall of Nineve, this fiery Judean proclaimed the joy both of the universe and of his own country in a short but very brilliant satire. The little book we have concerning him contains only fragments of the Prophet's preaching. The initial psalm (cf. Nah. 1:1-2:1) is of a different date from the oracle against the "city of blood." The latter (cf. Nah. 2-3) is a little, although highly admired, masterpiece of Hebrew poetry—a passionate description in which images tumble over one another in a sarcastic, breathless, almost savage pursuit. The Prophet is animated by a faith and a sense of justice which make him see the judgment of Yahweh in the total plan of history: the unforeseeable ruin of the most powerful nation in the world; the dazzling and absolute superiority of God; and the security of those who trust in God alone.[4]

Josias was killed at Megiddo in 608 B.C.[5] The king who "did right and justice," who "defended the cause of the poor and the needy," (cf. Jer. 22:15-16), for that very reason had to use authority and to oppose the forces of social oppression. Furthermore, his religious reform had met with resistance from the rural clergy, because it went against the profoundly pagan popular instinct. The sudden reversal at the time of his death seemed to nullify his work completely.

Pharaoh Nechao believed himself empowered to settle the royal succession in Juda as he pleased. He deposed Joachaz, the son of Josias, at the end of only three months of reign, and replaced him by his brother Joaqim (605-598 B.C.). To the despair of Jeremias, Egypt once more became the favorite of Jerusalem (cf. IV Kgs. 23:31-37).

Once the reins were loosened, the worst tendencies, which had been checked only temporarily, ran riot. Jeremias rose up against them, but he soon stood alone; from that time on, his soul knew only a long agony. Hence, the collection of his sayings retains many sorrowful pages (cf. Jer. 7-9; 25-26; 45). He was arrested and released (Jer. 20); his death was demanded and plotted (cf. Jer. 18:18-23; 26); and he lamented his fate. Nevertheless, his cruel duty remained, and he had to proclaim a disaster which could have been avoided.

At this same time,[6] another Prophet, Habacuc, of whom nothing is known except his great literary talent and the power of his thought asked himself the question, with utmost clarity: Why does the triumph of evil, that is to say, the Chaldean invasions, which were victorious and devastating, hatefully crushing innocent peoples, prevail? Why is justice checked if not because of God's failure to intervene (cf. Hab. 1:2-17)? The answer, which was to be taken up again by St. Paul, is given with an austere clarity: "The

[4] Thus, this little pamphlet, full of invective and revenge against a nation, takes its place as a teaching of faith and becomes a message of hope, thanks to the "prophetic" point of view that inspires it.

[5] Echoes of the mourning for Josias: cf. Jer. 22:10, 15-16, 18; II Par. 35:25; Zach. 12:11-14.

[6] Between the date of the battle of Carchemish and the end of the reign of Joaqin.

just shall live in his faith" (cf. Hab. 2:4); in other words, salvation is assured to him who puts all his trust in God and who clings to him without failing. Nevertheless, faith seeks to understand. Habacuc had raised an important question, one which concerned the general plan of history itself, and one which was to haunt and to disquiet more than one mind thereafter. The hope of the final victory of God is expressed in a magnificent psalm (cf. Hab. 3; compare with Judg. 5; Deut. 33:2; Ps. 68), which ends the little Book of Habacuc.

Jeremias himself always looked beyond the frontiers (cf. Jer. 25; 47-49); he commented on Carchemish (Jer. 46). He was greatly impressed by Nabucodonosor's accession to power, and proclaimed the formidable consequences of the authority thus established (cf. Jer. 13; 16:1-13, 16-18). Convinced of the absolute superiority of Babylon and of the folly it would be to resist her, he begged men to remain at peace, and, above all, not to put their hopes in a vain and perfidious Egypt. Nabucodonosor would even be called the "servant of Yahweh" by the Prophet (cf. Jer. 25:9; 27:6; 43:10).

Jeremias was considered a defeatist, despite which he was sure of the good sense his mission made. In such times, however, good sense depended on a higher wisdom. He had his prophecies of future misfortunes written down by his friend and secretary, Baruch, and had them read by him in the Temple before all the people. Informed of this, Joaqim, who would not believe the Prophet, tore up the manuscript and threw it into the fire (cf. Jer. 36).

The incident gives us valuable indications concerning the manner in which Jeremias had certain of his sayings put in writing. We can understand, too, why the work which bears under his name the witness of a long career full of clashes and ceaseless contradictions, has been greatly mistreated. It appears today in the greatest disorder. Not all of it is even by Jeremias. His faithful Baruch is the author of a certain number of pages,[7] and is probably responsible for certain textual arrangements. Moreover, his work as a compiler of Jeremian sayings had followers.[8] The work was not really

[7] We owe the accounts in which Jeremias is spoken of in the third person to Baruch: cf. Jer. 19:2-20:6; 28-29; 34:8-22; 36-45; 51:59-64.

[8] Cf. Jer. 10:1-16; 33:14-26; 50-51:28; 52. The Book of Jeremias is closely related to the events which put an end to the kingdom of Juda. Consequently, we shall call attention to many passages by the Prophet in retracing that history, and this will give us a start toward finding our bearings in this rather confusing book. For the dating of the fragments, we will follow A. Gelin, whose studies on Jeremias are truly outstanding.

"published" until sometime during the Exile; at that time it truly exercised its influence.

Did Jeremias compose psalms? A certain number of psalms are written in his manner and spirit. A reading of Jer. 12:1-6; 15:10-21; 17:5-18; 20:7-18, is sufficient to see how well qualified the Prophet was to sing in a poetic manner and, especially, in the elegiac style. Furthermore, psalms exist which seem to date from this era beginning with Josias and preceding the Exile. Even if some of the psalms were the subjects of later revisions or adaptations, and provided that assertions are not made too firmly, one may cite the following psalms as in some way Jeremian: Pss. 3; 4; 14; 22; 28; 42-43; 52; 55.

[FOUR]

THE CATASTROPHE

Nabucodonosor did not acquire supremacy over all the little states of the Middle East without also inheriting their hostile inclinations and their constant wish to rebel. It was well known that Joaqim was no exception and that he did not display constant fidelity to Babylon. Every year the Great King was forced to send a military detachment to collect the tribute and to discourage conspiracy. He allowed the pillaging bands next door to Palestine to ravage the little Judean kingdom. Joaqim disappeared in the year 598 B.C.[1] His son, Joakin, succeeded him, but only for three months (cf. IV Kgs. 24:1-9).

Jerusalem continued to pursue a pro-Egyptian policy, a rather stupid course because Nechao had just received another severe warning (cf. IV Kgs. 24:7) from Nabucodonosor, who was forced finally to again send his troops against Egypt. The Judeans took refuge in the city (cf. Jer. 35, the episode of the Rechabites). The besieged city surrendered at the end of two months and was subjected to pillaging and to the deportation of a select group of inhabitants (government workers, administrators, and specialized work-

[1] It is not known just how. According to IV Kgs. 24:6 and II Par. 39:8, the Greek text, he died at Jerusalem, but, according to II Par. 36:6, he had been taken as a captive to Babylon. Perhaps this latter text means that Nabucodonosor intended to take him, without having actually done so.

ers), among whom was the king (cf. IV Kgs. 24:8-16). Another one in the convoy was the man destined to become the "Prophet of the Exile," the priest Ezechiel, then about twenty-five years of age. Six years later, in exile, he was to hear the call of God to the ministry of the Word. Nabucodonosor created the third son of Josias (an uncle, consequently, of Joakin), Sedecias (597-587 B.C.), king. Jeremias, who had commented harshly on the conduct of Sedecias's predecessor (cf. Jer. 22:20-30; 13:18-19), would never cease exhorting this last king to be a loyal vassal of the invincible Babylon, without which all would be lost.

The accession of Psammeticus II in Egypt (594-588 B.C.) had the effect of arousing a new movement of revolt in the countries of the West (cf. Jer. 27); this fact and the Prophets in Jerusalem led many to believe in the fall of Babylon (cf. Jer. 28). Jeremias, on the contrary, wrote to the exiles in 598 B.C., advising them to settle down for a prolonged stay (cf. Jer. 29); besides, God would use them to refashion for himself a people by remaking their hearts (cf. Jer. 24). The Prophet was, moreover, not ignorant of the final fate of the neo-Babylonian empire (cf. Jer. 51:59-64).

Sedecias was a weakling, and his advisers were fools. The ten years of his reign consisted of nothing but evasions, blind audacity, and short-term calculations. The biblical text primarily saw in his reign "evil in the eyes of Yahweh."

Then came the days of God's wrath.

At the beginning of 588 B.C., a powerful Babylonian army surrounded Jerusalem. An eighteen-months' resistance began, which was as heroic as it was foolish and cruel. To influence Heaven, a favorable manoeuvre was about to be made: the freeing of the slaves. Just as Pharaoh Apries (588-568 B.C.) was about to effect this just decision in the south, it was revoked, and Jeremias proclaimed the divine punishment (cf. Jer. 34:8-22). At the same time, he expressed an amazing confidence in the future (cf. Jer. 32-33:13).

The Prophet no longer put his trust in anyone but God. Men were totally disappointing. The Torah had not been able to hold them up; besides, they had failed it either through lack of ability or lack of faith. If God wished to continue his work, he would have to endow men with a greater gift than the one he had given them through Moses, even greater than that form, so attractive and admirably renewed, which was Deuteronomy. This was what God was going to do: he would inscribe his Torah within each man (cf. Jer. 31:23-40). The Initiative of God, "a New Covenant," the interior law in the heart, a new "knowledge of God"—these were, from the viewpoint of re-establishment after the destruction, the promises which form the pinnacle of the Book of Jeremias. They made of him one of *the* great evangelists of the true religion, based on profound personal dispositions.

Jerusalem, starving and at bay, cared nothing for his lofty words. Although the king was favorable to Jeremias, he was ineffective. The Prophet was arrested, shut up in a dungeon, set free, thrown into a muddy well, saved again, and once more incarcerated (cf. Jer. 37-38). But, he was not silenced.

Finally, in the summer of 587 B.C., the walls of Jerusalem gave way. The king and his family fled through a breach in the wall, but they were overtaken and brought to the headquarters of Nabucodonosor. Nabucodonosor had the sons of Sedecias slain before his face, after which Sedecias' eyes were put out and he was sent to end his days in a Babylonian prison (cf. IV Kgs. 25; Jer. 2:52). During this time, the sack of Jerusalem took place; the destruction was complete. Nabuzardan, the executor of Nabucodonosor's vengeance, set aside everything of value; then he set fire to the Temple, the royal palace, and the city. Terror accompanied by despair beset the Israelites. The Dwelling of Yahweh disappeared from the midst of his people.[2]

A great number of prominent men were seized and executed by Nabucodonosor's order. From among the survivors, a selection was made for deportation. Those who remained, poor folk, were given a governor, an honest and peaceable man, Godolias. They were also given the little city of Mizpa, seven miles north of Jerusalem, for a capital. Jeremias was given freedom either to remain in the country or to rejoin his friends in exile. He preferred to remain with Godolias and work for the reorganization of the poor people who were in subjection to Babylon.

The cup of bitterness was not yet drained. An enraged nationalist, Ismael, assassinated Godolias and his court. A group of judicious men put an end to the cruelty of the murderous band, but fearing Babylonian reprisals, they decided to disregard the "word of Yahweh," which Jeremias had clearly declared to them, and to flee

[2] For an account of this and what follows, cf. Jer. 37-44.

into Egypt. The poor Prophet! He was taken by force to Egypt, where he had to struggle against the idolatry to which his companions succumbed. The circumstances of his death are unknown.

He had failed in everything.

In the eyes of God, however, he had not failed; for he had fulfilled his exceptionally thankless mission to the end, at the cost of the most heartfelt tortures.

He had been given the task, first to foretell and then to see the terrible Day of the Visitation of Yahweh (cf. Jer. 5:9; 6:15; 9:8; 21:14).[3]

He had foretold and had seen, but by faith alone, the rebirth of his people, cleansed and converted, a community of "the poor" like himself, who, for the moment, were on the banks of captivity. To them he bequeathed his soul, actually something more than a literary work because it was always alive. His message was a decisive turning point in divine Revelation. In his face and in his destiny were foreshadowed the features and the mystery of another suffering Servant.

[3] In the translations, *paqad* = "to visit," is often expressed by a word like "punish."

7 The Remnant

[ONE]

THE FACE OF THE WORLD CHANGES | The sixth century was one of the most extraordinary centuries in history.[1] The accession of Cyrus to the throne and the creation of the immense and gracious Persian empire would be enough to prove this. Simultaneously, however, people everywhere could be seen making progress. Even more remarkable was the fact that the human spirit reached one of its high points of maturation: religious wisdom and religious ideas suddenly appeared in various parts of the world to a degree of perfection previously unknown. Universal history was to be marked by them.

The Egyptian Renaissance, a product of the twenty-sixth dynasty, although real enough and valid certainly, should not be overestimated. The pharaohs during this period were Apries (588-568 B.C.) and, above all, Amasis, his rival and successor (568-525 B.C.). From then on, the future would be played out on the northern shores of the Mediterranean.

Italy was already on the road to her amazing destiny, although in an unpretentious way at present, and still on the margin of the more general history. At Rome, where the capitol was founded (508 B.C.), the Latin republic succeeded the kings (the story of the Tarquins) and triumphed little by little over the rival peoples of the peninsula, especially the Etruscans (cf. p. 95).

Greece was entering upon her finest period. She had seen the aristocracies disappear, the middle class become dominant (due to the appearance of money and the sudden revelation of its power), and the proletariat become conscious of its condition. Class struggles had broken out—on a city-wide scale only, but terrible nonetheless. Because of this an appeal went out to men who were called tyrants, but who were really the men of the hour. They ruled with

[1] In his *Origin and Meaning of History* (Plon, 1949), K. Jaspers makes it the "axial period" of the history of the world.

stern and absolute authority, which, all things considered, was both necessary and beneficent. Sparta (cf. pp. 94-95), with its own kind of organization, which resulted in a strange and dangerous natural austerity, would have to leave priority of influence to Athens. After having unified Attica, Athens had passed from a dynastic monarchy to an oligarchic republic. A series of social revolts, which were marked by vain attempts at order under the severe Draco and the wise Solon, ended in the prosperous despotism of Pisistrates and the solid "democracy" of Clisthenes. Athens was ready for one of the most extraordinary flowerings of humanity.

The Megarians founded Byzantium. The Phocaeans founded Marseilles. The Phoenicians continued to plough the seas, and Tyre (cf. p. 95) was still in its splendor (cf. Isa. 23; Ezech. 26-28). Miletus vied with Tyre in sowing merchant colonies throughout the Mediterranean and on the shores of the Euxine Sea. The Milesians, however, met with resistance in the interior of Asia Minor. The kingdom of Lydia, whose capital was Sardis, was already a figure of great power when Gyges created it in the seventh century. It still knew glory under Croesus (561-546 B.C.), a magnanimous potentate who was famous for his wealth and for the clever ways he kept it. He was also a generous protector of temples and a philhellenic friend of poets, scholars, and philosophers.

The sixth century saw the birth of philosophy [2] with the sages of Miletus, Thales, Anaximander, and Anaximenes: Heraclitus of Ephesus, the father of the "philosophies of evolution"; Pythagoras of Samos, mathematician and thinker, the initiator of a doctrine whose appearance was a capital event in the intellectual history of the West; and finally, the sages of Elea, Parmenides the metaphysician and his apologist Zeno.

The burgeoning of the spirit was at work also, although in a

[2] Pythagoras was the first, according to Cicero (cf. Tuscul. 5:8), to take the name of "philosopher" or "friend of wisdom." In regard to this appearance of philosophic thought, reference should obviously be made to histories of philosophy such as A. H. Armstrong, *An Introduction to Ancient Philosophy* (London: Methuen, 1957); Frederick Coplestone, S.J., *A History of Philosophy*, Vol. I: *Greece and Rome* (Westminster, Md.: Newman, 1946; New York: Doubleday Image Book, 1962); G. S. Kirk and J. E. Raven, *The Presocratic Philosophers* (Cambridge University Press, 1957); E. Zeller, *Outlines of Greek Philosophy* (New York: Harcourt, 1931). Cf. also the bibliography on p. 94, note 4.

different way, in the Far East. We can do no more than allude to the immense history of Asia. The steppes and the plateaus of central Asia contained an inexhaustible reservoir of men, which had already overflowed and was to overflow again in various invasions. The empire of China was in reality only a division into districts without much unity. India had no all-inclusive political regime and was divided into principalities and independent cities.[3] But, in the sixth century, these vast countries also reached a peak of cultural development.

In fact, Lao-Tse (605-520 B.C.), the founder of Chinese Taoism, and Confucius (555-479 B.C.), whose great wisdom was to become the dominant religion of China for twenty-five centuries, were contemporaries. The same was true in India where Mahavira, called Jina (599-527 B.C.), the founder of Hindu Jainism, an ascetic doctrine of escape and transmigration into Nirvana, was a contemporary of Sakhyamuni, called the Buddha (560-477 B.C.), the initiator of a religion whose development would be extraordinary; Buddhism was akin to Jainism, which advocated abstention from earthly things in order to attain to transcendent knowledge.

Israel, the exilic Israel of Ezechiel and of the Deutero-Isaias (of whom we are about to speak), was not touched by these great doctrines. The same, perhaps, cannot be said of Zoroastrian Mazdaism,[4] the religion of the Persians in the time of the Achaemenians.

Zarathustra, called Zoroaster (660-580? B.C.), was a sage like Confucius or Buddha. He undertook to reform the naturistic polytheism which formed the basis of the Iranian religion, and on which was erected the theology of Ahura-Mazda, the ancient divinity of the Iranians. The Persians of the sixth century traced their official religion back to the Iranians.

Ahura-Mazda (or Ormazd) was the supreme Being "who was, who is, and who always will be," omniscient, all-powerful, benevolent, merciful, and creator by his word alone of the material world and of the world of spirits. According to this doctrine, a whole

[3] For China and India, cf. J. Finegan, *Archaeology of World Religions* (Princeton University Press, 1952); George C. Ring, S.J., *Religions of the Far East* (Milwaukee: Bruce, 1950).

[4] Cf. J. Duchesne-Guillemin, "Iranian Religion," in Étienne Drioton, *et al.*, *Religions of the Ancient East, op. cit.;* R. C. Zackner, *Zurvan, a Zoroastrian Dilemma* (Oxford University Press, 1955), *The Teachings of the Magi* (New York: Macmillan, 1956).

world of hierarchized spirits exists, who play various parts in the visible world. The spirit of evil is Angro-Mainyush (or Ahriman), a cosmic power, who is the ruler of the world of shadows and of wickedness, and who has subalterns or demons; he is not a god. The universe is in the power of Good and Evil, who are eternal antagonists. Later on, for all practical purposes, Ahura-Mazda came to be identified with the spirit of good, although it was not possible to say that a dualist theology, properly so-called, or that belief in a genuine monotheism existed.

Mazdaism, moreover, was more a wisdom than a religion (no bloody sacrifices), an ideal for peace and for justice, a search for the good and for truth. A judgment of the merits of each man would take place at death; then, at the end of the world, a cosmic drama would take place, a struggle between the two opposed principles; the Good would be victorious, overthrowing all creation; then the general judgment of men, the liberation of souls, and the resurrection of the body would take place. A "savior" (Saoshyant) finally would restore all things to their original condition.

If one adds to this the fact that the Zoroastrian priests of the Achaemenians, who were called the "magi," and who were charged especially with the sacrifices and the guardianship of the sacred fire, were defenders of orthodoxy against popular superstitions and lived according to rules that were peculiar to them, making of them a caste quite distinct from the "laity," one cannot fail to perceive similarities between the postexilic religious thought of Israel and Zoroastrian Mazdaism. It seems difficult to deny that the latter helped the Yahwism of Israel to develop certain conceptions, which it already possessed but which later became more precise.[5] Supposedly, too, Mazdaism, which we know particularly from later texts and traditions, received influences from its contacts with Mediterranean Asia and with Israel; this explains certain resemblances. The

[5] It is not possible, within our little history of biblical literature, to treat this question in detail. The reader will have at least grasped the importance of Mazdean ideas concerning the following: the supreme God, creator and victor over evil; invisible spirits, angels or demons; individual and collective eschatology; even a kind of "messianism"; and the building up of a clergy. Our treatment of the exilic and postexilic biblical writings will make us think of it more than once. Note, however, that the apocalyptic writings, which inherited much from the Mazdean eschatology, would take only a minor place in the canon of the Scriptures. Furthermore, the only direct reference to Mazdaism that can be cited in the Bible is the "Asmodeus" in the book of Tobias.

historical cause of these contacts was the Persian elevation to the government of the whole of anterior Asia, of which we must now speak.

Nabucodonosor, who reigned for forty-three years, made a dazzling success of the neo-Babylonian empire. Babylon, rebuilt and extraordinarily adorned under his father and himself, enjoyed incomparable prestige at that time. It had become the world meeting place of wealth and of all the arts, the capital of intellect and of beauty, the crossroads of the great currents of thought, the most important religious center of the world.[6] Peoples and races met there and intermingled; when they left, they carried afar the fame of the brilliant metropolis. Biblical tradition would finally retain the image of Babylon as a symbol of all that is powerful and fragile in this world.

The new splendor of Babylon, however, would be short-lived. The successors of Nabucondonosor were insignificant and incompetent: Awelmardug (= Evil-Merodach, 561-560 B.C.); Nergalsharusar (= Neriglissar, 559-556 B.C.); Labashimarduk (556 B.C.). After Labashimarduk had been assassinated, Nabonidus, the son of a priest and a priestess, was raised to power by the sacerdotal party (556-539 B.C.). He had been a sexton, but as a monarch he was visionary, a weak and insane man, without care either for the government or for popular opinion.[7] In 548 B.C., he was forced to hand over the reins of power to his son Belsharusur (Balthazar). During this time, the mountaineers of the East were preparing an invasion.

To the south of Media, that is, east of Babylon and north of the Persian Gulf, a population little known until then, the Persians, vassals and allies of the Medes, succeeded in forming the little kingdom of Anzan in the region of Susa. In 553 B.C., the king of this minority, Cyrus, rebelled against Astyages. After many vicissitudes, Cyrus triumphed over Astyages, conquered all of Media, and had himself proclaimed king of the Medes and of the Persians (550 B.C.). He established a regime, whose benevolence toward conquered countries was unknown heretofore. He pushed on as far as Asia Minor, where Croesus organized a resistance (548 B.C.).

[6] It had fifty-five temples and many other sanctuaries. It held devotions of all kinds and great masses of worshippers came from all the corners of the world.

[7] He went against the piety of the people and aroused general dissatisfaction by having the divine statues from the various sanctuaries of Lower Mesopotamia transported to Babylon.

Cyrus, however, succeeded in capturing him in Sardis, Croesus' capital, and brought Lydia, as well as the Greek villages on the Ionian shore, under subjection. Cyrus launched some daring expeditions into the Siberian steppes and the plains of Chinese Tartary (545-540 B.C.). It was clear that he planned nothing less than the conquest of the entire world.[8]

Babylon, in the hands of the visionary and incompetent Nabonidus, was in danger. In 540 B.C., Cyrus set out, took over the cities of Lower Mesopotamia through which he passed, and in a fortnight, almost without striking a blow, without causing the city to suffer or even to interrupt its worship, took possession of Babylon. Apparently he respected the buildings, customs, and inhabitants of the city, announcing "salvation for all." He was acclaimed as a liberator (September-October 539 B.C.). Nabonidus was deposed but given his freedom; Belsharusur, however, the defender of the capital, was slain (which was to inspire Dan. 5). Cyrus returned the statues of the divinities, which Nabonidus had a passion for collecting, to their proper cities. The population saluted its new master as the "elect of Marduk," of Sin, of Nabu, of Ishtar, and of every other god. He did not have a divine effigy to return to Palestine; nevertheless, he was saluted as the "elect of Yahweh" by the Israelite exiles. He restored their liberty, as he did to all the peoples formerly conquered and "displaced."

After almost ten years more of campaigns, during which he never entered Egypt, although he was victorious over the nomads of the Iranian plateaus and penetrated as far as Turkestan and India, Cyrus died, apparently during an expedition against the Scythians, in 529 B.C.

He left to Cambyses, his son, an immense territory, conquered and subject, the most extensive empire that had yet been known in the Near East, and one marked by the innovation of a remarkable administration (roads, relay posts, prefectures). Most of all, he left his memory as a liberator and a pacifier, as a magnanimous man who had been won over to new and very humane ideas, as a man whose comprehensive policy was practical and tolerant. A Mazdean, like all the Achaemenians, his religion was flexible enough for him to be

[8] An easy and interesting work is *Cyrus*, by Champdor (A. Michel, 1952). It contains a great deal of information about the sixth century in the Middle East.

benevolent in regard to other beliefs and other traditions. Emphasis on monotheism, which tended to predominate in the Mazdaism which had been rethought out by Zarathustra, may have prepared Cyrus for a special understanding of the faithful of Yahweh.

[TWO]

A NEW ISRAEL | After the first capitulation of Jerusalem and the deportation of 598 B.C., Jeremias, in a striking vision in which he saw two baskets of figs of very different quality, was given to understand that there could be no hope of building the future with the Judeans still living in the country (cf. Jer. 24).

A final deportation was carried out in 582 B.C. (cf. Jer. 52:30). Juda was no more than a very poor territory surrounding a dismantled and ruined Jerusalem. Politically, it was reattached to the great Babylonia province of Syria-Palestine, but it had no precise boundaries and found itself at the mercy of ill-disposed neighbors: Philistines, Samaritans, and especially Edomites (cf. Ezech. 35:5-12; 36:2-5; Abdias 10-16). The population was not only reduced in numbers,[1] but the most valuable men had gone into exile. To be sure, no forced repopulation with strangers from remote countries had been carried out, as had happened with Samaria in the eighth century (cf. p. 113). Nevertheless, the hostility of surrounding settlements, their infiltrations, and their insolence toward this humiliated minority, which had been subjected and had been deprived of its borders, made a resumption of the collective consciousness or any effort at a common plan impossible.

[1] Perhaps barely a third was left. It has been estimated, for example, that Juda may have had from one hundred to one hundred and twenty-five thousand inhabitants before the destruction; that the victims of the war as well as the refugees in Egypt must obviously have numbered in the thousands; that the different deportations had totalled from forty to sixty thousand persons, perhaps more. These calculations are made on the basis of indications in the Bible (cf. IV Kgs. 24:14-16; 25:11-12; Jer. 52:28-30), in which only the men are counted. One cannot, however, arrive at exact estimates; those that have been made are widely divergent (A. Parrot, for instance, in the work cited on Babylon, says that "the great majority of the population had remained in Juda," p. 74, note 3; and he contrasts Jer. 52:30 with IV Kgs. 24:14; but in the same volume, p. 98, he speaks of "about fifty thousand" who returned after the Exile, according to Esd. 2:64-65!).

Deprived of its heart, Jerusalem, and of its clergy, Yahwism became an anemic religion, in great danger of deterioration. Worship, however, was kept up at the site of the Temple (cf. Jer. 41:5). It is also thought that ceremonies of mourning and of penitence commemorating, on anniversaries, the sad events of 588-587 B.C. very soon began to be celebrated in the Holy City (cf. Zach. 7:3; 8:19). The "Lamentations" ascribed to Jeremias, whose editorial work, properly speaking, is to be fixed about the end of the period of Exile, may have had their origin in these celebrations. Religious fidelity was also maintained no doubt, by virtue of the fact that the Judeans were not without contacts with their exiled relatives and friends, and messages from the Prophets thus came to them. It was only too necessary to recall them to the purity of the traditional faith. Their instinctive naturalism, the old basis of the Canaanite religion, and local superstitions were beginning to regain strength. The inclination toward naturalism was facilitated by the fact that the Babylonian representatives of the government were officially polytheists and foreign rites were celebrated at Jerusalem for them.[2]

The inhabitants of Juda certainly also corresponded with their brethren who were settled in Egypt. The refugees there formed a fairly important colony. They had been well received and had found employment in the towns of Lower Egypt. Their Yahwism, however, was soon corrupted and amalgamated with other devotions (cf. Jer. 44:15-30).

An interesting, but entirely different case, was that of the little Jewish colony which, as early as the seventh century, settled on the Island of Elephantine, an island at the first cataract of the Nile (opposite Aswan). A military colony, which enjoyed the favor of Psammeticus I, its mercenaries were charged with defending the southern bastion of Egypt against the Nubians. Numerous papyri have been found there testifying to the existence of a Jewish life in many respects similar to that of the Israelites in Palestine, but still hybrid. Yahweh was the great God, the first but not the only one. The most surprising fact concerning the faithful of Elephantine is that they had their own temple to Yahweh, although it is true that they had been installed on the island before the promulgation of the law which allowed only one sanctuary in Israel. A century and

[2] This can be seen from the exilic or postexilic literature; cf. for instance the idolatrous practices referred to in Isa. 65:3-5.

a half later, the temple of Elephantine would be destroyed by the non-Jewish inhabitants of the island. Then, Jerusalem's attitude would point up its privilege of possessing, thenceforth, the only Temple of Yahweh.

The colony in the Delta would develop in the centuries that followed, and became very important in the Alexandria of the third century. For the moment, Israel's destiny was not to be worked out in Egypt. The "basket of good figs" or, to use the expression so often repeated by the Prophets, the "remnant," would have to be looked for in Babylon (cf. Jer. 24:5-7; 29:10-14; Ezech. 11:15-20).

The exiles reached Babylon after an extremely painful march of almost 1,200 miles, having left the bodies of some of their company beside the sunscorched track. They may have been relieved when they finally arrived in Lower Mesopotamia; they may even have been agreeably impressed by the region. As Palestinians, they had known only harsh, mountainous areas; they discovered that their new home was a sunny land with broad horizons and numerous oases. There were gardens everywhere, irrigated by grassy-banked canals. The average man living among the dense population enjoyed a standard of living unknown in Juda. The images retained in their memories of Jerusalem faded at the sight of the large and beautiful cities they met on the shores of the Tigris or of the Euphrates, and especially at the sight of Babylon in all its magnificence. The exiles were all the more sensitive to the sight of these wonders because they had been chosen, generally, from the urban and cultivated circles, from among the socially elite and influential castes—politicians, officials, landed proprietors, technicians, artists, Scribes, Prophets, and priests.

They were put into camps at first and were, no doubt, employed on public works. Like all the ancient empires, however, excepting Assyria, Babylon showed tolerance toward the strangers, believing that they would soon melt into the mass of the population and would thus lose their own identity. The government, therefore, was not slow in relaxing its attitude, and the immigrants were able to seek employment immediately.[3] Some engaged in agricultural work, but the majority found work in the city, in trade especially; [4] others

[3] This explains the advice of the Prophet in Jer. 29.

[4] "It seems that this is an old sociological law, that by reason of their knowledge of at least two languages and their lack of attachment to a particular plot

pursued administrative careers.[5] Many knew the ways of becoming rich.[6] It should be noted that the Israelites from the ancient kingdom of Samaria, installed in Lower Mesopotamia for a century and a half, were able to ease the path of the newcomers.

The usual problems arose as soon as they arrived. Were the exiles to isolate themselves or collaborate with the people of the country? Should they wait for liberation, a dream which was still supported by visionaries, or should they adopt a realistic position in the face of new conditions? Undoubtedly, indecision plagued them at first, if not discouragement and a great deal of anxiety because of the difficulty in the beginning of adopting so many new things. Normally, circumstances should have led the Israelites to assimilation. Furthermore, their former hopes were crushed: the gods of Babylon had been the stronger; failure invited the rejection of the past, suggesting that they let themselves be forgotten as Jews and be recognized as Babylonians. Some Israelites decided on this course, or were led into it little by little. They claimed, no doubt, to be following the counsel given by Jeremias in a famous letter (cf. Jer. 29:5-7).

Nevertheless, the most remarkable fact of this history is that the Judean exiles as a whole did not let themselves be assimilated; they soon formed a solid and vigorous community of their own in Babylon. The breaking up of the former social framework, contacts made on the long road to exile and in the camps, the sharing of the same sufferings and the same work, the mutual aid given rise to by the circumstances, and the needs of their situation, rapidly brought about fraternal understanding and coalition among all the exiles, the leaders, workers, priests, Prophets, and Scribes. Former factions and divisions disappeared at a single stroke. In addition, besides

---

of ground, strangers become merchants rather than cultivators" (Baron, *History of Israel,* p. 146). We are, however, not relying on theory. Valuable information has been provided by the tablets (730 in number) of the "Bank of Murashu and Son," discovered in the ruins of Nippur, which date from the fifth century before the Christian era. They have preserved the names of many Jewish clients and have revealed their occupations or positions.

[5] Esdras and Nehemias would be well-placed officials; cf. also the case of Daniel.

[6] Cf. Esd. 2:65-69 and Neh. 7:67-72, in which the collection for the "National Relief" largely exceeded a million gold francs; according to E. Meyer, "170 million francs of today, with a purchasing power several times as high" (Baron, *op. cit.,* p. 148).

ties of blood, they held cherished memories in common. The remoteness of the homeland led to its idealization and to nostalgia for it. The result was a profound scorn for the pagan and impure land of exile. The religion of Yahweh had never ceased being preached by the Prophets, whose sayings haunted the memories of the people. The exiles knew the psalms by heart and sang them among themselves; this was their religion. Faith and piety once more seemed incomparable; everything else was nothing but an abomination and a defilement.

Even if a sanctuary no longer existed it was possible for the faithful of the Lord to form themselves into groups, since they were brothers of one mind. The Israelites possessed something which was strictly their own, something which could draw them together and nourish the common life: the Sacred Texts. Either known by heart or transcribed on rolls of parchment, the texts were the religious and literary treasures of the Israelites. They were made up of the great traditions, national and liturgical songs, writings of the Wise Men, and discourses and poems of the Prophets. The whole of Yahwism was contained in this literature—all that God had done for his People. The Sacred Texts seemed to be a Presence of the ever busy Yahweh; they were his living Word.

The Israelites, then, began to read these precious texts at meetings. They meditated and commented on them, seeking from them inspirations for living, for defending themselves from surrounding influences, and for the creating of a distinctly Israelite rhythm of living "in the midst of the Gentiles." A substitute liturgy was created for the prayer meetings on the Sabbath and on feast days.[7] Men with special qualifications naturally played particular roles in this liturgy: they became leaders or "elders," readers, and interpreters and preservers of the Scriptures.[8] A religious service of this kind, without sacrifices and consisting solely of prayers and readings, had undoubtedly never before been seen.

The remaking of Israel into a religious and fraternal community of this kind, so soon after the tragic and brutal disappearance of its

[7] Many, finally, were to be singers (men and women); cf. Esd. 2:65 (this text, however, which is the work of the author of Par., must be interpreted in accordance with his personal interests).

[8] Thus, the office of *sopher* or "man-of-the-book" was not far from being created.

traditional structures and of supports that had seemed indispensable, was a fact without precedent. It presupposes that the People of God possessed a special inner dynamism, of a kind (the Bible says a "spirit") which has never ceased to astonish the world. Ezechiel speaks of it in terms of "resurrection" (cf. Ezech. 37), and as a work of the "Spirit of God." The Deutero-Isaias would recall the days of Moses, when the Lord once before had made a people for himself. Was this not the "new Covenant announced by Jeremias (Jer. 31:31)?

Among the instruments God made use of for this work were the Prophets; in the front rank among them was Ezechiel, God's "watchman" (cf. Ezech. 3:16-21; 33:1-20) and one of the elders of the Golah.[9]

Before Jerusalem was captured and destroyed, he, like Jeremias, had announced the catastrophe and had emphasized Israel's general culpability for it (cf. Ezech. 1-24). He spoke in a personal way, as a visionary, employing strange and unconnected images (cf. Ezech. 1-3:15; 8-11), speaking in powerful allegories (cf. Ezech. 16; 17; 21; 23), and using gestures that were, to say the least, surprising (cf. Ezech. 3:22— 5:17; 12:1-20; 24).

When the fatal hour arrived, Ezechiel saw the divine Presence departing from the Temple in flames (cf. Ezech. 10:18-22). Where, then, would the Lord dwell? The following was revealed to the prophet: "Thus says the Lord God: Though I have removed them [the exiles] far among the nations and scattered them over foreign countries—and was for a while their only sanctuary in the countries to which they had gone . . ." (Ezech. 11:16). God in exile! God still in the midst of his own! From then on, men would know that where the faithful are gathered together, there God always is.

Nothing had ended for the People of God; rather everything was beginning: "I will give them a new heart," said Yahweh, "and put a new spirit within them; I will remove the stony heart from their bodies, and replace it with a natural heart . . . thus they shall be my people and I will be their God" (Ezech. 11:19-20; cf. 18:31; 36:26). Those who heard Ezechiel relate his visions understood that he was exhorting purification, penitence, and a profound interior renewal. Without mitigating the responsibility common to all (cf.

[9] This is a Hebrew term applied to the whole of the exiles or to the "emigration." For the deportation of Ezechiel, cf. p. 148.

Ezech. 16; 23), emphasis was clearly placed on individual responsibility (cf. Ezech. 18).

Ezechiel, faithful to the tradition of his predecessors and, like them, mindful of life on an international scale, commented on the attitude of the countries that were neighbors of Palestine (cf. Ezech. 25-32); their hostility to the People of God would be punished by destruction. We get this information from the Prophet's speeches concerning Tyre (cf. Ezech. 26:1-28:19) and Egypt (cf. Ezech. 29-32). That Yahweh should treat with a sovereign and rigorous authority nations whose greatest fault was their pride might well cause Israel also to take heed.

Returned to Yahweh and "reborn," thanks to the Spirit-of-life that had spread in the community (cf. Ezech. 37:1-14), no longer suffering from ancient divisions (Ezech. 37:15-28), Israel in exile would return to the Country of Yahweh. But things would no longer be as before: Ezechiel saw a new Dwelling place of God and a new Service of God, in a Holy Land which looked ideal, having the wonderful fruitfulness of a "terrestrial Paradise." The most striking thing in this "Torah of Ezechiel" (cf. Ezech. 40-48) (a theoretical plan for the rebuilding of the Temple and for laws of worship, set forth by a priest-legist), is the idea of "holiness," of the holiness of God and of everything that is connected with his Dwelling; of an "isolating" holiness, very different from the worldly kind, requiring of the members of the "consecrated" people, and primarily of its priests, a rigorous ritual "purity." This idea was to dominate the era beginning for the Jewish community.

The final section of the Book of Ezechiel is, like nearly a dozen of the oracles of the collection, dated (cf. Ezech. 40:1; 1:1-2; 8:1; 20:1; 24:1; 29:1, 17; 30:20; 31:1; 32:1, 17; 33:21). The Prophet noted down the day on which the revelations were made to him. These notes were collected, either by Ezechiel himself or by one of his disciples, into one complete whole made up of two parts; the two parts corresponding to the division of the Prophet's career. We have, therefore, as in the case of Jeremias, some oracles which were written before being spoken, and others which, perhaps, were only written.

From the viewpoint of style, Ezechiel is a mediocre writer; he was verbose, common, complicated, tormented, and obscure, more a writer of prose than of poetry. He usually proceeds by the simple means of repetition and the piling up of terms. Nevertheless, the very power of his inspiration makes him a great artist. The pictures he paints are extremely moving and his images never would be erased from the memory of the People of God.[10] He knew also how to write magnificent poems, which were masterpieces of the first rank because of their feeling, their freedom, and their evocative power (cf. especially Ezech. 27 and 31). Furthermore, he prepared the way directly for a literary form which would develop rapidly and would enjoy a great vogue in two or three centuries. This was the apocalyptic form, which announced the final and shattering victory of God over his enemies in an impressive scenario (cf. Ezech. 38-39). Ezechiel had a genius for using symbolism. His visions are bizarre, filled with intricate details, and, as a result, are difficult to follow.[11]

Anyone accustomed to reading Ezechiel, however, returns to him again and again. Not only is there something fascinating in him, but also his lofty reflections concerning the deep-seated conversion of the heart, on the responsibilities respectively to history and to the Lord, on the transcendence and the mystery of God, and on the "sacred" Dwelling of "the Lord is here" (Ezech. 48:35), never cease to be presented as basic ideas.

Prophet of the community in exile, true initiator of the "Judaism" that was being born, Ezechiel is also the father of the literature which is called "sacerdotal." We will treat sacerdotal literature in a separate section, but first we must note briefly the continuation of Isaian literature.

These additions to the collection of Isaias were occasioned by a situation which arose during the last days of Nabonidus (cf. p.

[10] Ezechiel put a whole wealth of new images in circulation. They will be found again in all the apocalyptic literature; the Apocalypse of St. John would make marvelous use of them. Ezechiel can also be said to have exercised a profound influence on the mystic tradition, both Jewish and Christian.

[11] One can become accustomed to it, however, and quite rapidly. Babylonian imagery (cherubim, hybrid beings) may have had some effect on the mind of the Prophet. On the other hand, visions of this kind must not be "construed" as coherent "tableaux," but the meaning of each descriptive element (for example, at the beginning of the collection: fire, metal, chariot, wheels, eyes, animals, and so on) should be successively grasped as if it were projected separately on a screen, one image being removed to make room for the next, with only the meanings joining one another. The visionary has, moreover, a very clear sense of the inferiority of his expressions in relation to an indescribable reality, and he multiplies the formulas of approximation and imprecision ("like," "aspect," "resemblance").

158). Babylon's destruction, the condition required for the liberation of the exiles, was foretold to them by a few Prophets whose names are unknown. Thus, we read in Isa. 13:1-14, 23, a strong and brilliant prophecy describing the disaster which would befall the capital and scoffing at the descent of its king to *sheol.* The same subject, and no doubt the same historical context, is found in Isa. 21:1-10. Here, more than just Babylon, a monarch drunk with self-love is condemned; all pride is condemned, and all opposition to the One Lord. Similar prophecies were added to the collection of Jeremias (cf. Jer. 10:1-16, and especially Jer. 50:1-51, 58). Was Isa. 34-35, a prophecy against Edom, and much like Isa. 13, also a product of the same period? It is difficult to fix an exact date, but they are specifically apocalyptic poems, in the tradition of Ezech. 38-39.

Notice the following prophecy of Isaias, which is quite different in scope and written in a new style: "Comfort, give comfort to my people, says your God. Speak tenderly to Jerusalem, and proclaim to her that her service is at an end . . ." (Isa. 40:1-2).

The exiles needed comforting. No doubt they had been courageous and had accepted their lot as expiation for past sins, but over a period of forty years courage weakens. They saw themselves growing old and ending their days in a foreign land; and they remembered Prophets like Jeremias and Ezechiel foretelling the end of the Exile and the re-establishment at Jerusalem. Surely the younger generation thought that the period of divine chastisements had come to an end. It felt that the worst was over, and it knew that its hopes and its ambitions could not be fulfilled in Babylon.

The author of the marvelous *Book of Comfort of Israel,* which today is usually called the Deutero-Isaias, corresponding as it does to Isa. 40-55, is anonymous. He must, however, have been a strong personality, one who enjoyed great prestige, who played a leading part in the Babylonian community, and who received exceptional enlightenment from God. The new prophecies, a product either of the Prophet himself, if his disciples, or of tradition, were written from the traditional viewpoint of absolute faith in a holy and saving God (cf. Isa. 40:31; 41:10-14; 43:1, 5, 10; 44:8; 50:10), and were attributed to the great Prophet of the eighth century.

It was the eve of the great successes of Cyrus; raised up in the

East and coming from the north (cf. Isa. 41:2, 25), he descended on Lower Mesopotamia. The Persian conqueror was hailed as the "Shepherd" of Yahweh, his "Anointed" (cf. p. 89). Although there were bold words, Cyrus would truly be the instrument of God by permitting the return of the exiles to the Holy Land (cf. Isa. 41:1-7, 25-29; 44:28; 45:1-6).

The Prophet foretells, in flowing and none too strict style, but one that is admirable for its enthusiasm and soaring passages, sensational and uncomprehensible "news": the return of the liberated exiles to the Land of the Lord in prosperity and happiness; a new "Exodus" through an irrigated and blooming desert; a meeting with the God of the Covenant who comes, formidable and magnificent, returning home to Jerusalem on a holy and royal road with his people, lifted up at last from its humiliations . . . (the entire work can be cited; hence, the entire work should be reread; on the theme of the new Exodus, cf. Isa. 40:3-5; 41:18-19; 42:10-16; 43:16-21; 48:21; 49:9-11; 50:2; 51:10; 52:8-12; 55:12-13). In reality, no change has taken place; the Deutero-Isaias shows very clearly by his words the continuity of history and the faithfulness of God to his Plan, recalling the fact that they are merely the fulfillment of things past, long since predicted by the messengers of God (cf. Isa. 42:9; 43:12; 44:8; 46:9-11; 48:3).

The benefits obtained by Israel through the Exile become evident in this Prophet: the opening to the world beyond; the universalization of Yahwism; the taking of definite positions with regard to polytheism. God is the creator of the universe (cf. Isa. 40:12, 22, 26, 28; 42:5; 44:24; 45:7-12, 18; 48:13; 51:13, 16); he is the One and incomparable Lord (cf. Isa. 40:18, 25; 42:8; 43:10; 44:6-8; 45:5-6, 14, 18, 21-22; 46:5-9; 49:9; 54:5). He is the one who "redeems" and who "saves" (cf. Isa. 41:14; 43:1-8, 11-14; 44:6, 22-24; 45:15, 21; 47:4; 48:17, 20; 49:7, 25-26; 50:2; 51:10-11; 52:3, 9; 54:8). Salvation is a gift of God and is part of his justice (cf. Isa. 41:10; 42:21; 45:8, 24-25; 46:12-13; 48:18; 51:5-8; 54:14, 17). The Chosen People are greatly encouraged by the idea that salvation belongs to them, even though the vision becomes more universal and includes the salvation of all men (cf. Isa. 42:6; 45:14; 49:6, 18; 51:4; 52:10; 53:11-12; 54:1-3; 55:5). Nevertheless, Jerusalem is the center for the gathering of the peoples—a renewed and happy Jerusalem, the "spouse of Yahweh" (cf. Isa. 49:14-21; 51:17-52:10; 54:1-17). One is struck by the constancy of these thoughts, and by the clarity, freedom, and purity of such a theology.

Special prophecies, currently called the "Songs of the Servant of Yahweh," can be seen in the *Book of Comfort:* Isa. 42:1-9; 49:1-7; 50:4-9; 52:13-53:12. To take notice of them does not imply taking them out of their related context and denying them to the author of Isaias 40-55. Who is this "Servant"? The question is so difficult and so complex that it cannot be treated here either in summary fashion or in a sufficiently definite way. In context, these songs evidently attribute the name "Servant" to Israel itself (cf. Isa. 41:8-9; 42:19; 43:10; 44:1-2, 21, 26; 45:4; 48:20; 54:17). Therefore, possibly the Servant is the Chosen People, the messenger and instrument of God among the nations. Furthermore, he may represent not only certain servants of God, but also a particular one; one who takes charge of his people before God and who accomplishes the mission of saving others; contradicted and persecuted, he becomes by his sufferings the savior of many. In this way, both the collective and individual character of the mysterious personage can be explained. Perhaps the songs were completed by disciples of the Prophet of the Exile. In addition, it seems that the theology of humility and of expiation found in Isa. 53 does not forget the impressive and sorrowful figure of Jeremias as the Servant of God. In subsequent eras, the "Songs of the Servant" would be proposed as new landmarks of the messianic doctrine: Prophet, master of wisdom, missionary, vicarious victim—such, in reality, the Savior would be. From that time on, the Gospel of the Redemption of the world by the sacrifice of an Envoy of God (who would include and sum up in himself the whole community of the People-Servant) was present in the religious thought and in the sacred literature of Israel.

The Exile, with its strong feelings, its sufferings, its fears, and its hopes, certainly inspired psalms. But since the psalms are not dated, and are part of a general tradition, it is difficult to state definitely exactly which were products of this era. No doubt they expressed feelings of humiliation and of pain, of bitter repentance, and of a converted faith, which characterized the spirit of the community in exile. Of particular note are Ps. 51; 74; 79; 85 (songs of a later date, like Ps. 126 and 137, retain the memory of the deportation). Because their authors were probably priests, these psalms were given a place immediately in the liturgy of the prayer meetings.

The songs contain reminiscences; they make use of texts composed at an earlier time, notably the works of the ancient prophets and of Deuteronomy, of Jeremias, Ezechiel, and of the Deutero-Isaias, as well as of other psalms. A fine example of this anthological process is the Canticle of Moses found in Deut. 32. A commemoration of the greatness of God the Creator and a commentary on the painful but privileged history of Israel, it is filled with passages suggestive of the prophets and especially of the Deutero-Isaias.

Anthological also, with reminders of Jeremias, of Ezechiel, and of the Deutero-Isaias, are the five poems called the Lamentations of Jeremias. They were probably composed at Jerusalem for the faithful there (cf. p. 160). These funereal complaints, written in the Hebrew elegiac mode, the *qinah,* sorrowfully recall the catastrophe of 587 B.C. and the sufferings endured by the inhabitants of the Holy City at that time. Their heart-rending lyricism makes them one of the most poignant expressions of human grief. They were not sung merely to mark the anniversary of mourning; they were meant to be, as it were, moral commentaries on sorrow; they were intended to help men become conscious of their responsibility for the misfortune, and to promote repentance and conversion to an invincible faith and hope in God who rescues from every trial.

Chapters 1-4 of Deuteronomy were undoubtedly added to the book at the time of the Exile and were its first preface. Probably Chapter 28:47-68, a good part of Chapter 31, plus some interpolations or reworkings constituted the definitive edition of the work. This great book, akin to Jeremias and also to the wisdom of Proverbs, was the messenger of the marvelous doctrine of the love of God for his people (cf. p. 139). Recalling the experiences of the desert but also the prospects of a happy life in the "good land" of God, it must have brought a powerful consolation to the Gola, since it served as a prelude to the birth of a "Judaism" in which God would dwell.

[THREE]

THE GREAT TORAH | The Deutero-Isaias does not resemble Ezechiel, either in style, in ideas, or in principal themes. But Ezechiel had founded a school; and a whole literature, called "sacerdotal," proceeds from this Prophet-priest. It held an important place in Israelite tradition and finally in the Bible. Composed in part during the time of the Exile, its composition was resumed and was completed in the fifth century. The Babylonian Gola was its true original environment, but since it is a homogeneous literature, we shall consider it here as a whole, anticipating somewhat the beginning of the postexilic period.

The historian will always regard the rapid rise of the Jewish[1] minority of Babylon as an absolutely extraordinary fact. The rise was due primarily to the consciousness the Israelites had of possessing a privileged and inalienable individual heritage. Deprived of a political structure and without a homeland, the People of God nevertheless saw immediately that it had something by which to live—the Torah, its true frame of reference and, at the same time, its guaranty of unity. It was understood that the Torah had to be defined and published among the brethren as soon as possible.

Adherence to the Torah was the best means of keeping the Israelites distinct as an ethnic and religious group from the other peoples with whom they had to live in exile. Several points drew the line of demarcation, safeguarding the faithful of Yahweh from pagan contamination: not to eat exactly like everyone else; to have rules of their own for distinguishing the sacred from the profane; to keep special days as holy days (notably the sabbath); to practice circumcision; and, to be strict in regard to the laws of conjugal union. One can see in the Prophets of the exile that the idea of the holiness of God was felt more intensely than ever among the Israelites, with the result that religious observances must have received a more fixed character. Perhaps the firm establishment of religious rites purely and simply, enabled the Jewish people to preserve itself.

In order for the Torah to play its part both as a safeguard and as a communal link among the exiles, who were unorganized except for local or neighborhood meetings, it had to be known by as many as possible and to be communicated to them in a written form that was easily obtainable, popular, and capable of being transmitted. Furthermore, it had to be presented as a religious instruction and as a rule of life sufficiently complete to characterize the different

[1] From now on, we can use the terms "Jew" and "Judaism," while continuing to use the words "Israel" and "Israelite" (just as, for ancient times, we spoke of the "Hebrews"). It is, in fact, only after the Exile that one can consider the Israelites as belonging to the territory of Juda.

aspects of Israelite life, leaving no room for the inventions of individual fancy. Thus, a vast collection of ancient narratives, ritual prescriptions, liturgical rubrics, customs, and a very elaborate system of laws, was built up, which was useful for keeping alive and for maintaining in the Israelite consciousness the great, living Hebrew religious tradition.

The priests had always been men of tradition in Israel as elsewhere.[2] They were the specialists of the Torah. A great number of them lived in exile, for they had almost all been deported. They were the only elements of the ancient Israelite society to retain a title of their own and to be able to play a part in the community. Their prestige in the community increased considerably; they became the counselors and teachers, the thinkers, and the writers. In addition, the clergy, unlike the Prophets, always remained anonymous, acting not through the impression that could be made by a striking personality nor by virtue of the sudden impulses of one inspired; rather, their actions resulted from long and patient group effort. A group such as the "sacerdotal circle," composed of theologians and archivists, of jurists and scholars, of historians and Scribes, produced the monumental work that is called, in the language of biblical criticism, the "Sacerdotal Code." [3] This Code is made up of the entire Book of Leviticus, half of Exodus, two-thirds of Numbers, and about one-fifth of Genesis.[4]

Once again the work was attributed to Moses, or, more exactly, presented as the words of Yahweh to Moses or as narratives set in the time of Sinai. The sacerdotal circle was accurate in ascribing the Code to antiquity, because some of the traditions represented did in fact go back to the very ancient periods of the history of Israel. In addition, the authors had the conviction that they were merely restoring or continuing what Moses had begun. Furthermore, a striking analogy existed between the position of the Hebrews in Egypt and at Sinai and that of the Israelites in Babylon, where they were a nation without a state or a territory. But if the

[2] Cf. pp. 73 and 125-26. In addition, the exiles had before their eyes the example of the great Babylonian clergy and, no doubt for them more strict and more impressive, the example of the Zoroastrian magi.

[3] Ordinarily designated by the letter P, from the German word *Priestercodex*, or "Book of the Priests."

[4] See the table of texts P on p. 178, the other texts of these books are Yahwist and Elohist (cf. pp. 106–7).

authors of both the ancient and new Torah considered the past which God had made for his people, they knew well also how to enact decrees covering the conditions under which Israel was going to live; and they did so not in the theoretical and even impractical manner of Ezechiel, their Prophet-teacher, but with a practical realism of the most detailed kind. Still, there could be no further fear of falling into mere rubricism, for the word of the Prophets was also preserved, which prevented religion from again becoming simply a formalistic system of practices.

The priest-writers of the new Code were concerned, then, with assembling, classifying, and arranging the liturgical and moral traditions, at the same time purifying them of the superstitions which contaminated them, simplifying what time had rendered too complicated, and infusing a spirit that was profoundly religious and at the same time communal. The synthesis was based on the predominant notion among the priests and the whole community—the concept which had dominated the message of Ezechiel in its last chapters: Yahweh is "holy" and "holy" is his people. Consequently, the persons, actions, and things related to the worship paid to the Lord claim particular attention, and hold the chief place in the sacerdotal literature.

Obviously, the problem of innovations did not arise. The worship and sacrifices of Israel, its feasts and its rites of purification were of ancient origin; sometimes they were older than Israel itself, having been inherited from the Ancient Near East.[5] Rites such as those that are described in Lev. 14:4-9, 49-53 and Num. 5:11-31; 19:2-10 are manifestly archaic. If one knows the levitical Torah well, doubtless one can discover a part of the history of worship in Israel. One can also perceive the successive efforts at "Yahwizing" ancient religious practices, which had been adapted from the surrounding environment, and the changes and precisions that came with time (during the course of the royal period particularly and in connection with the Temple of Jerusalem), as well as the reforms accomplished or, at least, attempted. One will recall (cf. p. 142) that the era of the

[5] The common basis of the Ancient Near East—Mesopotamian, Egyptian, and Canaanite remnants—can be seen cropping out in the P texts. Cf., for example, the notes of Cazelles in the section "Leviticus" in the Jerusalem Bible (ed. Cerf), concerning the following passages: Lev. 1; 3; 4; 14; 2:7, 13; 5:5; 7:10; 8:28; 12:3.

last reform, the reign of Josias, saw the birth of the literature that was now in the final phase of its compilation.

The most ancient group of texts is the "Torah of Holiness" (Lev. 17-26), which is not unrelated to the "Covenant Code" of Exodus 20-23 (p. 74). It also has perceptible similarities to Deuteronomy (notable, for example, in Lev. 19) and obvious relationships with Ezechiel (levitism of Ezech. 18:6-9; 44:20-31; Ezechialism of Lev. 26). It must have been completed between the years 570 B.C. and 540 B.C. approximately. The theme found throughout the book is that of the "holiness" or disposition required in order to approach God.

The "Torah of Sacrifices" (cf. Lev. 1-8) was composed next.[6] A remarkable systematization of a complex liturgical inheritance, it reduced the ancient sacrifices to a few types and classified them in the light of a more profound theology of sin, of expiation, and of communion with God.

The "Torah of the Pure and of the Impure" (cf. Lev. 11-15, including possibly the ritual of Kippur in Lev. 16) is another systematization which began with empirical ideas and with ancient practices, and followed a great religious principle: men may not eat just anything, nor may they touch everything; in particular, a man may not use the generative powers of life in just any way, because of the holy Presence of the God of life, and because he belongs to the living, holy People of God. The laws which concern the priests in Lev. 8-10 certainly come a little later and are dominated by the idea that the priesthood is representative and mediative. Finally, Chapter 27, which deals with the persons and things dedicated to God, was added.

Leviticus does not shine because of its literary beauty. The style is generally poor and dull; it was not worked on by great artists. In it, tediousness is often the penalty for carefully following a certain form. Among its characteristics can be noted a concern for technical detail and a seeking for schematic arrangements; in the other books, which are a part of the same literature and with which we shall deal shortly, collections and lists of names are added

[6] As far as can be determined, for if a detailed chronology is attempted, we are only in the realm of approximations and probabilities. The names given to the groups of texts are not biblical, obviously, but are usually accepted in biblical studies.

(genealogies, censuses), numerous topographical and chronological information is given, and a preoccupation with figures (ages, lengths of time, dates, dimensions) can be found. The language of Leviticus is verbos, monotonous, and never wearies of repetition. Although these characteristics are a mark of probity, Leviticus is not attractive to the reader who has not yet advanced far enough into its particular spirit, nor discovered, at the core of such technical but banal remarks and mountains of details, the high religious value of the message. In reality, the theological vigor and profundity of Leviticus are absolutely remarkable. Its religious thought has great stability, guided always by a strong concept of the divine Holiness. The care for details and for liturgical realism is, moreover, the expression of an orthodoxy which knew what the unfortunate experiences of laxness and of syncretism, of drifting and of anarchy in the preceding period had cost Israel.

Chapters 8-12 of Leviticus are closely connected with those things which pertain to divine worship in the second part of Exodus (cf. Exod. 25-31; 35-40). Ezechiel, and before long, Aggeus, Zacharias, and Malachias, will meet in some way in the central theme of the book: "They shall make a sanctuary for me, that I may dwell in their midst" (Exod. 25:8), the Lord said. The same idea of "holiness" can be found in Exod. 28:36-38; 30:29, 33; 31:14. The way the priests speak and their duties express exactly the lofty preoccupations of the clergy, whom the Exile had brought into being and had caused to reflect on things (cf. Exod. 25:22; 28:36-38; 29:42-46; 30:30; 40:14-15). The gifts and the contributions of work pointed out in Chapter 35 are not, perhaps, unrelated to the offerings of the exiles enumerated in Esd. 2. The holy Tent or Dwelling of Yahweh is conceived by men who remembered the Temple of Solomon, and is described with the care one brings to great and well-loved things. The furnishings of the Tabernacle and the required liturgical Service signify the sacramentalizing Presence of God in the midst of his own. Was this true even in the desert? Certainly, and in every similar situation, when the People of God are far from the permanent Abiding-place of God and on the way to it. The Deutero-Isaias begins to sing of the "new Exodus."

The Exodus is a journey: this idea would inspire the composition of the Book of Numbers. A large part of Numbers and its general arrangement are a product of the same theological and literary circle. The influence of Ezechiel is felt in the Book of Exodus, notably with regard to those things which concern the priesthood.[7] The sixth-century authors, and probably those of the next century[8] who continued their work, display in the book respect for the ministers of worship (cf. Num. 3-4; 8; 17-18; 25) and for their use of numbering systems, of genealogies, and of figures (cf. Num. 1-3; 7; 26; 33-34). In addition, they complete the Torah of Leviticus with ritual ordinances and with remarks on the law (cf. Num. 5-6; 9; 28-30; 35-36). But to describe the community of the desert, to arrange them according to rank around the Lord who was present among them, a people "tempted" and rebellious—and to what an extent! —condemned to forty years outside the Holy Land, but preparing to enter the Country of God, was not this the most opportune message for the exiles who had been called to rebuild the people around Yahweh at Jerusalem after the great trial?

Characteristic of the sacerdotal literature is the enunciation of a torah or a description of a law at the end of a narrative or in connection with a narrative. In this way, prescriptions, customs, and laws enter into the development of the history of Israel, for example: the establishment of the sanctuary at Sinai (cf. Exod. 25-40); the statute concerning the priesthood at Cades (cf. Num. 17-18); and the distinction which was beginning to be made between civil power and religious power on the steppes of Moab (cf. Num. 26-27). Similarly, the ritual of the Pasch (lamb and unleavened bread) was woven into the woof of the account of the departure from Egypt (cf. Exod. 12:2-20, 43-51).

Great literary contributions of sacerdotal origin are also found in the Book of Genesis: the laws concerning marriage and the sabbath found in Gen. 1; the prohibition of homicide found in Gen. 9; and the obligation of circumcision found in Gen. 17. In these passages can be recognized the demands made by the situation of the faithful, who had to keep apart from the non-Israelites with whom they were mixed. In order that the people might recognize one another, it was also necessary to attach great importance to the ties of origin and of kinship. The "genealogies" of the Torah recall these requirements (cf. Gen. 5; 11; 25; 35; 46; and the genealogies

[7] That of the Aaronide branch of Sadoc, of which there was never any question before Ezech. 44 and Num. 3 and 18.

[8] For certain developments have no relation to the postexilic restoration or even to the work of Esdras and Nehemias.

of Exod. and Num.). Even in the use of old Mesopotamian themes such as that of the Flood,[9] liturgical preoccupations are manifest: the ark of salvation has the same measurements as the Temple of Jerusalem; important moments, indicated in months and in days, are liturgical dates.[10] Gen. 1, the first chapter of the Bible, shows the universe as a temple in which all duties are regulated, with creation falling within the sabbatical framework.

Thus, a book appeared which, if not yet made up of the five scrolls of parchment (thus, the Pentateuch), that is, if not arranged into the Yahwist, Elohist, deuteronomic, and sacerdotal texts as we know it, at least was a "holy priestly History," which constitutes a large part of the Pentateuch and shapes its general structure.

Having at their disposal an abundant documentation in the form of ancient documents and numerous written traditions, the sacerdotal writers were able to construct a vast doctrinal synthesis on the canvas of history. The history of Israel was conceived according to the ideal to which the holy people, in the midst of whom God "had set up his Tent," were dedicated; the history of laws signified this holy Presence and the belonging of the hierocratic people to God. But the thought which dominates everything is still that of the Covenant (cf. especially Gen. 9; 17; Exod. 19; 24; see also Exod. 2; 24; 6:4-5; 31:16; Lev. 24:8; 26; Num. 18:19; 25:13), the holy Covenant which, from Moses to Ezechiel, and down through the entire era of prophecy, signified the living connection between Yahweh and his people. Passed on in a manner at once sacramental and practical, the Torah taken as a whole perpetually recalls the conditions, the meaning, and the spirit of the Covenant, while gathering up, in order to make them actual, the living memories of a past which was the very action of God in the People of the Covenant.

Such was the tremendous fidelity of Israel. And if the men who defined the condition of life for a people who aspired to rebirth were not Prophets, at least they were looking in the same direction as the Prophets, preparing, like them, for the Return, the Regeneration, the Community of God.

[9] It could be read in Babylon, and could be heard proclaimed in the liturgies (cf. pp. 10-11).

[10] As we shall see in the volume on Genesis.

THE SACERDOTAL TEXT IN THE PENTATEUCH

Gen. 1; 2:1-4*a;* 5:1-28, 30-32; 6:9-22; 7:6, 11, 13-16*a,* 18-21, 24; 8:1-2*a,* 3*b*-5, 13*a,* 14-19; 9:1-17, 28-29; 10:1-7, 22-23, 31-32; 11:10-27, 31-32; 12:4*b*-5; 13:6, 11*b*-12*a;* 16:1*a,* 3, 15-16; 17; 19-29; 21:1*b,* 2*b*-5, 23; 25:7-11*a,* 12-17, 19-20, 26*b;* 26:34-35; 27:46; 28:1-9; 29:24, 29; 31:18*b;* 33:18*a;* 34:1-2*a,* 4, 6, 8-10, 13-18, 20-24, 27-29; 35:9-13, 15, 22*b*-29; 36:1-14, 20-30, 40-43; 37:1-2*a;* 46:5*b*-27; 47:7-11, 27*b*-28; 48:3-7; 49:1*a,* 28*b*-33; 50:12-13. Exod. 1:1-5, 7, 13-14; 2:23*b*-25; 6:2-30; 7:1-13, 19-20*a,* 21*b*-22; 8:1-3, 11*b*-15; 9:8-12; 11, 9-10; 12:1-20, 28, 37*a,* 40-51; 13:1-2, 20; 4, 14, 8-9, 15-18, 21*a,* 21*c*-23, 26-27*a,* 28-29; 16: 1-3, 6-14, 16-18, 22-28, 31-36; 17:1*a;* 19:1-2*a;* 24:15*b*-18*a;* 25; 26; 27; 28; 29; 30; 31:1-18*a;* 34:29-35; 35; 36; 37; 38; 39; 40. Levit. in its entirety. Num. 1; 2; 3; 4; 5; 6; 7; 8; 9; 10:1-28; 13:1-17*a,* 21, 25-26*a,* 32*a;* 14:1-2, 5-7, 10, 26-30, 34-38; 15; 16:1*a,* 2*b*-11, 16-24, 27*a,* 32*b,* 35-50; 17; 18; 19; 20:1*a,* 3*b*-4, 6-13, 22-29; 21:4*a,* 10-11; 22:1; 25:6-18; 26; 27; 28; 29; 30; 31; 32:18-19, 28-33; 33; 34; 35; 36. Deut. 4:41-43; 32: 48-52; 34:1*a,* 7-9.

8 The Judaic Community

[ONE]

BACK FROM EXILE | Some Jews had established themselves permanently in Babylonia, either because they liked the country or because of self-interest or because of the force of circumstances and the obligations of life. They had recovered their positions and had established families; they considered themselves well placed, and they had discovered that it was possible to live as worshipers of Yahweh outside of Palestine.

Nevertheless, the literary evidence that has come down to us from the captivity shows that many other Israelites had an ardent desire to return to the land of the Lord. Furthermore, the return seemed to be necessary: Israel was not yet strong enough to live as a "Diaspora," that is, to be dispersed throughout the world, as was later to be the case. Nostalgia for Jerusalem, for the land of their ancestors and of Yahweh, forever commemorated by Ps. 137, only increased with time, looming large in their imaginations and in their thoughts.

In addition, the question was no longer open to reflection. In conformity with the word of its Prophets, Israel suddenly saw the end of its captivity in the coming of Cyrus. Just as he had set free the other peoples of regions he had conquered, in particular restoring the privileges of their own religious life, so also the conqueror of Babylonia published an edict in 538 B.C., the year following his triumph, that authorized the deported Jews to return to Jerusalem and to rebuild the Temple of Yahweh there (cf. Esd. 1:1-4).[1]

The decision to depart was made without delay. Caravans were organized, carrying with them a sizable number of gifts collected by the Babylonian community. The repatriates numbered in the

[1] The documentation on the events in Palestine during the second half of the sixth century is found essentially in the books of Esdras and Nehemias (concerning these books, cf. p. 192), supplemented by the prophecies of Aggeus and Zacharias. There are gaps in this documentation.

tens of thousands.[2] They had at their head a prince of the House of David, Zorobabel, who had been appointed by the Persians as high commissioner for the land of Juda, under the control of the governor of the Province of Transeuphrates. The religious leader was Joshua, to whom the people were beginning to give the title of high priest. Naturally, there were many priests in the returning caravans. Acting under official authorization, they carried back the vessels and sacred objects formerly confiscated by Nabucodonosor.

Well-prepared and well-organized in advance, the people were divided on arrival into families and according to localities, as the lists in Esd. 2 and Neh. 7 give evidence. How were they received? Feelings of friendship, fraternity, the desire to help, or selfish reasons caused some to welcome them with thanksgiving and pleasure. Reasons for dissension were not lacking, however. In particular, there was the question of property. The repatriates reclaimed their ancient rights and produced in their own defense genealogies which had been strictly up-to-date. The non-repatriates, on the other hand, considering that historical circumstances had changed everything, upheld the new, de facto state of affairs. Other troubles also arose.

The former exiles were imbued with a profound piety. Their first concern was to raise the altar of holocausts at Jerusalem and to reestablish daily sacrifice immediately. The first general religious gathering took place on the Feast of Tabernacles. The following year they decided to restore the Temple, and workers and materials began to be assembled. The foundations of the new sanctuary were laid amid great happiness and the most touching emotions (cf. Esd. 2-3).

Moved by the sight of such happiness, the Judeans who had remained in Palestine offered their help, but it was declined with contempt. They were regarded as impure for such a holy task, because they now belonged to a hybrid race and because their religion had become contaminated. The absolute rigorousness which had characterized Yahwism in exile was displayed immediately. The people who were rejected, however, would take their revenge by means of political intrigue, bribery of officials, obstructions and

[2] The exact number cannot be given, in spite of the statements in the Book of Esdras. The author of this book, who was also the author of Paralipomenon (cf. p. 205), writes according to a literary form and using ideas which do not require us always to take the figures he gives as mathematically exact.

strikes, to such an extent that the work could no longer be continued. At the end of the year 537 B.C. it came to a stop (cf. Esd. 4:1-5, 24).

Not much is known of the fifteen or eighteen years that followed. It was certainly a difficult period; many foundered in despair and in discouragement. A state of painful hostility became permanent between the "people of the homeland" and the repatriates. Economic conditions in that mountainous land, which is naturally poor in resources rapidly deteriorated; to make matters worse, the first harvest had not been a success (cf. Agg. 1:6, 10-11; 2:16-19), further aggravating the social unrest (cf. Zach. 8:10).

In addition, world affairs were in a bad state. Cambyses II (529-522 B.C.), the son and successor of Cyrus, continued his father's work of expansion by conquering Egypt; but he did not have the importance, force of character, or vision of Cyrus. He became intolerant and hard, his evil intentions being attributed to a pathological lack of balance. He died in Egypt while on his way home.

The succession to power caused widespread disorder, conspiracies, and violence throughout the empire. Supported by the partisans of order, Darius (522-486 B.C.) claimed to be a descendant of the Achaemenian family, and finally established his claims by force. His was another highly successful reign. He led victorious expeditions to Iran and India, and into the regions around the Euxine Sea and the Danube; he was defeated in Thrace, however, and this was the beginning of the Wars of the Medes and Persians.

Darius pushed to the limit the application of the universalist and centralizing principles of Cyrus. He put the finishing touches on the creation of a governmental framework which was both simple and flexible but at the same time firm and codified, uniting highly dissimilar ethnic groups without impairing their characteristics, rights, and individual customs. The whole empire was divided into twenty satrapies, each having at its head a kind of viceroy, who was very powerful. He was charged especially with collecting taxes and with watching over the police and the administration of justice. He himself, however, was subject to strict control and was bound to respect the local administrations. Finally, the great system of strategic and commercial roads inaugurated by Cyrus was perfected. A regular postal system, which made communication between the various regions possible, was also brought to completion.

At the beginning of Darius's reign Prophets were sent to Israel to sound the note of courage and to help drive back the demoralizing tide. Aggeus, a witness of the apathy that prevailed among his compatriots, began to speak in 520 B.C. Even though the terms he used were strongly theological, they were no less practical: it was absolutely necessary to build the Temple, to start the work again with ardor (cf. Agg. 1:2-11); a divine blessing would then be assured, that is, all would enjoy happiness and the divine favor; the glorious presence of God would dwell in the midst of his people (cf. Agg. 2:3-9); under Zorobabel, the servant of a royal race and the elect of Yahweh, perfect and happy times would come (cf. Agg. 2:23). The Prophet evoked eschatological and Messianic times in brief but remarkable terms.

In the little Book of Aggeus, which is composed of short fragments of sermons whose central theme was the Temple, the Levitism of Ezechiel, the views of the Deutero-Isaias, and also of the Trito-Isaias, who was, as we shall see, contemporaneous, are very evident. The few Prophets whom we have yet to meet would make extensive use of the works of their predecessors. Their principal effort would be to readapt ideas and tendencies that had been expressed already.

The discourses of Aggeus were effective. Work was begun again under the direction of Zorobabel, a man with high hopes,[3] and of Joshua, the high priest, both of whom were supported by the Prophets. Thanks to their prudent and clever policy, they succeeded in avoiding difficulties from the governor of the satrapy. He was suspicious of the great works that were being carried on at Jerusalem, and he came under the influence of malcontents who had united themselves with the Samaritans. A report was sent to the capital of the empire; it was effective in bringing about the rediscovery of the edict of Cyrus. Darius republished the edict and promulgated a decree favoring the reconstruction of the Temple (cf. Esd. 5:1-6, 13).

Aggeus was still prophesying toward the end of 520 B.C. when another Prophet, Zacharias,[4] intervened with similar intentions: to stir up the energies of the revival, and to give heart and spirit to his listeners. The collection which gives evidence of his purpose

[3] We would indeed like to know how he met his end and why these hopes were not realized in him. On this point, however, nothing is known.

[4] The author of chapters 1-8 of the collection. For Zach. 8-14, cf. p. 198.

is a series of small fragments, especially eight visions and a few brief discourses. The symbolism used by the visionary is difficult to interpret, and his angelology is more advanced than any yet seen; both of these characteristics make Zacharias a truly apocalyptic writer. Moreover, he is clearly from the same school of thought as Ezechiel and the sacerdotal literature.

His message was extremely encouraging. The holy city would be rebuilt and the enemies of the people of God would be annihilated. Yahweh would dwell in the midst of his own and would draw other peoples to himself (cf. Zach. 1-2). The priesthood would be regenerated and re-established, with a high priest at its head. At the same time, temporal power would be assured by a Messianic representative (cf. Zach. 3-4). Everything evil and injurious would be driven out and punished (cf. Zach. 5-6). Finally, in line with the most authentic prophetic thought, Zacharias showed the great prospects which the future held in store for the holy community (cf. Zach. 7-8).

With this encouragement, the Temple was completed (515 B.C.) and levitic worship guaranteed. The dedication of the house of God was celebrated, and then the Feast of the Pasch and of the unleavened bread (Esd. 6:13-22). In comparison with the splendors of the past, the building and ceremonies certainly were simple, but they were the fruit of a series of hardships and of a great faith.

Tradition has placed in the wake of Isaias a collection of various poems composed between 530 B.C. and 510 B.C., or more precisely, about 515 B.C. It may be thought that they had a single author, today called the Trito-Isaias, whose work corresponds to Isaias 56-66. Although he patterned his writing after the formulas of Deutero-Isaias, but in a new way,[5] Trito-Isaias is also indebted to Ezechiel. He knew, moreover, how to maintain a proper balance between the preaching of the Torah (cf. Isa. 56:1-2; 58:13) and the worship at the Temple (cf. Isa. 56:5-7; 57:13; 58:12; 60:7, 13; 65:11; 66:20), on the one hand, and a truly profound interior religion (cf. Isa. 58:1-5; 61:8), one especially guaranteed by the practice of justice and of fraternal aid (cf. Isa. 58:6-10; 61:1-3), on the other. The Judean community was in need of correction for several reasons: unsuitable and vice-ridden leaders (cf. Isa. 56:9-12); widespread corruption

[5] Compare Isa. 40:3 with 57:14; 41:19 with 60:13; 49:23 with 60:16.

(cf. Isa. 59:1-15); and the propagation by the people of the practice of idolatry and of syncretism (cf. Isa. 57:3-10; 65:3-7; 66:3, 17). The Prophet, therefore sent out a call for repentance and amendment (cf. Isa. 59). But he did so in the name of a good and merciful God, who was both Father and Spouse (cf. Isa. 57:16-19; 59:20-21; 62:1-12, and especially Isa. 63:7-64:11 [6]), and the God of the humble (cf. Isa. 57:13-15; 66:1-2). The return to the grace of Yahweh and to the glory of the new Jerusalem were sung with ardent and enthusiastic joy (cf. Isa. 60-62; 65-66). In an all-embracing vision of the world, the nations were invited to turn toward Yahweh (cf. Isa. 56:3-8; 60:1-13; 66:18-23), although Israel remained his well-beloved people, a people-priest (cf. Isa. 61:6; 66:20).

The composition of the prologue which forms the first nine chapters of the Book of Proverbs must also be placed at the end of the sixth century. It contains several ideas: an important and urgent exhortation to accept the wisdom of the wise men, especially by receiving instruction from the Master and by docility to their teachings (cf. Prov. 1-4); a persistent warning against every evil deviation, especially loose living (cf. Prov. 5-7); and finally, an admirable glorification of divine Wisdom (Prov. 8-9). The prologue differs in form from the ancient collections of maxims which it prefaces (cf. p. 127), and from those which were added to it later (cf. Prov. 22-24; 30; 31:1-9; 31:10-31). The form of the prologue is no longer that of little, disconnected *meshalim* set one after the other, but rather that of fairly extensive discourse-counsels with a single theme. Furthermore, it is newer by reason of its content. Even if it is preoccupied with practical, common sense ideas, or concerned with a pedagogy based on experience, and using the didactic method of repetition which is characteristic of the teaching of the Scribes, still wisdom is revealed in the prologue in a new and marvelous way. Wisdom is personified in the prologue and speaks in the first person (cf. Prov. 8:22-31). She introduces herself as born of God before every creature and co-operating in the creative action of God. Moreover, she announces herself as a type of prophetic word (compare Prov. 8:1-6; 9:1-6, with Isa. 55); she proposes to dwell with men and to give herself to them in fellowship.

It is easily understood that here opens a deep mine of revelation and of reflection.

[6] Isa. 63:7-64:11 is a psalm and can be compared with Pss. 74 and 79.

God gives his grace to the poor (cf. Prov. 3:34). The wise men whose maxims are collected in the Book of Proverbs are greatly concerned with the poor (cf. Prov. 14:20, 21, 31; 16:19; 17:5; 18:23; 19:1, 7, 22; etc.). This concern was already apparent in Deuteronomy (Deut. 15:4-11). We know, moreover, from the Prophets (cf. pp. 109-16, 121) and even from the old "laws" (cf. Exod. 22:20-26), that those who went through life handicapped in some way could always believe that God favored them.

Starting with the seventh century, the idea of the poor, like many other ideas which God had put into the heart of his people, began to be of interest. Sophonias had announced that the people of God, who made up the "Remnant," would be a people of poor men (cf. pp. 136-37). Jeremias himself had personally lived in poverty (cf. p. 151). Thus, the men of Israel were beginning to understand that it was a possible, and even a better, state of life: a state which must be truly lived. The harsh trial of 587 B.C. and of the Exile, commented upon by the Prophets, had contributed greatly to this understanding. The Hebrew language has a whole gamut of words to designate the unfortunate, the needy, the indigent, the weak, the afflicted, the abandoned, the humiliated, the humble. The most characteristic word used, one that was to become the most common, was *anaw* (in the plural, *anawim*). It designates a man who suffers in difficulties or who is undergoing a trial, and, primarily, one who is "bowed" down by adversity and who is under the hand of God.

The notion of "poverty" set aside its original meaning as a comparison of social or economic conditions and assumed a significance which was more personal, more profound, and more religious. The man, or the people, who lived in loneliness or under difficult circumstances, came to consider his unfortunate condition not merely as an inevitable fate which he had to accept or as a trial aimed at his correction, but as a sign and a call to a better state of life, which brought him closer to God.

The *anaw* or poor man knew that his relationship to God, who was ready to help him, was not the result of his own personal value. Deprived of everything, he was also poor in virtue. He was a sinner, and he knew himself to be one. It was, perhaps, through that knowledge that he became aware of his radical poverty: He could not justify himself, he needed to be saved. Ps. 51 expresses these sentiments in an extraordinarily profound manner. The song and the prayer of the *anawim* are especially heard in the psalms.

Discredited in the eyes of others and in his own eyes, the poor man is "humble." [7] Just as he has no possessions, so also he is emptied and deprived of himself. Since he no longer has nor is capable of having confidence in himself, he discovers, as no one else can, that the Lord is his refuge—sufficient and incomparable. He learns from experience, which obviously resembles the experience of the desert, that God loves him.

The "poor" man, then, is he who, in times of affliction and of trial, conscious of his complete helplessness, awaits in hope and with utter docility—and, in the end, with joy and complete gratitude—all of God's desires and actions. Expressing an attitude of mind which fastens itself to God in faith and love, the language of "poverty" unites with the language of the Prophets when they speak of "justice" and "fidelity," and that of the wise men when they write the words "wisdom," "obedience," "piety," and that biblical expression which characterizes the theological mood so well: the "fear of God." [8] Together with all these terms, the traits of soul which God implanted in his people throughout the patient course of history gradually take shape.

[TWO]

THE WORK OF REFORMATION

Darius was able to suppress the insurrection at the beginning of his reign and to establish order in his immense empire, but he met with failures in the West, which were to have an important effect: Greek resistance.

Two worlds confronted one another. Why did the enormous and all-powerful Eastern empire not use its tremendous forces to sweep away the dust of little cities, which were united temporarily only by danger? This, like many other historical facts, is a paradox. Ob-

[7] *Anaw* is translated, in French and English Bibles either by "poor" or by "humble." Here we see that such a translation is both possible and justifiable. *Anawah* may be translated: "poverty," "humility," "the state of one who is afflicted."

[8] On several of these terms, cf. *WG*, pp. 206-13.

viously, the Near East was beginning to doze. Because the stakes were either life or death, tiny Greece, on the other hand, bent all its energies in an enthusiastic but tragic effort, displaying the vigor of its youth and its clear-sightedness in the bitter struggle. It defended a civilization which was ready even then to be given to the whole world.

On the Greek peninsula human genius was attaining its most extraordinary achievements and its most harmonious equilibrium—the "Greek miracle," as it has been called. The names of Polycletus and of Phidias were prominent in the field of art; Aeschylus, Sophocles, and Euripides were the great tragedians; Anaxagoras, Socrates, and, before long, Plato and Aristotle ennobled philosophy; Herodotus and Thucydides shone as historians; and, the very symbol of the time, the gifted statesman, was embodied in Pericles. These names are impressive enough to evoke the grandeur of that fifth Greek century—the great classic century—under the influence of Athens.

We can give only a cursory summary of the principal stages of the Wars of the Medes and of the Persians.[1]

Darius fought at Mount Athos in 492 B.C., and at Marathon in 490 B.C. (First War of the Medes and the Persians). Hostilities began again under his successor, Xerxes (486-465 B.C.). The Athenian general, Themistocles, embodied the resistance and brought about the unity of all of Hellas, which was ratified at the Congress of Corinth in 481 B.C. The Persians succeeded in seizing Athens, but suffered reverses at Salamis and at Plataea in 480 B.C. (Second War of the Medes and the Persians).

These victories excited the Greek feeling of superiority over the barbarians. Athens was always a rival of Sparta; and under Pericles (470-433 B.C.) was at the summit of power and of influence, strongly asserting the greatness of her culture. Pericles signed a thirty-year truce with the other cities of Greece, which were so anarchic by nature. A truce was necessary, because the Persians gave no indication of disarming. After six years of campaigning in Egypt and on the sea against the Greeks between 459 B.C. and 454 B.C. (Third War of the Medes and the Persians), Artaxerxes concluded a peace, which gave to the Greeks the colonies they had held in Asia Minor for two or three centuries.

[1] So-called because the empire founded by Cyrus was known as the empire of "the Medes and the Persians."

This would have put an end to hostilities, except for the internal divisions of Greece. The variances played into the hands of the Persians, who were ever watchful and adroit in using gold to buy treachery. In the unfortunate Peloponnesian War, Sparta and its continental league made an alliance with Darius (425-405 B.C.). A contrary alliance would be made late between Athens and Artaxerxes II (405-358 B.C.). Sparta defeated its rival and seized its leadership. Still later, Sparta's claim to primacy was disputed by Thebes (400-358 B.C.), until, under Philip II and especially Alexander the Great, Macedonia dominated the whole of the peninsula and set out to conquer the world.

Palestine took part in these events only very indirectly—by paying, for example, like other regions of the empire, the contributions and taxes which supported the war budget. In the political geography established by Darius I, Judea formed part of the fifty satrapy, the Transeuphratene, which extended from upper Mesopotamia to the Egyptian frontier, with Damascus as its center. Judea was a tiny territory from 25 to 30 miles wide, much smaller than Samaria, to which it was at first subordinated. This subordination continued almost to the end of the empire, for Idumea, which then extended to the north as far as Lachish and Hebron, afterwards disappeared into the desert of Negeb.

The Judeans had suffered much from Edom, especially at the time the Davidic kingdom crumbled and Jerusalem was sacked. The Edomites had even joined the invaders and the devastators (cf. p. 159). The little Book of Abdias, which may be dated from about the year 500 B.C.,[2] recalls the events. It expresses feelings of indignation against age-old enemies, whose crimes, committed in contempt of the rights of humanity and even of fraternity (cf. vv. 10-11), will be rigorously punished by God. Like other prophecies of threat, this one is a kind of appeal to the justice of God and an act of faith in his victory.

[2] The ancient "confederates" of the Edomites, mentioned in Abd. 7, may be the Nabateans or Nabayot Arabs (cf. Gen. 25:13; Isa. 60:7), who, in the sixth century, won from Edom the mountainous territories to the east of Arabah and the Dead Sea, and created a central refuge for themselves in the strange eagle's nest of Sela, which was to become the curious Nabatean capital of Petra. There may also be an allusion to this drive against Edom in Isa. 63:1-6 and Mal. 1:3. Certain exegetes see two sections in the prophecy of Abdias, one of which would be earlier than the year 500 B.C.

But of which powerful "city," destined for complete ruin, did another Prophet, the author of Isaias 24-27, speak. The chapters are usually called the Apocalypse of Isaias. If it was Babylon, as one is quite generally led to believe, the prophecy was undoubtedly related to the destruction of that city by Xerxes in 485 B.C. The destruction was announced as the prelude to the deliverance of the world and to the coming of Yahweh; the judgment of the world is expressed in terms of cosmic catastrophes (cf. Isa. 24). One psalm celebrates the reign of Yahweh (cf. Isa. 25), and another proclaims peace and salvation from God for those who trust in him (cf. Isa. 26). The prophecy ends on a note of great hope: the regrouping of those dispersed into the city of God (cf. Isa. 27). This manner of speaking of general upheavals (cf. Isa. 24:1-6, 18-23; 25:7-8; 26:21; 27:13) is a direct preparation for the appearance of the genuinely apocalyptic form which would flourish in another two centuries.[3] Furthermore, the message of these enthusiastic poems, which were addressed to a small nation of poor people (cf. Isa. 25:4; 26:6), is certainly a most encouraging one.

Encouragement was needed. The reign of Xerxes, an ostentatious but incompetent monarch, was that of an oppressive tyrant. Men suffered because of it throughout the whole empire. Because Judaism was not ready for such a difficult trial, it would pass through a crisis. Economic difficulties never produce good effects. Excessive taxes cause men to be avaricious and petty: Yahweh noticed this in the offerings and sacrifices that were given to him (cf. Mal. 3:8-10). Moreover, the contrast between the hopes vigorously aroused by Ezechiel and by Deutero-Isaias and the mediocre condition in which Israel vegetated was obvious; and the realization of such a fact, becomes depressing after a time. Suffering and disappointment explain many things: social abuses (cf. Mal. 3:5; Neh. 5:1-5); evasions of the Torah, especially in regard to marriage (cf. Mal. 2:10-16; Esd. 9:2, 12; 10:10-11); failures of the clergy (cf. Mal. 1:7-2:9); and widespread religious torpor and tepidity.

Such are the miseries which Malachias[4] denounces and which

[3] We shall speak further of the apocalyptic form. Isa. 24-27 had a great influence on the Apocalypse of St. John.

[4] This name, which means "my messenger" (cf. Mal. 3:1), may be the name of the Prophet, but is more probably the name given later to a Prophet who has remained anonymous. The date of his work, a little before the reform of Esdras, is practically undisputed.

he wishes to remedy. A great Prophet-writer, who wrote between 470 and 450 B.C., he was a preacher of vigorous words, possessing a great and sensitive heart, and animated by a lively apostolic fervor. He owes much to Deuteronomy. For Malachias, as for Ezechiel and the sacerdotal code with which he too is imbued, religion is centered on the worship at the Temple. Little remains of the Prophet's work and yet he expresses boldly the highest truths: the paternal love of God for his People (cf. Mal. 1:2, 6; 2:10; 3:17); the Covenant (cf. Mal. 2:10; 3:1); the value of the Torah lived in spirit and in truth (cf. Mal. 3:7, 22); the holiness of the priesthood and its mission of teaching (cf. Mal. 2:6-7); conjugal fidelity (cf. Mal. 2:10-16); the value of sacrifice and of worship (cf. Mal. 1:10-14; 3:4), which is sometimes perfectly offered by the pagans; [5] Yahweh's terrible "day" of salvation, prepared by the precursor sent by God (cf. Mal. 3:23-24). Their responsbility for, and the odious character of, the general relaxation were vigorously made known in this way to a people faithless to its God.

Nevertheless, escape from the difficulty required something more than knowledge; it was necessary to act, to inaugurate reforms. Again the initiative came from the Babylonian Gola.

In the year 458 B.C., Esdras, a priest-Scribe whose faith was perfect and who was eminently worthy, set out from Babylonia with a decree from Artaxerxes appointing him the official inspector responsible for affairs of worship and law. Large sums of money, made up partly of grants from the royal government, and partly of collections from the Jewish community of Babylonia, were given to Esdras so that he could proceed to reorganize the cult. He had also, of course, full power to execute the program of reform (cf. Esd. 7-8). It must be noted that, the Persian decision to favor the frontier region and to promote good order there, coming as it did at the moment when a rebellious Egypt had been brought back in line (cf. pp. 187-88), was a highly politic measure.

Esdras saw at once that marriages between Israelites and foreign women were one of the principal causes of the reigning disorder. A general assembly was held at Jerusalem and it was decided to establish a commission charged with examining the licitness of the

[5] Mal. 1:11 seems to think in particular of the perfection of the Zoroastrian cult of Ahura-Mazda, the "god of heaven," for whom bloody sacrifices were no longer carried out.

marriages. Its decrees, however, were not carried out without difficulties. Nevertheless, thanks to the firmness of Esdras, the operation was brought to a satisfactory conclusion (cf. Esd. 9-10).

It had also seemed good to set to work to rebuild the walls of the Holy City, but the enterprise was the object of a false denunciation by the Samaritans. They looked askance at everything that might seem to indicate a desire for autonomy in their regard. They succeeded in their cause: about the year 450 B.C. an order from the king made it necessary to interrupt the work (cf. Esd. 4:7-23). Thus, once again things went wrong, resulting in great damage to the morale of the poorly consolidated Judeans and to the incomplete reform.

Nehemias, a noble Israelite who was an officer at the court of Artaxerxes I, learned of the situation at the end of the year 446 B.C. The king permitted him to leave Babylon, giving him letters patent with which to remedy the destruction of the Holy City (cf. Neh. 1-2). Some months later, Nehemias was at Jerusalem, where he secretly inspected the ruined walls and then made public his intent and his powers. Opposition, covert in the beginning, soon became violent. The reformer, however, cleverly organized both the works and the defense of the works against ambushes and sabotage, leading his people by his noble faith, by his prestige, and by his personal courage. They completed the work in two months (cf. Neh. 3-6).

But, this was not all that had to be done: the community of Israel had to be rebuilt on its traditional basis. Great assemblies were held in the autumn of 445 B.C. The Torah was read publicly by Esdras as a prelude to the renewal of the Covenant, which was celebrated with solemnity (cf. Neh. 8-10). These hours were among the greatest in the history of Israel. Furthermore, the ceremonies, which took place not in the Temple but in a great square in the city, and which consisted essentially in the reading of the Law, may be regarded as instituting, officially and actually, Judaism, properly so-called. From the ceremonies, it received its characteristic form, its consecration, and its spirit. Judaism has not forgotten this fact, and the Jews have always considered Esdras as their second founder, after Moses.

Shortly afterwards, they took a census of the repatriates and decided where each should live. The dedication of the walls was celebrated in grand style. The community was primarily a religious one, and the priesthood was its essential framework. Decrees were carefully enacted with regard to the position of the Levites (cf. Neh. 11-12). In 433 B.C. when his mandate lapsed, Nehemias returned to Babylon (cf. Neh. 13:6).

Some years later, however, in 425 B.C. he learned that the Israelite position had been compromised, and he returned. This time he had extremely strong measures put into effect: the absolute exclusion of strangers from the enclosure of the Temple; the assurance of funds for the Levites, who had abandoned their duties because of lack of resources; a strict obligation to observe the Sabbath; and the rigorous condemnation of marriages with non-Israelites (cf. Neh. 13:7-31). "Purity" of race and "separation" from strangers were then asserted to be indispensable for those who wished to remain faithful to Yahweh thereafter.[6]

Nehemias' end is not known. His work, which is confused with that of Esdras, was authoritative, essential, and definitive: the organization of the Jewish Community—a fraternal and uniquely religious society, a true "church" founded on the principles of the holy Torah of Moses.

The reform, whose stages we have just described, is known to us through the "Memoirs of Esdras and of Nehemias," as the autobiographical sections found today in the biblical books bearing the names of these two men are called. Their writings, then, are contemporary with the reform. A century later, they were inserted, along with a certain number of official documents—edicts, rolls, reports—from the same period, into the great work which is now divided into the Books of Paralipomenon, the Book of Esdras, and the Book of Nehemias.

The memoirs, especially those of Nehemias, rank among the finest pages of narrative literature in the Bible.[7] They are an admirable testimony of faith and of courage, and their value is inestimable for the knowledge they give us of an environment and of an epoch concerning which documents are otherwise lacking.

The book which Esdras read publicly was the Torah, "the Book of the Law of Moses" (cf. Neh. 8:1). It may be thought that it was the Sacerdotal Code. The great work of legislation and of religious in-

[6] From this came the importance given to genealogies. The Samaritans, the Arabs, the Edomites, and other ethnic groups with which the Israelites had to live from then on were of a kindred race, but diluted, not "pure."

[7] The story of David has been compared to them (cf. p. 86).

struction, composed chiefly during the time of the Babylonian Exile (cf. pp. 172-78) but continued later, as has been seen, was completed and, no doubt, organized as a whole during the second half of the fifth century. We have already noted the characteristics, the value, and the decisive importance of this work.

The book read by Esdras was also called the "Law of God" (cf. Neh. 8:8).

From very ancient times, every "Torah" was considered to enjoy divine authority (cf. p. 62). This conviction became more and more firm and clear. The Prophets contributed to it. They were received and heard as messengers from God (cf. p. 119) and their prophecies, even in written form, were preserved as the word of God. So, too, with greater reason, were the teachings and directives, recalled by the Prophets, which expressed the divine Covenant, the relationship, and, so to speak, the dialogue between God and his people.

The revelation of the sacred character of the traditional Scriptures was particularly helped by their reading in prayer meetings, and their recitation or their singing in the liturgical assemblies. The Jews had begun to do this in captivity (cf. p. 163), and they continued the practice in the Jewish communities outside Palestine; Jerusalem acquired the custom beginning at least with Esdras and Nehemias.[8] If the Scriptures enjoyed a privileged position and a genuine cult, it was, first and foremost, because men believed they came from God, but it was also because they were a means of defining, affirming, and of extending the faith. While we cannot yet speak of a "canon" or officially established list of the Sacred Scriptures, it is clear that as early as the fifth century they were read as the "Word of God."

[THREE]

THE GREAT LITERATURE OF THE POETS AND SAGES

The Sacred Texts of tradition were written in Hebrew (pp. 84-85). This very fact would distinguish them from then on, and would place them in a separate category. The Hebrew language, therefore,

[8] Readers of our preceding volume will remember, here, ideas which were forced upon us at the very beginning (*WG*, p. 47).

ceased to be the popular language, and Aramaic became generally predominant.

Aramaic, already spoken for a long time in the wide world known as Aram, which had become consolidated especially during the period between the eleventh and the eighth centuries (cf. pp. 91-92), became an alphabetized language on being brought into contact with the Phoenician region. Hence, since Aramaic supplied a much simpler and more rapid handwriting than the cuneiform, little by little losing its dialectal characteristics in order to become a "common" speech as the language of a shifting and widely disseminated population, it spread very rapidly, especially in Mesopotamia. It was known and written by administrative officers in Assyria and in the Palestinian regions in the eighth century (cf. IV Kgs. 18:26). Wars and banishments, political and commercial dealings continued to contribute to its diffusion. At the end of the seventh century, it had become, besides other local tongues, the language of international exchanges in the entire Near East. Already accepted in the Neo-Babylonian empire, it became, from the time of Cyrus and Darius on, the official language of the Persian empire.

Palestine in the north, more cosmopolitan than the south, was not long in becoming almost completely Aramaicized. The reformers of the fifth century in Judea seem to have made an attempt to maintain the use of Hebrew there (cf. Neh. 13:23-25). But the attempt was made in vain, for Aramaic was gaining widespread acceptance. Hebrew disappeared from everyday life, although it continued to be the sacred language of Israel—not only the language of the Sacred Scriptures which had been collected up to that time and of the liturgy of the Temple, but also the language of the greatest Prophets, sages, and of the Scribes dedicated to the study of the Torah.[1]

If the fourth century, the period to which we have come, has given us very little information about Jewish life and events in Palestine and if, because of this, Israel seems to have retired within itself and to have had no history, still the fact remains that it was a time of great literary fecundity for the little Judean community. Innovations and masterpieces appeared in such profusion that, in one sense, this period may be called the finest era of Judaism.

[1] With a few exceptions (cf. *WG*, p. 165), we have indicated the few biblical passages that were written in Aramaic. For the characteristics of Aramaic, cf. *loc. cit.*

The literature was always highly religious. It was inspired either by the desire to serve the Lord in his worship and in life, or by the active fidelity of the People of God to its great traditions. It was so faithful to the past that it utilized and cited many of the writings of the great prophetic era—and for that very reason lacked their originality and power. But it also bears witness to the deepening of an ever-living tradition which was always moving forward. It reveals the thoughts that haunted intellects, the interior crises that thoughtful and restless souls suffered, and the tendencies of a Judaism which was often sorrowful, although always ardent, profound, and full of hope.

The liturgy, which had profited much from the reforming action of Esdras and Nehemias, had completely regained its importance at Jerusalem. The sacred duties, the daily sacrifices, the numerous sacrifices of thanksgiving, purification, and expiation, and the ceremonies of feasts, which took place in the Temple and in its courts, occupied a substantial and vital place in Israelite life. The Holy City was the heart of Judaism. It was a loadstone which made up the happiness of every worshiper of Yahweh. It was *the* important, and only, center of pilgrimage. It was, above all, loved by the priests who were completely dedicated to the divine service. They studied, perfected, adapted, or renewed the traditional sacramentalism for themselves and for the people of the Lord, making it possible for men to "sanctify" themselves in order that they might approach the Holy God and "serve" him.

The men of the sanctuary did not content themselves with perfecting the details of the ritual within the larger theological panorama of history (cf. pp. 177-78); they also composed songs, hymns, and prayers. No doubt we owe a large part of the present-day psalter to them. Their poems were intended either for choral use in the Temple or for the crowds taking part in certain solmenities and pilgrimages. In the beginning, some were private prayers expressed by fervent souls. Later, however, they were taken up by others and became representative of the community in prayer before the Lord. This alone is enough to show that the psalms cannot be dated with precision and without reservation. Nevertheless, it is true that many psalms were composed during the epoch of the Persian empire.

Like other literary works of the time, the psalms were often indebted to earlier writings, in particular to prophetic literature. The influence of Deutero- and Trito-Isaias can often be discerned in them. Borrowings were made also from the Proverbs and from other wisdom writings (Job, for example), and, of course, from older psalms.[2] The *"style anthologique,"* so characteristic of the literature of that time (cf. p. 170), which undoubtedly is represented best in the psalter. Thus, Psalms 70, 71, 86, 96, 97, 116, 135, 138, 142, 145, and 147 are more or less made up of memorable experiences, or of well-known texts which have been put together.

The Lord, Yahweh, is praised admirably in these poems; hymns magnify his reign: Pss. 93, 96, 97, 98, 99, 100. The collection of praises which later would be called the "Hallel" consisted of Pss. 113 to 118, plus the psalm which was to become the "great Hallel" of the Jewish liturgy, Ps. 136, Ps. 138, and the five psalms at the end of our present psalter, Pss. 146 to 150. Another series, composed of Pss. 120 to 134 was also made a little later on; they are called Songs of Ascent (or gradual canticles, or Song of Degrees) and seem to have been used especially in pilgrimages going up to Jerusalem.[3]

Many psalms are similar to the wisdom writings and are, more or less, collections of *meshalim:* Pss. 32, 34, 37, 62, 101 (see also Pss. 7, 12, 13, 16, 25, 49, 90, 92, 94, 112, 127, and 128). The psalms with historical themes, in which the psalmist meditates on the past of Israel and in which lessons for the present are drawn from sacred history, are more in the line of prophecy; examples of this type are Pss. 68, 78, 105, 106, 114, and 136.

The soul of the People of God—the spirit given to it by God—nowhere is revealed better than in the psalms. They have been called the "literature of the Poor of Yahweh." The authors of these poems were not just close to the more humble classes, they formed part of them. They belonged to those lowly, dispossessed, and despised people who had passed out of the stage of dissatisfaction and found true liberty; whose anxiety had dissolved into complete confidence;

[2] The psalms, too, suffered a certain foreign influence, Babylonian in particular. One will find in the collections of Assyro-Babylonian texts (cf. Dhorme, ch.-F. Jean) interesting comparisons to make. One should, however, recognize that the Israelite inspiration which created the psalms was sufficient in itself, through its power, its originality, its beauty, and its superiority over all other literature of this kind.

[3] Among these last, Ps. 132 is a fine example of reflection on the past (cf. the prophecy by Nathan in II Sam. 7) made actual in new circumstances (reconstruction of the Temple, Messianic hope set on Zorobabel).

and who, more than any others, found themselves in the company of God, enjoying his friendship (cf. pp. 185-86). The psalmists had come through the trial; they had experienced insecurity and the lack of all human support. They had also experienced God as the only perfectly secure refuge, abandoning themselves to his divine "goodness and fidelity"[4]

They had learned to despair of the fidelity of man. Psalms like those concerning the Kingdom of God—Psalm 93, 96 to 100 (cf. also Pss. 29, 46, 47, 48, 68, 76)—express the presentiment of or the waiting for an "end." This "eschatology,"[5] if it does not concern the "end of everything," is a reflection on the end of the world as it is seen and the establishment throughout the universe of a definitive Kingdom of the Lord God. An event of this kind is outside the simple, logical development of history and escapes the determinism of facts: it heralds God's sudden invasion into the theater of the world; it points up his sovereign "judgment" of the universe, and the fact that "salvation" is a work of divine power; it shows the renewal of all things, and the establishment of an era of perfect peace. Cosmic phenomena and wars usually supplied the descriptive elements of these "last times." The Prophets spoke in the same way of the "Day of Yahweh" (cf. pp. 109, 122, 136).

Some still spoke in the same vein. The excellent poet Joel seems to have composed his prophecies toward the end of the fifth century. Essentially, he announced the "Day of Yahweh" by commenting on an invasion of locusts which fell upon the country and devoured the harvest. This scourge, which he describes in striking terms, is a sign of the coming of God, terrible for his enemies but merciful for his people. His coming must be prepared for by penance (cf. Joel 1-2; notice the "liturgy" of 2:17). God restores prosperity to the country, assures Israel of his presence, and announces the pouring out of the prophetic Spirit, not only, as before, upon certain inspired

[4] Mention of the "poor" in Pss. 9:10, 13, 19; 10:17; 22:25; 25:8-10, 16-18; 31:8; 34:7-8, 19; 35:10; 37:11; 40:18; 69:34; 86:1; 109:22-31; 113:7; 119:176; 130:1; 138:6; 140:13; 142:6-7; 145:4; 146:7; 147:6 (this list of citations is obviously not exhaustive).

[5] From the Greek word *eschaton*, that which is "last"; eschatology is the consideration of everything that pertains to the end of time or the end of a time. We became acquainted with it first, from the biblical point of view, in *WG*, pp. 248-50, where a preference, which we believe to be founded on the Bible, was shown for the word "completion."

men, but upon all (cf. Joel 3). Jerusalem will see the hostile mob of "nations" meeting within its walls, but Yahweh will save the Holy City, cleanse it of foreigners, restore happiness to it, and dwell in it (cf. Joel 4).

The "apocalyptic" character of passages like Joel 2:1-11 and 3:3-4 is immediately evident. Also evident is the fact that Joel imitates or makes much use of his predecessors, Amos, Sophonias, Jeremias, and, more especially, Ezechiel.

Written a hundred years later, about 300 B.C., the collection of Zacharias 9-14, called the Deutero-Zacharias, poses many questions and is very hard to interpret. In it the Kingdom of God and the happiness of his People are as the result of punishment of enemies (cf. Zach. 9). Purifications are imposed, and in particular the bad leaders are condemned so that order may be re-established (cf. Zach. 10-13). The salvation of Jerusalem, in the midst of great and bloody devastation, is due to God. Finally, the city will be completely sanctified (cf. Zach. 14). The collection does not seem to be the work of a single author; its style is entirely "anthological," and its form is the same as that of the apocalypses. It foretells the decline of the Persian empire and perhaps even the Macedonian conquest. The hopes of the Chosen People for liberation, victory, peace, and consecration to God are unlimited.

Deutero-Zacharias, whom we have anticipated, in order not to remove him entirely from prophecy and to bring him nearer to Joel, with whom he is similar, is not, properly speaking, a Prophet. For all practical purposes, the era of prophecy ended with the fifth century.

Nevertheless, the collection which would soon be made of the "Twelve (minor) Prophets" (cf. Sir. 49:10) and which has become canonical, also contains a document of a kind we have not yet encountered: the Book of Jonas. A short book, it may be dated from the same time as Joel. It owes its classification to its theme, although it does not represent the actual preaching of a Prophet. From the literary point of view, it is a narrative, an imaginary story,[6] that is quite astonishing, highly animated, charming, extremely subtle, and

[6] Among other reasons showing clearly that it is not a true story, are the artificial character of the composition and the several improbabilities, in particular the sudden and complete conversion of Nineve. Note, however, that in the "canticle" which Jonas is supposed to have sung "in the belly of the fish," the text actually means the "belly of sheol," of a danger of being swallowed up

not without humor. The message is one of exceptional universality: although a Jew may have ideas that are entirely narrow and that do not admit the possibility of anyone being saved besides those who enjoy racial and national membership in Israel, here Yahweh accepts the conversion of the men least likely to be saved in an Israelite vision of salvation—the Ninevites! This is equivalent to saying that the pagans, whoever they may be, can come to the true God. The fact that God loves all men and, consequently, that all men should love one another could not be better implied.

Less daring, the delightful little Book of Ruth,[7] which was composed at about the same time, is also a way of teaching that the community of Israel can and should open itself to strangers. It is the story of a Moabitess who is not only integrated into the People of God by marriage, but who even becomes an ancestress of David, thus providing the Messianic line. Another truth found in the Book of Ruth is that God cares for the humble (he does great things for a poor woman in trouble). We can see also in this very pure pastoral romance, the themes of divine providence and of family piety.

The author of the Book of Jonas uses for his narrative the name of a Prophet from the time of Jeroboam II (IV Kgs. 14:25). The story of Ruth is set "in the time of the Judges." Now, we are about to meet the Canticle of Canticles and Ecclesiasticus, which refer to the history of Solomon; the poem of Job, which takes up a traditional personage (cf. Ezech. 14:14), bringing him to life in the surroundings of the patriarchal era; and the story of Tobias, which purports to be connected with the events of the end of the eighth century. These references to the past are made freely. Thus, we are present at the appearance of a new literary form which came into vogue beginning with the end of the fifth century.

The main point is no longer concerned with history as such, but with the stories connected with a historic past which is made use of rather than faithfully related. The important thing is the teaching which is drawn from the stories. In line with tradition, the intention is to instruct, to illustrate a doctrine, to settle questions, to give examples of conduct, and to provide help in living. The past is so rich

in the water, of a shipwreck; fish, sheol, and danger of death are practically synonyms (compare Ps. 18:5-6, 17-20).

[7] Annexed to the book of Judges, in modern Bibles, because of the period in which the author sets his story. In the ancient tradition and according to the Jewish canon, Ruth forms part of the *Ketubim* (cf. *WG*, p. 24).

that it can be drawn from abundantly.[8] Imagination, however, plays a large part in writings of this kind, as well as the search for means to make their reading both agreeable and captivating.

Although this type of literature seems to be new, it must not be forgotten that in Israel history was never written solely to present history. Remember the Yahwist and the Elohist traditions, the "deuteronomic" history, and the "sacerdotal" history. Prophets, Patriarchs, and wise men did not scruple about making free variations on the basis of historical traditions. These latest works, however, go much further, clearly contributing to the development of a literary form which no longer falls within the properly historical domain.

Writings of this kind are connected with a form, which developed particularly during the rabbinical period, (beginning with the Christian era) and which is called *midrash.* The word comes from the Hebrew verb *darash,* which means *to seek.* The *midrash* is an investigation employed in connection with the study of the traditional texts in Israel. The *midrash* is a reconsideration, a meditation, an explanation of the Sacred Scriptures, a reinterpretation of them in view of new circumstances, and, therefore, a bringing up to date of traditional data. There were *midrashim* of Prophets and of kings existing at an early period (cf. II Par. 13:22; 24:27). The form could not, however, really exist until the Scriptures were fixed, that is, beginning with the fifth century. The reuse of texts since the Exile, which we have discussed so frequently, that bear witness to a new reflection on ancient assertions and to an effort to apply them to present situations, is already in the nature of *midrash.*

Among the People of God, then, men were now sure enough of the past to be able to speak of it freely. That past was regarded as an inexhaustible source of riches. It was not only a mine to be exploited but a history to be relived. Nothing shows better that the Word of God remains alive, that it continually offers itself (and always up to date) to the People of God, and that it ceaselessly calls on men for their reply, that is, for their fidelity and their promise.

In the literary form of edifying stories, the finest example of *midrash* is undoubtedly the Book of Tobias. In it, the author makes use of a tradition which was partly foreign in origin.[9] It is a simple

[8] The Western Middle Ages were to do the same for the Christian past.

[9] There is a connection between the book of Tobias and the wisdom-novel of Ahikar, which was well-known at the time. The *Histoire et Sagesse d'Ahikar*

family story, set flexibly enough in Media between the eighth and the seventh century.[10] The climate, recreated from the literary point of view, is that of the time of the Judges, or, better still, that of the time of the Patriarchs. The book imitates the narratives of Genesis, but one feels the sensitiveness of mature experience and the depths of a proven piety in it. A graceful and touching story, written in the style of the "wisdom" writings, and interspersed with prayers and canticles, it is of great artistic value. It knows how to borrow with ease from all the earlier writings. Unfortunately, we do not know its original text.[11] Nothing remains but versions—Greek, Syriac, and Latin—which are quite divergent. It is dated approximately from the fourth to the third century.

The Book of Tobias reflects the popular piety and the family customs found among the Jews of the postexilic period. Its principal purpose is to emphasize the duty of fidelity to the law of God, especially with regard to charity and love of neighbor. The problem of the suffering of the just man under trial receives a soothing solution. The grandeur of marriage is brought to light admirably. Angels and demons are presented with great simplicity and intervene much more than in the past (Persian influence). Reflections on duties toward the dead, prayer, fasting, and almsgiving are found also. The final canticle belongs to the great prophetic tradition, especially to that of Isaias, in proclaiming the glory of Jerusalem, a light for all nations and a cause of joy for all her children.

The Canticle of Canticles is a marvel of poetry, of passionate tenderness, and of lyricism. It extols the love of man and woman in all its fervor, delicacy, and beauty, with its tensions and anxieties, in its purity and in its strength. Nevertheless, a whole tradition, both Jewish and Christian, believes that the Canticle of Canticles does not concern itself with human love: following Osee, Jeremias, Ezechiel, the Deutero- and Trito-Isaias, it interprets the short lyric drama as the espousals of Yahweh and Israel (cf. p. 121), as the appeals addressed by God to his people and the delay of his people in responding to supreme love. An allegorical interpretation is not compulsory,

l'Assyrien has been translated from the Syriac into French by Fr. Nau (Letouzey et Ané, 1909). Tobias is the cousin of Ahikar (cf. Tob. 1:22; 2:10; 11:18; 14:10).

[10] The historical information in chapters 1 and 14 in particular is given freely.

[11] Some Hebrew and Aramaic fragments of the book were, however, recently discovered in the now famous caves of Qumran, near the Dead Sea.

however, for it is not suggested by the text. Furthermore, one need not choose, as one may often wish to do, between "divine" love and "profane" love: the love of man and woman is sacred, born of God. How fortunate that, after the Prophets who celebrated the "conjugal" alliance between Yahweh and Israel, another inspired singer, resuming the link with the Yahwist tradition (cf. Gen. 2:18-25) and profiting by the clarifications of the wise men (against false loves), should have magnified the mutual love which God puts into the hearts of man and woman.

The Canticle is short. Another poem from that period, the Book of Job (which, undoubtedly, can be dated from the first half of the fourth century) is as comprehensive as anyone could wish and incomparable in its literary luster. Between a prologue in prose, written in the style of the ancient narratives, and a brief epilogue, also in prose, which form the setting, large sections of discourse in verse make up the debate on "wisdom" between Job and, first, his three friends, then a fourth, and finally God. A work of striking genius, unique in the Bible, the Book of Job is classed among the greatest of universal literature. Its style is extremely varied, brilliant, and brisk; parts, like the first discourses of Job (cf. Job 3; 6-7; 9-10) or those of Yahweh (cf. Job 38-41), to cite only a few examples, reveal the finest artistic style: they sparkle with images and are animated by a vigorous inspiration. The vocabulary is like that used by sapiential writers, with numerous memories of things past and reworkings of texts (Isaias, Jeremias, Proverbs, Psalms). In addition, the author is a highly cultivated man in full possession of a rich personal style; and he has proven himself capable of constructing a poetic drama of unusual scope.

The foundation of the debate bears on "wisdom" itself and gives testimony to the ferment of minds in an Israel which was always seeking, always restless—restless for God. Among the wise men, selected to portray types, who is right? The defenders of the traditionally received theses, who follow Deuteronomy and Proverbs, or the man who, having had experience, finds them insufficient and gropes his way toward solutions still unknown? The length of the discourses is, as it were, a practical initiation into the experience of Job. The theoretical or moralizing replies appear ineffective and even painful as they are applied to a living man whose innermost being is laid bare, who is twisted by his suffering, and who is tortured by the unreasonableness of his position. Is the justice of God not involved? Like

Habacuc (cf. pp. 146-47), Job appeals to God. God does not answer the questions asked, rather he calls upon Job, giving him the proper perspective; that is, he draws him out of the boundaries within which suffering has imprisoned his thought, in order to place him in a more important but also a simpler reality, one which he should examine first. Job regains the silence of adoration and of acceptance, of humility and abandonment. The conclusion, then, is an appeal to acquiescence: "The just man, because of his faith, shall live" (Hab. 2:4), by a radical resignation and a total abandonment of himself to God. This is essentially *anawah* (cf. pp. 185-86). Job is the "poor man" at the stage of theological reflection, at the level of a wisdom which breaks all barriers in order to express itself before God; in order to try to hear and to see God (cf. Job 42:4-5).

The courage of the Book of Job lies in its having brought up a serious question and having rejected easy answers. Job is also the book of a living experience, with all its attendant tensions, clashes, and emotions.

Although it may perhaps belong to a century or a century and a half later, another wisdom writing can appropriately be compared with Job. This is the Book of Ecclesiastes (in Hebrew, *Qoheleth;* he who calls in order to gather together," the "teacher-lecturer"). The author of this book, however, is even less a conformist than the author of Job; hence, his writing is more astonishing.

He sees the problem of human life under opposite conditions: the insufficiency and deceptive character of an existence which is filled with all that man can desire, all that is considered agreeable, enriching, and fortunate. This problem is pushed to the ultimate limits of philosophical reflection. For the degree of criticism attained by the *Qoheleth* is one of philosophical thought, the only place that such thinking is expressed in biblical tradition. Hebrew, especially the late and Aramaicized Hebrew of the time, did not lend itself to abstract expression. Hence, the author of Ecclesiastes, who writes in rhythmic prose interspersed with sentences in verse, lacks enthusiasm. He compensates for the indigence of his language, however, by great simplicity, by the sly malice of a free spirit fond of paradox, by the vitality of well-coined and unexpected formulas, and by the balance and scholarly progression of the whole work.

Such a curious work can neither be presented nor analyzed without first being read over and over. It is a critique that puts everything in its place: happiness, knowledge, work, idleness, wealth, poverty, pleasure, occupations, society, solitude, worship, virtue, misconduct, etc. Undoubtedly, the first purpose of the *Qoheleth* is not to allow man to deceive himself. Experiences honestly acknowledged contradict views that are overreassuring, precautious, or very short-sighted. The *Qoheleth* is a true man, one strong enough to reject all illusions; but if he takes a cautious view of this narrow life, it is because he knows that man cannot be satisfied with it, that he is not attuned to this world only. The means must not be taken for the end, that is, this world must not be taken for something it is not. If the best, in any case the first, approach to the solution of a problem is to state its terms correctly, the *Qoheleth* enunciates the problem of the destiny of man as no one else had ever done. He thrashes it out, and places his questions, especially those in regard to death, eternity, and recompense—in short, on the reason for man's existence and the final meaning of his life—before God with the audacity of faith itself. Furthermore, this wise man, who did not mean to be "edifying" but who, in practice, is, consents with simple courage and without overestimating himself in any way to the life which God proposes for men and to his laws.

Job and Ecclesiastes, along with Proverbs and the Psalms, provide a whole documentary on their time, on their contemporaries, and on their environment.[12] Through them an interesting picture of the Jewish society of the time could be drawn, the psychology of the types of men who predominated or attracted attention in that society could be studied, and currents of thought could be uncovered. Even though we may know very little about the events that took place in Palestine during the course of the fourth and third centuries, at least the writings of the wise men enable us to know the Judaism of that time quite well, from within, so to speak, even to its deepest spirit.

[FOUR]

ISRAELITE LIFE FROM THE FOURTH TO THE THIRD CENTURIES | Judea had succeeded, after repeated appeals to the central government, in making itself politically independent of

[12] From Job's justification of himself, for example, in Job 29-31, we can draw many observations.

Samaria (cf. p. 188). From that point onward, it formed a distinct territory enjoying equality with the other subdivisions of the fifth satrapy, within which it was included administratively.

Nehemias seems to have been succeeded in the office of governor at Jerusalem by a man named Bagoar. Later, the juridical importance of the high priest took first place, and he was made responsible for public order to the royal agents. Thus, the regime developed into a purely ecclesiastical system, and Israel became a hierocracy. A sacerdotal assembly assisted the high priest with religious and juridical matters. In this way, the priests continued to fulfill their traditional functions as described in Deut. 17:8-12: they decided new or doubtful cases; they proclaimed the authority of their decisions as *toroth;* and they annulled earlier decisions when necessary (cf. II Par. 19:8-11). In this way the Law, possessing the capacity to reform and to rejuvenate itself, always remained alive.

The priesthood came from the family which, among the descendants of Aaron, was shown favor: the sons of Sadoc (cf. Ezech. 40:46; 43:19; 44:15; cf. II Sam. 8:17; III Kgs. 2:27, 35). By acquiring a quasi-political authority, however, it ran the risks accompanying such a development—the spirit of riches and of domination—to the detriment of the value and fervor of religion; hence, it drew down upon itself serious reproaches (cf. Mal. 1-2; Zach. 11:8; 14:21; Neh. 13:29-30). One cannot, however, be satisfied with this negative viewpoint; for thanks to the clergy, the indispensable structure of Judaism, the grandeur of its worship, and the conservation of its best traditions, were maintained.

Although it may be necessary to skip down to the year 300 B.C. (if not farther), for the date of its composition, the Book of Chronicles [I and II Paralipomenon] should be cited here as showing the characteristic notions of the sacerdotal society and, in a broader way, of representing ideas that were quite current in the period to which we have come.

The Book of Chronicles is a great work of *midrashic* history, which at first was one with the Books of Esdras and of Nehemias (cf. p. 192). The author, no doubt a Levite, was a disciple of these reformers. He wrote to commemorate their work and perhaps to excite or to back a similar effort at a time when the question of loyalties was coming up again.

His work makes use of the Books of Genesis and of Numbers, of

Samuel and of Kings, as well as of many writings not preserved in any other form, but which relate to the kings [1] or come from the Prophets,[2] family documents such as genealogies or official records, and, above all, the archives of the Temple. The Chronicler reuses his sources extensively and often contents himself with recopying texts.[3] His work, which incorporates ancient materials (sometimes large sections) and postexilic documents received from excellent sources, is scholarly and serious. Nevertheless, his purpose is not to write a history; and far from being a simple repetition or a merely supplementary re-presentation of an already written history, the Book of Paralipomenon simultaneously reveals theological progress, the mentality of an environment, and the intentions of the author.

To understand the originality of the work, we need only consider the passages which are not found in the Books of Samuel and of Kings (such as I Par. 1-9; 12; 15-16; 22-29, for example), or compare the presentation of the reigns in Juda in the Books of Kings with that found in II Par. 13-26. It can be seen at once that if the "Earlier Prophets" were inspired by a prophetic and deuteronomic spirit, Paralipomenon, besides being still very sympathetic to Deuteronomy and to its atmosphere of "joy before Yahweh," is also composed of a "sacerdotal" mentality, as the expression is used properly of the work "P," of which it is manifestly the heir.

David is the central figure of the work. Although a restoration of the monarchy was then inconceivable, the author seems unable to stop at a purely sacerdotal conception of Israel. Perhaps he thinks that the authority of the Sadocites is only temporary. In any case, for him the Plan of God leads normally to a kingdom, to the Messianic and eschatological kingdom of the Prophets.

The history of David is prefaced by the most extensive of the genealogies (cf. I Par. 1-9). Beginning with Adam, the tribes of

[1] Cf. I Par. 9:1; 27:24; II Par. 16:11; 20:34; 24:27; 25:26; 27:7; 28:26; 32:32; 33:18; 35:27; 36:8.

[2] Cf. I Par. 29:29; II Par. 9:29; 12:15; 13:22; 20:34; 26:22; 32:32; 33:19; 35:25.

[3] In Esdras, he went so far as to insert Aramaic documents without translating them into Hebrew: cf. Esd. 4:8-6:18. One may note, in addition, certain modifications of style and vocabulary (an obvious tendency to schematization and amplification), and some liberty with regard to the documentation which serves him as a basis: compare I Par. 18:7 and II Sam. 8:18; I Par. 20:5 and II Sam. 21:19; I Par. 21:1, 25 and II Sam. 24:1, 24; II Par. 8:1 and III Kgs. 9:10.

Juda are put at the head, and along with the tribes of Levi, which are put in the center, hold the principal place. The historical vision of Paralipomenon is universalist taking into account the non-Israelite peoples. No doubt these lists, which mean little to the modern reader (although they are expressive of the bonds which unite all men, presenting as they do a picture of their solidarity), evoked, for the author and his contemporaries, the living and complex condition of the Israel they knew. Hence, God's Covenant with the Patriarchs [4] and with David (cf. II Par. 13:5) had, for the author of Paralipomenon, the open character that prophecy perceived in it.

The chronicler traces back the cultic and levitical institutions (cf. I Par. 22-29) to David, who was considered the second lawgiver after Moses. These institutions are obviously his chief concern. Nothing relating to the persons and things connected with the Temple of Jerusalem and with the sacred service is overlooked. No better way could be found to show the hierocratic and liturgical ideal of post-exilic Judaism, or to justify the status and privileges of the Levites.[5] The reforms of Ezechias and of Josias (cf. II Par. 29-31; 34-35) are described at length and lovingly (compare also: II Par. 23 with IV Kgs. 11; II Par. 26:16-23 with IV Kgs. 15:8).

The chronicler, then, creates a synthesis of prophetic views and Levitical ideas. He sees Israel both as a theocratic monarchy and as an ecclesiastical community. Paralipomenon is many things: a bold commentary on the Sacred Scriptures; a meditation on the history of the People of God with a view to bringing certain aspects of it up to date for the needs of the times; a history written in order to place institutions in their historical setting (like "P"), and to show their Messianic meaning; and a very fine example of *midrash.*

Paralipomenon reveals to us the existence of an entire historical or documentary literature which has disappeared. Undoubtedly, the same, is true of other works, for example, poems, songs, and the "wisdom" writings. Nevertheless, the psalms we know are further valuable evidences of postexilic Judaism. They continue to express the piety of the priests and of the people, to make audible the voice,

[4] More than thirty times Yahweh is called the "God of our fathers."

[5] In the style of Ezechiel, the chronicler wishes to establish the distinction between the priests and the Levites, and to assert the rights of the latter. The question posed by this distinction, ignored by the Book of Kings and by Deuteronomy (in which one speaks of "Levitic-priests") is too difficult to be considered here.

charged with emotion, of the "poor of Yahweh," and to propagate the spirit of the Prophets and the wise men, all the while presenting a true picture of social life. The Book of Paralipomenon cites some of them (cf. I Par. 6:41-42; II Par. 16:8-36). However, the writings of the wise men, both of those we have met and of those we will soon encounter (Sir., Wisd.), especially enable us to understand this period to some extent.

The wise men were open-minded men, of broad culture, who protected human values. With them, a new dimension in the thought of Israel becomes evident. Their "wisdom" seems to speak more of justice and of rights than of history and of revelation; it takes more interest in the current life of men than in the Hebrew past. They judge more according to the sentiments of a conscience enlightened by faith than according to the prescriptions of a ritual. They do not draw inspiration from an intransigent mysticism; rather they propose a realistic and moderate morality. They call God, not so much Yahweh-Sabaoth (Lord of Armies), but rather the Creator of all things. Nevertheless, they did not break with tradition in any way; it shows its close relationship to the ancient Scriptures, which it uses and meditates on continually. Still, the wise men were convinced that their wisdom proceeds (although by a different road and under a different form) from the Spirit which inspired the Law and the Prophets. In practice, they even go so far as to identify their wisdom with the Torah (cf., for instance, Pss. 1; 19; 119) and to use the oratorical, exhortatory, and public language of the Prophets (cf. Prov. 1:20-21; 8:1-6). From now on, however, wisdom no longer addresses itself solely to Israel, for it does not wish to be a privilege jealously preserved for a closed community; rather, it desires to be a good propagated as widely as possible. Because of Israel's old connections with the wisdoms of the Ancient Near East, it already possessed a tendency toward universalism which the requirements of life with foreigners now propose to it as a program. Hence, Israel has become a missionary.

The Israelites were, in fact, in contact everywhere with non-Israelites and were even often subject to them politically. Many foreigners resided in Palestine. More important, more and more Israelites lived in foreign countries. Henceforth, in speaking of Israel, it will be necessary to look beyond the frontiers of little Judea.

Of course, the Diaspora, or dissemination, does not date only from the fourth century. Transplantations and emigrations had taken place as early as the royal period, notably at the time of the destruction of the kingdom of Samaria. Obviously, the great Babylonian deportations which took place the beginning of the sixth century played a more decisive part, for many of the exiles never returned (cf. pp. 161, 179). The regions in which the presence of the Jews can be noted at an early date are Babylonia, Syria, the Mediterranean coast, and Egypt. During the time of the Persian Empire, which gave the Near East two centuries of comparative peace and important means of communication, the Jews multiplied considerably. They learned quickly to adapt themselves, resolutely confronting coexistence "in the midst of the nations."

They did not follow similar patterns of life in the various places in which they settled, nor did they always develop at the same pace. Yet, in the different places where they lived, one can see the outline of an organization into little communities. Gathered around the "elders" or heads of families, priests, and Scribes, specialists in the knowledge of the Sacred Books,[6] they held regular meetings in secluded places or in houses. There they prayed together or acquainted themselves with the Law of God, learning to remain faithful to him. The "synagogues," essentially houses of prayer and of instruction, had their origin in these meetings. The existence of the synagogues will be discussed further when the Hellenistic period is treated.

Jerusalem, however, was not forgotten. The Israelites of the Diaspora paid tithes regularly to the clergy of the House of God. They sent offerings to be sacrificed at the One Altar. Insofar as possible, they made pilgrimages to the Abode of Yahweh on his Holy Mountain (cf. the Gradual Psalms, p. 196). Many kept a nostalgic desire for Sion in their hearts, and envied the fortune of their brethren who dwelt in the Holy Land. Communications were maintained by letters sent back and forth.

Nevertheless, they had to learn how to live far away from the Temple, doing without the sacrificial liturgy which expressed the religion of Yahweh. Fortunately, the Torah was the living witness of Yahweh's religioin. Hence, reading from the Torah assured that the dispersed communities would retain a surprisingly religious vitality.

[6] One function is specified, that of the *sopher*, the "man of the book," one who is learned in scriptures, the *grammate* (cf. I Par. 27:32; Esd. 7:6, 11; Neh. 8:1).

Although they found themselves in pagan environments[7] and in conditions that were sometimes highly "secular," the Israelites as a whole remained true to their faith. The spiritual life of a great many was even intensified because of their reaction against the influences of their surrounding. Consequently, fraternal life among the Jews became closer and more profound, and at the same time great personal piety developed.[8] However, they ran the risk of withdrawing again into themselves and of excluding others.

Obviously, the life of Israel at Jerusalem and in the Diaspora should not be oversimplified. Although the people more and more showed itself to be exceptional, it was still composed of men—of poor men. Social injustices, especially in Judea, had not disappeared as if by magic. Much is said concerning the "evildoers" and the "impious" in the writings of the wise men, and the complaints of the *anawim* show how harsh their oppressors could be. With regard to religious observance, some, as is usually the case, were fervent, while others, who could not always work up enthusiasm or anxiety, must be considered as merely "practicing" Jews. Tensions are inevitable between the strict and the complaisant, between traditionalists and men of a new era. A time was approaching when the "world" and its requirements would give rise in Israel to the most serious problems and to an extreme crisis.

[7] Cf. p. 161, note 4, p. 162, note 5. The stories of Queen Esther and of Daniel, the page, were inspired by realities that had been lived.

[8] This is extremely evident in reading the Book of Tobias.

9 Facing a New World

[ONE]

ALEXANDER AND THE HELLENIZATION OF THE ORIENT | The reign of Artaxerxes II lacked energy and suffered from disorder. Egypt had freed herself from Persian rule. Certain satrapies rebelled. The government of Artaxerxes III (358-338 B.C.) was stronger: Egypt was retaken and Syria subjected, and the Persians held their positions firmly against the Greeks. A change took place after the accession of Darius III (338-330 B.C.).

The kingdom of Macedonia had intruded itself upon the Greek republic at a time when internal rivalries were dissipating Greek strength. After his victory at Chaeronea in 338 B.C., Philip II (359-336 B.C.) made himself master of the whole Greek peninsula, and he was planning to conquer the Eastern peoples when he was assassinated.

His son, Alexander the Great (336-323 B.C.), would carry out his program by conquering the world. Everyone is familiar with Alexander's extraordinary career; it was an adventure more wonderful than a dream, and a romance that was truly lived. He progressed from victory to victory: Granicus in 334 B.C.; Issus in 333 B.C.; Tyre in 332 B.C.; Palestine surrendered without a struggle; Egypt was annexed and Alexandria founded; victory over Arbela in 331 B.C.; the capture of Babylon, Susa, Persepolis, and Ecbatana in 330 B.C. (death of Darius III); and the expedition to the delta of the Indus in 325 B.C. Two years later, Alexander died of malaria in Babylon at the age of thirty-three, leaving behind him a Persia which had suddenly become Greek, and the beginnings of the important work of civilization.[1]

Alexander was a man of universal genius. As a conqueror he was kindly, humanistic, and interested in cultural development. He had set himself the task of raising the standard of living of all men and

[1] For a more complete study of Alexander the Great, cf. William W. Tarn, *Alexander the Great* (Columbia University Press, 1948).

of uniting them by making them participants in Greek culture. He knew, however, that the world unity which he dreamed of creating could only be realized if respect were shown for local differences and for foreign courage from the very beginning. Keenly aware of the fascinating grandeurs of the Ancient Near East, he did not wish them to be annihilated, but rather assimilated.

Undoubtedly, certain influences had already come into play between the Greek peninsula and the Mediterranean Near East, especially since the Greeks had acquired a superiority in the Egyptian Delta with which the pharaohs had to reckon (cf. p. 133). Nevertheless, Greece had never been anything but a small country. If one considers the general development of the world as it was then known, its cultural leadership was of recent date. Previously, as far as the Near East was concerned, Greece had been chiefly a beneficiary. Having reached the summit of its success in the fifth century, it had become too proud and too jealous of its achievements to consider the "barbarians" capable of receiving anything from it. This feeling of superiority was to be a further obstacle to the uniting of the two worlds.

These facts point up the greatness of Alexander's intelligence, audacity, and skill. In spite of the shortness of his life, he was able to start a movement throughout the entire Near East which brought about profound changes, making a new world of it. In fact, only from the time of the Macedonian conquest on can Hellenization be spoken of in the sense of Greek culture penetrating the Oriental World, even to the systematic penetration of every thought and action of men's lives. The successors of Alexander followed the same program, but they were not able always to carry it out with the same flexibility or with the same spirit of benevolence.

The Greek language was to be one of the most efficacious means, of bringing about the Hellenization of the world. Greek was the most beautiful and the most perfect language that had yet been invented. It was a creation of reason and of proportion, embodying the grace and the harmony, the delicacy and the balance which characterized the Greek spirit itself. Born a little after Aramaic, Greek, like it, came from the Phoenician alphabet. It developed rapidly and in an original way, giving rise to a variety of dialects, among which Attic finally prevailed.

Beginning with Alexander and continuing under his successors,

Greek spread rapidly throughout the Near East, putting an end to the international career of Aramaic. The latter, however, did not disappear completely (especially not in Palestine, where an effort was made to resist Hellenism by keeping Aramaic alive). The Greek adopted by the entire civilized world was no longer the Attic dialect; rather, it was an evolved form of Attic, although less polished and mixed with other dialectal elements, especially Ionic. According to the normal laws of linguistic development, this Greek, on becoming popularized, lost its clarity and its stability, and tended to do away with the complexities and the difficulties of the classic tongue.[2] In calling it the *koine,* or "common," language, men recognized that it had a somewhat universal character, and that it possessed the power of becoming, quite simply, the universal language. It was adapted to the requirements of everyday life, and was used easily for daily intercourse and for business. Because it was the language of both the common people and of cosmopolitan circles, Greek finally reached to the very frontiers of the empire.

The establishment of cities patterned after Greek cities was also a powerful transforming agent in the Near East. The cultural penetration could not have taken place unless the centers of the new civilization multiplied. Thenceforth, then, there would be not only Athens, but also Antioch-on-the-Orontes and Seleucia-on-the-Tigris, Pella and Rhodes, Ptolemais and, primarily, Alexandria. Other centers would appear later, especially under the Seleucids. These foundations also answered the needs of those living in colonies, for the Greek did not feel at home and could not live except in a *polis.*

Endowed with the privileges and the franchises that were enjoyed by the cities of the metropolitan peninsula, the Greek cities of the Near East, some of which arose and developed with astonishing rapidity, offered many facilities for living and exercised a strong attraction. Because of their attractiveness, they brought together different races and cultures. Naturally, Greek pride was opposed to assimilation; the Greek citizen's intention was to maintain his superiority by discrimination and by preserving a special status. Life and its complexities, however, and the practical requirements of politics and of the economy, were continually opening a breach in

[2] On the principal characteristics of this common Greek of the Hellenistic epoch, cf. *WG,* p. 166 f.

this basic position. Many of the people of the Near East were to attain positions similar in almost every way to those of the Greeks, and were in the end to obtain even juridical citizenship.

Thanks to a common language and to coexistence in the urban areas, intellectual and cultural influences were capable of making themselves felt, although this would take time, if indeed a true osmosis was even possible. For this was an encounter between profoundly different age-old and strongly marked mentalities, of psychologies, and of states of balance, all profoundly different. Recall the discussion of Semitic thought (pp. 19-32; cf. also, *WG*, pp. 158-62). Could it be reduced to the Greek spirit? Had it enough affinities for the love of logical reason, of beauty and of order, of abstract and impersonal knowledge, which the Greeks cultivated? The Near East had never been satisfied with humanism, because instinctively it perceived humanism's essential shortcomings. Could it, then, be coaxed by philosophical doctrines?

Alexander, the pupil of Aristotle, marched toward the East accompanied by philosophers and scholars, with the intention no doubt of pursuing his conquest also in the domain of thought. With Greek colonization, the philosophies inevitably spread. Those of the third and fourth centuries represented a development of the thought of the preceding period (cf. p. 187): they became rationalistic in the extreme, and were, above all, preoccupied with morals. A delicate balance of this kind was sought by the Epicureans, the asocial asceticism of the Cynics, the volutarism of the Stoics, and the skepticism of the Pyrrhonists. Naturally, the various schools opposed and argued with one another. It cannot be denied that new and valuable ideas were born in this way, but there was little consistency and little security in systems which were tainted with relativism and subjectivism. Indeed, some of them refused to admit any value to knowledge and any meaning to life. Although Greek thought was rarely atheistic in theory, in practice it was completely atheistic. It distrusted the gods and meant to get along without them.

The Near East would not be a pupil in the school of Greek thought. It possessed something better by reason of its immemorial customs, its powerful traditions, its solidly rooted laws, and especially its metaphysics, which was unknown to the brilliant but often shortsighted Greek reason. Attempts were made, especially by Jews, to unite the two forms of thought—Greek rationalism and the religious metaphysics of the Near East. Evidence of these attempts can be found in the Judaeo-Hellenic teachings, of which Aristobulus in the second century and Philo in the second are the best-known representatives. These, however, were the attempts of intellectuals, chiefly in Alexandrine Egypt. From a more general viewpoint, Hellenism did not invade the Near East through philosophy. Still less did it make inroads through its religion: the Near East had nothing to gain from the civic, artificial, rudimentary, and hollow devotions of a Greece which did not know how to answer the most profound anxieties of the human heart.

Hellenism made greater advances by means of its externally visible accomplishments—buildings and art; morals and civic life; education; and, above all, entertainments, the theater, and sports, which were Greek specialties. Habits and exterior ways of life are never changed in vain; little by little, men conform to the changes in a deeper manner. A harmonization and a leveling off took place, which tended to lower the barriers of ethnic groups, putting men on the same level and in communication with one another, and transforming the peoples of the Near East into the new citizens of the modern world.

Understandably, acceptance or rejection of the externals of the new civilization became a current problem, capable of receiving various solutions. It was a serious problem, too, for the new civilization symbolized and carried with it a state of mind and particular tendencies. Each aspect of the new civilization was closely related to every other aspect. It called for fundamental choices, even if this fact was not immediately apparent. As an aid in thinking on this subject, consider the position, for example, of a young Israelite. He was brought up in a sound traditionalism, but a traditionalism that was stubbornly closed to every exterior influence and that was rooted in archaic, outworn practices, which constantly hindered natural development. When such a man discovered, quite close at hand and offering itself to him, a pleasant and easy manner of living, full of truly human values, flexible and sanguine, immediately sociable, intelligible, and practical, a crisis had to arise.

Nevertheless, if we compare the Hellenization of the East with the Romanization of Europe in the first centuries of the Christian era, we can see that the Latinization of the West was comparatively easy and conclusive, whereas the East was never to show itself either readily or completely or permanently receptive to Greek culture.

Consequently, the Eastern world would some day, during the Roman period, reaffirm its own characteristics and its natural tendencies, finally rejecting Greek civilization. It would not do so, however, without having benefited from contact with Greek civilization. Nor would it do so without having infused into that civilization, in return, some of its own religious dynamism and without having awakened in the Greek breast a sensitivity to a spiritual world of which it was unaware. Interaction of this kind would not, however, always be simple or peaceful. We have not yet come to the period when interaction between the two cultures began. The course events would take depended largely on those who presided over the destinies of the peoples. For example, the rather easygoing manner of governing which characterized the Ptolemies in Egypt was quite different from the more systematic Hellenizing of the Seleucids. History was to give Palestine, that eternal pawn of international policy and strife, first to Egypt and later to the Seleucids. Hence, even though all of the Near Eastern peoples did not passively undergo penetration by the Greek spirit and ways, Judaism was the bastion par excellence of the resistance, singularly obstinate and finally irreducible.

After the death of Alexander, his empire was divided between his generals (*diadochi,* or "heirs"). Phrygia was given to Antigonus; Assyria and Babylonia to Seleucus; and Egypt to Ptolemy; while Macedonia was given to Cassander, and Thrace to Lysimachus.

From 323 B.C. to 301 B.C. more than twenty years of disputes and wars were carried on between these competitors. Antigonus and his son, Demetrius Poliorcetes, prevailed temporarily over Seleucus and Ptolemy in the Near East, but these two united to triumph in the end (Ipsus, 301 B.C.). Then, only two Eastern kingdoms remained, and they were vowed to perpetual rivalry.

The ancient satrapy of Syria was divided into two parts. Seleucid Syria was attached to the northern kingdom (Antioch was founded in 300 B.C.), and Coele-Syria, to which Judea belonged, was subjected to the Ptolemies. During the Egyptian tenure, which was tolerant and comparatively tranquil, life was not too difficult. Greek culture was not introduced in an authoritarian manner; nevertheless, it penetrated, naturally enough, by force of circumstances, with the Jews showing themselves more resistant than the rest. The Israelite community took little part in politics and was not yet subject to the restraints that were imposed upon it after its transference to the Antiochians. Therefore, it was able to carry on the work of plumbing its own depths, which was so characteristic of postexilic Judaism.

Judaism, at this time, spread with extraordinary rapidity throughout the whole Near East and to the shores of the Mediterranean. Such an expansion was made necessary by virtue of the considerable numerical increase of the Jews, an exceptionally prolific race. Israel, however, did not owe its development to biological vitality alone. The number of its adherents of foreign origin also increased greatly. The religion of Yahweh, infinitely superior to all the mythologies, was attractive, and its representatives were now traveling throughout the world: preachers and propagandists were working to win sympathy and to secure conversions [3]; Jewish colonists testified to their faith by the mere fact of their existence; and many merchants carried it throughout a world in which communications were becoming more perfect. Israel had become a missionary, whose ardor and ingenuity produced surprising results.

Most of the Jews and proselytes [4] of the Diaspora spoke the Greek of the *koine*. Communications and exchanges with foreigners were greatly facilitated by this fact, but the Jews had ceased to know Hebrew and Aramaic. Consequently, they ran the risk of losing contact with the Sacred Scriptures, which were preserved only in the ancestral language, and which inspired and regulated their whole religious life. They came to realize this early, especially in Egypt. A large number of Jews settled in Alexandria, a great modern city, founded by Alexander and built principally under Ptolemy II, which was now the greatest center of Hellenistic culture. They constituted two-fifths of a population that exceeded 500,000. Their flourishing colony obtained special privileges, as well as real autonomy, from the Ptolemies. Such a community could not persevere in the faith

[3] We have no knowledge of any other ancient religion which sought, systematically, to spread outside the natural environment of its worshipers and to recruit new members. Israel inaugurated, in history, and largely through its own efforts, the evangelical mission, the apostolic conquest, which was to become among Christians the diffusion of their "good tidings."

[4] The word "proselyte," which comes from a verb meaning "to come toward," seems to have been invented by the Seventy to designate a foreigner who lived in the country; it came to designate the non-Jew converted to the Jewish religion (and in modern language every new convert to a faith or to a doctrine).

and live in the tradition if its members were unable to understand the texts read at the hours of prayer and during the explanation of the Sacred Books.

Thus, the version of the Scriptures called the Septuagint[5] came into existence at Alexandria. The translation, a work of pioneers, was a gigantic undertaking. The feat appears even more novel and daring when one considers that the translation was made from a Semitic language into a language which had an entirely different spirit and mode of expression. The completion of the work was an event of considerable importance in the history of antiquity. From the religious point of view, its consequences were to be immense. The Greek Bible would quickly become the world-wide vehicle of the Revelation given to Israel.

The work was not accomplished at a single stroke. The Greek Pentateuch seems to go back to the time of Ptolemy II Philadelphus (284-247 B.C.), that is, to about 250 B.C. The other translations followed little by little, which accounts for certain differences in literary value. The Pentateuch enjoys the best translation. The Earlier Prophets are almost equally well translated, but the translation of the Prophet-Writers is of lesser quality. The version of the poetic and sapiential writings, is rather poorly done.

In the meantime, some of the Israelite writings (which we shall soon encounter) were being composed directly in Greek. The Hellenized Jews read them as they would read the traditional Scriptures, and indeed completed their collection of the Sacred Writings in this way. The Jews of Palestine, however, acknowledged only the books that were written in Hebrew. This is the origin of the distinction between a somewhat abridged list and a somewhat longer list of inspired books—the origin of the question that would arise one day under the title, the "Deuterocanonical Books" (cf. *WG*, pp. 65-67.

The entire work called the Septuagint is believed to have been almost complete at the end of the second century.

Among the later writings, which were added to the collection of the Holy Books during the Graeco-Egyptian period, is a work commonly called the Wisdom of ben Sirach or of the Siracid (cf.

[5] This designation (called also the *Septante*) comes from the legend contained in the *Letter of Aristeus,* attributing the accomplishment of the work to seventy translators. It is often abbreviated in writing: the LXX.

Sir. 50:27; 51:30), afterwards named the Book of Ecclesiasticus.[6] Its composition should be dated between the years 190 B.C. to 180 B.C., with the Greek canonical text being translated from the original about 130 B.C. by the grandson of the author (cf. Prologue).[7]

A congenial work, it is both a summary of Judaic "wisdom" and the most emblematic memorial to that "wisdom." It is composed of short pieces of *meshalim* plus some longer literary sections. It utilizes and often quotes the writings, especially the wisdom writings, currently read in the Jewish communities of the time. In comparison to all the Scriptures, the Book of ben Sirach is a work of adaptation, a new presentation of wisdom, and a commentary.

Following the lead of the Book of Proverbs, with which it is so closely related, the Book of ben Sirach portrays wisdom as the art of living happily by doing what is pleasing to God. In other words, the work is a manual of religious and moral instruction for a well brought up and pious Israelite, set down by a prudent professor. This master, however, is not a passive man; he is not as bourgeois as has been often said. His misgivings recall those of Job and of Ecclesiastes (cf. Sir. 11:14-26; 17:22-27; 40:1-11; 41:1-4); he knows that humility and poverty are a prerequisite for grace before God (cf. Sir. 2:17; 3:18-19; 11:1, 11-13; 19:21; 21:5; 34:10); and his "fear of God" (cf. Sir. 1:11-2:18; etc.) is quite close to what we call the "theological virtues."

Ben Sirach is a true and genuine scribe of Israel, a man conscious of the greatness of his vocation (cf. Sir. 38:24-39:11). He has a fine mind, is well informed, and is a realistic observer (he has traveled: cf. Sir. 34:9-12; 39:4; 51:13). To experience, he adds the noble quality of judgment. His mind is so profoundly religious, a religion whose ruling element is charity, that he is devoted to liturgical worship (cf. Sir. 34:18-26; 35:1-20; 50:1-21); he loves and venerates the priesthood, the liturgical functions, and the rites,

[6] This name is of Christian origin and seems to come from the fact that the Wisdom of ben Sirach was much read in the Church of the first centuries, unless the intention was to show that the book was received by the Christians contrary to the usage in the synagogues. In any case, there is no connection in origin between this title and that of the Book of Ecclesiastes.

[7] The fragments of the Hebrew text rediscovered in our times represent about three-fifths of the book. Considering the variations of tradition in the presentation of the text, differences will sometimes be found in the numbering of the verses in modern Bibles, and it is well to be on one's guard in this respect.

without cluttering up his devotion with any of the rubrical or legalistic exaggerations which were established at a later date. Quite simply, he belongs to those of the faithful who were resolved to observe the Holy Law; he is one of the *Hasideans,*[8] who challenged the popular current of ideas.

The Siracid was fully aware that the paganizing influence of Hellenism exercised a real fascination over his contemporaries and was making dangerous progress. It had not yet begun to employ troublesome methods, although many minds were already in danger of being disturbed. The new wisdom is the reaction of an intelligent man who is determined to defend the traditional values and the sacred patrimony of the People of God. A disciple of the exilic and postexilic theologians whose thought centered on the mystery of creation, he sings beautifully of the wisdom of God at work in nature (cf. Sir. 16:22-18:13; 42:15-43:33). The religion he proclaims is capable of impressing even minds which are not Israelite. He also knows, however, the way to present a synthesis of everything worthwhile from the past. He writes a "Sacred History" which clearly shows the election and the destiny of the people of Israel (cf. Sir. 44-49), and which expresses a profound faith in the fidelity of God to his plan of salvation. Finally, ben Sirach exhibits an extremely noble idea of Wisdom; not only is she from God and anterior to creation (cf. Sir. 1:1-10), not only does she identify herself in some way with the Torah, as she did previously in certain Psalms (cf. Sir. 24:22-23; cf. p. 208), but she seems to be the Spirit of God himself and a divine Person (cf. Sir. 24:1-21; notice the connection with history and with worship). A revelation which was later to be made more complete is foreshadowed here even more than in Prov. 8.

The magnificent unfolding of the wisdom (cf. Bar. 3:9-4:4) which comes from God, which is given to his people, and which is identical with that of the Torah, is found in the collection of various writings that have been attributed to Baruch, the secretary and disciple of Jeremias. They may be dated from either the third or the second century. Unlike the work of ben Sirach, which was Judean, the texts of Baruch came from the Diaspora and are im-

[8] From the Hebrew word *hesed:* "love," "attachment," "fidelity," "devotion," "zeal"; hence, men who are pious, devoted, fervent. In a Westernized form, the word has become "Assidean."

portant witnesses to the life of the Jewish communities outside Palestine. Besides the poem on the divine wisdom cited above, a fine psalmic prayer of contrition and of supplication, of praise and of hope (cf. Bar. 1:15-3:8), and an encouraging twofold prophetic exhortation, carries on the best themes of prophetic tradition (cf. Bar. 4:5-5:9). In addition, a letter attributed to Jeremias and supposedly sent to the exiles of Babylon is included. The letter is a polemic against the idolatrous cults (in the manner of Jer. 10:1-16 and of Isa. 44; 46), and manifests a perfect knowledge of the religious institutions of Mesopotamia during the Greek period.

[TWO]

FROM THE REVOLT OF THE MACHABEES TO THE KINGDOM OF HEROD

During the course of the third and second centuries, a power—Rome—advanced on the West with giant strides. During the three centuries preceding, the consular republic, which had superseded the regime of the kings (cf. p. 95) by making war on the powerful Etruscans, the Samnites, the Umbrians, the Gauls, and the Greek cities of the south, had succeeded in establishing the unity of the Italian peninsula to the advantage of Rome alone. Now this force could and would impose itself on the whole Mediterranean coastline. In two hundred years, one by one in rapid succession, other powers would be compelled to yield: in the second century, Carthage (the Punic Wars), Spain, Macedonia, Numidia, and the Cimbrians; in the first century, Pontus, Syria and Palestine, the Gauls, and Egypt. At the same time, however, the Roman republic was passing through the most terrible internal crises. Having undergone the Plebeian Revolutions, attempts at democracy, and social efforts (Cato, the Gracchi), an aristocratic dictatorship was established by Sulla. Then came the re-establishment of the consulate (Crassus and Pompey in 70 B.C.) —the final step toward the regime of personal government by a single man (Augustus), which turned into an absolute empire.[1]

[1] Obviously, even the least detailed history of Rome and of the beginnings of the Roman empire cannot be given. It is equally impossible to give a complete bibliography. Accounts of this history will be found in *Cambridge Ancient*

Rome, whose external policy at the beginning of the second century consisted more in preserving its superiority where it was already established than in making new conquests, was, however, unable to maintain diplomatic peace in the East. Antiochus III, the Great (222-186 B.C.), the sixth of the Seleucids, defeated Ptolemy V at Panion. Then, never doubting his own power, he entered Greece and attacked the Romans. He was vigorously expelled and completely beaten at Magnesium in 189 B.C., being forced to yield a part of the territory of Asia Minor and to pay an enormous indemnity during the next twelve years.

After Panion, the Palestinians passed from the control of the Ptolemies to the government of the Seleucids. At the beginning, they felt no great change or disturbance. Since the Seleucids ordinarily recognized the local governments in their various colonies and annexed territories, they sanctioned the authority of the Council of Elders. In addition to the priests, whose assembly was the original nucleus of this Council (cf. p. 205), eminent or influential laymen, Scribes or lawyers, now held seats in it. This was the origin of the Sanhedrin of Jerusalem. Councils of this kind existed in all the important Judaic communities, but the Council of the Holy City was obviously the chief one.

The situation, however, soon grew worse. The Syrian empire, going from crisis to crisis, lapsed into the most profound decline. Naturally, it was always on the lookout for money, and because of this its sovereigns, although cultivated and even refined men, often became shameless brigands capable of looting anything they could find. Therefore, after Magnesium, at a time when the Antiochian government needed money, suspecting that the treasury of Jerusalem contained great riches, Heliodorus, the minister of Seleucus IV (186-174 B.C.), was sent to pillage it. The mission failed, however (cf. II Mach. 3).

Another cause of difficulties in Judea was the continuation of Hellenization. To the Israelites, who, like the Hasideans, were deeply attached to the Law, the new civilization seemed essentially impious. Because they were men of merit and were united among themselves, they were ready to play their part in presenting opposition if affairs grew worse. Affairs did grow worse.

History, Vols. IX-XII (New York: Macmillan, 1932–39); A. E. R. Boak, *A History of Rome to A.D. 565* (4th edition; New York: Macmillan, 1955).

After Seleucus IV was assassinated by Heliodorus, he was succeeded by his brother, Antiochus IV Epiphanes (174-164 B.C.), an unscrupulous opportunist. Skeptical and mentally unbalanced (he was nicknamed "Epimanes," the "madman"), as prodigal as he was rapacious, he sometimes had good intentions, even though he was clumsy and brutal. He resolved to use force in Hellenizing the small Jewish nation which was proving to be extremely intractable. The reason for Antiochus' insistence was primarily political in nature. Judea was now the frontier of the Seleucid empire. Since men were always found in it who dreamed of the less strict regime of the Ptolemies or who actually looked for anti-Syrian support from Egypt, it seemed to Antiochus that, if it could not be won over voluntarily, he had to subject it to himself either by violence or annihilation.

The Jews, who were divided politically into the friends of Egypt and the partisans of Antiochus, were also divided with regard to the modernizing movement. Some were receptive to the new humanism, in comparison with which the traditional conservatism seemed old-fashioned, narrow, and harsh. There were also matter-of-fact and practical men, opportunists and profiteers, who found it to their advantage to enter actively into the political aims and the venalities of the Syrian government. The aristocrats in office and the propertied bourgeoisie also had good reason to curry favor with Antiochus. Finally, there were the insignificant, the indifferent, or the resigned; once the persecution started, the danger of widespread apostasy would be kindled.

Fighting this tide of surrender, a party of opposition rose up. The party was made up of men who felt that an important loyalty was at stake, and that the hour had come to choose for or against Yahweh. These genuine disciples of Moses and of the prophets were of two kinds: the martyrs, whom the impious power called upon to renounce their faith and who preferred to die; and the "resisters," those who took up arms and fled to the bush, stirring up and organizing the revolt, and declaring a "holy war." They could count on public opinion being on their side and on the support of the people of humble station, the "poor," who were truly religious in spirit and faithful to the traditions of the faith. Thus, when the revolt broke out, it came from the very heart of Judaism.

The stake being fought for was the Temple of Jerusalem. To a foreigner, the Temple was a place of worship much like those of other countries, and not one of the most important places of worship either, since Judea was only a small canton (a hexagon 44 miles in diameter) in the large province of Coele-Syria. But for the Jews, not only of Judea but everywhere, it was a supreme prize to be loved and defended: it was the reason for the existence of the one Holy City—the very Dwelling of God.

The high priest was the recognized leader of the Jews and, for all practical purposes, their defendant before the royal government. In 175 B.C., a just and pious man, Onias III, was high priest. Such a man could not be part of Antiochus' intrigues, but Antiochus had no difficulty finding helpers. First came Jason, the brother of Onias (who was deposed); he was supplanted by Menelaus, a man who was not of the Sadocite line (cf. p. 205) and who perhaps even came from a nonsacerdotal family. Both Jason and Menelaus bought the sovereign pontificate from the monarch and worked for the Seleucid while lining their own pockets (cf. II Mach. 4).

A gymnasium was built in Jerusalem so that the youth could engage in sports. It was a success; Hellenism became the fashion, especially among the leaders and the priests. Disturbances took place, however, resulting in the first pillaging of the Temple by Epiphanes, who was making a tour at the time in Egypt. Then, the king, seeing clearly that every Jewish act was a religious act, decided to suppress the religion of Yahweh. A great persecution, painful to remember, followed upon his decision. Jerusalem was stripped, the Temple was profaned, the practices of worship banned, circumcision and the Sabbath prohibited, and the keeping of the Sacred Books forbidden. Sacrifice to idols was made obligatory; a pagan altar was set up on the very altar of Yahweh in the Temple. The faithful were massacred, and there was a reign of terror (cf. I Mach. 1; 2 Mach. 5-7).

In 167 B.C., the revolt broke out in the countryside. It was begun by a valiant sacerdotal family known to tradition as the Machabees—Mattathias and his five sons, among whom Judas was particularly famous.[2] They were supported by the fervent movement of the

[2] They are called the Machabees by general application of the surname given to the most famous among them. Perhaps this surname means "mallet" or "hammer"; in this case it might be translated, by analogy with the Frankish prince of the seventh century of our era, "Judas the Hammer." Mattathias de-

Hasideans (cf. p. 220, note 8), among whom there was a group of priests of the family of Sadoc, which had been deprived of the sovereign pontificate (cf. I Mach. 2). Guerilla warfare, and then open war, as well as politics and intrigues among the people of the country and on the international plane—all of this is so complex that only the principal facts can be mentioned here.[3]

First of all, Judas (166-161 B.C.) undertook to liberate the territory from the tyranny of the Seleucids. One by one he defeated the envoys or the generals of Antiochus IV: Apollonius, Seron, Lysias, Gorgias, and Nicanor. The Temple was purified, and worship resumed in 165 B.C. (cf. I Mach. 3-4; II Mach. 8; 11; 12). He was then forced to defend the independence he had won against Israel's neighbors: Transjordania, Idumea, Philistia, and Galilee (cf. I Mach. 5; II Mach. 10; 12). Hostilities on the part of the Syrians were resumed under Lysias, Gorgias, and a new Seleucid, Antiochus V (cf. I Mach. 6; II Mach. 9; 10; 13). During the time of Demetrius I, a traitor called Alcimus, who had had himself named high priest, won over the Scribes and the Hasideans. Judas carried on the conflict against Nicanor and Bacchides, the protectors of Alcimus, and formed an alliance with the Romans (cf. I Mach. 7-9; II Mach. 14-15).

A second phase of the conflict, led by Jonathan (161-143 B.C.), was centered around the struggle for political independence. Jonathan consented to having his authority recognized by a usurper of the Seleucid throne, Alexander Balas. From Alexander he also received the pontifical dignity (152 B.C.), although it was considered to belong only to the Sadocites (cf. I Mach. 9-10). The illegitimate appropriation of the supreme sacerdotal office had its consequences: some Sadocites formed a dissident group with a certain "doctor of justice" at their head and withdrew into the isolated region of the mountains of Juda. Their attitude and their manner of living asserted both their opposition to the Hasmoneans, who were judged to be corrupt, and their rigorous fidelity in observing the Law of the Covenant made with the Fathers.[4] Believing that he could no

scended from Hasmon or Hasamon, whence the name of "Hasmoneans" given to his descendants.

[3] It goes without saying that the only way to get an idea of Palestinian events between 167 B.C. and 134 B.C. is to read the two Books of the Machabees.

[4] Such, at least, is one of the hypotheses, which seems to be plausible as an

longer continue without the support of the Syrian government, Jonathan attached himself again to Demetrius II and to Antiochus VI, and kept up the alliance with Rome and with Sparta (cf. I Mach. 11-12).

The war came to an end under Simon (143-135 B.C.), another son of Mattathias, who obtained from Demetrius II, and later from Antiochus VII, a charter of liberty which was recognized by the Romans (Roman control was inevitable from this time on in the whole Near East). Simon became hereditary high priest, ethnarch of the new, independent, and enlarged state of Judea, and, consequently, the founder of the dynasty called Hasmonean (cf. I Mach. 13-16). There is good reason to think that under the pontificate of Simon the members of the Sadocite sect were harassed, their rigorism being considered as the holding of a hostile position and as the extremism of fanatics. Apparently, their admirable and venerated master, the doctor of justice, died during this persecution. A group of them then fled to the country of Damascus to seek refuge. There they founded the "Community of the New Covenant," basing the foundation on an oath of renewed fidelity to the Law according to the old sacerdotal tradition.

At his death in 135 B.C., Simon left the power to his son, John Hyrcanus (135-104 B.C.)—"high priest, head of the society of the Jews." Things were difficult in the beginning, for Antiochus VII seemed to want to reopen the entire issue. On the death of the monarch, however, Hyrcanus won back the prerogatives of the little state and was able to govern it with intelligence and energy, enriching himself considerably in the process and increasing the territory.

The hereditary enemies of the Judeans paid dearly for their opposition to the Machabean efforts at liberation. Idumea was annexed

---

explanation and co-ordination of the various facts supplied by the documents discovered since 1947 in the caves at the site of Qumran, close to the northwest shore of the Dead Sea. The bibliography on these documents is large: articles in learned journals are numbered by the hundreds. Photographic publication of the manuscripts is in progress and its completion must be awaited so that the many questions raised since the discovery can be treated with as much prudence as possible. Cf. Millar Burrows, *The Dead Sea Scrolls* (New York: Viking Press, 1955), *More Light on the Dead Sea Scrolls* (New York: Viking Press, 1958); T. H. Gaster, *Dead Sea Scriptures in English Translation* (New York: Doubleday, 1956); J. T. Milik, *Ten Years of Discovery in the Wilderness of Judea,* English trans. by J. Stingnell (Naperville, Ill.: A. R. Allenson, 1959); Geza Vermes, *The Dead Sea Scrolls in English* (Baltimore: Penguin Books, 1962).

and its inhabitants forced to submit to circumcision under pain of death (in 110 B.C.). The Samaritans, separated from the Judeans by age-old enmities, were also subjected by force and severely punished. The temple they had built on Garizim at the end of the fourth century to compete with the Temple of Jerusalem was demolished in 128 B.C. In 107 B.C., after a year's hard siege, Samaria fell and was destroyed.[5]

Rich, happy, worldly, receptive to innovations, Hyrcanus held, from the religious point of view, an orthodox but moderate position, so that, and this is the irony of fate, the Hasmoneans had gone over to the side of the modernists and the Hellenophiles—the party of the Sadducees.[6] The Sadducees was now a confirmed and established party. Originally favorable to the Syrian kings, liberal, opportunistic, and holding a good position, it was represented principally by the higher clergy and the aristocracy.

By rallying to this trend, Hyrcanus alienated the strict and the fervent—the Hasideans, the party of those who had supported the Machabean revolt. Their concern for purity and fidelity to the Law had become more and more defined and rigid, until it hardened into prescriptions which were added to those of the Torah. Thus, they were distinguished from the rest of the Jews to the extent of deserving the name of "Pharisees," that is, "separated" or "separatists." Little concerned, at least at first, with political factions, they were Hellenophobia personified. Many people regarded them as "saints," and admired and loved them. Their influence, which was quite extensive, would make itself felt in many writings.

Hyrcanus left five sons. Aristobulus, the eldest, reigned only one year. His youngest brother, Alexander Jannaeus (104-77 B.C.), succeeded him and assumed the title of king, while remaining high priest. He further enlarged the territory considerably by annexing

[5] Herod rebuilt it in 26 B.C. under the name of Sebaste (in honor of Augustus). It is to be noted that the Samaritans regarded only the books of the Pentateuch as Sacred Scripture; their schism was complete as early as the fifth century, when the prophetic texts and the other writings had not yet been joined to the Torah.

[6] If this name, as seems to be the case, comes from Sadoc (p. 205), it indicates that this was the party of the priests. We must not, however, confuse it with the Sadocite sect which we saw withdrawing from public life about 150 B.C., in the time of Jonathan. Others think that the word comes from *sedaqa:* "justice"; this would make it the "party of the just."

the Shephelah, the borderlands of Idumea and of Nabatean Arabia, Transjordan, and Upper Galilee. His dissolute ways, however, prejudiced the Pharisees and the people against him, to such an extent that they attempted, and this is another paradox in a troubled history, to overthrow him by appealing to the Seleucid Demetrius III. Nevertheless, national sentiment finally prevailed and, after having severely punished the Pharisees (the war lasted six years and claimed tens of thousands of victims), Alexander Jannaeus ended his days in peace.

Under Alexandra (77-68 B.C.), the widow of Aristobulus I, and later Alexander Jannaeus, a reconciliation with the Pharisees was effected. Now they were able to be members of the High Council, along with the aristocracy and the priesthood who formed a part. They also went into political life, and the influence of the Sadducees was ruined (68-64 B.C.). Alexandra had two sons: Hyrcanus II, the elder, already high priest, enjoyed only a short reign at first, having been forced to abdicate in favor of his younger brother, Aristobulus II, who had taken up arms against him and whom the Sadducees supported. The Idumean Antipater urged Hyrcanus to reclaim his rights by force, with support from the Pharisees, and the struggle was resumed.

But Rome was now present in Palestine. The consul, Pompey, who had just conquered Mithridates in Pontus, undertook to pacify and to organize the Near East. In 63 B.C., he was in Syria and Palestine. Aristobulus and Hyrcanus found themselves forced to submit their rival claims to his judgment. After some hesitation, Pompey chose to support the party of Hyrcanus. The priests who had been faithful to Aristobulus withdrew into the Temple. The Temple was besieged and taken. Hyrcanus II then became high priest again, but Judea ceased to be an independent state. It was cut away from its recent non-Jewish annexations; that is, it retained only the Judean territory properly so-called: Galilee, Perea, and a narrow Transjordanian strip. It was subjected to paying tribute, and Hyrcanus no longer governed except under the control of a proconsul.

In the years that followed, disturbances broke out again, and the Roman governor of Syria divided the country into five districts, each with a council of elders at its head. Hyrcanus retained only the office of the sovereign pontificate (57 B.C.). During this time, the Idumean Antipater had continued his intrigues and had become a kind of grand vizier to Hyrcanus II, all the while working for the Romans.

Rome was in the thick of political rivalries (the conspiracy of Catiline). The period from 62 B.C. to 59 B.C. saw the first triumvirate, made up of Crassus, Pompey, and Caesar. Later, while Caesar was occupied in Gaul, there was a return to the consulate under Crassus and Pompey (55-54 B.C.). Then, when Crassus was defeated in the Near East, Pompey became the sole consul (51-49 B.C.). Caesar returned, however; he rebelled against the senate and declared war on Pompey, who fled with the government. Caesar made himself the master of Italy and of Spain, crushing Pompey in a terrible battle in Greece (cf. Pharsalus, 48). Pompey was assassinated at Pelusium. Caesar carried the pursuit as far as Egypt where he was seduced by Cleopatra. She was the daughter of the second to last Ptolemy, and had been kept from the throne by her brother. Caesar restored her rights as queen.

Encamped on the border of Egypt, Caesar needed support. In 47 B.C., he arrived in Syria. He nullified the arrangements made by Pompey and restored authority to Hyrcanus II by naming him ethnarch. Then, to stand by Hyrcanus' side (indeed over Hyrcan for all practical purposes), he made Antipater proconsul of Judea, while the two sons of Antipater became *strategi*—Phasael at Jerusalem and Herod in Galilee. Caesar then returned to Italy where intrigue, civil wars, and the deaths of famous men followed one another. In February of 44 B.C., the senate was forced to name Caesar dictator for life. On March 15th, however, senatorial conspirators assassinated him. The following year, the second triumvirate was established with Antony, Octavius, and Lepidus. Antony left for the Near East (where he was to let himself be ensnared by Cleopatra), and Phasael and Herod had him name them ethnarchs, while Hyrcanus was again no more than the high priest.

The invasion of Syria by the Parthians gave Antigonus, the son of Aristobulus II, an opportunity to become king of Jerusalem for a time (40-37 B.C.). Hyrcanus was removed from office and Phasael committed suicide. Herod, on the other hand, fled to Rome, where he pleaded his cause so well that he was recognized as king of Judea by the senate. He was met by the outbreak of war on returning to Palestine, but, with the aid of the Romans, he seized Jerusalem in 37 B.C. Thus was begun a reign that lasted thirty-four years; one that was both glorious and sad, powerful and tragic. By marrying a granddaughter of Hyrcanus II, Mariamne, Herod entered the family of the Hasmoneans and regarded himself as their heir.

[THREE]

THE STRUGGLE OF THE WRITERS

Information concerning the period from the insurrection of Mattathias to the establishment of the Hasmonean kingdom is particularly abundant, because the events that took place were written down (some even in duplicate) in the Books of the Machabees.

The First Book of the Machabees, written toward the end of the second century, is by an unknown author. His personality, however, can be discerned to some extent in his work. A cultivated Jew, he writes pleasantly and simply, in good Hebrew style. His work, however, is known only in the Greek version, the Hebrew original having disappeared almost entirely. He narrates the events which took place during the course of some forty years, from the accession of Antiochus IV to the death of the high priest Simon. He is a real historian; knowing perfectly the facts and the setting in which they took place. He has drawn upon the official archives for documents of a diplomatic nature, which he reproduces conscientiously, especially numerous letters exchanged with foreign authorities (cf. I Mach. 8:20-32; 10:18-20, 25-45; 11:29-37; 12:6-18, 20-23; 13:36-40; 14:20-23; 15:2-9, 16-21). Thus, he has left a solid firsthand work, and one of the best historical books of antiquity.

This, however, is not an adequate description of his work. Its literary style is, if one may so put it, quite simply biblical. He knows the "Holy Books" and venerates them (cf. I Mach. 12:9; cf. 1:59-60); he quotes them and imitates their style (cf. for example, I Mach. 2:51-64; 3:19, 55-60; 4:24, 36-51; 8:73; 14:6-12). He allows himself to be carried along by the traditional cadences and takes off on long digressions (cf. for example, I Mach. 1:26-29, 38-42; 3:1-9; 14:4-15). He establishes himself still more in the biblical tradition, especially in that of the Earlier Prophets (he makes one think of the histories of Joshua, of the Judges, and of David) by his intention, which is to narrate history in relation to its meaning. If foreign persecution and oppression were a result of God's anger with his faithless people, the liberating victory was no less due to divine intervention in favor of the Chosen People. Consequently, events are looked at with the eyes of faith, and are recounted as a continuation of "Sacred History," possessing certitude of Israel's divine vocation.

A man of his times, the author is very much in favor of the Romans (cf. I Mach. 8:1-16), but he detests Hellenism, against which, in his own way, he writes a book in opposition. He writes of the glory of those who have triumphed over Hellenism—the Machabees, of whom he is a convinced and enthusiastic partisan, whose noble characteristics and heroic deeds he magnifies, and whose courage is contagious. Hence, his book was one of the most comforting and stimulating messages for the children of Israel.

The First Book of Machabees is entirely independent of the work known as the Second Book of Machabees. The second work is not a continuation of the first; rather, it counts in its own way a certain number of the facts reported in I Mach. 1-7. Written in a good Greek of the late period, in a verbose and grandiloquent style, which is ornate and affected in the manner of the time, the second book presents itself as a summary of a larger work written by a man named Jason (cf. II Mach. 2:19-32). Nothing is known concerning Jason, except that he must have written shortly after 160 B.C. The work of the man who made the summary dates from the years after 124 B.C. (which is mentioned in II Mach. 1:9). A Jew, who patterned himself after the Alexandrine orators, he is an extremely fervent and pious believer, whose intention is obvious. He addresses his brethren of the Jewish communities of Egypt, taking advantage of the Machabean history to interest them in the religious affairs of Palestine, especially in the Temple and the annual feasts (cf. II Mach. 1:9; 2:16; 10:8 the conclusion of the first part of the book; 15:36 the conclusion of the second part). In this way, he reminds them of their privilege of being the one People of God and of their inalienable patrimony—the House of God, his Law, and his worship.

He speaks with an enthusiasm, which does not deprive the book of its historical value (it is well documented and often supplements I Mach.), although it does explain certain liberties he takes with the history. Preacher and panegyrist, he takes sides, expresses his opinion, speaks out in regard to men and to events. He has been classed among the historians of "feeling."

In addition to the ideas it holds in common with other books and to those it has received from tradition, the Second Book of Machabees contains teachings which had never before been expressed. These teachings, which were to take their place in the current of Jewish thought, developing there, included affirmations regarding the resurrection of the dead (cf. II Mach. 7:9; 14:49; also, however, cf. Daniel, hereafter), retribution in the life beyond (cf. II Mach. 6:26), the value of prayer for the dead (cf. II Mach. 12:41-46), and the intercession of the just, who are already with God, in behalf of the living (cf. II Mach. 15:12-16).

The fact that the work was written in Greek was one reason why it was not received as a Sacred Scripture in Palestine (cf. p. 218). Furthermore, due to the unpopularity of the Hasmoneans in Judea, from the end of the second century on, books which glorified the heroes of that family were in disfavor. The same feeling was not held in the Diaspora and in later tradition. For this reason, the two Books of the Machabees were placed in the Septuagint side by side with the other books, whereas they did not form part of the Hebrew collection of Sacred Scriptures.

The armed resistance of the years around 160 B.C. had not been, and could not have been, the doing of all the Israelites. For one thing, the Hasmoneans had not won them all over. Besides, the leaders were soon seen to be imitating the very men against whom their fathers had fought. Israel was far from satisfied. Since its soul was fed constantly with the greatest hopes because of the habitual practice of reading its Prophets, it could not fail to feel increasing impatience at the contempt and harassment with which it was treated by foreigners. The destructive character of Hellenism, on the one hand, and political corruption, on the other, led to rebellion in the minds of some men, although they had no inclination for revolt, nor any way of expressing it in action.

Naturally, they kept the faith—faith in the promises of God to his people—even to the point of exasperation. They believed in God to such an extent that they no longer believed in anything except him, to the exclusion of all human interventions. Hence, they began to expect everything from God; and to expect it suddenly, as the result of a sudden interference in history. Thoughts of this kind had already been manifested; in fact, they were one of the aspects of prophecy (cf. pp. 197-98). Now, however, they assumed an important and even predominant place in the thoughts of men. Because of this, a whole literature of hopes and dreams in a close-at-hand, unforeseen, and sensational future, cropped up, being represented by the apocalyptic writings.[1]

This type of literature, which was extremely prolific and which met a general need, enjoyed great success.[2] Only by reading the apocalyptic writings, those at least which, luckily, have survived, or which have been accidentally recovered, can one understand their style, their content, and their spirit. The most representative piece, and one of the most ancient, is the Book of Daniel. A discussion of this book must be postponed, however, until some consideration has been given to the common traits of apocalyptic writing. Two hundred years later, the Apocalypse of St. John will be found among the Christian writings. Among the other books of this kind, which have not been entered into the canon of the Scriptures, we can mention here only the principal ones and then reflect on their general characteristics.[3]

One of the finest apocalyptic works, a truly beautiful piece of writing, is the collection of texts grouped under the title of the Book of Enoch. Interesting also are the Book of Jubilees (called also the Apocalypse of Moses), the Testament of the Twelve Patriarchs, and the Preface and the Third Book of the Sibylline Oracles. These writings may be dated from about the second century, although certain additions were inserted later. Several of the apocalyptic writings, for example the Parables of Enoch, the Jubilees, and the Testament of Levi, are apparently the work of the Essenes

[1] "Apocalypse" means literally: "the act of uncovering," "unveiling," "revelation"; it indicates that it is concerned with hidden things, secrets, and, in particular, the thing that is mysterious to the highest degree, the future.

[2] One may compare certain literary vogues through the ages, such as the courtly romances of the Middle Ages, and the love stories or detective stories of the present day. But perhaps the best comparison would be, all differences being taken into account, the explosion of romanticism in France in the nineteenth century, a kind of manifestation of revenge and of escape in the face of the paralyzing, deceptive, and humiliating Restoration.

[3] Cf. examples in R. H. Charles, *The Apocrypha and Pseudepigrapha of the Old Testament in English*, Vol. II, *Pseudepigrapha* (Oxford at the Clarendon Press, 1913); cf. also H. H. Rowley, *The Relevance of Apocalyptic* (2nd edition; London: Lutterworth Press, 1947; reprinted, 1961).

or of the "Sectaries" whose center was at Qumran.[4] The same is true of the Book of the War of the Sons of Light and of the Sons of Darkness, which is dated from the first century before the Christian era. At the end of that century the Life of Adam and Eve (also called the Apocalypse of Moses) was set down.

The first century of the Christian era saw the appearance of the Assumption of Moses, the Book of the Secrets of Enoch (or Slavic Enoch), the Fourth Book of the Sibyl, the Fourth Book of Esdras, the Apocalypse (Syriac) of Baruch, the Ascension of Isaias, the Apocalypse of Abraham, and an apocryphal Ezechiel.

The second century of the Christian era produced the Apocalypse (Greek) of Baruch, the Fifth Book of the Sibyl, the Testament of Abraham, and the Apocalypse of Sophonias.

Naturally, after the beginning of Christianity, these writings often included Christian interpolations. On the whole, the texts cited above, with the exception of the fragments discovered in the Dead Sea caves, have scarcely ever been handed down except in various translations (in Greek, Syriac, Ethiopian, Arabic, Armenian, Georgian, Slavonian, and Latin). Consequently, serious critical studies are needed before the texts can be used. The knowledge we do have of them, however, will enable us to define the apocalyptic style to some extent.

The apocalypses were connected in a way with prophecy. The older Prophets, beginning with Amos, had often spoken of the "Day of Yahweh" in terms of catastrophe on an almost universal scale. We need only to read Sophonias to understand this. Oracles of this kind developed particularly during the Exile (we many mention, for example, Ezech. 38-39; Isa. 34-35; Aggeus; the First and Second Zacharias; Isaias 24-27; and Joel). The Prophets who made these somber pronouncements, however, were aiming at the amendment of their contemporaries, and they counted on the present contingencies. Apocalyptic literature, on the contrary, showed little faith in the fortunes of history. Instead of being a literature of realistic involvement like prophecy, apocalyptic literature was a literature of supernatural escape.

[4] If the religious of the "Sect" of Qumran cannot yet be positively identified with the Essenes (known by Philo, Flavius Josephus, and Pliny), still their relationship cannot be doubted.

It was generally presented in the form of stories, which were both biblical and transhistorical.[5] Characters from sacred history[6] and celestial beings moved or spoke in scenarios that were intended to be a commentary on the contemporary history of the readers,[7] as well as announcements of upheavals which would lead to the deliverance and the dazzling triumph of Israel.

To write such "revelations," one had to be a "seer." For this reason the apocalypses are often "visions"; and to obtain credence in them, they had to be presented, not as the product of human knowledge, but as reavealed by God, either directly or through the medium of angels. For the same reason, the dialogues found in the apocalypses had to be attributed to famous persons, Patriarchs, or Prophets.[8]

The visions are almost always described in stereotyped images which had become classic. The most frequent symbols are the stars, the cosmic elements, meteorological phenomena, calamities and disturbances of all kinds, colors, large numbers of animals, the parts of the human body,[9] clothing, weapons or other instruments, trees or other plants, and so forth.[10] Numbers are obviously choice figures. Persons and events, races and countries were evoked in a language

[5] We return to the world of the myth again, but with important differences.

[6] Adam and Eve, Henoch, Noah, Abraham, Jacob and his twelve sons, Moses, Isaias, Sophonias, Ezechiel, Esdras, Daniel, and others. The Scriptures are, obviously, quoted profusely.

[7] For instance: in the parables of the Book of Enoch, allusions to Alexander Jannaeus and to Herod the Great; in the Apocalypse of the Weeks, in the same Book of Enoch, allusions to Antiochus IV; in Sibyl III, allusions to Alexander the Great and to Antiochus IV; in Esdras IV, grief of a Jew over the destruction of Jerusalem by Titus in 70 B.C.

[8] Whence the name of "pseudepigrapha" often given to these writings (for example, by the Protestants; Catholics usually call them "apocrypha").

[9] For example, to give only a text which can easily be found: Apoc. 1:13-15, which, furthermore, derives from Dan. 10:5-6.

[10] Frequent symbols: star = angels or men; white oxen = the just, the Messias; black oxen = the impious; heifers = women; calves = children; elephants, camels, or asses = the giants of Genesis; wild beasts and birds of prey = Gentiles; lions, leopards = Assyrians and Babylonians; dogs = Philistines; wolves = Egyptians; hyenas, wild boars = Edomites; foxes = Ammonites; vultures, falcons, crows = Syrians; eagle with twelve wings and three heads = Rome; forests, cedars = enemy kingdoms; sheep = sons of Jacob, Israel; lion = Messias; vine, fountain = kingdom of the Messias; lightning = time of the Messias; house, desolate old woman = Jerusalem.

which was deliberately obscure and enigmatic. Riddles and allegorical arithmetic was used; only a circle of initiates possessed the key to their interpretation, and then enjoyed the heady satisfaction of understanding them while they remained unknown to their enemies.

The scenes usually take place in "heaven" or in the "heavens," and in a universe peopled by angels. The stories are set at the "end of time" and during the days preceding it. Descriptions and narratives aim at creating an impression; they seek the grandiose, the fantastic, the terrifying; the wonder in them takes many paths.

This literature is feverish, sometimes to the point of delirium. The intemperance of the imagery destroys its charm and exhausts its strength. The piling up and interweaving of symbols often produces, at least for the modern reader, the effect of disconcerting and fatiguing incoherence, sometimes almost becoming a nightmare. Nevertheless, apocalyptic literature must not be judged too hastily according to present ways of thinking. The form is by nature paralogical. It is much like dreams, and its unfolding must be understood as a succession of meanings.[11]

The biblical "canon," which retained Joel, Zacharias, and Daniel, rejected the apocalypses mentioned above. This fact lessens their importance in the development of Israelite thought, and limits the need to know them.

Nevertheless, because they are contemporaneous with certain books of the Sacred Writings and came from the same circles, they are extremely valuable for a knowledge of those circles and for an understanding of the apocalyptic form. On certain points, they are almost the only evidence of ideas which were in the process of maturation and would be manifested during the first Christian century; for example, the doctrine of retribution after death (cf. II Mach.) and, especially, the expectation of the Messias (cf. the

[11] These dreams have grandeur and communicate a kind of vigorous poetry to the literary descriptions. Moreover, to repeat a comparison already made in connection with Ezechiel (cf. p. 166, note 11), the images must be seen as appearing separately and disappearing one after the other, each being sufficient in itself for the expression of what it has to say. Thus, in the example given, Apoc. 1:13-15 (cf. p. 235, note 9), the person is not drawn with descriptive elements that supplement one another; rather, these elements simply express, one by one, his sacerdotal character, his kingdom, his eternity, his divine manner of knowing all things, his terrifying power, his majesty.

"Son of Man" in Enoch). In addition, they possess exceptional moral qualities and they constantly advocate the highest virtues.[12]

Finally, it must not be forgotten that the fundamental theme of the apocalypses is the struggle of the powers of evil against God, with the just enduring the trials of this struggle. It ends in an unforeseeable manner by the sudden victory of God, which is the catastrophe that puts an end to the world itself, that is, to the world as it then is. Men are judged, punished, or rewarded according to what they were and did. And this is the inauguration of the Kingdom of God, with whom the just, who have risen, shall live eternally.

Of particular note is the fact that a kind of parallel apocalyptic movement is evident in the literature and in the religious or popular circles of Greece and even Rome. This movement, however, was much less extensive than Israel's, and was undoubtedly the result of Oriental influence. It was directed toward a universal eschatology, the waiting for a return of the "golden age." Hence, it was to some extent similar to the Jewish apocalypses: it revealed the excitement of men's imaginations at that time, the curiosity of their minds concerning the secrets of the world and the mysteries of the hereafter, and their taste for an esoteric language and for "revelations" presented allegorically or in mezzotints. In paganism, too, this literature was the work of special religious currents. Among other signs, it was one of the manifestations of the similarity of beliefs and of the mysticism which so strongly affected men's minds in the Near Eastern and Mediterranean world at the beginning of the Christian era.

Everything that has been said with regard to the apocalyptic form is valid for the Book of Daniel. Especially in its second half, Daniel is one of the best representatives of this form. Written by an unknown author (as the form required) it seems to have been set down during the heroic hours of the War of Judas Machabeus, that is, about 165 B.C. This does not mean that the materials of the book are all so late. On the contrary, the author used sources which were already written and which made it easy for him to attribute his visions to a seer of the time of the Babylonian captivity. The work is composed of two kinds of writings: *midrashic* accounts of the story of Daniel and his companions (cf. Dan. 1-6); and dreams

[12] Some of these writings, like the Testament of the Twelve Patriarchs, may be considered as preparations for and remarkable approaches to the Gospel.

and visions, which constitute the genuinely apocalyptic part of the book (cf. Dan. 7-12). Each of the visions speaks symbolically of the same kingdoms or dominions from the postexilic period up to the time of the author.

The entire work is a powerful criticism of the Oriental paganism of the time. Its primary purpose, however, is twofold: to strengthen the courage of the Jews, who were being persecuted by Antiochus IV, by means of miraculous narratives and edifying examples; and (in a sense even more valuable), to rise far above the eddies of past and present history, to bring out the providential movement of history, and to give signs of the end that God will put to it. An uncommon power of thought and intuition went into the Book of Daniel. No doubt the writer took advantage of the great Prophets, especially Ezechiel, whom he utilizes. Nevertheless, he was the first to embrace in a single glance a vast period (four centuries) of the secular history of the Near East. He did not attempt to recount secular history; rather, he showed its significance, bringing out the ephemeral character of the successive empires, their swift disintegration, and, above all, their complete collapse in the person of Antiochus IV, whom he regards as the last of the Seleucids. In his eyes, this cruel and monstrous tyrant, over whom God finally triumphs at a single stroke, epitomizes all the forces of evil (cf. Dan. 8:19-25; 11:36-45).

Two camps, two worlds, in fact, confronted one another: the camp of God and the camp which pretended to make itself divine in opposition to the true God, seeking to suppress him. The opposition could not be humbled, and the combat, which was to form a prelude to God's victory, was inevitable. From out of the struggle, pious and faithful men would emerge saved. The angelic powers are mobilized with a view to this triumph, and "dominion" and "glory" are given to a "Son of Man," whose "kingdom will not pass away." The "saints" who have been resurrected will reign eternally with him, while the "sinners" are given over to eternal punishment (cf. Dan. 7:13-14, 18; 12:1-4). Nowhere previously in the Sacred Scriptures had the theology of Judgment and of the Messianic Kingdom, as well as reflections on the hereafter, been pushed so far.

Some prayers (cf. Dan. 3:24-90) and three *midrashim* (Susanna, Bel, and the Dragon: Daniel 13-14), which were added to the Book of Daniel, show, by means of heavy irony directed against paganism, that the observance of the Law always saves the just in the end, through the ruin and shame of their enemies.

Two *midrashic* works represent, as do the Books of the Machabees and the apocalypses, the characteristically defensive attitude of an Israel which found itself threatened on all sides, and which imposed upon itself a rigoristic fidelity to the Law of its God: the Book of Esther and the Book of Judith.

The Book of Esther is hard to date with certainty; its composition is often set at the end of the Persian period. It seems more probable, however, that it was composed during the time of the Hasmoneans, that is, about the middle of the second century, if not later. The book recounts the extraordinary events which won for the Jews, who were settled in Persia and who were suddenly threatened with extermination, miraculous salvation and a complete reversal of the situation: elevation to honor. The form of the Book of Esther, however, is not historical: the story was merely inspired by history. And it is a fine story, too, in which the characters are well delineated and the action dramatized with remarkable artistry. Many passages have a recognizable sapiential character. A relationship to Esdras, Nehemias, and Daniel, can also be perceived, while the anecdotal background is not unrelated to a story of Persian origin, which is found in Herodotus. The theme is the mastery of God over events which are directed to the punishment of the impious pagans and the salvation of the just Israelites. This theme, completely traditional in Hebrew literature, is sufficient to explain a book which would otherwise seem spiteful and bloody. The facts are constructed and arranged in relation to the general idea of the triumph of Israel and to the comfort it brings to the readers. The improbabilities of the antisemitic persecution forecast in the first part of this "novel" are balanced at the end by the massacre of the Persians on the order of their own king. The exaggeration, like the ostentation, is so great that it leaves the reader untroubled.

The Book of Judith also has an ardent and fighting spirit. Although the events it relates are entirely different, it is still the history of a miraculous deliverance of the People of God. This book, too, can reasonably be dated from the second half of the second century; it may perhaps even be appropriate to assign its composition to the beginning of the following century. Made up of narratives, discourses, and prayers or psalms, it is well-balanced, the development of the story leading up to the conclusion in an admirable way. The Book of Judith is an "edifying" story that seeks to capture the reader's attention more for the instructive value of a religious drama, rather than for the historical content. Indeed, what historical content there is seems a pretext, and is treated with complete freedom.[13] Once again, literary and thematic likenesses to Ezechiel, Joel, and Daniel are evident. The book is related to the apocalypses in its fundamental idea: the struggle between God (and Israel) and the impious; between the sovereign Master of the world and a paganism intoxicated with itself. The crushing victory of the Lord in the most unforeseen manner is intended to give confidence to the Israelites. In this book, as in that of Esther, only fanaticism and cruelty are revealed, unless it is understood as it was intended to be, that is, as a sermon, an exhortation, an exemplary history lesson. A note of universalism can be found in it—the conversion of Achior, the Ammonite! Understood in this way, the work expresses great faith in the destiny of the Chosen People, in spite of the disastrous appearance of its present position and the meagerness of its human forces; and it shows the willingness of the Israelites to maintain a scrupulous fidelity to the observances of the Law, while exhibiting deep hatred of the impious.

The collection of psalms called the Psalms of Solomon has not entered into the definitive canon of the Bible, but is preserved in the Greek Bible. The work is related in spirit with the two preceding books, although it is very different in form. The eighteen poems that comprise the Psalms of Solomon can be dated with accuracy between 63 B.C. and 48 B.C., for some even describe particular circumstances (for example, the taking of Jerusalem by Pompey). They are very beautiful. In them are found prayer and exhortation, polemics and wisdom, and a well-defined doctrine of Messianism and of eschatology. Primarily, however, they are undoubtedly one of the most typical expressions of the fanatically separatist attitude and, at the same time, the admirable piety of the Pharisees, in

[13] Stylizations, generalizations going beyond the actual, effacing the concrete outlines; gratuitous and generous admixtures of historical and geographical data, without the slightest fear of the greatest improbabilities; personifications: weak Bethulia = Israel; Nabuchodonosor and his army = the pagan world.

whose ranks belongs the author of these psalms. They represent the most characteristic tendencies of the Jewish soul—above all, an indestructible faith and hope. Justice and wisdom, combined with humility and poverty, are set up as principles of life. The author also shares and propagates his belief in the resurrection and in immortality. These ideas constituted the doctrinal and spiritual climate of Israel when Christianity made its appearance.[14]

The Book of Esther has, as it were, a counterpart in a Hellenic version, a work called the Third Book of Machabees (apocryphal). In the Hellenic version, a Ptolemy decides to exterminate the Jews of Alexandria, but is diverted from his plan by a miraculous intervention: fate thus turns against the Egyptians, who are handed over to the vengeance of the Jews. A historical romance, which borrows facts from actual history and mixes them with fiction, it must have been composed about the beginning of the Christian era.

Like the Second Book of Machabees, and some of the apocalyptic writings, the work is Alexandrine in origin. It is connected with the isolationist and xenophobian resistance movement, which was represented by several other books of the Hasmonean period. This tendency, however, was much less marked and much less vital in the Jewish centers of the Diaspora than in Palestine. For Palestine was the home of the First Book of Machabees, of most of the apocalypses, and of the books of Daniel, Esther, and Judith. Living conditions were very different for the Jews living in Jerusalem or within its canton from those who lived in colonies or in districts in foreign countries, especially in Egypt.

The Jews living outside Israel remained solidly attached to the traditions of the Fathers and were resolved to protect their wonderful heritage. Nevertheless, they thought they could go beyond a merely conservative and defensive attitude. They realized not only that they must live as Israelites whenever they lived among men with backgrounds and ideas other than their own, but also that Israel had a mission: to make itself known, to reveal the true God; and, toward that end, to carry on discussions, to expound, and to bear witness. Thus, a whole literature of apologetics was born. It sought to reach the pagans, desirous of explaining to them, in language they could understand, the content of the faith of Israel.

[14] These very remarkable poems can be read in R. H. Charles, *op. cit.*, pp. 625-52.

History, epic poetry, philosophical demonstrations, even drama (not many, but it is a crowning touch!)—all forms seemed useful to the defenders of Judaism. Penetrating Greek culture, they wished to show to the peoples with whom they lived, the anteriority and the universal superiority of Israel in every order of excellence. Thus, the noble ancestors of the Hebrews were reputed to be the source of all important discoveries and of every extraordinary enterprise of humanity. Philosophers such as Philo were ingenious in synthesizing ideas fathered by Pythagoras and Plato with the Revelations of Moses, seeing nothing but harmony between the Academy and Sinai. Even the classic authors of Greece were presented in such a way that they became the apologists of Judaism; and there was no shrinking from the falsification of names or from the worst sort of interpolations. Jewish writings which extolled everything Judaic were attributed to famous Greeks, whose authority and fame served as guarantees. If such procedures shock us, it must be remembered that they were the common and accepted practice of that time. They give evidence of an extraordinary broadmindedness and of the vital dynamism that animated Israelite propaganda.

A curious example of the lengths to which the Israelites went, is a collection of oracles attributed to a legendary pagan Sibyl. Of special note is book three of the oracles and its Prologue (which unlike the other books does not seem to have been retouched by Christian hands). In the obscure manner of apocalyptic literature, the Sibyl was made to predict the history of the world according to a Judaic perspective and ideology.[15]

A short historical romance known as the Letter from Aristeus embroidered the story of the Greek translation of the Hebrew works. It did so in order to make the event seem marvelous in the eyes of the sages and scholars of Alexandria (cf. p. 218, note 5). The letter is another interesting example of the schemes and of the efforts of Egyptian Judaism.

The attempt to meet pagan thinkers on an intellectual plane was the reason behind another work, the Third Book of Esdras (Greek). Although the book is a reworking of the story of Esdras and of Nehemias, it contains an instructive addition: chapters three and

[15] It was through something like the "Sibylline" writings that Virgil is thought to have known of the Messianic and eschatological hope evoked by him in Isaian terms in the Fourth Book of the Bucolics.

four describe the wager made by three servants of Darius on the subject: What is the most powerful thing in the world: wine, the king, women, or truth? "Truth is the greatest and is superior to everything else." In this story can be seen the influence of the traditional wisdom of Egypt, as well as the philosophical ideas of the Alexandrines. A Latin version of the Third and Fourth Books of Esdras are preserved as an appendix in the Catholic editions of the Vulgate.

The Fourth Book of Machabees (apocryphal) may also be mentioned. Written in the form of a discourse, it comments on the story of the martyrs in II Mach. 6-7, and in so doing expounds and defends the philosophical thesis: "Pious reason is capable of dominating the passions."

The best representative of Israelite literature in the Hellenized territory is the important and beautiful work currently called the Book of Wisdom. Also called the Wisdom of Solomon, it is chronologically the last book of the Old Testament.

Its author, a cultivated Alexandrine Jew, probably wrote between 80 B.C. and 60 B.C. Although his purpose was to show, in the manner of the other Israelite "sapiential writers," that neither wisdom nor happiness exist apart from the way of God, from whom all good proceeds, and to help his brethren to defend themselves against the pagan influences of their environment, he was, nevertheless, receptive to profane values. He possessed encyclopedic knowledge; and he wrote as a Hellenist in a style that was easy, elegant, and somewhat affected. His message was completely in the traditional Hebrew line. In order to convey it, however, he employed a manner of speaking, a cast of thought, and acquisitions of human ideas which enabled him to express himself as no one had ever done before, at least in the writings that had become canonical (continuous discourses, definitions, descriptions, analyses, summaries, and chains of reasoning).

The book is, as it were, a continuous meditation on the theme of man and of wisdom. Its subjects include: final happiness or unhappiness according to whether one has lived well or ill (cf. Wisd. 1-5); the prerogatives of divine wisdom and the means of possessing it (cf. Wisd. 6-9); the role of wisdom in history and in the judgment of men (cf. Wisd. 10-19). The Book of Wisdom taught that it is necessary to preserve oneself from idolatry, to accept the lot that God has given to each man, to do the will of God, to choose "life" instead of sin and "death." Although the idea of the immortality of the soul was not unknown in the Judaism of the time, nevertheless it is expressed in this book with a clarity and a logic which have benefited by contact with Greek thought (cf. Wisd. 2:23; 3:7-10; 6:18-19; cf. 9:15). Faith in God is always faith in the living and historical God of Israel; but human intelligence is believed to be capable of attaining him if it is honest and if man lives as God requires. The notion of God-Wisdom is spoken of as Prov. 8 and Sir. 24 interpreted it, but in terms that are more metaphysical and more humanistic (cf. Wisd. 7:25-27; 8:1-3). Finally, the commentary on the past made by the book is a good example of *midrashic* literature, in which history is treated with the greatest freedom (for example, it adds legendary facts, makes new interpretations of facts that were understood in a different way up to that time, and uses poetic licence).

Like ben Sirach, the author of the Book of Wisdom makes use of all the preceding writings which constituted the treasure of Israel and inspired its life: the Sacred Scriptures.

But likewise, it is important to note also that, with books of this sort, Sacred Scripture and, simultaneously, biblical tradition, henceforth opened to an intelligent and wise universality, begin to integrate new and foreign values. Israel, endowed with such an incomparable heritage, was called upon now, while faithfully preserving it, at times to modernize its formulas and to break out of its limitations.

10 The Critical Era

[ONE]

THE GRAECO-ROMAN WORLD [1] | In two centuries, the world had become Roman (cf. p. 221) and, for the first time in history, found itself unified in an empire entirely centered at Rome. This unity, the inclusion in the empire of the rich provinces of the Near East, and the building of the famous Roman roads which spread out from the capital to the Indies, to Mauretania, and to the British Isles, permitted an extraordinary economic and cultural development in the newly created world.

The Hellenization of the Near East had paved the way for Roman unity, and when unity was realized, it was completely impregnated by Hellenism. Although the world which had been built by the victories of the republican and the imperial legions, and by the methodical tenacity of a policy of successive intervention, control, and annexation, was Roman in its administrative structure and governmental centralization, it was Greek in civilization. Greek thought and art were found everywhere, and the Greek language was the universal speech.

Rome had brought order and peace to the world. More precisely, the new era had begun with the accession of Octavius to imperial power.[2] The preceding century had left unpleasant memories. It had

[1] Not to mention in some way the Graeco-Roman world as it appeared at the beginning of the Christian era would show a lack of fidelity to our purpose, which is always to make a preliminary reconnaissance of the environment in which the biblical writings appeared and to take it into consideration when dealing with their origin. We cannot, however, give more than a rapid and summary presentation of it here, and even this is a gamble. This world is immense and complex: how can one speak suitably and at the same time briefly of history and society in the dimensions of the universe then known? We must, therefore, be satisfied with a partial view, even of what concerns the religious life, to which we attach more importance. Studies on the subject are not lacking. We can cite nothing better than Michael Grant, *The World of Rome* (New York: Mentor Books, 1961); Jerome Careopina, *Daily Life in Ancient Rome*, English trans. by E. O. Lorimer (Yale University Press, 1960).

[2] Concerning the emperors who succeded one another during the first century, see the note on pp. 253-57.

seen anarchic rivalries, bloody contests between men for control of the government, and the ravaging of provinces by the armies. Therefore, the cult paid to Augustus was one of gratitude for the great benefit of unity and peace, which were a consequence of his taking over the reins of power.

Possessing absolute control over the army, having the right to make laws as he pleased, and exercising the sovereign office, which gave him absolute power in the religious and moral order, the emperor had almost unlimited authority. He was represented in the provinces by a hierarchy of governors and officials, chosen for the most part from men who were highly cultured and broadminded, whose administrations were generally very humane (there were, of course, exceptions). Nevertheless, the emperor kept in close contact with municipal and provincial assemblies, which enjoyed great liberty in practice with regard to local customs and organizations: these, in return, were devoted to the emperor and insured the continuance of his cult. In this way, the ruler found the means of counterbalancing the power of higher officials, which carried the risk of becoming excessive.

The army, which depended directly on the emperor, was obviously a decisive force. It was made up of nearly 400,000 men (20 to 25 years of service), organized into a stable military hierarchy. Enlistment in the army took the form of a religious *sacramentum.* It had its gods, represented by insignia, the imperial eagle, and other images, to which strict worship was due.

Even more than in the Hellenistic world, the concept of city, which had indeed sprung from that world, was the basic element in the Roman universe. Only the "citizen," that is, a recognized member (by birth or by acquisition of the right) of a city, was a human person. Every citizen formed part of the assembly of the people or the *ecclesia.* The assembly, however, was dominated by a council of rich citizens, the *boule;* hence, the city was really governed by the wealthy aristocracy. Nevertheless, independent of and superior to the *boule* was the *gerousia,* or the corporative council, which was supported and protected by the state. Like every organized body, the *gerousia* had its religious duties and upheld the imperial cult. The city was a complete organism, all of its structures and activities being linked with piety toward the gods. Resident foreigners, aliens, or travelers (thus, merchants, industrialists, professors, philosophers, physicians, diviners, magicians) did not enjoy the rights proper to citizenship, but were, like the citizen, free men.

The slave was only a chattel in the power of his master, a kind of domestic animal. Never before had there been so many slaves as in the Roman Empire. Besides bankrupt debtors who no longer had anything to give but themselves, and the children of slaves, the wars had put on the market considerable numbers of prisoners to be sold. Because of their harshness and their contempt, the Romans (with some, perhaps many, exceptions) had lowered the state of the slaves to a degree previously unknown in history. Since the tremendous number of the slaves greatly outbalanced the number of free men, the safety of the latter could be secured only by iron discipline and punishments such as torture and death, sometimes even mass slaughter.

Slavery, especially in the form it took in Roman society, was a grave injury to the human person and a disgrace in history. Nevertheless, we must not be guilty of an anachronism. Although inhumanness must always be condemned, slavery in the Roman world was an institution that had become customary. Each age and each environment regards certain of its institutions as natural and indispensable, not realizing that they may later be judged as blemishes. The question of the continuance or the disappearance of slavery as an institution did not arise in the Graeco-Roman world of the first century.[3] And one should not conclude too readily from this fact that the Romans had no sense of the dignity of man.

Rome had in some way universalized the Greek ideal of seeing to it that men become truly men. And she had propagated the institution born of that ideal—the *paideia*, the education of the young. The careful and methodical education of youth began with the children six or seven years old, who were just learning to read, but gave more particular care to the *ephebes* (youths 18 to 20 years old). The *ephebes* were provided with a firm civic formation and were trained chiefly in the exercises and competitions of the gymnasium. Their education, from beginning to end, involved an initiation into and a participation in cultural life. It aimed to form men who would be

[3] The Apostle Paul, whom no one will suspect of lacking esteem and love for men whoever they may be, did not oppose slavery. The Church, which was to abolish it, did not do so until centuries later. Remember the recent history of Negro slavery. Are men more conscious now, in "Christian" countries, of the debasing condition of the working classes than a hundred years ago?

faithful to their country and to their religion, and at the same time be eager to participate in the public games.

Cultural pursuits, however, were solely the privilege of a special caste, the *honestiores,* who were favored both by birth and by the government. They were allowed to pursue their studies in the great intellectual and artistic centers, notably Athens. The masses of the people were denied this humanistic education. They were the *humiliores,* those who worked so that the small number of the privileged could satisfy their tastes and their needs, and be assured of success and of leisure. In reading the classics of Latin literature, the danger exists of forgetting this multitude, which made up the bulk of society, and of seeing society only as a small aristocracy, which was wealthy in goods or in ideas.

The philosophical currents which had spread with Hellenism (cf. pp. 214-15), acquired, so to speak, a colder, more purely rationalistic aspect, when they came in contact with Rome. Epicureanism, which saw in the world only matter and chance, without any intervention by the gods, who were themselves of a material nature, taught prudent moderation with regard to needs and a healthy search for pleasures. The most popular doctrine, however, was that of the Stoics. It was highly suited to the Romans, because they were practical men, devoid of metaphysical sense. The Stoics taught an austere morality, a morality void of excess or enthusiasm. Their wisdom was a medicinal one, which had several objectives: freeing man from suffering by an asceticism that would dominate pain; suppressing desires; attaining a state of imperturbable equilibrium, that is, ataraxia or apathy. Stoicism held a pantheistic conception of the world. It also possessed a notion of the equality of all men, conceived as members of one large and unique body. It contributed to the development of virtues which were quite Roman in concept: temperance, fortitude, wisdom, the autonomy of the individual, probity, and justice; not to mention a certain preoccupation with self, which is part of the self-sufficiency of the wise man.

The intellectuals' concept of morality, however, could not keep the multitude of common people alive; rather, it seems to have provoked or to have stimulated an anti-rationalistic reaction. The Graeco-Roman world of the first century generally preferred the fires of Eastern mysticism to the icy water of the philosophers. To be more precise, the religions, which had come from Egypt, Syria, and

Phrygia, played an important role in synthesizing the various cults and pious societies (an example of syncretism).

Cicero, in a speech to the Senate in the year 56 B.C. (cf. *De Haruspicium responsis*, 9, 19), declared that if the Romans did not have all the qualities observed in other peoples, they did surpass all others in piety and religion. His statement is at least a testimony to the consciousness the Romans had of being very religious.

From the very beginning, especially in country districts, nature religion, which had been received from more ancient times, was preserved. That this is true seems to be a universal human fact. As social life progressed, religion became more defined, more specified and diversified; it was found everywhere in daily life. No doubt the *penates* of the family hearth, the *genii* of particular locals, the *lares* of the crossroads, and all the secondary divinities of the poor, held a more important place than classic mythology as we know it. All the religious practices were observed: prayers, oaths, sacrifices, votive offerings, manifestations of repentance, consultation of oracles, recourse to the gods of healing and of divine cures. Furthermore, religion was a social and a public affair. Every civic function and every assembly was begun or accompanied with sacrifices. Certain associations, circles, and brotherhoods, held sacred banquets. The priesthood, a purely ritual ministry, was an official duty. Sanctuaries were arranged much like those of the Near East: a temple or house of God situated in a consecrated enclosure or plot, with a sacred wood or grove and a fountain containing lustral water. Numerous feasts were observed throughout the year, at which time the various liturgies were performed, and which deeply affected the common life of the people.

The advent of the empire precipitated the notion of emperor worship, an idea that developed side by side with the development of the city of Rome. Emperor worship was concerned primarily with deceased emperors, whom death had placed among the ranks of the gods; occasionally, however, a reigning emperor would desire to be made a god during his lifetime. The power and the extent of this new worship should not be minimized (with the exception of Rome itself, however; there, people were generally quite skeptical of emperor worship, and of many other practices as well). The forerunners of this type of cult were found in the Near East, especially in Egypt, which divinized its pharaohs, and in Alexander's notion that he himself was of a divine race. The profound purpose of the imperial religion was world unification, the turning of the world into a large city, a plan which would necessitate a divinity common to all the citizens and uniting them. Emperor worship went beyond the person of the emperor: he might disbelieve in it and refuse adoration, as Tiberius, Claudius, and Vespasian did; or, he might accept and even demand worship, as Caligula, Nero, and Domitian did. In any case, the emperor could not disregard it without undermining public order and the structure of the regime. The worship of the Augustus was civic worship on a universal scale, a natural prolongation and the hierarchical summit of all the traditional religions. In addition, the imperial apotheosis met the need of having a concrete god, a visible benefactor (*epiphane*). The cult was usually spontaneous on the part of the people, and neither imposed by the government nor fabricated by the provinces. Such a religion, however, is purely external; it is the act of a man living under certain political and social conditions; it does not lay hold on his inner being. The Caesars bestowed benefits and amusements on the people; but they could neither touch nor change their souls.

Despite the fundamentally permanent character of the popular religions and despite the great number of divinities officially recognized and honored, it is certain that a profound skepticism had become widespread, especially after the diffusion of the fickle and critical Greek spirit. The jibes of Juvenal and other wits with regard to the nonexistence of the gods, and the open incredulity or the dilettantism, which left many traces, were manifestations either of a loss of contact with the spiritual world or of despair or confusion. The extension of the frontiers of the empire brought about a remedy to this situation.

By pouring out its products and its slaves, its merchants and its emigrants, into the entire Mediterranean world, the Near East provided, through its religions, an answer to the anxiety and the profound aspirations of the Graeco-Romans. Eastern cults were often imported along with slaves who communicated their religions to their masters, even reaching into the cultivated and governing circles of society. Because slaves did not enjoy civil or religious rights (at least until the Antonines, at the beginning of the second century), and because they were often foreign born, they were spontaneously the devotees of nonofficial, noncivic, and international religions, of religions which were both attractive and sensual. By the very fact that international religions were not linked to municipal religious systems, they possessed a personal character which struck a respondent chord in men who were searching and waiting.

Within two centuries, that is, especially after the time of Alexander, the Eastern cults were at home in almost every part of the civilized world. There scarcely existed a locality of any importance in the empire created by Augustus, which did not have, publicly or clandestinely, its chapel or its temple dedicated to a new god, with its group of initiates and their special rites. Among the imported divinities, the principal ones, Isis and Osiris, came from Egypt. Serapis, also an Egyptian import, was the result of a confusion between the Syrian Atargatis and Adonis, and the Phrygian "Great Mother" and Attis.[4] In addition, there are similarities and mixups made which caused some divinities to be more or less identified with each other; hence, Isis, Cybele, the Great Mother, and Aphrodite were similar; Adonis, Attis, and Dionysus have resemblances; and Serapis was the same as Osiris and the Sun, and he was to become Jupiter and Pluto. The cult of Dionysus, originating in Thrace, was more Greek than Eastern, but because of its orgiastic ceremonies, its frenzied races, drunkenness giving rise to "sacred" hallucinations, and frantic dances producing "ecstasy," it can be likened to the Eastern "mysteries." In spite of the cult's extreme aspects, it was a search for liberation and, through the purification of the soul, for access to a superior life. Very close to the Dionysus of the bacchanalia was the Zagreus of Orphism. Having a double origin, it, like neo-pythagoreanism, also practiced purification, in order to liberate the imprisoned soul and to bring it, through transmigrations and metempsychoses, to union with the divinity.[5]

Without entering into details, we must consider the characteristics of the Eastern cults at the beginning of the Roman empire. Truly, in their developed forms, these cults were a continuation of the ancient agrarian, seasonal, naturalistic, and vitalistic myths, which

[4] We do not mention Mithra, who had a great vogue, but only beginning with the second century.

[5] The study of Orphism is difficult. A presentation of it was made by Lagrange, *Les Mystères: l'Orphisme* (coll. Etudes bibliques, Gabalda, 1937). One can also consult histories of religions or histories of Greece.

had provided an outlet for the secret urges, the fundamental anxieties, and the profound intuitions of man (cf. pp. 22-26). They have been given the name "mysteries," which evokes both their requirement of an initiation and their secret character. In general terms, the religious actions they practiced were the product of an isolated environment. The worshipers of the god, possessing an esoteric doctrine, met secretly and celebrated their cult by means of rites known only to themselves. They did not admit postulants into their group except after a gradual process of initiation, a progressive revelation of the mystery, and the fulfillment of a certain number of ritual prescriptions (abstinences, baths, trials, and oaths [6]).

One can readily grasp the many differences between the mystery cults, which laid hold on the whole man, engaging his innermost life, and the official, public, and conventional religion. The question no longer revolved around ancient Oriental mythism. An innovation had arisen: while the ancient liturgies of the Near East were a collective celebration, with a generally magic character (rites of fecundity, in particular), of a myth of nature, the new cults incorporated a personal religion. The worshiper relived in himself the drama symbolized by the mystery. When the mystery, as usually happened, celebrated the "passion," the death, and the rebirth of a god, the initiate experienced these events liturgically within himself. He passed ritually through death, and acquired the certainty of a new life, which would be his after his real death.

Not all of the mystery religions were so extreme. At times, they were practiced in such a sensual atmosphere that man's lower instincts could find satisfaction in them. Often, obtaining the favor of the gods in the present life, curing evils, or finding happiness was satisfactory enough "salvation" for many of the devotees. Many also found consolation in sensing the immediate presence of divinity. Nevertheless, some initiations promised a more durable union with the divinity, a salvation beyond the tomb, and a happy immortality. In their fervor and exaltation, the faithful discovered a meaning for human existence and received assurance of survival.

Experimental theosophies, religious psychoses, and quests for a

[6] There is actually very little detailed documentation on the practices of initiation; by definition, they have remained secret.

superior "knowledge" ("gnosis"[7]) were dramatic "mysteries," with powerful emotional overtones. They opened to the human soul vast horizons by exerting a profound interior and mystical appeal. Because of their character, they exhibited a great attraction and enjoyed considerable success. Their most notable traits—a kind of practical monotheism, a doctrine of the god-savior, a bodily asceticism, a moral perfecting, a spiritual search, and a personal and universal religion—constituted a striking advance in religion and an astonishing approach to God. Christianity, having come from the Near East also, about the middle of the first century, would discover centers into which the mystery religions had penetrated and which were more or less prepared for Christianity, although it was profoundly different. Judaism had been faced with and skirted these mystery cults before, and it was radically distinct from them. Against the complex, syncretic, and ever moving background of pagan mysticism, solid historical Yahwism retained its truly original form.

Note on the Governmental History of Rome During the First Century

In the year 4 A.D., Augustus "adopted" his son-in-law Tiberius, who became coregent in 13 A.D. All of the Mediterranean countries, as well as a part of western and central Europe, were subject to Roman authority. Augustus died in 14 A.D., leaving a magnificent reputation as the pacifier of the world. The realization of political unity for the first time, facilitated religious syncretism. Although Israel did not enter into this union, the emperor was benevolent toward the important group of Jews living in Rome.

On the death of Augustus, Tiberius (14-37 A.D.) was his acknowledged successor. He deserved this recognition because of his personal ability. At first his reign was glorious and happy, but later, the difficulties strewn in his path made him a tormented and cruel man. His nephew, Germanicus, the conqueror of the Germans, after becoming governor general of the Near East, died there suddenly. His wife, Agrippina, accused Piso, the governor of Syria, of the crime;

[7] Not to be confused with gnosticism, which would not appear until a little later.

later, encouraged by her supporters, she suspected Tiberius himself, who withdrew to Capri (26-37 A.D.). Other troubles followed in the wake of the Germanicus affair: the rivalry and conspiracy of the powerful and ambitious minister, Seianus (who was executed); and serious disturbances at Rome. Seianus detested the Jews and he seems to have been chiefly responsible for the short-lived persecution of the Jewish colony in Rome. After the death of Seianus, Tiberius restored to the Jews the privileges that had already been granted to them. Before his death, Tiberius "adopted" the son of Germanicus and Agrippina, Caligula, who succeeded him.

Caligula (37-41 A.D.) was a good-for-nothing and a monster, a prodigal madman who wasted the riches accumulated by Tiberius and brought dishonor to the imperial office. Wishing to play the great Oriental despot, he was the first emperor to claim adoration as a god during his lifetime. He married his sister Drusilla, to whom he intended to bequeath both his empire and his divinity. He was assassinated. The senate considered abolishing sovereignty and returning to the consular republic, but the praetorians acclaimed Caligula's uncle, Claudius, Germanicus' brother, "emperor."

Claudius (41-54 A.D.) was an emperor whose government was excellent, although it was constantly contested. His wife was the detestable Messalina, who engineered a conspiracy and disappeared during a great disturbance. Then, he married his niece, Agrippina the younger, the daughter of Germanicus and of his wife, Agrippina. She was a widow and already had a son, Nero. An intelligent and energetic woman, popular but unscrupulous, she had Claudius adopt her son Nero in the place of Britannicus, who had been born of the marriage between Claudius and Messalina. Afterwards, she had Claudius poisoned. Nero was immediately acclaimed by the praetorians, despite the fury of the senators. About the years 49-50 A.D., while Claudius still reigned, some of the Jews began to create disturbances because of their involvement with a new movement—"Judaeos impulsore Chresto assidue tumultuantes," says Suetonius (Claud. 25)—Christianity. To combat them, Claudius wrote a decree of expulsion, which, however, was not very strictly applied.

Nero (54-68 A.D.), a frivolous aesthete who thought only of amusing himself, soon found himself at odds with his mother. The severe Agrippina, seeing that she could expect nothing good from her son whom she had thrust into power, now set her hopes on the first son of Claudius, Britannicus. Britannicus, however, died suddenly (55 A.D.). During the years 58–60 A.D., a war sprang up in Armenia, led by Corbulon, who had been commandant in Syria. It ended, after new difficulties with the Parthians, in the creation of a vassal kingdom. The period was also marked by the institution of the "Neronian games," at which the clownish emperor sought to have his talents as a poet and an actor admired, but succeeded only in exhibiting his debauched morals. Nero married his mistress Poppaea after he had his mother, Agrippina, assassinated. Although Poppaea does not seem to have been an adherent of Judaism, she does seem to have been favorable to it. Nero was hateful to the people. Against this backdrop of hatred and of orgies the fire of Rome broke out. Nero, searching for someone to blame for this terrible catastrophe, unleased the first great persecution of the Christians, which resulted in the horrible scenes of August, 64 A.D., and in those which apparently took place in several parts of the empire. In 66 A.D. revolt broke out in Judea. When the Jews resisted the government of Syria, Nero, then engrossed in the theatrical festivities which were part of a pompous journey through Greece, sent the strong and prudent general, Vespasian, and his powerful army against them. Vespasian, with his son Titus, at first warred with a terrible vengeance against the Jews for two years, circling in from the periphery of Judea to the outskirts of Jerusalem (66-68 A.D.). When, however, he learned that Nero had been deposed by the senate, deserted by all, and had been slain, the prudent military leader halted his troops not far from Jerusalem and decided to wait for changes in governmental policy at Rome. His wait lasted for a year (June 68—June 69 A.D.).

The governor of Spain, Galba, was at first acclaimed emperor by his legions, then he was elected to the throne. He was an earnest man and had good intentions, but he was old, narrow-minded, and harsh. He fell out with everyone. Assassinated at the end of six months, he was replaced by Otho, a friend of Nero's.

Otho ruled for only three months. The legions from Germany, who wanted their own leader, Vitellius, to be emperor, revolted and invaded Italy. Otho committed suicide.

Vitellius, an incompetent, stupid creature, became emperor, and thought of nothing but plunder. Vespasian, however, although still in Palestine, was also proclaimed emperor and recognized as such by the whole Near East. He let his son Titus complete the siege of Jerusalem and sent an army before himself into Italy. It defeated the troops of Vitellius and Vitellius was slain amid the horrors of civil war.

Vespasian (69-79 A.D.), well-prepared to assume the reins of government because of his long and honorable career in the administration and in the army, was called the "emperor with common sense." He was one of the greatest men to hold that office and laid the foundation for the outstanding century of the Antonines. He put an end to both the internal and external disorders that he had inherited from Caligula and Nero. He used prudence in reforming the institutions, and he used moderation in restoring to the imperial authority all its force. As his partner in this beneficent government, he took his son, Titus, who succeeded him.

Titus (79-81 A.D.) was an attractive personality, who was not highly virtuous but well-endowed and liked. He had been given the difficult task of taking Jerusalem when Vespasian departed for Rome. He was certainly worthy of his father, carrying on Vespasian's governmental work in a praiseworthy manner. His reign was short-lived, however, for he died worn out at the age of forty, leaving behind a haloed and lasting memory among the Romans.

His brother Domitian (81-96 A.D.), who was twenty-eight, immediately had himself elected and acclaimed emperor. He had inherited the noble qualities of his family, but he lacked sufficient experience. Arrogant in character, he was authoritarian and caused antipathies. Domitian's difficulties in Britain and in Germany, his disagreement with the senate, and finally the hard campaign he undertook against the Dacians, gradually ruined his prestige. He was restless, became maniacal with suspicion, and finally sank into a kind of despotic delirium. He had himself proclaimed a god, exacting a cult which no one at Rome would recognize. Because of force exerted by the aristocracy and the intellectuals, he declared war on the Christians, whom he intentionally confused with the Jews, ordering them to pay the didrachma which the Jews formerly had sent to the Temple of Jerusalem and now sent to Rome. His violent persecution (92-96 A.D.) brought Nero's persecution to mind. It came to an end when the persecutor had been assassinated, the consequence of a vast conspiracy to which his behavior had given rise.

An old senator, Nerva (96-98 A.D.), was chosen as Domitian's successor. His government was honest and prudent, but it was weak. He shared his rule with Trajan, the governor of Germany, and left him the reins of power on his death.

Trajan (98-117 A.D.), the "Optimus," the "Father of his country," was truly an excellent man, whose reign was well-balanced and prosperous. Unfortunately, under his reign, as under that of the three good Antonines who succeeded him, the persecution of the Christians, an endemic malady in the empire, however censured it might be (cf. a letter from Pliny and the reply of Trajan), continued. Under Trajan a revolt of the Jews who were scattered throughout the whole of the Near East began.

Trajan's nephew and successor, Hadrian, ordered Jerusalem to be rebuilt as a Graeco-Roman city. The command aroused a fanatical and bloody insurrection, which was led by the pseudo-messias, Bar-Koseba, between the year 132 A.D. and 135 A.D. The insurrection was put down in a definitive way by Hadrian's forces.

[TWO]

ISRAEL IN THE ROMAN EMPIRE | Herod (37-4 B.C.) was the son of Antipater, the Idumaean vizier of Hyrcanus II, and the husband of Hyrcanus' granddaughter, Mariamne. He owed his fortune to Rome, under whom he had been able to manage his own affairs cleverly, without the least scruple. Ever a faithful partisan of Rome, he always managed to be on the side of the victor of the moment. Thus, at first he rallied to Antony, whom he had met at Antioch in 41 B.C. We have seen how he had obtained the government of Judea and the title of king from the senate (cf. pp. 229-30).

In 31 B.C., a conflict broke out between Octavius and Antony. Antony was defeated at Actium and pursued into Egypt, where he committed suicide with Cleopatra (30 B.C.). Herod hastened to meet the conqueror, who returned from Egypt through Palestine. Octavius reached Rome as the undisputed master of the whole empire in 29 B.C.; two years later, he was proclaimed "Augustus," and then

"Princeps."[1] The king of Judea had maneuvered perfectly to keep himself in the good graces of the court.

Herod, surnamed the "Great," was in fact a very great man. He owed his greatness to an unlimited ambition, that was served by an appalling and ingenious energy. His reign left memories both of magnificence and of horror. His servility toward Augustus won many favors for Palestine: an enlargement of Palestinian territory; exemption from tribute to Rome; and interior autonomy with regard to finances, justice, and the army. Herod's royal powers, however, were limited by several factors: he was unable to act outside Palestine without Rome's approval; his throne was nondynastic in character; and, because of the general political control Rome held over him, he was condemned as king of the Jews always to be careful not to displease the emperor.

Primarily a politician, Herod was a skeptic who knew how to make religion a means of governing. Hence, even though the splendid work of building the Temple of Jerusalem was due to him, elsewhere he built pagan temples. His policies also explain why he showed real respect for the religious prescriptions of the Jews, although at heart he remained pagan and dissolute. The people, however, under the guidance of the Pharisees, were not deceived; they detested Herod. The king knew of their hatred and was haunted by it; and he took his revenge for it. He was without doubt one of the most bloody men in history. The number of individual murders and collective slaughters for which he was responsible is shocking. His victims were picked as much from among his own family (his wife Mariamne, his mother-in-law Alexandra, and his three eldest sons) as from among the Jews, among whom were included many notable personages.

Herod's unhappy end brought relief, but it gave rise to other fears. In his will he divided the kingdom between his three last sons.[2] His will, however, was valid only to the extent to which

[1] For a summary review of the beginnings of the imperial era, see pp. 229-30 and 253-57.

[2] He had seven sons. Doris gave him Antipater; Mariamne the Hasmonean gave him Alexander and Aristobulus. These were the three sons he had slain (the last, Aristobulus, had had two children: Herod-Agrippa and Herodias). By his second wife, Mariamne, Herod the Great had Herod Philip, who lived as a simple private individual at Rome, having married his niece, Herodias. By the

Rome would approve it; besides, the Jews had asked to be directly attached to the empire, in order to free themselves from the Herodians. Augustus, besieged by the petitions of the competing rivals, thought he should make a trial of Herod's successors, for what the experiment was worth, giving them, not the title of king but that of tetrarch. Archelaus was put in charge of Judea, Samaria, and Idumaea; Herod Antipas, of Galilee and Perea; and Philip, of northern Transjordania.

Philip was an excellent servant of Rome, a peaceable character, and a good administrator, but his career was uneventful. He had married his grandniece, Salome (the Salome of Mark 6:22-28), the daughter of Herod Philip and Herodias. Dying without offspring, Herod Agrippa I inherited his lands.

Herod Antipas was less peaceful. A great lover of things Roman, he was Tiberius' friend and accomplice in the affairs of the Near East. Unhappily, his fame comes from having married his niece Herodias, already the legitimate and unrepudiated wife of his brother Herod Philip, in spite of his marriage to the daughter of Aretas IV, the king of the Nabatean Arabs. The public scandal he caused was denounced by John the Baptist, who paid for his courage by an ignominious death. Antipas' action was also the cause of war with the Arabs, the injured wife having taken refuge with her father (in 36 A.D.). Tiberius wished to intervene in favor of his man, but the legate of Syria in charge of the matter, Vitellius, was prudent enough not to want war. He let things drag and Tiberius died in the meantime, leaving the situation unchanged.

On his accession to the throne, Caligula elevated to royalty one of his companions in debauchery, Herod Agrippa I, the brother of Herodias, and a man whose checkered past marked him as an adventurer. He received as his lot the territories which the tetrarch Philip had left at his death. Consumed by ambition and jealousy, Herodias incited Herod Antipas to go and request the same kind of advantages from Caligula. But Caligula, forewarned by Herod Agrippa, sent the petitioner into exile, accompanied by Herodias, who was unwilling to leave him; his tetrarchy was annexed to the kingdom of Herod Agrippa I (in 40 A.D.).

Samaritan, Malthake, he had Archelaus and Herod Antipas; finally, by a Jerusalemite, Cleopatra, he had Philip. These last three were made heirs of the kingdom by his will.

Archelaus, a cruel tyrant, did not govern southern Palestine long. After a new appeal by the Jews to Rome, he was removed from office. His territory, annexed to the Empire, was thenceforth entrusted to the rule of Roman procurators (in the year 6 A.D.), of whom there would be fourteen.

The procurator was an administrator who worked in conjunction with the legate governing the Roman province of Syria and who was dependent on him. He resided at Caesarea, but went up to Jerusalem and remained there whenever circumstances or necessity required it. He was responsible for public order, and for that reason had four military contingents at his disposal. He was charged with collecting taxes, and carried out the job by means of a complicated bureaucracy of judges and publicans, whom the populace naturally detested. He had to render judgment on Roman citizens and, in major cases, on Jewish defendants.

Apart from political sovereignty, the institutions, customs, and traditions of Judaism were respected, along with the exceptional privileges which had been conceded to the Jews (cf. pp. 264-65). The emperor himself protected the cult of Jerusalem, even sending offerings to be sacrificed for his intention. The privileged position of the Jews was not always the case, however, as we shall see in connection with the reign of Caligula. Nor did the procurators observe all the Roman decrees of liberality toward the Jews. The Jews, on the other hand, became more and more difficult to govern.

The first procurators, Coponius (6-9 A.D.), Marcus Ambivius (9-12 A.D.), and Annius Rufus (12-15 A.D.), were named by Augustus. Tiberius first appointed Valerius Gratus (15-26 A.D.) to the post. Valerius deposed the high priest in office, Annas (designation to the sovereign pontificate was a prerogative of the procurator), and after trying three others, finally came to an understanding with Caiaphas. Valerius' successor was Pontius Pilate (26-36 A.D.), whose reputation is known. He was a harsh man who hated the Jews, and used his ingenuity to harass them and exasperate them in the religious domain, making many victims before he was removed from office. Under Caligula the procurators were Marcellus (36-37 A.D.) and Marullus (37-41 A.D.). During this period, while a violent persecution broke out against the Jews of Alexandria on the pretext that they had refused to worship the divinized emperor, things also were going from bad to worse for the Palestinian Jews. Caligula had given the order to erect his statue in the Temple of Jerusalem; if his command had been carried out, an uprising would have occurred, followed by bloodshed. This stupidity was avoided by the prudence and courage of Vitellius's successor as governor of Syria, Petronius. The assassination of Caligula was celebrated as a holiday by the Jews.

Herod Agrippa I, who, as has been seen, owed his fortune to Caligula, also profited by the accession of Claudius. Claudius was equally his friend, and was indebted to him for aiding him to accede to the supreme power. Claudius added to the territories of Herod Agrippa (to the north and east of Palestine) those belonging to the procuratorship of Judea, which included Samaria and Idumaea. In this way, the kingdom of Herod the Great was reformed under his grandson (41-44 A.D.). The grandson's short reign, was a happy period for the Jews, whose religion the Herodian ostentatiously respected (although without himself believing). This benevolent arrangement, however, had a counterpart in the minor persecution of the dissident community spurned by the Pharisees—the Christians of Jerusalem (cf. Acts 12:1-3).

Herod Agrippa died suddenly, leaving only three daughters and a boy who was too young to rule; consequently, Claudius placed his entire territory into the hands of the procurator, Cuspius Fadus (44-46 A.D.). The choice was not a bad one, nor was that of his successor Tiberius Alexander (46-48 A.D.). The assigning of subsequent procurators was difficult because the people were so irritable and insufferable. The situation became more and more awkward, and in less than twenty years the Jews were driven to the most rash and most desperate of their revolts.

Whether it was governed by a Herod or by a procurator, Palestine was considered by the Jews, wherever they were, as their religious center, their spiritual homeland, and the heart of their existence. The Jews who did not live in Palestine dwelt, for the most part, within the Roman empire. The empire itself now included almost all of the countries bordering on the Mediterranean and extended from the Atlantic to the Persian Gulf. This situation was doubly favorable to the expansion of Judaism: it provided facilities for communication, travel, and cultural exchanges, and it insured the protection of the Romans, from whom the Jews had won favors since the time of the Machabees. Because of the high birthrate among the Jews and of their ability to adapt to the customs of foreign lands without letting themselves be assimilated, and also because of the large number of conversions from paganism to Judaism,[3] their expansion was extraordinary.

The growth of Israel was noticeable primarily in the Holy Land itself. The Israelites, who, at the beginning of the second century before the Christian era, occupied only the small mountainous area of Judea surrounding Jerusalem, had finally established themselves, by virtue of the Hasmonean conquests and the policy of the Herods, in almost every region of the Palestinian territory. They even reached into "Galilee of the gentiles," that is, into the district with the largest foreign population. The Jewish population of Palestine is estimated to have been about two million in the middle of the first century of the Christian era.

The development of the Diaspora was even more surprising. Large colonies of about a million each were found in Mesopotamia, in Syria, in Asia Minor, and in Egypt. More settlements had been made in other countries. The text of Acts 2:9-11 is one of the most revealing from this point of view. According to reliable estimates, almost six million Jews lived outside of Palestine. Hence the total number of Jews in the Roman empire was nearly eight million. The total population of the Roman empire is set at about seventy million. In other words, one Roman in ten was a Jew; and since the Jewish colonies were less numerous in the western regions of the Mediterranean, the Hellenized Near East counted one Jew in every five inhabitants.

The Jews lived especially in the cities, and, arriving in poverty, dwelt for a long time in the hovels of the most wretched sections. In this way the first "ghettoes" were formed. On the other hand, it often happened, as has been pointed out, that many of the Jews found lucrative positions for themselves, practiced intellectual professions, and entered administrative organizations. By the very fact that Judaism was solidly established everywhere, it showed little fear of its surroundings and became more receptive to those whom it attracted and whom it might welcome.

[3] The words of Jesus in Mat. 23:15 show the missionary zeal that animated the religious élite in Israel.

The non-Israelites who became converts to Judaism were of two kinds, according to the degree of their adherence: the "proselytes" (cf. p. 217, note 4), who were incorporated into Israel by circumcision and who were subject to all the obligations of the Torah; the sympathizers or the "God-fearing," who had not committed themselves to Judaism, but who frequented the synagogues. The latter group were not circumcised, nor could they be considered to be "practicing" Judaism. Nevertheless, they were more than interested in the Israelite religion, and attached themselves to it by their faith in the One God of Revelation, as well as by the piety of their characters and their fulfillment of certain observances.

Judaism was not modified or mitigated because of outside interest in it. Every Jewish community could be recognized because of its unity, its strictness, and its strong interior organization; seen from without, it seemed closed off from the rest of men. The life led in each community was an enigma that disturbed the eyes of the profane. The requirements of the Jewish Law had immediate practical consequences in everyday life: dietary regulations (rules of purity) forbade the taking of meals in common; circumcision, which prevented the Jews from participating in sports and which occasioned low jests; and the Sabbath rest, which had no parallel in Graeco-Roman life. Jewish customs of this kind were aggravated by a chauvinistic cult that had become atavistic of Jewish separatism, and by their taking of a stand, which was both intellectual and sentimental, against the pressures or the dangers of pagan infiltration.

The social influence of the Jews (their numbers, the strangeness of their customs, the success of their transactions in the economic and financial world, the strength of their esprit de corps) was enough to give rise to a widespread hatred for them that would rapidly become general and serious throughout the whole civilized universe. In the Hellenized Near East, furthermore, it was common knowledge that the Jews were supported by the Roman newcomers and that they were favorable to the imperial power, readily becoming its auxiliaries, for example, by accepting positions as taxcollectors. This "antisemitism" (more precisely, it was anti-Judaism), was particularly noticeable at Rome and at Alexandria, both among the common people, as shown by certain insurrections (the first of the "pogroms"), and among the upper circles and intellectuals.[4] It is not surprising that opposition to Judaism became impassioned, exaggerating its reasons for existence to the point of creating legends like those of "ritual murder" and the cult of the ass,[5] and distorting the traditional history of Israel.[6]

Jewish apologies, which had been published and circulated beginning two centuries before (cf. pp. 241-42), replied to these attacks, but they were scarcely read by the non-Jews. In fact, they were intended chiefly to sustain the morale of the Jews who might become depressed under the valley of defamation, hatred, and humiliation. They kept alive among the children of Israel the idea of their election, the hope of a kingdom in which they would be over all the nations, and a contempt for and a profound detestation of the *goym* (nations). With what deeply felt emotion they must have savored the psalms of malediction, while their imagination reveled in the triumphant notes of the apocalyptic songs.

Undoubtedly, in the Diaspora, relations and contacts with other men had been practiced for a long time, and attempts were made to propagate the Jewish faith and to obtain adherents to it. Nowhere, even in Palestine, had the holy community been completely closed to non-Israelites. Nevertheless, the Jews did not usually even consider the turning of the *goym* to Yahweh except in terms of conversion under pain of extermination. This attitude was often foolish and unjust; however, it was understandable, and saved Israel more than once from being assimilated.

The Israelite attitude had forced Rome to give the Jews a special status in the empire. The empire had become a mixture of many nations, races, cultures, and even religions. The Roman religion, as has been pointed out, was a kind of a soulless state in-

[4] Cicero, *Pro Flacco,* XXVIII; Seneca, quoted by St. Augustine, in *The City of God,* VI, 11; Apion, in the *Contra Apion* of Fl. Josephus, II, 11; Juvenal, *Satires,* XIV, 103-104; Tacitus, *Historiae,* V, 5. Part of our documentation on the conditions to which we refer comes from S. W. Baron, in his *History of Israel, op. cit.,* pp. 225-85.

[5] These legends, born in the time of the Seleucids, claimed that the Jews secretly sacrificed a pagan every year while pronouncing an oath of hostility to strangers, and that they paid religious worship to an ass (similar accusations were later made against the Christians).

[6] For example, the Exodus was explained by saying that the Israelites had been expelled from Egypt because they spread leprosy there.

stitution, which the state could not get along without; and although it had its adherents (it was compulsory to be one), scarcely any of them were truly faithful. Nevertheless, the Roman religion had annexed the gods and cults of other countries to itself, and had acclimated itself to other regions by coming to terms with local religions. Israel alone was able to stand apart, without making concessions. When a procurator like Pontius Pilate wished to infringe on the regulations against displaying graven images, and still worse, when Caligula spoke of having a statue erected to himself in the Temple of Jerusalem, the whole people rose up, ready for the most desperate resistance, prefering death rather than the "contaminations" and the "abominations" other nations accepted.

Rome, then, allowed the Jews a certain autonomy in their internal affairs, which consisted of a real independence on the religious level and, insofar as it pertained to religion, in the civil domain. The privileges conceded to the Jews varied, however, depending on the changes in central authority and according to whether the Jews were those of Judea or of the Diaspora. Among these special privileges, the following can be mentioned: exemption from worshiping state or the city; the proscription of statues as objects of worship; the protection of the synagogues by Roman law; the right to keep the Sabbath; civil equality of the Jews among themselves; and, the privilege of special tribunals. In each regularly established Jewish community, a local Sanhedrin watched over the administration of the affairs of the group, and was empowered to make judgments in secondary cases.

At Jerusalem, the great Council or Sanhedrin, which had originated two hundred years earlier (cf. p. 222), could render judment, with a few exceptions, in all cases falling under the Jewish Law. Rome, for example, reserved the right to impose capital punishment. Presided over by the high priest, the Sanhedrin was composed of seventy-one members, who were divided into three groups: the priestly aristocracy, called the "chief priests" (cf. p. 272); the leaders of public life, that is, the lay nobility or the ruling and propertied social class, called the "elders"; and the intellectuals, theologians, and jurists, called "Scribes" or "doctors of the Law." The first two groups were Sadducees, who were unpopular with the people because they showed their dislike for the masses, and did nothing for them. The third group was composed primarily of Pharisees; it was, from the beginning, highly popular among the people, and was the progressive, active wing of the Council.

[THREE]

THE JEWISH COMMUNITY | By nature, Palestine had always been an agricultural country. In the first century, essentially it still was a farming community, but because of a considerable population increase and the attainment of a certain unification, Palestine was systematically exploited as never before. The land had grown very fertile, producing wheat and especially barley to such an extent that large quantities could be exported. Its fruits—dates, figs, olives, grapes, lemons, pomegranates—were not only superabundant but were of a quality that was highly appreciated everywhere. Papyrus was also cultivated, and the balsam trees of Jericho were world famous.

To increase the production of the various crops to the maximum, the raising of small animals that might be destructive to the fields was prohibited as far as possible. Cattle raising, however, continued, especially in Transjordania. Although there was little meat, fish was consumed in enormous quantities. This led to the establishment of important fishing and fish-preserving industries on the Lake of Genesareth. The Jews of Palestine were, therefore, primarily rural workers.

Small industries had, as everywhere, a raison d'être, especially in certain quarters of the towns. Nevertheless, the only notable one was the textile industry, which produced wool and linen. Few Jews devoted themselves to work in banks, because of their repugnance for lending at interest (a repugnance inculcated by the Torah: cf. Ex. 22:24; Deut. 23:20-21; Lev. 25:35-37); in a world of capitalism and usury, however, some were more realistic. Some men engaged in major commerce, establishing firms and chartering ships; but they comprised a very small minority and lived somewhat on the fringe of the community.

A consideration of the natural riches of the country might lead one to believe not only that Palestine was self-sufficient, but also that its population was wealthy. This was not at all true. There were rich men, even some who had great fortunes, but these were the tyrants and the exploiters, beginning with Herod, who possessed unheard of riches and profits. Most of the Jews were oppressed in a shameful and pitiless way by the men in power or by extortioners in government. Contributions of natural products, requisitions and forced labor, regular taxes and occasional deductions, indirect taxes, customs and tolls, as well as the sacerdotal tithe, offerings and other taxes for the Temple—all of these were more than was needed to impoverish the country. The bulk of the population formed a proletariat that bordered on indigence.

Such a situation did not contribute to the unification of the country. Besides being naturally made up of diverse regions that tended to be separate from one another, the people's long history had also sharpened certain differences or contrary views among them. John Hyrcanus and Alexander Jannaeus had restored to Palestine the frontiers it had had during the most glorious years of the royal period (cf. pp. 226-27). The Idumaeans had not acquired, merely because of their forced incorporation into Judaism, a spirit similar to that of the Palestinians, their hereditary enemies in the Judean mountains. The Samaritans, who also had to yield to force and whose sanctuary had been destroyed, only felt more deeply at odds with Jerusalem (cf. John 4:9). The ancient Philistine coastal region, a country which dealt in trade, had responded to Hellenization more than the other. The creation of the great port of Caesarea accentuated the cosmopolitan character of this flat and fertile region, pointing up how different it was from the mountainous central area. Even though Judaism had penetrated into the Transjordanian regions, Iturea and Gaulonitis to the north, Decapolis and Perea in the center, and Nabatean Arabia to the south, they were never truly Jewish regions.

Finally, a very noticeable difference could be seen between the Jews of Judea, who had been Jews from time immemorial, so to speak, and those of Galilee. Galilee was also a fairly recent annexation; its inhabitants were Jewish by race, and although they were geographically part of the frontier region and counted many foreigners among their fellow countrymen, they had become true Israelites by faith and by religious practice. Galilee was, because of its products, the richest district of Palestine, but it was overpopulated and suffered from systematic exploitation by the rulers of Jerusalem and by the landed proprietors who lived there. A population of laborers, the Galileans were despised by the learned rabbis of the Holy City, who considered themselves the sole custodians of orthodoxy (cf. John 7:52). The Galileans were less inclined, or less accustomed at least, to submit to the yoke of legal minutiae; they were less scrupulous about observing them, and were more broad-minded.

A haughty scorn for the common people [1] was professed particularly by the Scribes, the Pharisees, and the Sadducees. The first of these three groups of men filled an office; the other two each represented a kind of party which was both religious and social.

Like wise men of times past, the Scribes or *sopherim* (cf. p. 209) gradually became entrenched in Judaism. It was due largely to them that the writings which formed the sacred patrimony of Israel had been collected. At the beginning of the postexilic period, they were not yet distinguished from the priests (cf. pp. 190, 209); but later they were recruited from the laity (like ben Sirach, p. 219). The Scribes acquired the teaching authority for themselves; hence, finally, the clergy retained only the duties connected with liturgical worship, and its hierarchical privileges, while the Scribes were charged with instruction. It was their duty to preserve, to transmit, and to comment on the traditional Law.

During the period presently under discussion, the Scribes held an important place in Jewish life. Called "men of the sacred Scripture" (*grammates, hierogrammates*), they were acknowledged as "masters" (*didascali*), and "masters-of-Law" (*nomodidascali*, lawyers). From their childhood they devoted themselves to the study of the sacred texts, giving all their time to them during a lifetime of labor, austerity, and of poverty. Their principal task was to interpret the Torah, defining its precise application in diverse concrete cases, whether these cases were ordinary or exceptional. Therefore, the lay Scribes were moralists, subject to the dangers of all specialization and particularly, in their case, excessive casuistry. The

[1] The "men of the country" or "people of the land," as they were called. This expression, which had designated, on the return from exile, the hybrid population, Samaritan especially, to distinguish it from the repatriates (cf. pp. 180-81), had retained a pejorative connotation. Now, however, it was used to designate the uncultivated people, considered by the "just" as a clumsy peasantry, superstitious and entirely sinful.

people liked these doctors and directors of conscience, these catechists and spiritual fathers who were anxious to instruct them; they trusted them and had recourse to them more often than to the priests. Many of the Scribes were Pharisees and played predominant roles as members of that group; they were called "Rabbi," that is, "great one."

The Pharisees' viewpoints, mode of living, and their practical attitudes began to become apparent during the time of the Hasmoneans (cf. p. 227). They were heirs or successors to the Hasideans, men who vowed a rigorous fidelity to the Law (cf. p. 225). From early times, they had assumed the task of studying and commenting on the Torah. Anxious to perform their work perfectly, they sought, like the good Scribes or disciples of Scribes they were, to define it in terms of everyday life. The ritual prescriptions, in particular, posed problems to which solutions had to be given in the light of tradition and according to the wisdom of the masters. Under Alexandra, the decisions of their doctors were considered as authentic extensions of the Torah, and had the force of law. They formed an association in which the members obliged themselves to the strict observance of the legal precepts as they were interpreted or supplemented. Estimates put the number of the Pharisees at about six to eight thousand in the middle of the first century of the Christian era.

The Law they sought to impose may be called oral in the sense that it was no longer made up solely of the Scripture found in the Sacred Books, but also consisted of the "traditions" established by theologians and moralists. The traditions now formed an impressive total of minute and complicated prescriptions, which went beyond and even above the Torah, for example, the rules concerning ritual purity (cf. Mark 7:3-4), the sabbath rest (cf. Mark 2:24; 3:2; Matt. 12:2, 11; John 9:16), and the cultic dues (cf. Matt. 23:23). The whole effort of the Pharisees and of the Scribes belonging to their school was to show the value of the traditional religion. They wished to accentuate its uniqueness by comparing it with other modes of living that were not rigorously Israelite; they wanted to surround it with an enclosure that would defend it from destructive influences. The existence of Pharisaism can be explained, therefore, by the circumstances of Palestinian life after the invasion of Hellenism and the presence of foreigners among the Jews.

Because exaggeration was possible, some of the Pharisees dealt in it. The Gospel denounces the religion of legal practices which causes the spirit of the Law to be forgotten. Jesus Christ was often severe, and on one occasion (cf. Matt. 23) angry with the formalism, the foolishness, the subtleties, the blindness, and the hardness of a certain number of the Pharisees. Do not forget, however, the highly stylized form (like that used by the ancient Prophets) of Christ's reproaches. Of special note is the fact that Jesus spoke out so vigorously against the Pharisees only because of the esteem he had for them and the influence they exerted.[2] He felt himself quite close to them on many points, and approved of their work. Many similarities can be found between the maxims of the Pharisaic doctors and the message of the Gospel. The similarities make the points of divergence even more conspicuous, and these differences were all the more noticeable and all the more painful to Christ because something fundamental was at stake: freedom of spirit; the progress of the People of God in history; and the true fulfillment of the Law (cf. Matt. 5). The conflict will be taken up again when the Apostle Paul is discussed.[3]

The Pharisees must not all be judged alike. Many of them, like the Scribe praised by Jesus (cf. Mark 12:28-34) were "not far from the Kingdom of God." Many were leaning toward Christianity, and some of them even rallied to it (cf. John 3:1; 19:38-39; Acts 5:34-40; 15:5; 23:6-9). Historians have observed that, in the middle of the first century, the Pharisaic movement passed through a crisis, because of the lack of great men and the poor qualifications of the lesser ones. The Pharisaism of the Hillels and of the Shammais, some decades before the preaching of the Gospel, and that of Johanan ben Zakkai, of Ismael ben Elisee, of Akiba ben Joseph, and of so many others after them, seems to have been of a different class. Even though the Pharisees were men of God who were profoundly faithful to the Spirit, many of them were criticized (by Jesus and sometimes by others before him) for what can be called, in the pejorative sense, "Pharisaism."

[2] Just as today, clergy, religious, and church members are criticized more than the rest; more is expected of those who have received more.

[3] The Gospel best formulates the essential reproach: cf. Mark 7:8-9, 13. One can say in regard to the ritual ablutions, the fasts, and all other observances, the same thing that is said of the Sabbath in Mark 2:27 (compare II Mach. 5:19; I Mach. 2:32-42).

In general terms, a Pharisee was primarily a man who was very religious, a guardian of God's holiness, and one who tried to show that the relationships of man with such a Lord, although they are possible and marvelous, cannot be reached easily. He was a disciple of Ezechiel.

What has been said above, explains the political attitude of the Pharisees. Under Herod, to whom they refused an oath of loyalty, they did not take part in public affairs; rather, they devoted themselves solely to their mission as religious guides. They preferred a purely theocratic government, but during the regime of the procurators they accepted the Romans and advised submission to them.

As has been pointed out, they treated the common people, who were illiterate and ignorant of the Law, contemptuously. This form of pride was the primary fault held against them, although it can be explained as a kind of psychological logic of those who seek purity and perfection, and who fall into self-justification. Regardless of the Pharisees' pride, the people, with a sure instinct, felt the Pharisees to be on the side of God. They always gave them their approbation and their confidence. When all of the buildings were destroyed in the year 70 A.D., the Pharisaic party remained the principal, and almost the only, inspiration of Judaism; in a very real sense, it was Judaism's animating and productive element, its leaven.

The foremost ideal in the minds of the Pharisees was to bring about a theocracy. Certain partisans of this plan, however, were not as reserved as the Pharisees; some were determined, through a revolution if need be, that the austere principles of the Pharisees would be accepted on a political plane. Their participation in acts of resistance against the Romans and their ardor in behalf of the ideal caused them to be called Zealots. As extremists they would never be satisfied until they were able to fight openly the holy war they were fomenting. To hasten this end, they rebelled on the occasion of the census of Sulpicius Quirinus, when Judea was annexed to the empire (cf. p. 259). Even though their revolt was crushed, they continued to arouse hostility against the foreign authorities. They refused to "render to Caesar what was Caesar's" (cf. Mark 12:17). Some of them seem to have been followers of Christ, although his attitude must have disconcerted them.

In the vanguard of the Zealots, in the service of the resistance, were bandits called "Sicarii," or "dagger men," because they stabbed the Romans whenever they had a chance. The administrative power, understandably enough, was haunted by these dangerous men, whom they knew to be always out of sight. Hence, the Romans lived in a permanent state of irritation, and often struck back by brutal repressions. The Sicarii and the Zealots were the principal causes of the insurrection in the year 66 A.D. and the disaster of 70 A.D., which they did not survive.

Few priests could be found among the Pharisees, because the priesthood did not share in the esteem enjoyed by the Pharisees. The period of the priests' greatest prestige in Israel (which indeed they deserved), was far distant. A high priest headed the clergy, but his importance was defined only after Nehemias (cf. p. 205). The Hasmoneans had been in charge of both the sovereign pontificate and the kingdom (cf. pp. 226-28). After their decline, the high priests were elected or designated by civil authority from among the members of important or influential sacerdotal families. After Herod, the office of high priest was the object of shameless bargaining. The pontiffs did not always remain in office long (cf. p. 260), but, in subsequent eras they constituted, along with their relatives, the essential element of the sacerdotal aristocracy, which finally came to be called as a whole the "high priests." Forming part of the influential world of politics and of finance, exhibiting an unscrupulous covetousness, and taking scarcely any part in religious movements or doctrinal discussions, this high clergy never enjoyed popular sympathy; rather, it was publicly criticized and held in scorn.

A distinction must be made between the hated official class of priests and the fairly large body of priests [4] of modest means and of Levites with slender incomes, who formed, obviously, a lower level of clergy and who were quite close to the people. Because

[4] "It has been calculated that there were some 18,000 adult priests and Levites in the country. If one accepts this figure as approximately exact, the whole class would represent about three per cent of the Jewish population of Palestine and would not exceed one or two per cent of the number of Jews in the world. Ten thousand at least of these Palestinians were Levites, while the majority of the others were priests of low rank, who did not feel any less indignation than did the masses of the laity before the excesses committed by the few influential families placed at the top of the ladder" (S. W. Baron, *op. cit.*, p. 365).

they had not been given the mission of teaching, they did not share in the important role of the Scribes. They were, on the whole, religious men, however. Although they attracted scant attention and were seldom the objects of discussion, they performed their duties and lived their lives in such a way that they kept alive the great faith by which Israel lived. They could not help but suffer, however, from public disregard for the priesthood, in spite of the efforts of the Scribes, the Pharisees, and of their adversaries the Sadducees, to uphold the honor of the sacrificial function, which was the very heart of the life of the People of God.

From its beginning (cf. p. 227), the party made up of Sadducees was linked to the clergy. Because they favored the Seleucids and the pro-Hellenic movement, the Sadducees were despised by the Machabees and by the Hasideans; and hence, they were in opposition to the Pharisees by reason of fundamental preferences. During the course of two centuries, the Sadducean party had been the victim of the vicissitudes of politics. With the arrival of the Romans, however, the high priest became the official representative of the Jews. Thus, the Sadducees, members of the priestly party (cf. Acts 5:17), aligned themselves with the political rulers; and there they remained until the destruction of Jerusalem (and of the clergy) in the year 70 A.D. They virtually controlled the activities of the Temple, which was sufficient to show their power.

In one sense, the Sadducees were conservative, and in another sense they were progressive. They were the official defenders of the Law, but they did not acknowledge it except in its ancient and written form. They would not accept the books composed after the wise men of the fourth century. Consequently, they rejected the "traditions" of the Scribes and the doctors, which were so important in the eyes of the Pharisees. Apart from the Torah in its simple and established form, the Sadducees had no other loyalties. They were liberals who were receptive to all human values, and to all progress that did not relate to Revelation.

Their position explains the fact that, although they were won over to humanism and its innovations, they refused "modern" doctrines like personal immortality, the resurrection of the body, and the existence of angels (cf. Acts 23:8). In general, they also concerned themselves very little with eschatology and Messianism. In the view of the Pharisee, however, these were the very points which must be believed. The Sadducean outlook also explains their intransigence with regard to the penalties for failing to observe the Torah. They interpreted the Law literally, with the result that, for example, they sanctioned condemnation to death for adultery or for blasphemy. The Pharisees, on the other hand, looked for extenuating circumstances and a way to soften the penalties. It seems paradoxical that the meticulous rigorism of the Pharisees was easier than the laxity of the Sadducees.

The Sadducees represented a kind of fidelity to the past. Israel, for several centuries, had been conscious of its missionary vocation with regard to other nations. To isolate itself, purely as a means of defense and as a desire to remain apart, would be to stop the advance of history and to obstruct the Plan of God. The too uniformly legalistic tendency of the "pure" had to be rectified by the more universal character of the other movement. The Sadducees, therefore, were most discerning; had they been more faithful to the "sources" and to the needs of the times, they might have been able to play a necessary and decisive part in converting the world to the true God. For this, however, their understanding of the existing situation would have had to be based on their faith; as matters stood, however, everything about them—their ideas and behavior—came from the fact that they did not have a religious spirit; they were not men of God. Jesus himself felt extremely far removed from them, and they could not comprehend anything that this messenger of the Spirit preached.

A truly religious attitude was formed and organized by a group of fervent souls, who were opposed to the Hellenized priesthood because it had become worldly and lax since the middle of the second century. Philo, Flavius Josephus, and Pliny, referred to this group as the "Essenes." [5]

At present, the recent finding of the Dead Sea Scrolls leads us to believe that in them new traces of the Essenes have been rediscovered. Indeed, it has been thought that the site of Qumran was their place of origin and their center (their "motherhouse"). From there they formed into groups, for Essenean communities were known in other parts of Palestine, as well as in Egypt and in Syria. Persecution forced them to establish a place of residence at Damascus. Philo says that there were four thousand of them. At Qumran,

[5] Cf. bibliography, p. 225, note 4.

they built living quarters for three hundred (the buildings were used for the common life—prayer, study, meals, manual work—but the "monks" had for their "cells" the caves in which the famous manuscripts were discovered). The structures found on the shore of the Dead Sea date from the end of the second century or from the beginning of the first century before Christ. They were abandoned during the first years of Herod the Great's tenure of office, following an earthquake which ruined the whole region in the year 31 A.D. Then, they were reoccupied in the time of Archelaus, at the dawn of our era. During the course of the Jewish War, in 68 A.D., the Tenth Roman Legion put the community to flight. The buildings were destroyed by the Romans, but a part of their library was left or hidden in the caves of the cliff.

The Essenean congregation constituted a true Jewish religious order. Although they were closely related to the Pharisees because of their origins and their inclinations, the Essenes were clearly distinct from the Pharisees in three ways: like the priests of Jerusalem, they were from sacerdotal stock, and the basis of the community was composed of priests but they were separated from the priests by a more rigid fidelity to the Law of Moses; they kept aloof from active life, both political and social; and they lived in a closed community, under a complete, detailed, and strict conventual rule.

The Essenes were vowed to celibacy (perhaps, however, at one time or another there were married Essenes). They renounced all personal property. The goods turned over to the community and the fruits of the work of the brethren were administered by the officials of the congregation. Possessing a good framework and hierarchy, the community was both a hierocracy because of the principal role given to the priests, and a democracy because of the manner in which everything was decided in common. To enter the community, the aspirant had to pass through the various stages of a rigorous formation: a year's novitiate; baptism; two years' probation; definite affiliation; solemn vows.

Above all, the Essenean ascetics were strict observers of the Law, especially of the statutes regarding the rite of purification. They performed ablutions several times a day and took multiple precautions against defilement. But they did not allow bloody sacrifices, either because they wished to keep themselves apart from the priesthood at Jerusalem, or because they considered their meals taken in common, according to a set ritual, as true and sufficient sacrifices. They practiced the virtue of religion to an admirable degree; they loved God and served him with fervor, and prayed long hours in common. The hymns found in the texts of Qumran are very beautiful and show a profound piety. Among themselves, they also practiced the highest degree of fraternal charity; but their charity did not extend to other men, who were considered reprobates and, hence, were hated.

Although Essenism was rooted in Judaism and was completely Jewish, it is suspected, nevertheless, of having shared in certain heterogenous currents of thought (Iranism, Pythagorism, Egyptian asceticism). Their participation in alien thought may be explained by the travels made by exiled members of the community, and the influences to which they were subjected abroad. Outside influences would also explain certain of their positions, and in particular the deep-seated dualism of Essenean doctrine. In its broad outline, the doctrine of the Essenes was the same as that of Judaism itself. Of particular note, however, was their special insistence on the election and predestination of the members of the community. They considered community members to be sole heirs of the "New Covenant," and they called them "sons of light," men set apart from all the "sons of darkness." The Essenes believed, furthermore, that God chose certain men to play the role of mediators—Moses, Sadoc, the "Doctor of Justice"—to obtain the graces necessary for "justification." They expected two Messiases to come at the end of time: one from the sacerdotal race, and the other from among the descendants of David. Finally, they believed that two "spirits" of equal power, one of truth, the other of iniquity, had been placed by God in this world for the sanctification and happiness of the elect, and for the damnation of the impious. With regard to the interpretation of the Scriptures (their interpretation was entirely allegorical) they held that the hidden meaning of the Sacred Writings had been revealed only to their "Master" and that it concerned the community alone. They possessed a highly developed angelology. From what has been said of Essenean doctrine, a part of the apocalyptic literature (cf. pp. 233-34) must have come from them.

The Essenes were accepted by Judaism, and no doubt enjoyed some prestige in it, but they were distrusted by the less strict Jews.

Their manner of living kept them apart from other men to such an extent that their influence was probably exercised only on the elite. Indeed, the conviction is growing stronger that they exerted an influence on Christianity itself. Many similarities have been found between the Essenean texts and the New Testament, in particular the Johannine writings and the Christian literature of the beginning of the second century. John the Baptist certainly knew and visited his neighbors at Qumran. His doctrine, although different from theirs, nevertheless is reminiscent of it on several points. Furthermore, some of the disciples of John the Baptist were also disciples of Jesus, and many members of the sect seem to have entered the first Christian communities.

Clearly, Jesus was not an Essene. However much he appreciated the spiritual and moral quality of the religious of the desert, he did not preach the gospel of a private and privileged sect, or of an entirely ritualistic religion. Jesus preached salvation for all men, even sinners.

The poor listened to him. A "poor" man was one who belonged to the postexilic period and who had been formed by it (cf. pp. 185-86, 196). The term, then, does not evoke merely economic poverty, or numerous members of a minority, or the outcasts, such as the lepers, the infirm, the mentally weak, and the variety of beggars. The poor were the common people, those who were often in need, and who knew full well that one can bear the burden of every kind of want, except the need for God. The poor were the humble, whose souls were calm and ardent in spite of their lowly state, and whose way of living had brought about detachment from self, turning them toward the coming of the Kingdom of God. They were the pious believers, men nourished on the Holy Scriptures which Israel commonly gave to her children, who in misery and in hope waited for God to bring salvation and to reign. Some of the poor were Pharisees; others undoubtedly belonged to the various other strata of Israelite society. To be poor meant to possess a profound disposition of heart, something which is not necessarily dependent on a state in life, family background, or a particular profession. Nevertheless, the poor were found especially among the common everyday world of workers, among men who held mediocre or even inadequate positions. Although not acknowledged by the rest of the world, they were a profound group who lived their faith openly and put themselves at the service of the Lord. Obviously, they were not discussed by the other classes. The Psalms, however, and many other prophetic and sapiential pages of the Holy Book, continually bore witness to their spirit. Before long, names such as Zacharias and Elizabeth, Simeon, Anna, and Joseph and Mary, would cause some of them, who were part of the minor clergy or of the world of piety, to be known by many of the needy who lived in the fields and on the roads.

[FOUR]

THE FAITH OF ISRAEL

| Every historian has been struck by the vast superiority of the moral life and religious convictions of the Jews over ideas and customs then current in other nations and among men living in other environments. Israel stood out clearly from other nations of the world in the first century. It was keenly aware of that fact, and possessed a firm and courageous determination to remain distinct. Although Rome was able to integrate other nations without destroying them, and to come to terms with the various religions in its immense empire (at least politically), it had been forced to grant Judaism a special status. Rome not only had to recognize Judaism as a "licit" religion, but also it had to exempt the Jews from obligations incompatible with their faith, such as the worship of the city and of the emperor.

Israel received this special and distinctive privilege primarily because of its faith. A complete picture of the religious life of Israel in the first century cannot, of course, be presented.[1] However, a quick sketch of a few characteristics of the Israelite faith and of its practices will add depth to the preceding study of Judaic institutions. A consequence of this new consideration will be a better understanding of the living climate in which Jesus appeared and in which Christianity was born.

To understand the faith of Israel better, it is sufficient to look at

[1] Cf. G. F. Moore, *Judaism in the First Centuries of the Christian Era* (Harvard University Press, 1927–30); V. Tcherikover, *Hellenistic Civilization and the Jews* (Philadelphia: Jewish Publication Society, 1959).

the Bible. The Bible is the same today as it was then. It is the book in which the People of God expressed and still expresses itself—the book which gave Judaism its basic thoughts and customs. Recall some of the most traditional words of biblical language: Covenant — word — Law — justice — benediction — creation —newness — election — liberty — salvation — conversion — Redemption — judgment — holiness — Spirit — glory — truth — wisdom — Kingdom — dwelling — prayer — praise — service — sacrifice — expiation — poverty — fidelity — mercy — love — knowledge — neighbor — people — inheritance — mission — perpetuity — joy — peace — life. All of these words and more express the vital relationship uniting God to Israel and Israel to its God, according to the fundamental principles that date from Sinai.

An Israelite believed first and above all in God, the One God, the Living God of history, the God who acts in his people and leads it to salvation. God is the great Presence; he is Holiness and Goodness. He is adored in the humility of the faithful soul, and in the sorrowful perplexity of the sinner; he is loved with complete confidence, with eager and jealous attachment, and with overflowing piety and joy. And who can say how far, during conversation with God, that is, during the authentic religious experience of one who, accompanied by divine Wisdom, approaches the ineffable Lord with trepidation, how far his many *hassidim* and *anawim* have reached? How close have the words of the learned Rabbi, who is perpetually absorbed in meditation on the Sacred Word, or of the humble young girl, who simply "keeps in her heart" what she has heard of that Word and what the Spirit of God teaches her, come to God.

The exceptionally frequent visiting of God and the lively sense of his "holiness" had a practical consequence, which characterized the Jewish world in a visible way: Judaism's extraordinary concern for ritual "purity." Since the advent of Christianity, this excessive and material characteristic has often been denounced. Naturally, exaggerated customs crept in; this was true with regard to the Pharisees and with regard to certain obsessions of the religious of Qumran. However, both the Pharises and the Essenes were among the most devout of man. Does not the fact that Ezechiel and his disciples were responsible for this tendency immediately reveal its profound purpose? The minute and multiple rites of purification were symbols which sought, through acts in which the body was involved, both to show and to awaken an acute sense of the "sacred," which is a meaning of God.

These rites were prayers. Through them and through the "Benedictions" which the Jewish rituals still retain, actions and objects were made sacred, and the life of the faithful was sanctified. The Sabbath, feasts, and days of fasting sanctified Israelite life. Prayer (essentially the Psalms), impregnated and accompanied daily life. Israel lived by faith.

The manifestation of this faith was especially striking at Jerusalem, in the Temple where God dwelt. The Temple was a magnificent structure that had been built by Herod during the years 20-10 B.C. It was, at that time, certainly one of the finest monuments in the world.[2] The Israelites considered it the Holy Place, excluding all others. They all venerated the Temple and were linked to it by an intense love. Pious men, of course, might regret seeing the "Court of the Gentiles" crowded on certain days with sacrificial animals for sale and with tables for the exchange of foreign currency. Nor were all disposed to listen to the instructions or the discussions of the Rabbis, who gathered under the sumptuous porticoes (Greek rather than Semitic in style), which surrounded that court. Nevertheless, men found the essential things they came to the Temple to seek: participation in the ceremonies and in the sacrifices; the profound emotions caused by the holy liturgy; the silence of the reserved enclosures; the recollection of prayer, the happiness of being near the Lord.

The feasts on which pilgrimages were made—the Pasch, Pentecost, and the Feast of Tabernacles—and other feasts—the Atonement, Dedication, Purim—brought joyful and fervent crowds singing. The feasts took place amid fine displays of piety and of fraternity. The large attendance,[3] the active and enthusiastic participation

[2] Its treasury contained a considerable fortune. It was supplied by the didrachma (corresponding to two gold-francs) paid annually by every male Jew beginning after he had reached the age of 20 (Cf. Ex. 30:11-16) and collected by the local Jewish authorities throughout the whole world (the celebrated case of Valerius Flaccus, defended more cleverly than honestly by Cicero, resulted from the misappropriation by this governor of Asia Minor of a large sum gathered by the Jewish authorities).

[3] Regular pilgrimages came from all countries and were organized in great caravans. At certain feasts, especially the Pasch, the pilgrims could be counted by the hundreds of thousands. In spite of the size of the outer sanctuary, the

in the actions of worship, the generosity of the offerings, were all expressive of a powerful religious life which was truly interior. The psalms still bear witness to it. The feasts, moreover, provided an opportunity for certain meals to be taken with members of the family or with friends, using a liturgy of "blessings" and "thanksgivings" that were full of meaning and solemnity, and ceremonies filled with the most venerable traditions of Israel.

The Temple was unique; replicas of it could not be constructed, nor were branches allowed. Sacrifices could be offered only in Jerusalem. Each village in Palestine, however, and each concentration of Jews in the Diaspora, had a synagogue, where the people met on the Sabbath and on other occasions. The synagogue was a house of prayer and of study; a place where the texts of the Sacred Scriptures were read, chanted, explained, and meditated upon. The texts provided words, actions, and themes for prayer; they were the very substance of the liturgy of the synagogue and of the one religious teaching.

All things came to the Jews through the Sacred Scriptures. The Sacred Writings were regarded as the Word addressed by Yahweh to his people. A theologically constructed doctrine on the "inspiration" of the sacred books certainly did not exist, but evidence abounds to show that their divine origin, their absolute authority, and their sacred character were admitted by all. The Jewish literature of that era could not have existed without faith in the Scriptures, for Jewish literature was usually a mere commentary on the undisputed text. Since the New Testament is always citing the biblical texts, obviously it considers that God speaks through them.[4]

The list of the books accepted as "Sacred Scripture" was determined in its entirety. As has been pointed out, a difference between Palestine and the Diaspora concerning this matter arose (cf. p. 219). In Palestine, some fluidity in the determination of the list still existed. Thus, a decision made by the Synod of Jamnia in the year 90 A.D. was needed to remove all doubt concerning ben Sirach and the Canticle of Canticles. An absolute conviction, however, pointed up

ceremonies had to be repeated several times in order to satisfy everyone. Everything was done in the Holy City to facilitate the pilgrims' stay: exchange service; free protection (it was necessary only to give the hosts the skins of the animals offered in sacrifice); permanent centers for people of the same region (for example, the synagogues of Acts 6:9).

[4] We meet again, here, the statements made in *WG*, pp. 49-54.

the fact that there was a "canon" and therefore a radical difference between a certain number of traditional books and all the others: the former were "holy books," the others were not. The distinction was not made by a constituted authority, as for example by the authority of the Rabbis; it was the work of an entire history, of a whole collective life. The People of God itself, thanks especially to its prayer, its piety, and its liturgical worship had discovered the inspired books as if by a deep-seated instinct, in which the very Spirit of God can be seen.

The Sacred Scriptures could not be used without some peril. To possess writings that had emanated from God, to venerate them, and to take them as the supreme law and a rule of life might cause the people to forget that God had spoken through the intermediation of men and that, in consequence, the manner in which those men had expressed themselves should be taken into account. They might forget that Revelation had taken place in history, according to a certain progressive economy, and therefore that it was necessary to take into account the period in which the texts were composed.

Neglect of the human and historical aspects of the Scriptures resulted, so to speak, in seeing only the material make up of the text as something distinct from its meaning, and yet still divine. Thus, any verse taken out of context, or any word considered apart from the sentence in which it was contained, possessed an absolute value and enjoyed divine authority. The abuse thus described is called "literalism," a focusing of the reader's interest on the "letter" to the detriment of the meaning and of the true content.[5] Although this danger was not always voided in Israel, nevertheless, to say that the exegesis of the doctors was carried out only in this fashion is a calumny. They had sufficient knowledge of God and of Tradition to understand the true meaning of the Scriptures. Judaism never officially proclaimed that a man could satisfy the purely blind requirements of the "letter" without first considering the teachings expressed and the spirit signified by the texts.

Evidence of this, moreover, is not lacking. A whole contemporary Jewish literature existed apart from the apocalypses and the apologetic works, which had been written one or two centuries previously. These were the so-called "rabbinical" writings. They constituted a literature written in Hebrew, and sprang from the learned circles

[5] We have also had to touch on this point before; cf. *WG*, p. 97.

of Judaism, either in Palestine or Babylon. They had been collected not earlier than the second century of the Christian era, but they contained much older elements, notably numerous maxims of the first-century doctors and scribes.

The Scribes, who had been working with the Scriptures since the time of the Exile, continued their detailed exegesis of the Sacred Texts and of the Israelite traditions, giving explanations and practical conclusions for the various cases that arose. The *midrashim* (cf. p. 200) (called *aggadoth* when they are glosses on history) were composed in this way. Written in a narrative and homiletic narrative style, they had the characteristics of homilies, and aimed at pious instruction or edification. They are called *halakhoth* when their chief task is of analyses of and deductions based on juridical texts of the Scripture, in a style related to scholastic controversy, and resulting in the formulation of precise rules in the ritual or moral order. The halakha form was more developed, and produced the *Mishna* (= repetition), which is a collection of cauistic solutions, the *Tosephta* (= addition), which re-edits and completes the Mishna, and the Talmud (= study), which is a commentary on the Mishna. Mention must also be made of the Targum (= translation), which is not only an Aramaic version of the Hebrew Scriptures but also a paraphrase of them.

As a whole, the rabbinical literature seems to be a written report of the discussions that took place in the schools or the circles of moral theologians. Hence, it is not surprising that repetition and diverse, even contradictory, opinions are found in it. The form disconcerts those who are not completely familiar with it.[6]

Rabbinical literature not only provides concrete knowledge of the Jewish environment at the beginning of the Christian era, it also reveals the major tendencies of Jewish thought. It remained an authentic part of Tradition. Although the rabbinical writings make constant references to the Bible and adheres faithfully to it, they sometimes, as has already been noted, are guilty of providing nar-

[6] Nothing equals direct personal experience. Very few of the texts have been translated; cf., however, Leo Auerbach, editor and translator, *The Babylonian Talmud in Selection* (New York: Philosophical Library, 1944); H. Danby, *The Mishnah* (Cambridge University Press, 1933); C. G. Montefiore and H. Loewe, *A Rabbinic Anthology* (New York: Macmillan, 1938; reprinted, 1961); Herman L. Strock, *Introduction to the Talmud and Midrash* (Philadelphia: Jewish Publication Society, 1945).

row interpretations of the Scripture. Bearing witness to the unparalled moral spirit of the Chosen People was the most important single contribution of the writings. This moral spirit would not be found among other contemporary peoples, excepting, however, certain philosophical circles like the stoics (cf. p. 249).

Jewish morality was represented essentially by the Decalogue, and was understood according to the teachings of the Prophets and the wise men. Primarily religious it flowed from the relationship between God, whose rights were acknowledged above all others, and who manifested himself as much by his demands as by his compassionate goodness, and free men living in a community made up of the special People of God. Jewish morality, therefore, was founded on the Covenant.

Several particularly noteworthy views can be seen in this morality: the concern and respect for truth; the search for justice; a sincere and effective love of one's neighbor, considering him as a "brother"; respect for women; a horror of slavery; a sense of renunciation; and a real cult of chastity (this is the meaning of the numerous prescriptions relating to sexual morality). Thus, an acute sense of liberty and responsibility developed. Thus also, the value of personal actions and the value of solidarity among men, for their salvation or their perdition, grew in stature. Nowhere had men a greater sense of sin and of its gravity. Indeed, without having to stretch the point, it can be said that Israel taught the meaning of sin to the world. The discovery of the universality of sin provided a tragic aspect to human life. Israel, however, through its God, and through a developed doctrine of expiation and of the acceptance by God of substitute victims, discovered a profound dynamism and a robust moral health. The insistence on the necessity of "conversion" shows how this doctrine of life penetrated to the very depths of man, to his purpose in life and to the heart of his freedom.

On one point, however, the Jews never attained a well-balanced outlook: they detested foreigners and made little effort to understand them. Their blindness in this matter is both understandable and regrettable. The "Chosen" People had arrived at a snobbish overestimation of themselves. Hence, obliged to defend themselves in the midst of a world which was scandalized or irritated by their peculiarities, they had become so hostile to foreigners that they imagined them to be hated to the same degree by God and excluded them from all hope of salvation.

This attitude toward foreigners found support in Messianism and eschatology, at least as these ideas were envisaged by the mass of the Jewish population.

The expectation of the Messias was an established fact, and signs of his coming were found everywhere. The belief in the expectation was ardent and widespread, although much keener among the popular and profoundly religious circles than among the aristocratic and intellectual circles of the Sadducean variety. The figure of the Messias, however, was not very clearly defined in this great hope. It was known that he was to be raised up by God, endowed with exceptional prerogatives, and was to be the glorious king and leader of his people, the liberator of a triumphant Israel, and, seated at the right hand of God, the judge of all men.

Attention seems to have been fixed less on the person of the Messias than on his time and his work. The "days of the Messias" were usually conceived of as an era of extraordinary happiness. They would be inaugurated by victory over the "Gentiles" and the restoration of Israel in the Holy Land. The preliminary signs were those of the classic apocalypses: tribulations, cataclysms, and disorders of all kinds. Vigilance and endurance had, therefore, to be practiced, after which would come the Reign of God, the manifestation and glorification of the Messias, the punishment of the impious, the conversion or destruction of the pagans, and the gathering of the "saints" around God, in joy and in the superabundance of all goods. But the "last days" were also to be an era of interior and moral renewal, of new life for the spirit. Men expected at that time a "redemption," and they expected it from a "savior." All of these notions concerning the Messias were in vogue, but few of them were clearly understood.

Nor did the Jews have clear ideas of what lies beyond the present life and the end of time. *Sheol,* the dark, subterranean abode to which mortals go, held no more attraction than it had in the ancient traditional Israelite notions. The important thing was to have progeny "on earth" at all times. Men were always thought of collectively, as a people. But it is certain that, because of an intellectual evolution, which had been going on since the era of the postexilic wise men, now there was also preoccupation with the lot of the individual beyond the tomb. "Eternal life" was the object of solid faith and firm hope, after the manner in which the Apostle Paul expresses himself concerning it (cf. II Cor. 5:1-8; these terms are as much Jewish as Christian). In a general way, men remained faithful to the strong Semitic idea of the material and indivisible man (cf. pp. 28-29), against which the concept of the immortal soul "separated" from the body after death, borrowed from Greek thought, had not been able to prevail. From the Semitic motion arose the belief, which had become common, in the resurrection of the body. Intellectuals of little faith, like the Sadducees, did not accept it, but it was clearly professed by the Pharisees and by the people who followed them. Naturally, personal destiny was not conceived of apart from a collective destiny or without reference to the completion of history: it was to be realized within the Kingdom which was coming.

11 The New Covenant

[ONE]

JESUS [1] | "Now in the fifteenth year of the reign of Tiberius Caesar, when Pontius Pilate was procurator of Judea, and Herod tetrarch of Galilee, and Philip his brother tetrarch of the district of Iturea and Trachonitis . . . during the high priesthood of Annas and Caiphas, the word of God came to John, the son of Zachary, in the desert. And he went into all the region about the Jordan, preaching a baptism of repentance for the forgiveness of sins" (Luke 3:1-3).

Israel was a country which had known many disturbances and had been shaken up by many blows. Its only concerns were resisting foreign interference and national liberation. And, although it had seen the public displays of wandering preachers or men able to collect a crowd many times before, nevertheless, enough people were still willing to go to the low valley of the Jordan and there listen to words that flattered no one. For he was a blunt man, this "baptist." He set the ax of his words to the root of the evils from which sinners suffer, and plunged those who came to him in the river as a sign of a change in their lives, telling them of a coming: "Prepare the way of the Lord."

The inhabitants of the region bordering on the Dead Sea were acquainted with the ascetics who were devotees of the purifying

[1] Never before have we felt so inadequate: how can one speak with exactitude, moderation, and profound fidelity of Jesus Christ? There is no need to say that we must reread the Gospels (without taking them, however, as "biographies"). Contrary to our custom, we will not emphasize our statements or descriptions by references to the texts; this would create a web of numbers; everyone can find the texts for himself. Among the "lives" of Jesus, we may mention Henry Daniel-Rops, *Jesus and His Times,* English trans. by Ruby Millar (New York: Dutton, 1954); Leonce de Grandmaison, *Jesus Christ* (New York: Sheed & Ward, 1961); M. J. Lagrange, O.P., *The Gospel of Jesus Christ* (London: Burns, Oates & Washbourne, 1938); Jules Lebreton, S.J., *The Life and Teaching of Jesus Christ Our Lord* (London: Burns, Oates & Washbourne, 1934); Giuseppe Ricciotti, *The Life of Christ,* English trans. by Alba I. Zizzamia (Milwaukee: Bruce, 1947).

water and who led an austere life in common. The ascetics, however, did not attempt to attract crowds; rather, they sought to avoid the common people (cf. p. 275). The new preacher, on the contrary, addressed everyone, without distinction. Certainly, John must have known the monks, for their main convent, situated a few miles from the Dead Sea, dominated the lifeless beach. He must also have profited from his observations of their severe rule, their profound piety, their concern for perfection, and certain of their practices. He was not, however, an Essene; he went about preaching as one inspired, conscious of a new mission, blazing a new trail. Disciples gathered around him and were formed by him.

Later, John permitted some of his disciples to follow another young teacher, Jesus of Nazareth, who had come to be baptized by him.

In this insignificant village of Lower Galilee, Jesus had spent the years of his youth, and, according to his own wishes, it was a youth lived in simplicity, unnoticed by others. His family, descendants of David, lived in modest circumstances. Although little is known about Mary, the mother of Jesus, she played a secret but extraordinary role in his life. The evangelists, especially Luke and John, would impart precious information concerning her. As yet, however, the circles in which Jesus moved knew nothing of his family and early life.

He had not been a student in the rabbinical schools; he was not a disciple of any of the teachers currently in vogue in Israel. Nevertheless, people soon began to see that, during the long preparation of a youth lived withdrawn from the world, this man, now on the threshold of maturity, had assimilated both the Sacred Scriptures and the doctrines of the most avid circles. Indeed, he possessed a thorough enough knowledge of the sacred sciences to be able to make judgments about them and to speak of them decisively. People soon saw, too, that he belonged to the slighted but profoundly religious group of the "poor," who desired nothing but the fulfillment of the Plan of God for his people, who sought to do his will and who prayed with all their hearts for the "deliverance of Israel."

"The time is fulfilled," he said, "and the Kingdom of God is at hand. Repent and believe in the Gospel" (Mark 1:15). With these words a preaching career began which would last only two or three years, and which would be carried out almost exclusively in Jewish territory. Jesus preached principally in the countryside of Galilee, on the northwestern shore of the Lake of Gennesareth. He sometimes visited other regions and "went up" to Jerusalem. Before his arrest and execution as a criminal, about the year 30 A.D., he spent the last days of his life in the Holy City.

The young Prophet attracted attention from the beginning. Although he repeated the penitential message of John the Baptist, his style was different. He said things in a way no one had ever used before, and he spoke of things that had never been spoken of before. Nevertheless, it was evident that he remained well within the traditional faith of Israel. He invoked the Sacred Scriptures, of which he seemed to have an amazingly sure knowledge, constantly, and he spoke in such a way that he could be heard by everyone.

"Miracles" were multiplied at his word and in his presence: the sick and infirm were cured; "evil spirits" were cast out; even the dead rose at his command. Extraordinary events accompanied him and became everyday occurrences. The witnesses to his miracles were extremely impressed; although they were enthusiastic and filled with admiration, they were also troubled and frightened. They went in crowds to meet him; they laid the sick in the town squares so that he might touch them and restore them to health. He asked only that they have faith in him.

He used discretion in everything he did, refusing public acclaim and any personal glory. He acted without the slightest pretense; honesty, frank behavior, and sincere words were among the most striking traits of a personality that was both appealing and masterful. He could not tolerate evil; his passionate remonstrances reminded men of the Prophets of old. He was kind, however, always and tirelessly kind, and he possessed a quiet strength. He proclaimed peace and joy, and he performed only good works. The common people gathered around him immediately. When he spoke to the disinherited, or to those who suffered trials, or to the lonely, his sensitivity and understanding, his simplicity and tenderness were admirable; he was always ready to give help.

He appeared openly as a man of God. His "works," performed in an extraordinary way, were the "signs" of his claims. He prayed a great deal, both in the Israelite manner and in a way that was peculiar to himself. It was evident that a unique relationship existed between God and himself; they carried on an almost uninterrupted communication, although its exterior manifestations were simple and unspectacular. Men received the impression that no one else had ever loved God, or "known" him in a religious experience, as Jesus did—so spontaneously, so continually, to such a high degree, and with such interior purity. His whole religion was to "do the will of the Father."

His language was Aramaic, the tongue of his fellow countrymen. He spoke, like them, in a rhythmical flow of phrases, employing concrete and picturesque expressions. He used familiar comparisons, which he took from everyday life and from nature. His collected sayings vary according to particular circumstances of life. The style of his discourses varied; at times he delivered exhortations or expositions, and sometimes he spoke conversationally or merely answered questions. Some of his discourses were public, others were given in intimate conversations. Jesus sometimes cried out in the manner of the Prophets, and at other times he uttered the simplest words.

He delivered his discourses in the same way that the public speakers of Israel always did, in rhythmical form, with balanced, parallel propositions, which made them particularly suitable for memorization and repetition. Jesus used the same style when he instructed his disciples or disputed with objectors. His concrete and vivid answers, his simple and well-formed sentences, impressed themselves upon the mind and thus were preserved for later generations. In short, he spoke primarily, after the manner of the wise men, in *meshalim*. He is famous for his comparisons, which he unfolded in story form—the "parables." The form was used customarily by the Rabbis, but on the lips of the Master, it reached incomparable heights, and always served as a commentary to his preaching of the Kingdom of God. Because of the rules of the form the parables were always slightly enigmatical. Jesus said that he had chosen this form of expression purposely, because his hearers could not all immediately grasp the meaning of his message (cf. Mark 4:11). In any case, never before had anyone been heard to speak as this man spoke.

The "gospel" thus proclaimed was the announcement of a religion that established a filial relationship with the most good "Father" of all men. It was a gospel of fraternal love among men, without restrictions being set up and without compromises being made with evil.

Salvation was offered to all, especially a "Kingdom," inaugurated with the very coming of Jesus, was in the process of being established—a plan to be realized, and the free gift of God.

Jesus gave to the themes that had been traditional in Israel since the prophetic and sapiential preaching their full force and value, their total dimensions, and their precise purpose. Freed from the paralyzing web of additions, which the theologians of Jewish morality had spun, the holy Law of God reappeared in its essential declarations and according to its authentic inspiration. With Jesus, the Revelation made to the Fathers and to the great spokesmen of God recovered its authority and its purity, its precise and tranquil moderate character.

He agreed with the best teachers of Israel on many points. He borrowed from the teaching of the Scribes and the Pharisees, developing doctrines that would always be valid and profound; for example, truth and fidelity, interior dispositions, right intention, humility, prayer, and charity in all its forms. Nevertheless, he spoke of these things in a new and personal way. The most important evidence of this fact can be found in the "Sermon on the Mount" (Matt. 5-7).

He did not, however, merely demand a "return to the sources." Jesus was not only a reformer. If he went back to the sources in his search for the meaning of the Scriptures, if it was felt that he moved always within the holy Tradition of his people, still he also proposed, beyond the accepted truths and positions, and in his own name, a new teaching. That "salvation comes from the ews" (John 4:22), was in the Plan of God; his plan of grace in the history of men crossed through Israel, but was to go far beyond. Jesus knew that he had been "sent" to his people. However, he chose to deal first with the humble and the weak, with sinners and the lost, including even the taxgatherers, those destested publicans. Furthermore, he spoke of non-Israelites, of foreigners, of men of every kind, as being also among those "invited" to the Kingdom; they were to participate in a "salvation" which, from that time on, would be offered to all men without distinction. This salvation, whose purpose would not be to attain political ends, would be given to anyone who believed. Belief, however, implies fidelity, which is a promise, and charity. In order that a man believe, a profound conversion of heart must take place, a renunciation of self, according to the example of the

Master himself, who made the precept *to love* a "new commandment."

Also new in Jesus' teaching was the way in which he spoke of *his own person.* He demanded that a man have faith in him. He assigned himself a mysterious role, not only with regard to his unique relationship with "his Father" and with regard to his role as mediator between the Father and mankind, but also with regard to his relationship with all humanity, insofar as it concerned the salvation of the world. In the "Kingdom" of which he spoke, he held a determined place, which was indispensable and supreme. Was he the Messias, "he who was to come"? He did not answer the question directly; he allowed minds to mature, to seek, to discover. No one was more respectful of the liberty which is a part of every man than he. Nevertheless, he acted as if he were the "Christ." He referred to himself and permitted others to refer to him in terms which leave no doubt on this point. The title he preferred was the mysterious expression "Son of Man," a title which had a special Messianic meaning. It had come into Jewish tradition with the Book of Daniel (cf. pp. 237-38), but it remained an enigmatic expression. By using the title, he focused attention on his divine origin and on his transcendence, at the same time preserving his mysterious character, which faith alone could recognize.

Many understood something of his intention, and were more or less resolved to "follow" him and to put his words into practice. Many, too, never arrived at an understanding. No doubt, as soon as they actually began to accept him as the promised Messias, their state of mind perplexed them. He had no external affectations, no political ambitions; he said nothing against the foreign occupation. He was not interested in overthrowing the government and in national liberation; the magnificent deeds which haunted the imaginations of many (and not only just those of the populace) and which they expected as part of the "last days," were not even mentioned by him.

Jesus not only preached, he began something. He chose for himself disciples who were to be bound to himself in a special way, true friends in whom he had complete trust. The twelve he selected were not learned doctors; they were workingmen taken from among the people of Galilee. Some of them, however, undoubtedly had been members of the fervent groups of Essenes, of Zealots, and of other similar associations, which desired the fulfillment of God's promises above everything else. With them, then, the Master founded his *ecclesia,* that is, a fraternal community in which all those who were to believe in him would come together. He told them the conditions for membership, which were essentially faith and charity, and especially the law of forgiveness—God's forgiveness of the sins of men; men's forgiveness of one another. Taking all the time necessary to form them, Jesus gradually unfolded to the minds of his disciples a new vision of the world and of the salvation that he came to accomplish. In progressive stages he gave hints of the drama in which all this was to be accomplished, preparing them to be, in their turn, announcers of the same "gospel," the messengers and the sowers of his Church.

Crowds, which often were enthusiastic, flocked to him. They were to remain sympathetic to him until the end. He could not count on them, however, nor on an adherence which would really bind them to him. They were incapable of accepting his mystery so quickly; they were not ready truly to enter into a new life. The fidelity of the little group of his friends was sufficient success for the moment.

Among the doctors of Israel, some respected and liked the remarkable young teacher. In general, however, Jesus met only with difficulties, contradiction, resistance, and rejection from the Jewish intellectuals and leaders. Truly, as he himself said, a man could be only for or against him. Those who were against him, once they felt he was immovable, openly became his opponents. Many of the Pharisees adopted an attitude similar to that of the Sadducees and of the high clergy in regard to him.

The great cause of complaint was that Jesus was an innovator. The people in authority and the teachers always considered themselves the representatives of orthodoxy and the licensed guardians of Tradition, even though they easily confused one with the other because of their personal opinions and because they opposed everything new. Certainly, the preaching of the Galilean Prophet would require changes to be made. Jesus seemed to them to interpret one point in particular too much as he pleased: the ritual observances. Of course, he remained faithful to the Law of Moses and sustained its authority absolutely; but he gave an interpretation of it which the Pharisees did not accept. In particular he did not confuse the Law with excessive ritualism, as they did. This freedom irritated them. Furthermore, his habit of mingling with all comers, the predilection he showed for the ignorant and for all those who suffered (regarded by the "pure" as sinners and chastised), intensified the conflict. Finally, the incontestable success of his preaching, of his miracles, and of his goodness among the people, the influence he had over those whom the leaders of opinion reserved the exclusive right to direct, aroused their jealousy.

The opposition showed itself early and grew in numbers. The adversaries of Jesus systematically set about the task of contradicting him and of combating him. They were undoubtedly not numerous, but they were powerful. They finally decided to rid themselves of the man who was disturbing them.

Jesus knew their plans. The most surprising thing is that their plans seemed to be part of his own plan, of his own mystery. He neither avoided nor provoked them; he went toward something that "had" to come, his "hour." Of this, he made, from a certain time forward, something for his friends to reflect on. He used strange words, which they did not understand, which scandalized them, but which he repeated. The words he spoke made men think of the "suffering Servant" of the Deutero-Isaias. Jesus seemed consciously to be going toward a mysterious sacrifice, of decisive importance. His followers rejected such ideas.

In Galilee, far from the high priests and the ruling circles, he was relatively safe from a serious attack on his person. Now, however, he went up to Jerusalem, and this time he did not hesitate to enter the city amid public acclamation as the Messias. The leaders of the opposition realized that this was the time for intervention. At the end of a few days, he was arrested one evening, and taken before the Sanhedrin, which condemned him as a blasphemer for claiming to be the Messias and the Son of God. Since capital punishment could not take place without the decision and the cooperation of the Roman procurator, Pontius Pilate was solicited. Allowing himself to be convinced that he had been asked to pass judgment on an agitator dangerous to the security of the state, he too condemned him. Jesus was crucified, and in the presence of a few friends, with Mary his mother nearby, he died.

The disciples had fled, terrified, sick at heart. It was over. There was nothing to look forward to now except fear and shame, the emotional reaction of the other witnesses, the nightmare and the uneasiness of those responsible, and the hope of many people that everything would soon be forgotten.

Israel had seen and heard other pretenders to the office of Messias. Christ, it is true, could not be compared with them. He had put the gravest questions to Judaism; he seemed to solve its problems and to precipitate a crisis within it. Jesus had proposed to Israel, a land encumbered and weighed down by custom like a financier by his accounts, and played upon by forces which came as much from heredity and restlessness as from the heart and from prayer, a peace that was not of this world and a Kingdom of the blessed for the poor.

On the day after the crucifixion, however, Judaism was still the same. It still possessed certain values—primarily its faith, which was ardent, unique among all the peoples and always subject to harassment. Those who had hoped, listening for a moment to the words of the young Prophet, had nothing to look forward to except more waiting. He had not been lucky, this Messias; failure serves as a verdict among men. And what was this little adventure in history's broad picture? The majority of the people heard nothing concerning it. History, then, prepared to go forward without Christ.

But Jesus too went forward. Two days after that fatal afternoon, extraordinary news suddenly spread among the circle of his friends: Jesus had *risen* from the dead! He had been seen and recognized. True enough, he had foretold the event, but it was, nonetheless, overwhelming. Furthermore, it was a revelation: what the Master had told his disciples had come to pass. And immediately they made the essential discovery—the discovery not only of the true Messianic character of Christ, but also of his transcendence, his divinity.

Within the course of the next few weeks, during which he appeared to them a certain number of times, Jesus completed his teaching. He gave his disciples their instructions, assuring them that the Spirit of God would come to them in an extraordinary way and that he himself would abide permanently with them. Then, he sent them out into the world "to preach the Gospel to all men." Afterwards, he ceased to appear among them. The Church was founded and its history began.

[TWO]

THE CHURCH [1] | After the departure of their Master, the disciples and the friends of Jesus, the "Twelve" and a certain number of others, with Peter at their head and Mary beside them, did not cease to be good Jews. They remained pious, faithful to the customary observances of Judaism, and assiduous in prayer and in the religious services of the Temple. They did not attempt to separate themselves from their brothers in the faith of Israel. They caused no uneasiness with regard to orthodoxy; they seemed to be even more conformist than Jesus had been, and they did not have his confusing personality. Their humble situation had, moreover, the added advantage of attracting scarcely any attention to themselves. True, they made strange speeches, speaking of the Nazarene as if he were the Messias sent by God to Israel, risen from the dead, and having entered into the phase of heavenly existence in conformity with the Messianic prophecies (cf. Acts 2:32-33; 3:13-26; 5:30-32). They also conducted themselves in a peculiar way, especially with regard to the meetings they held among themselves and their custom of living in common (cf. Acts 2:42-47); in addition, they preached salvation by conversion and baptism (cf. Acts 2:38-40). Nothing they did, however, went outside the various ideas, activities, and ways of living which were commonly accepted as part of the multiple elements of Judaism.

The priestly aristocracy, it is true, and the Sadducees, was not entirely at ease on the subject of these people who imitated and glorified a man, whom they had recently condemned, even to the point of working miracles, as he did (cf. Acts 3:6-11; 5:12-16; 8:7). A few warnings and punishments made the disciples aware of their displeasure (cf. Acts 4:1–32; 5:18, 40). The Christians, however, enjoyed the people's favor and made converts among them (cf. Acts 4:21; 5:13-14). Many of the Pharisees and priests who were not Sad-

[1] The sources on which we draw are, naturally, almost all Christian. Among them, the Acts of the Apostles occupies a privileged position. Its historical value is of the first order, taking into account, of course, its literary character. To understand this, we are obliged to wait for the next chapter, in which we shall treat it explicitly. The many pages given to the activities of St. Paul comes from the fact that we are particularly well informed on this point, and know very little with regard to others.

ducees were sympathetic to these pious and courageous men; and they were converted to their viewpoint and way of living (cf. Acts 6:7; 15:5).

The number of people who heard the Gospel preached by Peter and by the other Apostles and who joined their community grew rapidly (cf. Acts 2:41, 47; 4:4; 5:14; 6:1, 7). They organized themselves into groups for prayer and instruction (cf. Acts 5:42), for the holding of property in common (Acts 4:36-37; 5:1-2), and for works of charity (cf. Acts 6:1-2). The apostles soon devoted themselves exclusively to the "ministry of the Word."

Through their teaching, as can be seen in the first addresses of Peter, their great exhorter (cf. Acts 2:14-40; 3:12-26), they sought to express their faith in Jesus Christ. They made use of traditional biblical terminology, especially because they could cite incessantly texts of Scripture which Jesus applied to himself, and whose prophetic import they now understood (cf. Joel 3:1-5; Ps. 2:1-2; 16:8-11; 110:1; 118:22; Deut. 18:15, 19; Isa. 53:7-8). Their essential assertion was that Jesus is the "Lord"; he is "at the right hand of God"; to him as to God are given the "power" and the "glory." A man prays to Jesus in the same way that he prays to the Lord God (cf. Acts 7:59; 8:24); baptism is performed in his name (cf. Acts 2:38; 8:16); miracles are worked invoking that name (Acts 3:6, 16; 4:10-12, 30). As early as during the first few months that followed the resurrection, the "religion of Jesus," "Christianity," existed and spread. Furthermore, the apostles and all of their disciples were conscious of having received the "Holy Spirit," whom Jesus had promised to send them and some of whose works were particularly notable (cf. Acts 1:5, 8; 2:4; 4:31; 5:32; 6:5, 10; 7:55; 8:15-18).

In comparison to the traditional faith of Israel, Christianity was obviously something more than just a degree of that faith; it was something new. Conflicts with official Judaism were going to be hard to avoid.

They began, naturally, among the Christians recruited from the Jews. Some of them held less strict views about the Law and were fairly broadminded; they came from Hellenized families or circles which had embraced the Greek language and culture. Far more advanced than the Twelve and the Christians who were recruited from Palestinian Judaism itself, these "Hellenists," as they were called, thought that many things in Israel were out of date. If they had not yet considered leaving Judaism, they were at least starting a movement of emancipation, which would become more pronounced, toward the Judaeo-Christian community.

The "Hellenists" seem to have formed their own distinct group, having at their head the "Seven" (cf. Acts 6:1-7). One of them, Stephen, who was particularly outspoken in discussions with other Jews of the Diaspora at Jerusalem, was arrested and taken before the Sanhedrin. His violent speeches, directed particularly against the Temple, caused him to be condemned to death by stoning, and he was killed.[2] The group associated with him was driven from the city by the Jewish authorities. The Twelve and the other Christians, whose more conservative tendencies were known and who, without condemning the "Hellenists," had kept out of their difficulties, were not disturbed by the Sanhedrin. (cf. Acts 6:8-8:3).

The dispersal of the Hellenists was the occasion of the first spread of Christianity outside Judea. In Samaria, along the Mediterranean coast, as far as Antioch and Cyprus, the Greek Judaeo-Christians proclaimed the Lord Jesus (cf. Acts 11:19). Hence, in pagan territory, and in particular in the great Syrian capital, communities were founded, that is, little groups of believers, centers of Christian life and evangelical expansion. Other Christian centers appeared fairly rapidly; in Galilee, at Damascus, at Alexandria, and at Rome. The Twelve Apostles and the church at Jerusalem gave their approval. The apostles themselves began to carry the Gospel outside the Holy City (cf. Acts 8:4-40; 9:43). Then Peter took an important step at Caesarea: he baptized a non–Jew, the centurion Cornelius, and the act was accepted by the community at Jerusalem. Although as a baptized convert Cornelius lived practically as a Jew and although his case may seem exceptional (cf. Acts 10:1-11:18), nevertheless, the question of the direct adherence to Christianity of non–Jews gradually arose. Then, at Antioch, pagans were evangelized and entered the Church (cf. Acts 11:19-26).

In the meantime, a young and ardent Pharisee, who was a native of Tarsus in Cilicia (cf. Acts 22:3; 26:4-5), therefore belonging to a milieu that was both Jewish and broadminded, and who had been

[2] The chronology is hard to establish: The affair of Stephen took place, according to some, at the end of a few months after the death of Jesus, as early as the year 30 A.D. or 31 A.D.; according to others, several years later, about 36-37 A.D. This latter date seems preferable: the development of Chris-

at Jerusalem at the time of the conflict precipitated by Stephen (cf. Acts 8:1) and who had set himself among the most fanatical adversaries of the disciples of Jesus (cf. Acts 8:3; 22:4-5; 26:9-12; Gal. 1:13; Phil. 3:6; I Tim. 1:13), suddenly became, from a persecutor of Christians, a Christian himself. Paul had met Christ on the road to Damascus (cf. Acts 9:3-8; 22:6-11; 26:12-16), in the year 36-37 A.D.[3]

Immediately Paul became a propagator of his new faith, evangelizing Damascus itself and the neighboring regions of Nabatean Arabia (cf. Acts 9:20-22; 26:20; Gal. 1:17), in the year 37-38 A.D. Then he traveled through Tarsus and its surroundings, from 39 A.D. to 42 A.D. (cf. Acts 9:30; Gal. 1:21), until, with his friend Barnabas, he became one of the five officers of the Church at Antioch. In that active community, in which the number of uncircumcised Christians was becoming greater than that of the Judaeo-Christians, he spent a year (43-44 A.D.) in fruitful apostolic work (cf. Acts 11:22-26). The problem of allowing pagans to become members of the Church was resolved in practice.

Learning that a widespread economic crisis was affecting the "brethren" of Judea particularly, the Christians of Antioch collected money and sent Barnabas and Paul with it to the authorities of the Church of Jerusalem (cf. Acts 11:27-30; 12:25).

At the same time, Herod Agrippa I, wishing to humor the Jews, began to harass and to mistreat certain members of the Church at Jerusalem (cf. p. 261). James, the son of Zebedee, one of the first of the Twelve to be chosen by Christ, was put to death. Peter, imprisoned, succeeded in escaping and left Jerusalem (cf. Acts 12:1-19). Then, a relative of Jesus, also named James,[4] who had joined the apostles after the resurrection, as other members of the family of Nazareth did, and who quickly rose to a fairly considerable authority,[5] became the head of the community of Jerusalem (cf. Acts 12:17; 21:18; Gal. 1:19; 2:9, 12).

The community of Antioch afterwards sent Paul, along with

tianity at Jerusalem seems to require a fairly long time, and the removal of Pilate from office in 36 A.D. would explain how, contrary to the case of Jesus, Stephen could be condemned to death by the Sanhedrin alone.

[3] We adopt the chronology which seems to us to be most certain. Others prefer the date 33-34 A.D.

[4] Not one of the two apostles of this name: cf. Mark 3:17-18.

[5] This is understandable. The "dynastic" idea had not entirely disappeared

Barnabas, to preach Christ at Cyprus (cf. Acts 13:4-12) and in the central part of southern Asia Minor (cf. Acts 13:13-14, 26). The various stopping-off places in their journey—Perge in Pamphylia, Antioch of Pisidia, Iconium, Lystra and Derbe in Lycaonia—can be read in the narrative of the Acts. It will be noticed at once that they were faithful to a plan which almost all the apostles followed in the beginning; that is, benefitting by the centers of Jewish faith created by the Diaspora and its missionary spirit (cf. pp. 217, 262-63), the preachers began by first addressing the Jews in the synagogues of the localities where they went. Reactions varied; they found adherents, but often also opposition. Thus, Paul and Barnabas soon took up the cry, which indeed would become the very basis of Paul's program: "We now turn to the Gentiles!" (cf. Acts 13:46). They left behind them communities in which Christians of Jewish origin and Christians of Gentile origin were united.

On their return to Antioch, "they called the church together and reported all that God had done with them, and how he had opened to the Gentiles a door of faith. . . . But some [Christians] came down from Judea and began to teach the brethren, saying, 'Unless you be circumcised after the manner of Moses, you cannot be saved.' And when no little objection was made against them by Paul and Barnabas, they decided that Paul and Barnabas and certain others of them should go up to the apostles and presbyters at Jerusalem about this question" (Acts 14:26; 15:1-2).

This question was not only important, it was decisive for the future of the young Church. We must also understand how difficult, painful, and tragic it could be for a Jew who, having given his faith to Christ, knew how much he owed to the sacred Law that had led him to God and to the Messias himself. Such a man might well think that the best way to go to the Lord Jesus was still through Israel, with its sacred observances, and in particular circumcision. The problem was to find out whether all of the Judaic observances were definitive in Israel; whether the Torah did not contain within itself everything necessary for further development, even to surpassing itself (cf. pp.

among these Israelites. Besides, whom did they hold more dear than the relatives of Jesus, beginning with Mary, his mother (concerning whom, however, no information is given us after Pentecost in the year 30 A.D.)? The successor of James was also a relative of Jesus (cf. Eusebius, *Hist. Eccl.*, 4:22:4).

61-62); whether the teaching of the Prophets and the wise men did not demand precisely the breaking of the boundaries that had been necessary up to that time; and whether the Covenant ought not now to extend, out of fidelity to the Lord who had revealed himself as the God of all men, beyond its past historical dimensions, to other peoples, to all men. Truly, every Jew converted to Christianity had to pass over a kind of road to Damascus; the pain experienced is part of every crisis in growing up. To refuse to make changes that demanded the renunciation of a past that was gone and the renewal in all of the newness of Christ, was to go against the history of the People of God.

Such was the teaching of Jesus (cf. pp. 291-94). No one had understood it like Paul, and now he began to defend a cause which was henceforth to be the purpose and the work of his life.

At Jerusalem, then, Paul expounded his point of view on the "gospel to the Gentiles," and he produced a living example of an uncircumcised neophyte: Titus. Peter shared Paul's way of thinking and defended it: "We are saved through the grace of the Lord Jesus, just as they are." James, the head of the Church of Jerusalem, was in full agreement: "My judgment is not to disquiet those who from among the Gentiles are turning to the Lord." Using his proposition, a favorable decision was made with regard to Gentile Christians. Neither circumcision nor any other prescription of Jewish origin would be demanded of these converts; they were simply to show the tenderness of their charity toward their Israelite brethren by abstaining from what was particularly odious to them: they were not to eat meat sacrificed to pagan idols, nor blood, nor meat not drained of blood; they were to abstain from any misconduct between men and women (cf. Acts 15:4-34).[6] Thus, with the apostolic decree of Jerusalem in the year 49 A.D. the "Pauline thesis" triumphed. The door opened wide to every Gentile who had been touched by grace, while at the same time the timid consciences of traditionalist minds were charitably spared.[7]

[6] It has been asked, however, if these last clauses were in the "decree," or if, on the contrary, they were adopted, after the departures of Paul and of Peter, by James, as head of his local church and in order to make the relations between the two kinds of Christians easier.

[7] Everyone can see that the various aspects of the difficult problem of that day are those of all time: traditionalism and progress; religious rites and interior

Nevertheless, the problem was to arise more than once; for example, in the "conflict of Antioch," Peter was rebuked by Paul for his ambiguous attitude and too great complacency toward the partisans of Judaic observances (cf. Gal. 2:11-21). Above all, the "Apostle of the Gentiles" suffered to the end of his life from the hostility, sometimes masked and sly, often open, but always tenacious, of the "false brethren" (cf. II Cor. 11:26; Gal. 2:4), men who were only halfhearted or barely converted Jews. It should not be too surprising, then, that he sometimes seems to include under the same rebuke the disciple of the Law who, having become a Christian, has not succeeded in integrating it with his new faith, and the traditional practicing Jew who has never believed in the Gospel. Similarly, we must know how to take his sometimes excessive impatience when he speaks against the Law (which he loves) with a vehemence which may lead us to believe that he was blaming divine Revelation itself (no doubt the most typical passage of this is Rom. 7).

The Gospel continued to spread throughout the world. For lack of documentation, little is known about the work of each of the Twelve, or about a great number of anonymous missionaries, except by the results, which were soon seen everywhere in the Roman empire. Luke, at least, has made it possible to trace the route of the great Pauline mission.

The second missionary journey of Paul (49-52 A.D.) began with a visit to the communities already established in Syria, in Cilicia, and in Lycaonia. Paul's reason for making the journey was to "strengthen" them (cf. Acts 15:36-40). He took Timothy with him as a traveling companion (cf. Acts 16:1-3; II Tim. 1:5; note that Paul was not obstinate in his position concerning circumcision since he had his disciple circumcised); then he journeyed through the territory of the Galatians, in the central part of northern Asia Minor, a rough and deeply pagan region, where his preaching met with great success and where, when he became ill there, he was cared for with extreme devotion (cf. Acts 16:6; Gal. 4:8-15). From there he went to Macedonia and founded, at Philippi, a community which was particularly dear to him (cf. Acts 16:7-40; Phil. 1:3-8; 2:12, 28-29; 4:1-4, 10-16). New foundations were made at Thes-

religion; law and liberty; institutions and events; acquired revelation and new breaths from the Spirit. Syntheses and balance were rarely to be successful.

salonica and at Beroea (cf. Acts 17:1-15); but he failed at Athens, where Paul compared all vanity with "worldly wisdom" (cf. Acts 17:16-34; I Cor. 1:17-2:16). From Athens he went to the capital of Achaia.

Paul spent eighteen months at Corinth and in the region round about. It was one of the most typical cities of the Graeco-Roman world. A center of important commercial dealings and of uninterrupted trade, Corinth was a market for all the products of the Near East and of the West. An enormous cosmopolitan city, it was celebrated both for the Isthmic Games, which were held there every two years, and for a sanctuary of Venus, the latter being symbolic of moral corruption pushed to the extreme, winning for the city the reputation of being the capital of immorality. In addition, all the cultural and religious characteristics of the time were represented in Corinth by its philosophical circles, its religious societies, its adherents of "gnosticism" and the initiation rites of its "mystery" religions (cf. pp. 253-54). Nevertheless, the gross sinfulness of Corinth was a lesser obstacle to the Gospel than the intellectual sins of sceptical Athens had been. In any case, Paul understood the apostolic importance of implanting the Church in this superior crossroad of the civilized world, and he took the time to form in it a center of intense, if not always tranquil, Christian life (cf. Acts 18:1-18). We shall hear the Apostle himself speak of it in his letters to the Christians of Corinth.[8]

Paul's third journey (53-57 A.D.) covered almost the same route, but he made stops of various lengths of time (cf. Acts 18:19-23). He spent an especially long time at Ephesus, where the brilliant Alexandrine convert, Apollos, had preceded him (cf. Acts 18:24-28). Ephesus was the capital of the Roman province of Asia, the third city of the world at that time, after Rome and Alexandria. In addition to commerce, wealth, sports, and amusements, the famous temple of Diana, one of the "seven wonders of the world," had been erected there. There, too, Paul spared no pains to win men for Christ, to instruct them, and to establish a solid and living church (cf. Acts 19:1-22). He did not forget, however, to watch over the communities he had left, because news of them was not always good.

[8] The attitude of the Proconsul Gallio, in Acts 18:12-16, shows us what a Roman was capable of understanding concerning the youthful Christianity, as seen from the outside.

Corinth, in particular, caused him grave anxiety, as can be seen in his correspondence. Youthful centers of Christianity, they had grave faults that had not yet all been corrected. Passions were strong and fraternal understanding was difficult. The surrounding environment, very unwholesome morally, constituted an insidious and permanent temptation to relapse. The neophytes, too easily influenced, passed from excessive enthusiasm to crises of depression. In addition, Paul, who was already suffering terribly from discords between Christians, found his own views questioned and was met by opposition. He was forced to utter severe words and sometimes had to forego being understood. The whole period was particularly painful and trying for the Apostle (cf. Acts 20:18-20, 31; I Cor. 4:11-13; 15:32; 16:8-9; II Cor. 1:8-10).

From Ephesus, Christian preaching spread—either the preaching given by Paul in person, or the words of the missionaries he sent out. To it was due the foundation of the communities of Colossae, of Laodicea, of Hierapolis, of Miletus, and of Smyrna (cf. Col. 1:6-8; 4:12-13, 15-16; St. Polycarp to the Philippians 3:2; Ap. 2-3). The sojourn of the Apostle at Ephesus ended with the celebrated uprising of the silversmiths (cf. Acts 19:23-40).

He had the intention of pushing farther into Europe, of going as far as Spain, and of passing through Rome (cf. Acts 19:21; Rom. 1:11-15; 15:22-32). First, however, he wished to go to Jerusalem to take there the moneys collected in his Christian communities for the benefit of the "saints" of the City, who were always in great need of material resources (Rom. 15:26-27; Gal. 2:10; I Cor. 16:1-3; II Cor. 8-9). He expected nothing good, however, from the Jews, who hated him (cf. Acts 20:3), and he feared a certain distrust on the part of the Judaeo-Christians. For, although Antioch and the other churches founded by Paul on the shores of the Aegean Sea represented the missionary spirit of the advance guard, the community of Jerusalem held opinions they believed to be wiser. It is true that the Church of Jerusalem was not situated in a pagan or Hellenized environment but was actually in the heart of an underdeveloped Judaism. Hence, the Christians felt constrained to spare the feelings of their former coreligionists; this, in part, justifies the difference in behavior.

After having revisited the Christians of Macedonia and Greece, making a series of stops along the coast of Asia Minor and then along the Phoenician and Palestinian shores, Paul arrived at Jerusalem in 58 A.D. (cf. Acts 20:1-21:16). Although he had in his hands the proof of union, the collection made in his communities, he was not received without caution by James and his associates. The Apostle did all he could to show his desire for harmony by agreeing to fulfill, with his traveling companions, a ritual service at the Temple (cf. Acts 21:17-26). But he went to meet something worse: recognized, he was howled down by the crowd and barely escaped being slain on the spot (cf. Acts 21:26-22:23). The chief of the Roman police protected him by arresting him and, after various dramatic events, he was sent to the procurator, Felix, at Caesarea (cf. Acts 22:24-23:35). He remained a prisoner there for two years while his trial dragged on (58-60 A.D.).

The perverse and ignoble Felix was succeeded by the Festus, who was an honest man (cf. p. 309). He was embarrassed by Paul's case. Paul, to avoid being turned over to the "religious authorities," thereby falling back into the power of the Jews, made an "appeal to Caesar" by virtue of his status as a Roman citizen. He then had to be taken to Rome as soon as the opportunity arose (cf. Acts 24-26).

The voyage was stormy and filled with terror; a shipwreck occurred at Malta (cf. Acts 27:1-28:12). Finally, more than six months after his departure, Paul was greeted with great affection by the Christians of Rome. His case was settled for the moment by a *custodia militaris,* that is, he was given liberty but was under the surveillance of a soldier whom he could not leave while awaiting the outcome of his trial (cf. Acts 28:13-30). Two years (61-63 A.D.) of on the spot apostolic activity followed; the Apostle was surrounded by or visited by many friends (cf. Eph. 6:21; Col. I:1, 7; 4:7-15; Philem. 23-24), and he took advantage of their comings and goings to send letters to his communities, such as Ephesus and Colossae. His trial ended in a dismissal of the charges.

Undoubtedly, it was at this time, about the year 62 A.D., that the Church of Jerusalem lost its great "bishop," James. A friend and protector of the poor and severe toward the rich, this pious descendant of the Prophets and of the wise men, who was both a relative and a disciple of Jesus, was unfortunate in being unable to please the high clergy of the Jewish capital. He was put to death on the orders of the high priest (cf. p. 309).

One year after Paul had left Rome, in 64 A.D., the persecution of Nero against the Christians broke out there (cf. p. 255). According to an established tradition, it was about that time, perhaps shortly after the outbreak of the persecution, that the Apostle Peter also died a martyr at Rome. He had been given the leading role among the Twelve from the time when Jesus was with them, and afterwards, by his preaching of the Gospel, and by inaugurating the community at Jerusalem and the communities of many other places. Nevertheless, we have little information about the second half of his apostolic life. The New Testament writings, however, as well as the primitive Christian tradition, are in agreement in recognizing the pre-eminence which Jesus had conferred upon Peter in his Church.

Hardly anything is known about Paul's fourth journey, which took him back to the Near East, between the years 63 A.D. and 66 A.D., or about the circumstances of his second captivity at Rome in 66-67 A.D., or about the details of his martyrdom, which undoubtedly took place in 67 A.D.

Palestine had, at that time, just rebelled against Rome. The foolish undertaking would continue through four years of horror and would end in a sea of blood. Halfway through the year 70 A.D., the walls of Jerusalem gave way under the pressure of Titus' soldiers; the Temple was burned, and on its ruins the Roman legions offered sacrifice to the divinities of Rome. Judea no longer enjoyed political existence, becoming simply the personal property of the emperor.[9]

These events were also grave for the Christians who were Israelites by birth or by sympathy. In Paul's apostolate, which ran beyond the year 60 A.D., the Jews were always uppermost in his thoughts; the same was true, and no doubt even more so, with regard to the apostolates of Peter and the other apostles. Distressing though it was to all the Christians, the ruin of Jerusalem, nevertheless, had some value: a sign for the destruction of Jerusalem appeared to them as a sign of the Coming of the Lord in his "Day," and the dramatic manifestation of the beginnings of the new era. The crisis which had, between the years 50-60 A.D., caused them to reflect on the problem of fidelity to the Chosen People and to the

[9] See note below on the Jewish War and the end of Jerusalem.

Judaic observances, had been resolved at a fairly early date by virtue of the Message of Christ and the dynamism of the Spirit in the Church, in the sense of breaking of bonds, which Paul called "freedom." Now, with even greater reason, Christians from all over, Jews as well as non-Jews, felt themselves freed from Judaism, and became conscious of their difference and their religious autonomy.

A slight distinction must be made with regard to the Judaeo-Christians of the Mother Church. As early as the beginning of the Judean insurrection, and before destruction became imminent, they had left Jerusalem and withdrawn to Pella, on the border of Transjordania, where, taking no part in the war, they were not disturbed by the Romans. They had retained from their place of origin, from the environment in which they had lived, and from the direction of James, a much more traditionalist and conservative spirit than the rest of Christendom. Their form of Christianity, which followed the Jewish customs, does not seem to have known how to adapt itself to the rhythm of the Church's development as a whole; rather, it seems to have wished to keep its unique character. Nevertheless, it barely outlasted the beginning of the second century. Sects which afterwards made use of the Judaeo-Christian name, like Ebionism, were no longer Christian.

Outside Judea, Christianity had made progress during the second half of the first century. Although there is evidence of expansion, its extent is not known in detail. Christianity was well established in Syria and in Asia Minor (where, before the year 70 A.D., and no doubt quite early according to tradition, the Apostle John had settled, with Ephesus as the center of diffusion), in Macedonia and in Achaia, in Egypt and in Cyrenaica, in Italy, and perhaps in Gaul and in Spain. The route of Christianity followed along the coast. It was marked by cities, for primitive Christianity was almost exclusively urban. From the social point of view, it had no prejudices, nor was it the work of one class to the exclusion of another; rich men and aristocrats, businessmen and government employees, soldiers and workmen and slaves were to be found in it. It is evident, however, that the majority of members were the humble and the needy, that the communities were established mostly in the parts of the city where the common people lived, and that the Gospel was preached spontaneously, so to speak, to the poor.

The recalling of the history of the Jewish War and of the destruction of Jerusalem is extremely painful because it was marked by widespread and frightening slaughter. It was one of the most horrible and savage spectacles the world has ever known. One who belongs to the People of God, or who is conscious of a deep relationship with Israel, cannot bring it to mind without having his soul deeply saddened by the recollection.

In the eyes of the Romans, the Palestinian insurrection could not resemble anything other than suicide. Among the Jews, their excited state of mind no longer permitted wise judgment. Certainly, during the four years of combat, admirable deeds of self-denial, fervor, strength of soul, and boldness were performed. On the other hand, if there were cowards, they should not be confused with those men of good sense, who had become too rare or who had too little influence, but who understood perfectly that after a certain point had been reached, courage and heroism no longer fired the energies of the rebels, but rather the most unbridled fanaticism, intoxicated pride, and a savage-like madness. The Pharisees, who had agreed in principle to the resistance, but who no longer approved of the means employed, found themselves thrust aside. Undoubtedly the most sorrowful among so many reasons for sadness, was the internal division, with brothers killing brothers.

It would be unjust to portray the scene as the true Israel. A person is not to be judged according to a paroxysm of madness that has laid hold on him. Furthermore, not all of the Israelites were involved.

Those chiefly responsible were the men who, according to the Jewish historian, Josephus, could be called "bandits," Zealots, especially those murderous and extremist Zealots, the Sicarii (cf. p. 272). Animated by an implacable hatred for foreigners and by a merciless thirst for vengeance, they were determined to use any means, even the most shameful, to attain their ends. They were the hidden and irritating arousers of popular sentiment. Popular sentiment, however, did not need to be enraged because it was already passionate and furious. They kindled the desire for a dazzling victory over Rome, which was pure madness for anyone who was not blind, and for a resurrection that would be a triumph in the eyes of the whole world. Obviously, such aspirations took on the appearance of a most Utopian Messianism, and was not likely to lead to a saner view of things.

All the evils, however, were not on the Jewish side alone. Rome, which certainly wanted peace, was not fortunate in the choice of the procurators she sent to Judea after the re-establishment of that office on the death of Agrippa I (cf. p. 261).

The first two, Cupius Fadus (44-46 A.D.) and Tiberius Alexander (46-48 A.D.) were suitable choices. They had to show their authority by executing a few rebels or bandits, but they did not have too much trouble.

Under Cumanus (48-52 A.D.), incidents began to set the Jewish masses into motion. They replied to the brutal laws of the procurator with reprisals worthy of criminals. Rome proposed conciliatory measures, which the Jews took for personal successes and which inflamed the unruly.

Felix (52-60 A.D.) was just the wrong man for the office. An opportunist who was as ambitious as he was base, he disgraced the office. The Zealots and Sicarii redoubled their activity. They promoted knifings, set fires, created panics, spread on unlimited aggressiveness, and gave no rest to anyone who did not share their frenzy. Addled brains excited the nerves of the multitude; the "envoys of God" led groups that were bewitched and that were destined for the Roman blades. Felix reacted with his usual clumsy brutality, but also with the duplicity of a profiteer. Complications at Caesarea brought about his recall by Nero.

His successor, the honest and peaceful Festus (60-62 A.D.), worked to restore quiet, but died before he had had time to introduce a little order into disorganized Judea. Before his successor arrived, the High Priest Hananos, a frantic Sadduccean, succeeded in putting to death the head of the Christian community at Jerusalem, James, and some other Christians (cf. p. 305). He aroused the indignation of the people and was removed.

Albinus (62-64 A.D.) seems to have come to Judea solely to get money. There were no means this thief would not use to acquire it; in particular, he raised money by liberating prisoners who were held under the common law or even under other laws. His greed played into the hands of the Sicarri, and disorder was found everywhere.

It was left for Gessius Florus (64-66 A.D.) to crown the evil. A shameless and avaricious criminal, he seemed, by his various methods of obtaining plunder, to have set himself the task of driving the Jews to the extremity of terror and of leaving them no alternative but rebellion. It was ready now to break out; tension was extreme, and a trifle could cause it to snap.

Only a summary of the course of events can be set down here.

May, 66 A.D.: serious rioting at Caesarea; a few days later, an uprising at Jerusalem; cruel repression (several thousand victims); resistance en masse at the Temple; an attempt, which was useless, at mediation by the moderates (Pharisees and priests) and by Agrippa II (son of Agrippa I and king of Chalcis in the interior of Lebanon); massacre of the Roman garrison of Massada; a cessation of the daily sacrifice for the emperor, which was equivalent to an open and official rupture.

September, 66 A.D.: war in Jerusalem between the moderates and the Sicarii; the latter won, and burned the palace of the high priest, who was slain; massacre of the Roman garrison; almost everywhere anger was aroused against the Jews and they were massacred in various cities, notably in Caesarea and Alexandria.

November, 66 A.D.: military intervention by the governor of Syria, Cestius Gallus, who proceeded as far as Jerusalem, but was driven out of Palestine and suffered enormous losses; the rebels fairly shouted their victory (money was coined as a sign of liberation!); organization of the defense of the territory by the priestly party, but in a mitigated and cautious manner that did not suit the hotheads; Josephus (the future historian) was put in charge in Galilee, which he made ready for war, but the extremist John de Giscala opposed him; similar preparations at Jerusalem, which were hampered by another extremist bandit, Simon bar Giora.

The beginning of 67 A.D.: Nero named Vespasian governor extraordinary of Judea with the mission of either pacifying it or subduing it; painstaking preparation of an army of 60,000 men; in the summer, war in Galilee, with the taking of the strongholds one by one (resistance of forty-seven days at Jotapata under the orders of Josephus); at the end of the year, Galilee and Samaria were conquered. The Roman successes in no way quieted Jerusalem, which was definitely in the hands of the terrorist Zealots, under John de Giscala; the extremists presided over a systematic slaughter of thousands of leading men, priests, and suspects (institution of an expeditious revolutionary tribunal), with the worst kind of bloody rage; later, this degenerated into a horrible debauch.

Spring of 68 A.D.: Vespasian occupied the coast, the valley of the Jordan (and the site of Qumran), and Perea, methodically encircling Jerusalem; death of Nero, halting of the operations for a year (p. 255). In Jerusalem, the bands of John de Giscala and Simon bar Giora, and later a new group of dissidents under Eleazar, disputed the leadership, dividing the city and the Temple between them like declared enemies; a furious civil war ensued, especially in the outer courts of the sanctuary; many were killed, and quantities of food stocks, which had been accumulated in view of the siege, were destroyed.

The beginning of 70 A.D.: Titus began his activities (cf. p. 256), reorganizing the army; at the Pasch, he encamped around Jerusalem; proposals for surrender were rejected; beginning of the siege, with full military machinery; breach of the outer north walls; impetuous and effective counterattacks by the Jews, resulting in the destruction of the Roman works. But famine set in. Titus had the city surrounded by a wall of ramparts, which made the blockade complete. The hunger became terrible and degrading; people died by tens of thousands.

July, 70 A.D.: taking of the Antonia, which was razed; the Temple was directly exposed to the onslaught of the assailants; cessation of the perpetual sacrifice (on July 12, forever!); another fortnight of efforts by the Romans to breach the Temple precinct wall, which was furiously defended.

August 9 A.D.: the gates were burned (localized fire), and the way was open, but orders were given by Titus to respect the Temple.

August 10 A.D.: engagements and hand-to-hand fighting in the courts of the Temple. A soldier, acting without orders, threw a flaming brand through the window of one of the rooms surrounding the sanctuary; fire burst out and engulfed the whole building; the confusion kept men from obeying the orders to extinguish it (only a few objects of the sacred furnishings were to be saved). The soldiers, in spite of Titus, stampeded and slew like wild beasts; they seized an enormous quantity of booty (gold especially); corpses were piled in heaps, and the ground was soaked with blood.

A few days later, the Roman eagles assembled in the sacred

enclosure; the legions offered a sacrifice of thanksgiving to the divinities of Rome. In the weeks that followed: "cleansing" of the city; massacres; the herding together of the captives (thousands died of want) destined for the slave markets; decision to raze the city (leaving enough of it to house a Roman garrison). Later, a few rebel strongholds were subdued (especially Massada, in 73 A.D.).

Judea no longer existed politically; it became the personal property of the emperor, managed by a legate. The Jews had died by hundreds of thousands. The country was in a state of desolation. The dwelling of Yahweh was annihilated and with it worship and the priesthood had come to an end; the city was definitively profaned. A special humiliation was the forcing of the inhabitants thenceforth to pay the didrachma, reserved for the Temple of Yahweh, to the Temple of Jupiter Capitolinus at Rome.

But Israel is never finished.

Purged of its utterly impractical Zealots, freed from the Sadducean influence by the disappearance of the sacerdotal aristocracy, it still had the Scribes and the Pharisees, who were its most important religious elements and who had known the way in which to keep themselves on the sidelines of the insurrection. As early as 68 A.D., Vespasian had authorized them, at their request (especially that of Johanan ben Zakkaï) to gather at Lydda and at Jamnia. Jamnia was the center of the spiritual resurrection. The learned Rabbis set about, with incomparable faith and care, gathering up the immense heritage of Sacred Tradition (the Synod of Jamnia in 90 A.D. was to exclude from its Canon a certain number of books written in Greek; cf. pp. 281-82). They made a study of the ways in which it would be still possible to maintain the cult and established them. They sought to organize a Judaism which, in spite of having ceased to be a political reality (though not in aspirations), could preserve its unity in the world.

For Israel existed everywhere, and the Jewish communities of the Diaspora had not rebelled (although they had suffered from persecutions because they were Jews). They were strongly fraternal among themselves, keeping up their connections with one another. They lived within an excellect structure, which was represented by the synagogue, in which the love of God and zeal for his Law, a profound spirit of prayer, and the sense of belonging essentially to the same people were maintained.

Although it lies outside the scope of the present history, a few words should be said about the subsequent rebellions, the final ones, which took place in the first part of the second century.

The sudden arresting of the nationalist fever in 70 A.D. was not a cure; the terrible lesson had not sufficed. Once again, prudent men were unable to control public opinion. And the apocalyptic writings had not ceased to keep dangerous illusions alive in the minds of the people, especially the desire for a Messias belonging solely to the Jews, who would crush their adversaries; an avenger, who would be utterly triumphant.

Under Trajan, agitation and uprisings broke out, which stretched from Cyrenaica as far as Mesopotamia. Repression was prompt and led to great slaughter (116-117 A.D.). The world came more and more to detest the impossible Jews, trying its hand at massacres which were thenceforth to be a natural occurrence in history.

Finally, under Hadrian, the most formidable of the insurrections broke out in Palestine. It was supported by intellectuals, encouraged by the Diaspora, and crystallized by a "messias," Bar Koseba, an adventurer who won widespread authority. Three years of pitiless war followed (132-135 A.D.). Naturally, Rome triumphed, although it paid dearly for victory. Jewish losses seem to have exceeded greatly those of 70 A.D. (more than half a million slain in battle; a still larger number of victims succumbing to privation; slaves sold in numberless quantities). Hadrian made a new city out of Jerusalem, renaming it Aelia Capitolina; it was entirely pagan, Graeco-Roman, and anti-Jewish by decree (Jews were forbidden to enter it under pain of death). On the site of the Temple of Yahweh, they raised the Temple of Jupiter, erecting both his statue and that of the emperor there; on Golgotha the temple of Aphrodite was built. Many Rabbis were martyred, dying for their faith. Jewish privileges were suppressed and all the Jewish practices—worship, circumcision, the Sabbath, teaching of the Torah—were forbidden.

These severe measures were abolished by Antoninus Pius (138-161 A.D.), the successor of Hadrian, in order not to provoke new wars. Judaism, tireless, set about the task of restoration and began to assume the shape it would thenceforth have in history.

[THREE]

CHRISTIAN LIFE | From the beginning the essential aspects of Christian life were evident.[1]

He who believes is a Christian (cf. Acts 4:4; 6:7; 8:13; 13:12; 14:1, 27; 15:7; 18:8; 19:18). Faith is to believe in the Lord Jesus Christ, in his "name" (cf. Acts 3:16; 5:14; 9:42; 11:17; 20:21). Christians are "believers" or "faithful" (cf. Acts 2:44; 4:4, 32; 18:27). One becomes a Christian by having "heard" the evangelical Word (cf. Acts 2:37; 4:4; 10:44; 15:7), and by having "accepted" or "received" it (cf. Acts 2:41; 8:14; 11:1).

Faith is the recognition of Jesus as the "Lord"; adherence to his Word, which is proclaimed and taught by his "witnesses," immediately creates a living and entirely new relationship with the Person of Christ the Lord, requiring a total pledging of oneself to him. Thus, faith begins by a "conversion," that is, by a change of soul and of behavior, and a renunciation of sin (which are "remitted"; cf. Acts 2:38; 3:19; 5:31; 11:18; 17:30; 20:21; 26:20). In this way faith "purifies the heart" (cf. Acts 15:9) and believers are "saved" (cf. Acts 2:47; 11:14; 15:11; 16:31).

Christians are "baptized" (cf. I Cor. 12:13; Rom. 6:3). Baptism is the rite which signifies entrance into the community of the faithful. The rite of "incorporation" into the Church, it is administered to all (cf. Acts 2:38, 41; 8:12, 16, 38; 9:18; 10:48; 16:25, 33; 19:5; 22:16). Distinct from the baptism of John the Baptist (cf. Mark 1:8), the baptism of which Jesus spoke (cf. John 3:5; Matt. 28:19) requires immersion in water and then a rising out of the water (the mode may vary in practice), according to a ritual formula, which signifies the participation of the neophyte in the death and resurrection of Christ (cf. Rom. 6:3-10; Gal. 3:27; Eph. 5:26; Col. 2:12-13; Titus 3:5-7). The lines of Christians are linked to the life of Christ.

They also receive the Holy Spirit, either at the moment of baptism,

[1] Essential documentation: the Acts of the Apostles. Concerning their historical value, cf. p. 353. We shall make some use of the epistles of St. Paul, but not in a systematic way; only a quick summary can be given.

or sometimes before or after. This "gift" of the Spirit (cf. Acts 2:38; 5:32; 10:45-47; 15:8) is sometimes signified by the rite of the imposition of hands (cf. Acts 8:17-18; 9:17; 19:6). Like the Spirit of Yahweh in ancient times, he may rush in suddenly (Acts 2:4; 4:31; 10:44-47; 11:15), and "fill" the new men of God (Acts 2:4; 4:8, 31; 6:5; 7:55; 13:52).

United to Christ, "risen" in him, animated by the Spirit of God, placed in the community of the Lord, the Christian "walks in a new life," he is a "new creature" (cf. II Cor. 5:17; Rom. 6:4; Gal. 6:15). Essentially this is a life "according to the Spirit" (cf. Rom. 8) and not "according to the flesh"; that is, it is a going out of self, a refusal of all forms of egoism.[2] Although Jewish morality seemed very lofty (cf. p. 284), "life in Christ" gives it its perfection. To become aware of the manner and the plan of *Christian existence*, it is necessary only to reread the exhortations which close almost all the letters of St. Paul (cf. for example, I Thess. 4-5; Rom. 12-14; Phil. 3-4; Eph. 4-6; Col. 3-4), particularly his beautiful "canticle to charity" found in I Cor. 13, and also the letters of James, Peter, and John. By way of antithesis, St. Paul made up lists of denounced vices and of sins to be avoided (cf. I Cor. 5:10-11; 6:9-10; II Cor. 12:20-21; Rom. 1:29-31; 13:13; Gal. 5:19-21; Eph. 4:31; 5:3-4; Col. 3:5-8; I Tim. 1:9-10; II Tim. 3:2-5). Gal. 5:19-23 should be reread especially. "Love therefore is the fulfillment of the Law" (Rom. 13:10).

Understandably enough, conversion to Christianity had quite a different meaning for Jews than it did for pagans. A Jew became a disciple of Jesus without changing his religion, properly speaking. He remained inside Yahwism, inside the Covenant, inside Israel. He continued to pray to Yahweh with a piety that was characteristic of all his people (pp. 280-81), and with a fervor that was increased by the fact that he called God "the Father" under a new frame of reference, "the Son," who is Jesus the Christ. The Torah had been his "tutor unto Christ" (Gal. 3:24); and Christ "fulfilled" both the traditional Scriptures and the history of Israel. In the beginning, almost all of the Christians came from Judaism. At first, they did not feel that they were leaving Judaism; rather, they felt that they were continuing it, in a new way, which certainly was neither foreseeable nor imaginable. All of this must be considered in order

[2] For the meaning of the words "flesh" and "spirit," cf. *WG*, p. 240.

to understand what Christian life was like for them, "who had the adoption as sons, and the glory and the covenants and the legislation and the worship and the promises; who had the fathers, and from whom is the Christ according to the flesh" (Rom. 9:4-5).

There was a difference, however, between the conversion of the "average Jew," the conversion of the "Hellenized" Jew, and the conversion of those affiliated with a movement like that of the Pharisees, the Zealots, or the Essenes. It has been noted that some Pharisees had become Christians, and that Zealots were numbered among the disciples of Jesus (cf. pp. 270, 290-91). Essenes like those who lived at Qumran (cf. pp. 274-78) probably came over to Christianity in large numbers. This explains not only certain characteristics of Christian community life, which suggest the Rule of these religious (Matt. 18:15-17; Acts 5:1-11; I Cor. 5:4-5), but also the lofty quality of the spiritual life attained to so rapidly by certain Christians, and the way in which St. Paul and especially St. John speak of it.

Conversion outside of Judaism must have been quite different. A genuine change of course, a radical change of "way," was involved in the conversion of a non-Jew. If the Jew who compared himself to the pagan had to be careful not to give way to pride (cf. Rom. 2), the former worshiper of idols or the skeptic of earlier days was obliged to break with a world that was deeply depraved (cf. Rom. 1:22-32). He had to abandon the "darkness" of error (cf. Eph. 5:8), and to renounce the "wisdom of this world" (cf. I Cor. 1). "Bear in mind," said St. Paul to the pagans "that you were at that time without Christ, excluded as aliens from the community of Israel, and strangers to the covenants of the promise, having no hope, and without God in the world" (cf. Eph. 2:12). Although the Asian or the Egyptian, the Greek or the Roman, did not have the benefit of a religious culture and of a spiritual heritage similar to those received by every Israelite, the shock of his conversion may have been the more decisive and possibly more effective. Perhaps he discovered more fully and felt more keenly certain values to which the other was too much accustomed. In any case, through him it became possible to think of the pagan world in a Christian way; and it was he who was able to become the messenger of Christ "to the ends of the earth."

The Christians prayed. They prayed at Jerusalem by participating in the customary liturgical rites of Israel and by assiduously frequenting the Temple (cf. Acts 2:46; 3:1; 5:12, 25, 42). Because of this, no doubt, they retained the manner of praying and of celebrating the worship (psalms) which would pass gradually into the specifically Christian liturgy when it was established. They prayed in common or privately, according to circumstances and particular occasions, to give thanks to God or to petition him (cf. Acts 2:42; 4:24-31; 6:4; 8:24; 9:11, 40; 10:9; 11:18; 12:5, 12; 13:3). They joined their Jewish brethren in the synagogues (St. Paul almost always began his preaching in a synagogue, where, of course, he prayed along with the others); and there too they took part in a worship that was composed of prayers, readings, and instructions —all of which would inspire the sacred Service carried on in the meetings reserved for Christians alone. They would be seen "speaking to one another in psalms and hymns and spiritual songs, singing and making melody in their hearts to the Lord, giving thanks always for all things in the name of our Lord Jesus Christ to God the Father" (Eph. 5:19-20). No doubt this was at least the "ministering to the Lord" (cf. Acts 13:2).[3]

The Christians also had meetings of their own, which were conducted in homes (cf. Acts 2:46; 4:31; 5:42; 9:19; 12:12; 18:7; 19:9-10; 20:7, 20; 28:30). Although they may have observed the Sabbath at first (cf. Acts 16:13), perhaps they began to consecrate the following day, the "first day of the week," in honor of the Resurrection of Christ (cf. Acts 20:7; I Cor. 16:2)—the day which would become the "Lord's Day" or Sunday (cf. Apoc. 1:10). In addition to prayers at their meetings, instructions were given to the faithful and to the neophytes (cf. Acts 5:42; 19:9-10; 20:7). Sacred reading held an important place; the Sacred Scriptures were assiduously listened to and studied, usually in the text of the Septuagint (cf. p. 218); they were explained in the light of the fulfillment of all things in Christ, who, it was discovered, had been foretold everywhere. The Gospels were to find their first form in the catechesis of the Christian assemblies; later, they were read in them, along with the apostolic letters. St. Paul insisted on this being done (cf. I Thess. 5:27; Col. 4:16).

[3] Elements of Christian liturgical poems seem to appear in Eph. 5:14 and I Tim. 3:16.

"Continuing steadfastly in the teaching of the apostles," the Christians were also faithful "in the communion of the breaking of the bread" (cf. Acts 2:42). If the rite they used was borrowed from the religious character of Jewish meals (cf. 279-80), and if there is some hesitation about simply identifying this "breaking of the bread," which one finds in Acts 2:46 and 27:35, with the "Eucharist" as it was to be celebrated and defined starting with the next century, still a comparison must be made with "the bread that we break, is it not the partaking of the body of the Lord," "eaten to proclaim the death of the Lord," and with the "Lord's Supper" and the "Lord's bread" in the community of Corinth (cf. I Cor. 10:16; 11:20-29). Since the event related in Acts 20:7-12 took place three years after Paul wrote to the Corinthians, then the sacramental and community Repast, which signified participation in the dead and risen Christ, was already being celebrated quite widely in conformity with the Lord's precept (cf. I Cor. 11:23). The Apostle saw in the Repast the sacrament of the unity and of the charity of Christians among themselves.

The love the first Christians had for one another has left a profound impression. Like the members of the community of Israel, they called themselves "brothers" (cf. Acts 2:29, 37; 3:17; 7:2; 13:15, 20; the word is found 130 times in Saint Paul). And especially, they behaved like brothers: "All the believers lived united and put everything in common; they sold goods and properties and divided the proceeds among all according to the needs of each. . . . They had but one heart and one mind; no one called what belonged to him his own, but all was in common between them" (Acts 2:44-45; 4:32). This made it possible to organize a program of regular aid (cf. Acts 6:1). Recall also the large collection taken up by St. Paul at the time of the economic crisis in Judea (cf. p. 304). There were many forms of fraternal devotion among the fervent disciples of the Lord. Their mutual affection was perhaps the greatest and most efficacious testimony (cf. John 13:35).

Does this mean that difficulties never existed between the "brethren"? The few examples of tension mentioned in the first communities (cf. Acts 6:1; 15:2, 39), the stormy course of St. Paul, full of snares even within the Church (cf. II Cor. 7:5; cf. p. 304), his severity toward the arguments between Christians at Corinth (I Cor. 3:3; 11:17-19), and especially the great difficulty of reconciling the traditional point of view of some with the more progressive view of others, show that differences of birth and of background, of purposes and of methods, did not disturb the unity of primitive Christianity. For the real unity of the early Christians was not based on uniformity and did not arise from a lack of vitality. Of particular note is the fact that the charity found in the Church of the One Lord was a vital thing; it was in full flight, completely developed, fairly bursting with energy, creativity, and initiative. "But all these things are the work of one and the same Spirit who allots to every one according as he will. For as the body is one and has many members, and all the members of the body, many as they are, form one body, so also is it with Christ" (I Cor. 12:11-12).

Because of natural conditions and of the inner workings of the Spirit of God, there was a great variety of activities and of roles in the Church. A great deal of evidence can be found concerning works and *charisms* (= gifts) in the primitive communities. They cannot, however, always be identified; indeed, Paul was forced at an early date to try to judge the worth of the lively spirituality found in his fervent Church at Corinth (cf. I Cor. 12-14).

The incomparable and irreplaceable original "witnesses" of Jesus (cf. Acts 1:22; 2:32; 3:15; 5:23; 10:41; 13:31), who were called the "foundations" of the Church (cf. Eph. 2:20; Apoc. 21:14), were the Twelve, the apostles. Their role as "the ones sent" (= apostles) and their "mission" (= sending) from Jesus (cf. Acts 1:8; Matt. 28:-18-20; Mark 16:15-16) made them essentially the "missionaries" of the Gospel. Peter was their visible head. When he left Jerusalem in order to accomplish the "ministry of the Word," his role as head of the original community was given to James (cf. p. 299). Paul seems to have acted in the same way at the end of his life; he confided the care of the communities founded by him to his disciples Timothy and Titus.

Since the communities multiplied rapidly, their members growing more numerous, some kind of organization was necessary. They do not seem to have had a strict and uniform inner structure. In each group or in each region they let themselves be guided by the requirements of particular situations, taking their inspiration from the existing modes of life, with the assurance that they were being led by the Spirit of God. The "Hellenists," for example, were led by the "Seven"; undoubtedly, the account of the institution of "deacons" (= servants) was due principally to the recognition of this community organization by the Twelve (cf. Acts 6:1-6). The way in which Jewish "parishes" were organized around the synagogues must have been widely imitated (cf. pp. 280-81). "Presbyters" (= elders), also called "bishops" (= guardians), who were the assistants of the apostles in the beginning, sharing their teaching authority, were entrusted with the responsibility for and administration of Christian communities (cf. Acts 11:30; 14:23; 15:2, 6, 22-23; 10:4; 20:17; 21:18; Phil. 1:1).

Paul enumerates the "ministries," as they were divided up among the members of the communities, in lists which are neither complete nor elaborated upon nor entirely in harmony with one another (cf. I Cor. 12:8-10, 28-29; Rom. 12:6-8; Eph. 4:11; see also Acts 13:1). The following is a catalogue of the various ministries: presidents or governors; pastors; evangelists; prophets; doctors; teachers; preachers; assistants; servants; healers. Each of these ministries fell into one of three possible categories: government; teaching; assistance. All of them, however, continued the work of Christ and the Twelve. The propagation of the Gospel and the "planting" of the Church was the primary task to be accomplished. The revelation of the Christian Message was made in two ways, corresponding to two stages of initiation: the first announcement, or *kerygma* (= crying out), to those who had never heard the Word of Christ; then teaching, properly so-called, or *catechesis,* that is, more complete instruction of the faithful by doctrinal or other kinds of study.

The matter taught cannot be easily or rapidly summarized: it consisted of the whole theology of the "New Covenant." A sufficient acquaintance with this doctrine will be had after acquiring some knowledge of the first Christian writings. The first Christian writings proceeded from Christian life and bear witness to it. Primarily missionary in character, they are the means of communicating what the apostles had received from Christ in the light of the Spirit given to the Church.

12 The Message of the Witnesses

[ONE]

THE EVANGELICAL TRADITION [1] | "He was journeying through towns and villages, preaching and proclaiming the good news of the Kingdom of God" (Luke 8:1). The word *gospel* (evangel) did not at first designate a text, a book. It meant primarily, according to its etymology and its biblical usage (cf. Ps. 68:12; Isa. 40:9; 52:7; Rom. 10:15), "good tidings," an "announcement that brings happiness." "Gospel," in this primary sense, which should never be forgotten, is to some extent synonymous with the term "evangelization": it is the preaching of the Kingdom of God, the word announcing the Message which will bring liberation and joy to those who receive it. The gospel "is the power of God unto salvation to everyone who believes" (cf. Rom. 1:16).

At first the gospel was made up of the words of Jesus. No one had ever spoken like him (cf. John 7:46); the things he said caused men to act, penetrated the heart, produced reactions, won men over, were decisive—lives were changed by them. His words were one with his person, with his actions, and with his life; they also pointed up the depth of his knowledge and the secret of his appeal. At his word miracles took place, which were divine and revealing "works" par excellence. Finally, his passion and his resurrection manifested the full meaning of his coming among men and of his dazzling victory over death. Such, then, was the first gospel.

The apostles were the listeners and witnesses who were "evangelized" to the point of being completely filled with the Word and the Spirit-and-Power of Jesus. At Pentecost they became, and remained ever after, the "evangelizers" or "evangelists" of the Kingdom, the messengers of salvation through Christ Jesus. Like their

[1] For knowledge of the "Gospel before the Gospels," read Lucien Cerfaux, *The Four Gospels*, English trans. by Patrick Hepburne-Scott (Westminster, Md.: Newman, 1960).

Master, they preached action and life. "For our gospel was not delivered to you in word only, but in power also, and in the Holy Spirit" (I Thess. 1:5). They did not write their message; they "made disciples," according to the very terms of their mission (cf. Matt. 28:19). The difference between them and Jesus was that they had to propose not their own word or their own persons, but Christ. Their gospel was the Lord Jesus; it was "all he had done and taught" (Acts 1:1), all they had "seen, heard, and handled of the Word of Life" (I John 1:1). If they wrote, it was "not with ink but with the Spirit of the living God, not on tablets of stone (like Moses) but on fleshly tablets of the heart" (II Cor. 3:3). They made men conscious of the presence of Jesus and of the complete renewal his presence produces.

Since they spoke Christ Jesus, and wished to communicate their experience of him and their love for him, they had to choose what to say. Their essential doctrine is expressed many times in the letters of Paul, which were written before the Gospels and which were an echo of his oral preaching: Christ dead and risen again (cf., for example, I Thess. 1:9-10; 4:14; I Cor. 15:3-4; Rom. 1:2-5; 4:24-25; 8:34, and especially 14:8-9). The apostolic gospel, however, was not reduced to such an extreme abridgement. It was necessary to present, and therefore to tell of Jesus—not all of his teachings nor everything that concerned him; that would have been impossible (cf. John 21:25)—through some of his words and actions.

Whether it was a question of a first announcement or of more advanced instructions (cf. p. 320), the apostolic preaching, through repetition, rapidly resolved into fixed formulas and into outlines; or rather into an outline, which is immediately apparent from the first discourses of Peter (cf. Acts 2:22-24, 32-33; 3:12-16, and especially 10:36-43, which is, as it were, the plan of the three synoptic Gospels). Note that the schema used has constant recourse to the Scripture, not so much to show, by apologetics, the truth of the assertions concerning Christ, but rather to place them in the whole of Revelation and in the History of Salvation, as the fulfillment of the Plan of God.

This fundamental credo was adapted according to the circumstances of preaching and according to the varieties of audiences. Peter, speaking to the Palestinians, emphasized Jesus as the Messias. Paul, in his mission to the Gentiles, primarily spoke of Jesus as

Savior and of the universal character of the Redemption. John, addressing Christians who were already instructed, showed how the events of Jesus' life were valuable as signs.

The audience, or more exactly, the community, the Christians who desired to know the Lord and his message well, reciprocated by asking questions concerning problems they were particularly interested in. They asked what Jesus had said and done about a variety of subjects: marriage, widowhood, and divorce; laws in regard to the Sabbath, purifications, tithes, taxes; classes of men like the publicans, sinners, and non-Israelites; the inequality and abuses of public power; the world outside and the realization of the Kingdom. The narratives and words of the Master, which entered into the "evangelical tradition," and the choice of scenes, deeds, maxims, and discourses were based on the kinds of questions asked by the Christian communities (many things, then, were passed over in silence or summarized after the manner of Mark 1:34, 39; 6:55-56).

Jesus spoke in the rhythmic style characteristic of Eastern wise men, which lends itself well to repetition and memorization (cf. p. 290). The preachers of the gospel and the catechists who aided them or elaborated their teachings needed only to reproduce the words; if certain teachings required development, this was done in short discourses. The narratives they told were short. Gradually, these little wholes, set in a fixed form, became joined and fell into a general chronological sequence, with details being added in a flexible and free manner. Thus, the apostolic teaching contained principally the following subjects: the preaching and baptism of John the Baptist; the ministry of Jesus in Galilee; his miracles, discourses, and controversies; his Judean ministry; his principal actions and his teaching; finally, the last days of the Savior, his passion and his death, described with care and in detail, his resurrection and his appearances to the apostles and disciples.

The need for fixing the elements of evangelical tradition in writing was apparent at an early time. The ancient world was extraordinarily endowed with the ability to transmit oral traditions faithfully. Because of the fact, however, that the messengers of the gospel were becoming more numerous, writing was obviously a sure and convenient method of preserving the Message in its original purity, and of easily diffusing it. Thus, "notebooks" were composed, "memoranda," so to speak, or *small collections,* which missionaries and catechists carried with them and which they used as outlines or reminders.

Some faired better: "Many have undertaken to draw up a narrative concerning the things that have been fulfilled among us, even as they who from the beginning were eyewitnesses and ministers of the word have handed them down to us" (Luke 1:1). The authors of these narratives are unknown, however, and nothing is left of their works, except what may be found repeated and fused into the canonical Gospels. The value of the canonical Gospels—the authority of their authors, and the importance of the communities whose catechesis they reproduce—gave them a predominant place, which rendered other accounts useless and caused them to disappear. It remains true, however, that if the canonical Gospels were composed (at least in a partial way and according to some kind of order) during the seventh decade of the first century, other versions were in circulation earlier and preceded them.

There is good reason to believe that two collections in particular were compiled at that time: one of them was a gospel series written in Aramaic, which was undoubtedly used in connection with the preaching of Peter at Jerusalem and reworked into the Gospel according to Matthew; the other recorded the various apostolic traditions. At this point, the difficult problem of the sources, the similarities, and the composition of the Gospels according to Matthew, Mark, and Luke is touched upon. The "synoptic problem," as it is called, can be treated only briefly here, with only a summary and approximate solution being given; a more extensive study will be reserved until later.[2]

The problem arises on the basis of twofold observation. A comparison of the Gospels of Matthew, Mark, and Luke reveals, on the one hand, astonishing similarities between them, even to the extent of complete verbal identity in many places, and, on the other hand, differences that are just as surprising, which manifest purely and simply the impossibility of reducing one text to another.[3]

[2] Besides the work cited in the note on p. 321, there is an extensive study by Xavier Léon-Dufour, *Concordance of the Synoptic Gospels* (Paris: Desclée, 1957); cf. also Alfred Wikenhauser, *New Testament Introduction*, English trans. by Joseph Cunningham (New York: Herder & Herder, 1958), Section 26, "The Synoptic Problem," pp. 221-53.

[3] X. Léon-Dufour, in the work mentioned above, invites comparison of Mark 4:19 with Luke 8:14; Matt. 22:25 with Mark 12:20; Matt. 28:1 with

To find an answer to the problem, it is necessary first to propose some simple hypotheses. Could not one of the Gospels have been the source of the other two? In this case, is it the one that seems to be the earliest, that is, Mark? On the other hand, Matthew and Luke have added a great deal. Where did these considerable additions come from? Would it be better to conclude that the three Gospels came from one source earlier than themselves, their differences being explained by their own purposes and their own spirit? The puzzling point in this hypothesis is the extensive and usually surprising exclusions of Mark (all the more so because he is generally the most spontaneous and complete of the narrators; compare Mark 10:46-52 with its parallels). Having delineated the problem somewhat by these questions, its solution can be considered in the following way:

Mark seems preferable as the original source, for he best echoes the teaching of Peter at Jerusalem and later at Rome (cf. p. 306). Matthew seems to have known Mark and made use of him; but he also uses, and primarily, another source, which seems to have been none other than the "Aramaic Matthew," mentioned above as being known in the primitive tradition of the Church.[4] Luke follows Mark very closely, but his many similarities to Matthew show that he also drew on the "Aramaic Matthew." Finally, it must be supposed that Matthew and Luke together profited, through some Aramaic or Greek source, from evangelical traditions not contained in the Aramaic Matthew and, separately, from information each had gleaned himself (this is true of Luke especially).

A general notion of the *creation of the synoptic Gospels* can now be formed. To begin with, the preaching of Peter at Jerusalem and in Palestine, as well as the preaching of other apostles and disciples, who belong to the first generation, can be noted; this was the "oral gospel." Afterwards some written efforts appeared (cf. Luke 1:1), the first records of the teaching of Peter and of the other preachers, in the form of little booklets—summaries for missionaries and catechists; rubrics for liturgical use in community

Luke 24:6; Matt. 19:16 f. with Mark 10:17 f. The passages are closely parallel, "only the subject of the sentence or the person speaking is different" (cf. p. 53, note 10).

[4] Especially the testimony of Papias, bishop of Hierapolis in the second century, which is reported by the historian Eusebius of Caesarea (264-340 A.D.), in his *Ecclesiastical History,* 3:39.

meetings. Between the years 40 A.D. and 50 A.D., the Apostle Matthew wrote his Gospel in Aramaic; no doubt, even then it was constructed to some extent as the canonical Matthew would be. It disappeared after the dispersion of the Judaeo-Christian communities of Palestine, but before that, it may have been translated into Greek (in the years 50-60 A.D.?). Another collection of evangelical traditions not retained by Matthew must have been compiled at the same time and, perhaps, was translated into Greek. Shortly before the death of Peter at Rome, the evangelist Mark composed his work, which was made up chiefly of the original record of the Palestinian catechesis of Peter, and completed by repeating the preaching of the same apostle at Rome. A little later, the text of Matthew as we know it appeared, its principal twofold source being the "Aramaic Matthew" (perhaps already translated into Greek) and Mark, with other apostolic sources, as well as personal information, used to supplement the work. Finally, the evangelist Luke produced his own work. Its principal source is Mark, athough the "Aramaic Matthew" also was used, together with the apostolic source; Luke had, in addition, a whole set of sources which were proper to himself.

The literary similarities suggest personal relationships; meetings between preachers and evangelists. Luke was a disciple of Paul; toward the end of the Apostle's career they worked together, and hence saw each other a great deal. Mark, who at first had been connected with Paul, later attached himself to Peter. It is possible and even probable that, about the years 62-64 A.D., Peter, Paul Mark, and Luke were together in the Jewish quarter of Rome. If this is true, any borrowings between the evangelical compilations and their dependence on one another in certain cases, are quite natural.

Although the synoptic Gospels were not written out in a definitive form until a comparatively late date (at the time Peter and Paul were ending their apostolic careers) they contain and transmit the most ancient Christian preaching. They have retained its essentially Semitic character, its popular and missionary qualities, and they are the authentic witnesses of the dawning of the Christian Message. In this sense they are anterior to most of the letters of St. Paul, although they were set down in definitive form after them. The Gospels are linked to their original apostolic source and to the oral catechesis of the first decades, and are made up of fragmentary and schematic narratives, selections, and summaries. Furthermore, their practical purpose is always preaching: they are intended to teach, to deliver a message, which must be accepted and lived—in faith; they aim less at imparting information than at forming a world animated by the redemptive work of Christ; they present the Lord Jesus so that men may meet him and become his disciples.

The canonical Gospels impart a teaching which is earlier than themselves, having been composed some time after the facts set down in them; indeed, their composition shows the stages of their formation. Although the work to be done in this field requires careful handling, it is certain that the elements integrated in the canonical Gospels are not all of the same date. They are mixed together now, but it is possible to discern strata in their compilation, and improvements. These observations have been made possible because of a recent exegesis whose critical method is called "history of forms."[5] Although the method employed is necessarily cautious and hesitant, only slowly going forward with its work, at least a debt of gratitude is owed to it for making possible fruitful progress in reflecting on Christian life in the first century. In a very minor but interesting way,[6] the Gospels are witnesses to the added detail which Christian life brought to the original Message, and they are an echo of the faith of the Church. A work, in this sense, of the Church itself, they are all the more precious and are vouched for with the greatest fidelity. No one can speak of Christ like the one whom St. Paul calls the spouse of Christ (cf. Eph. 5:23–32); no one can communicate as she can the Word of her Lord. The Gospels, like all of biblical literature, are the fruit of the activity of the Spirit of God in the People of God.

The fourth canonical Gospel differs greatly from the other three and only rarely does it parallel them. Nevertheless, according to the testimony of primitive tradition, it is the work of an apostle, of one of the earliest disciples, and of an immediate witness to Christ. Appearing late, it represents a stage of theological reflection that was already advanced. Although its carefully detailed passages were slow in being produced and were composed gradually, the fourth

[5] In German: *Formgeschichte*. Most of the originators and specialists in this critical method are Germans.

[6] Absolutely impossible to illustrate here; it pertains to the exegetical study, properly speaking, of the Gospels, and will come later.

Gospel contains very ancient elements; perhaps even the primitive preaching of the Apostle John is found in it. Because of its literary form, its study has been placed at the end of this history of biblical writings. In one sense, however, it is also a witness to the oral gospel, which was preached, if not actually written down, before the Gospels that were definitively accepted by the Church.

[TWO]

PAUL AND THE LETTERS TO THE COMMUNITIES

The life of the Apostle Paul is one of the greatest adventures ever lived. He traveled thousands of miles on foot, visited the most important centers of the civilized world, encountered the most diverse kinds of environments, met multitudes of people, carried out the boldest missionary activities, and lived through the dramatic vicissitudes of an extraordinarily eventful career (cf. II Cor. 11:23-28). The principal stages of his career have already been presented, but now greater attention must be given to him.[1] Although the history of Paul, seen from the outside, seems extraordinary, what can be said of the spiritual adventure of this man of God? He reveals himself in his letters. Before taking them up in the order of their appearance during the life of this astonishing missionary, his personality, his temperament, his ideas, and his literary gifts must be considered.

Paul was a natural *genius*, under the influence of God for the service of the Church. As in all truly great men, the personality of this superior man was filled with contrasts. His temperament had been endowed with the richest and most dynamic elements that can be found in human nature, and yet he felt his limitations more keenly than anyone else. He had an intelligence which was both intuitive and logical; although he possessed indomitable energy he

[1] There are many excellent biographies of St. Paul; cf. especially, Joseph Holzner, *Paul of Tarsus,* English trans. by Frederick C. Eckhoff (St. Louis: Herder, 1944); Fernand Prat, S.J., *Saint Paul,* English trans. by John L. Stoddard (London: Burns, Oates & Washbourne, 1928); Giuseppe Ricciotti, *Paul the Apostle,* English trans. by Alba I. Zizzamia (Milwaukee: Bruce, 1953); Justo Pérez de Urbel, O.S.B., *Saint Paul, the Apostle of the Gentiles,* English trans. by Paul Barrett, O.F.M. Cap. (Westminster, Md.: Newman, 1956).

could still experience feelings of impotence and depression. Sensitive to the point of irritability, yet delightfully tender of heart, he combined impatience and perseverance, openness of speech and, on occasion, subtlety. He was headstrong, but his authority, which was united with an innate gift of sympathy and a delicate tact, drew like a magnet. His ideas were vigorous and far-reaching, but also intricate and difficult; His speech was eloquent, although he scorned eloquence, and its ardor was contagious. He was filled with an ardent and always active love for the Church and for all men. His was a holy soul, in constant communion with God, but it had passed through darkness and anguish, and had experienced the burden of sin that weighs down human nature, and the interior difficulties caused by the incongruities inherent in the life of this world. His dominant trait was a total faith in Christ Jesus and the certainty of the mission confided to him.

He was a saint and a man inspired. The historian cannot place this operation of God, which was a primary factor in his Apostle, and which was the secret of Paul's incomparable work, on the same plane as other causalities.

Paul was a man of action. God had put into his heart the desire to make himself all things to all men (cf. I Cor. 9:22), and primarily to carry the gospel to the Gentiles as far as this was possible (cf. Acts 22:21). His mission, which was a personal one (cf. Eph. 3:1-9), was accomplished with the help of outstanding qualities: his methods of working; his ability to organize; and his practical intelligence. It has been pointed out already that he knew how to choose strategic positions for his apostolic conquest: Antioch, Ephesus, Corinth, and Rome. He was, of course, a victim of misconceptions, tactical errors, and disappointments. Athens ridiculed him; Corinth cost him many tears; he did not know how to make himself understood in Jerusalem. These were but the price of his boldness and of his participation in the mystery of the Cross. His audacity, however, usually was accompanied by a tireless patience and by shrewd judgment, enabling him to do what no other had ever done. When one says "the Apostle," one means Paul.

He was not only a great traveler for Christ, he was also the first *theologian* of the Church. His initial religious formation, that of a young Rabbi, had been excellent, and had prepared him for reflecting on ideas as well as for expressing his thoughts. His conversion constituted a fundamental revelation for him: Christ living in his disciples (cf. Acts 9:4-5). Even at this time the whole Pauline doctrine of the Body and the members, Christ in the Church, can be seen. As his experience, contacts with others, and the requirements of his apostolate forced him ceaselessly to deepen and to communicate his ideas, everything became integrated in a comprehensive vision of man, the world, and history.

Paul reconsidered the mystery of Israel and the Judaic values in the light of the complete Revelation. He reorganized "in Christ" his whole thought, his heritage as a Pharisee, and the elements of Hellenic culture he had acquired. He understood both the fundamental position of the redeemed Christian (redeemed but not yet perfected), the Mystery of the Church (whose members are concretely involved in the usual human manner of living and whose life-giving "Head" is Christ, who "dies no more"), and the movement of the whole of humanity and of the cosmos toward its end in the plan of universal Redemption through Christ.

This was an essential synthesis, not a systematic and complete construction. It was a line of thought that was constantly searching, seeking expression. It was delivered through approximations and fragments, whose elements are not all on the same plane and whose coherence is in motion, like the spirit that experienced it.

The fact that such a man, apparently the only one capable in his time, should have succeeded, twenty or thirty years after the death of Christ, in achieving such an elaboration of the entire Christian mystery, is truly extraordinary. The fact is even more extraordinary because this converted Rabbi, who had become a wandering missionary, never wrote a doctrinal "treatise" and never let his thoughts come to the surface, except in occasional letters whose purpose were chiefly practical and which were usually written in haste.

His literary genius was, nevertheless, undeniable and most exceptional. One cannot, of course, deny that he was influenced by his native country and by the regions in which he often lived. He handled the Greek language perfectly and brought it easily into the service of his personality, making it a good instrument for his apostolic task. Nevertheless he remained deeply "Hebrew" in thought and in expression; he is incomprehensible to anyone ignorant of the traditional and typical characteristics of the Semitic mind or of the classical anthropology of the Ancient Near East. Paul's words, his ideas, his mental patterns, are those of the Bible, which he knew perfectly (usually following the text of the Septuagint), and without which he could not explain himself. He belongs to the family of biblical writers, although this did not prevent him from using the texts in a rabbinical way (cf. Rom. 4; Gal. 4).

Free in the use of the artifices of expression, he well knew how to render himself no less free with regard to the "wisdom of words" and "pretentious speech" (cf. I Cor. 1:17-31; 2:1-4). Some of his literary characteristics are noteworthy.[2] His thought is often expressed in parallel statements and in repetitions which perfect it, as if it were gradually being focused on a central idea (for example, cf. Rom. 6:2-8; I Cor. 13:8-12). The logic of its development is frequently "verbal," that is, it proceeds according to the association of ideas or the linking of words one to another (cf. Rom. 1:1-5; 8:28-30). Because of his taste and his temperament, and also because of the impossibility of expressing a reality in its totality and of showing its contrasts in any other way, Paul makes uses of antitheses a great deal (for example, cf. Rom. 5:15-19). The following opposites are examples of this practice: flesh—spirit, death—life, light—darkness, sin—grace, slave—son, works—faith, bondage—freedom, old—new, judgment—justification, letter—spirit, folly—wisdom, strength—weakness, one—all. From time to time he employs a style that is moving or rhetorical (cf. Rom. 8:35-39; 9:1-5; Eph. 3:18-19). It may also happen, however, that he breaks off suddenly, leaving a sentence unfinished (cf. Rom. 5:12-14; 9:22-24). He likes to use personifications, which help him to show the dramatic aspect of the Christian Mystery; for example, he personifies the Law, Sin, Death, the Gospel, the World. He is not always strict in the use of words (in Rom. 7, the word "law" is taken in nine different meanings) and he creates words (for example by means of the prefix "syn" = with; cf. Rom. 6:4-8).

To speak of St. Paul the "writer" is a misuse of the word, and the Apostle would have ridiculed it. To be sure, he composed a few great letters, which were well constructed (especially Rom.; also Eph.). Usually, however, he wrote because circumstances demanded it. This is shown by the way he addresses the letters and closes them,

[2] On this point, cf. Fernand Prat, S.J., *The Theology of St. Paul*, English trans. by John L. Stoddard (Westminster, Md.: Newman, 1952), Vol. I, pp. 62-71; Giuseppe Ricciotti, *Paul the Apostle*, *op. cit.*, pp. 135-50.

by his use of interpellations, by his concern with giving practical advice, and by his many references to precise concrete situations. His letters are the missives of a missionary who wishes to keep in contact with those whom he has had to leave, to answer questions that have been put to him or that have been posed by circumstances of life or events, to continue the instruction of these Christians, to correct them when necessary, and always to encourage them. He usually dictated the letters to one of his disciples, a friend who acted as his secretary. They were composed at the end of a day of exhausting work. Because of the fact that it took several evenings to complete each letter,[3] sometimes resuming the work after prolonged interruptions, gaps in the development of Paul's thought were inevitable (compare for example chapters 8 and 9 of I Cor.; Rom. 16 was obviously added afterwards). The letters of St. Paul, therefore, reveal not only the passionate and vibrant temperament of a man who speaks with his whole heart, but also the vicissitudes of a life spent in traveling and working.

Paul is, therefore, not easy to read, as anyone who has done so knows. Nevertheless, once the reader begins, he cannot give up: the apostle is powerfully engaging; he makes a disciple and a friend of every reader, letting him share in his enthusiasm, in his earnestness, and in his promise to Christ. Paul is always lively.

The first known letter written by him (and therefore historically the first Christian writing and the first piece of New Testament writing[4]) was composed and sent at the time of his arrival in Corinth in the year 51 A.D. or 52 A.D., during his second missionary journey (cf. p. 302). The First Epistle to the Thessalonians is addressed to one of the little communities the apostle had founded on a recent visit to Macedonia, of which Thessalonica was the capital. The Christians whom Paul had formed there were a happy, fervent, and courageous community, even though certain points of their faith needed to be clarified and strengthened. The words he wrote to them came joyfully from his fatherly heart, which loved them so tenderly; he gave solid and practical counsels with aplomb; every-

[3] It has been calculated that, because of the manner of writing then in use, at least a week would have been needed for the transcription of a short letter like First Thessalonians, and one or one and a half months for the Letter to the Romans (cf. Riciotti, *op. cit.*, pp. 151 and 333).

[4] If, that is, the Epistle of James had not been written one or two years earlier, as we would gladly think it was (cf. p. 338).

thing he said was meant to encourage them. The marvelous thing about this short message of Paul's affection and esteem is that even though it was written early in the history of a youthful Christianity, it expressed many of the most important theological ideas. Even at this early date, the letter revealed the essential structure of Christian thought with regard to God, Christ, the Spirit, the Church, the coming of the Lord, and the Christian's attitude toward faith, hope, and a militant life. St. Paul treats only the coming of the Lord explicitly, for he wanted to calm the anxiety of his hearers on the subject of the dead. He tells them that they have nothing to fear; those who are dead will see the Lord, just like those who will still be alive at his coming. Paul expresses himself in the familiar language of the prophecies of the Old Testament, but in a way unlike that of the apocalypses. Although his ideas are directed eagerly toward the Advent of Christ, he has not yet acquired the force and assurance on this difficult question that will be found in his later letters.

The great Christian hope, a hope that reaches beyond death, is founded on the Coming of the Lord (cf. I Thess. 4:13-18). During the period of waiting, the Christian must be vigilant, preparing himself by practicing sobriety and the other virtues (cf. I Thess. 3:13; 5:1-11, 23). The time of waiting explains the violent opposition encountered by Christ and all the evil that proceeds from this struggle (cf. II Thess. 2:3-12). A Second Epistle to the Thessalonians was necessary a few months later to clarify this last point. The tone of the second letter is the same as the first, and it contains similar ideas. In the first, the feeling that the community was meant to suffer from its surroundings, but that it would hold firm, was evident. The second letter expresses the same notion, but adds that these difficulties might be a strain on them. Perhaps for this reason certain of the faithful expected to see the "parousia" (= presence, or coming) of Christ even in their lifetime; some expected him to come soon, without their having to do anything. Paul declares bluntly that they have not reached that point; they must not allow themselves to become idle: "If any man will not work, neither let him eat!" (II Thess. 3).

The Second Letter to the Thessalonians, like the preceding one, lets us glimpse the richness and profundity, the fineness and firmness of the Apostle's oral preaching, which can be seen in the text.

The two messages were sent from Corinth at a time when Paul, anxious to carry Christ to the most important parts of the world, was establishing a community in that enormous and bustling capital (cf. p. 302). Up to that time, his greatest apostolic success was reached in Corinth. A vital group, the Christian community there was composed essentially of workers and of the poor (Corinth retained slaves by the hundreds of thousands), and in them the Spirit of God manifested himself in an extraordinarily superabundant way. The creation of a Christian settlement in Corinth also took great daring. The new Christians, who only yesterday were still pagans, (for Jewish neophytes were only a minority among them), lived in permanent contact with all that was most seductive to mind and body in Hellenism; with all that would most disturb and complicate everyday life. They lived among people who were free and happy in a human way, among men who were in love with beauty and who were highly skeptical. They lived in the midst of the depraved, who flocked to Corinth because of the opportunities it offered for giving vent to their lust, and among adherents of religious groups, who were bewitched by the inebriating mysticism of cults of foreign origin. Thus, both on the intellectual and on the practical plane, the problem of faith and Christian development in a completely pagan environment was squarely posed. And however fervent these believers were, they were not angels. To the difficulties inherent in the surroundings were added misfortunes which were proper to the community itself: the infatuation of some people for divergent opinions, giving rise to dissensions; some regrettable moral weaknesses; failures in fraternal charity; excessive solutions for the problem of the sexual appetites (license or rigorism); exaggerations or deviations in the use of the divine gifts. Was paganism taking its revenge? Was not the integrity of the Christian Message at stake? In any case, the news that came from this community was not always good.

Paul had had to leave them and time had not straightened things out. His intervention was absolutely necessary, even from a distance, in order to bring to an end the troubles in his beloved Church of Corinth. From Ephesus, to which his third great mission had taken him (cf. pp. 303-4), he had sent rather strong counsels (cf. I Cor. 5:9). This letter—which has not been preserved—was not sufficient, however; or rather it brought up a series of questions. In 55

A.D. Paul wrote—on several occasions, it seems—what is for us the First Epistle to the Corinthians. The answers, for they are only answers, to the questions that had arisen parallel the happenings or incidents that had occurred in the community. Admonitions, directives, counsels, all are seen from one essential point of view: their relationship to Christ, in whom the whole of Christian life finds its animation and its coherence. Each question provides an opportunity for an important teaching: the Gospel; the union of Christians in one Lord; the apostolic ministry (cf. I Cor. 1-4); marriage and virginity (cf. I Cor. 5-7); sacrifice and the Eucharist Mystery (cf. I Cor. 8-11); the gifts of the Holy Spirit (cf. I Cor. 12-14); the resurrection of the body (cf. I Cor. 15).

Undoubtedly, the First Epistle to the Corinthians letter is the most representative letter written by St. Paul. It contains inexhaustible riches and is one of the most important Christian documents. The style, direct and vigorous, has a vivacity and a completeness, a kind of strength that reveals the author as being both passionate and strong. In it Paul shows himself to be in full possession of his power and of his style. His genius can be recognized.

Order had returned to the community of Corinth, but the elements of division were not all eliminated. Some men questioned the very authority of the Apostle and discredited him in a contemptible and malicious way. This became serious. Paul made a "painful visit" (II Cor. 2:1) to Corinth, which did not settle anything. From Ephesus, to which he had returned, he wrote "in tears" (II Cor. 2:4) a severe letter (it has been lost). From Ephesus again (unless he had left there and was already in Macedonia), in 57 A.D., after having at last received better news from his beloved Corinthians and as a token of reconciliation before going back to them, he wrote what was later to be called the Second Epistle to the Corinthians. The second letter is characterized by the manner in which Paul, who had to set matters straight once and for all this time, notably in regard to himself, entered into it personally to such an extent that no other testimony concerning the Apostle in more revealing and more concrete, more perceptive and more surprising. It lays bare his natural temperament and the depths of his soul. Difficult because of his allusions to the problems which had arisen, rich in valuable historical information, strewn with reflections and incidents which are of the highest doctrinal value, this astonishingly passionate letter gives an especially incomparable picture of the apostolic ideal.

The date of the composition of the Epistle to the Philippians is hard to establish. Usually it is placed during the time of Paul's Roman captivity. Nevertheless, good reasons incline the scholar to think that the letter was written at Ephesus in the years 56-57 A.D. (some say even earlier), at the same time the Apostle was dictating the Second Epistle to the Corinthians and the Epistle to the Galatians. The question also arises whether a combining of several letters which Paul sent at different times to his friends at Philippi make it up. The Philippians had known Paul for seven years (second journey) and had seen him twice more (third voyage). They had often helped him materially, something which Paul had not accepted from others. Hence, very special bonds of affection and trust existed between them. The letter bears eloquent testimony to this fact; to no one did the Apostle, whose feelings were always so obvious, speak with more tenderness—his soul wide open—with more joy and simplicity, revealing the depths of his perfect union in the Lord. In the second chapter, a kind of liturgical hymn is found, which is one of the great passages concerning Christ, showing him humbled even to the death of the cross, "emptied" of himself, but afterwards exalted above all creatures in heaven and on earth.

The Epistle to the Galatians seems to have been written from Macedonia or from Corinth, unless indeed it came from Ephesus. Composed in 57 A.D. it is no less moving, and even more vehement and pugnacious, than II Cor. It was directed, however, to an entirely different audience. Galatia was a Roman province located in the center of Asia Minor. Paul had visited it in 50 A.D., leaving behind a Christian community. After his departure, however, others had sown bad seed. Some Jewish converts wanted the pagans who had become Christian also to become Jews through circumcision and the observance of the Mosaic precepts. In fact, they proposed their wishes in this matter as a necessary condition of salvation. Since Paul had taught just the contrary, they tried to discredit him by calling into question his apostolic mandate itself. Thus, the great conflict, which was the crisis of the Christian communities in the middle of the first century, broke out in Galatia. From the outset, the Apostle sprang to the defense of the Gospel which they wished to alter or to replace, presenting the credentials of his mission and showing his agreement with the other apostles (which provides us with valuable autobiographical notes). Then he denounced, in terms whose apparent excesses and oversimplifications are explained by their context, by the heat of the discussion, and by the drama of the situation, the desire to return to Judaic practices after experiencing Christianity as a step backward, a conversion in reverse. "Liberty," which is "life in the Spirit," alone counted and sufficed. All of this is expressed in a fiery and brusque way, using direct questions and appeals. Paul's genius sparkles in the fire of anger and love.

Paul was now at the end of his apostolic ministry in the Near East. During his fifteen years there he had striven to increase the centers of Christian life, not only by converts from Judaism, but also, in accordance with his own mission, by baptized persons coming straight from paganism; God knew what the task had cost him. Nevertheless, he did not consider the work finished. He was not satisfied with having planted the Church throughout Asia Minor and in Greece; he wanted to go to the West, as far as Spain. An opportunity would thus be given him to visit, in passing, the community already existing at Rome, whose members he knew. Before beginning this journey, however, he had to take to the Church of Jerusalem (cf. p. 304) the help offered by his communities.

From Corinth, where he again spent three months before taking the road to Syria and Palestine, desirous of preparing his meeting with the brethren at Rome, he sent them a letter which would inform them of his intentions and would, especially, tell them the way he understood the gospel. In doing this, the letter was explained at length. In it are set down the great problems which occupied Paul's thoughts, notably the problem he had just treated in his Epistle to the Galatians. Thus, because he dictated the Letter to the Romans carefully, it became a theological synthesis, showing the dimensions and power of its author's maturity.

The fundamental theme is the gratuitousness of the salvation given by God to all men by means of faith (cf. Rom. 1:17). Paul first shows the universal need of salvation: the Gentiles were guilty of having strayed lamentably (cf. Rom. 1:18-32); the Jews were guilty of having grown proud of their privileges and had become hardened (cf. Rom. 2:1-3, 20). "All have sinned . . . all are justified freely by the grace of God through the redemption which is in Christ Jesus" (Rom. 3:23-24). The example of Abraham, a typical instance of "Christian" faith, proves that a man is given grace before having merited it (cf. Rom. 4). Once justified, the Christian lives by the love infused in him by the Spirit of God, a superabundance of grace (cf. Rom. 5). Justification, which is accomplished at baptism —death and resurrection in Christ for a life of liberty and of service (cf. Rom. 6)—is shown by the example of a dramatic situation (cf. Rom. 7). The gift of God is "life in the Spirit," a filial life, hope of the created universe, the beginning and promise of the accomplishment of the Plan of God, from whose love nothing can separate a Christian (cf. Rom. 8). Of course, the history of salvation has a tragic aspect: the temporary absence of Israel which has not accepted Christ. Again, however, there is a mystery of love and of mercy; Israel will resume its place in the Plan of God (cf. Rom. 9-11). Finally, Paul speaks openly and most tenderly of Christian life in the community, whose principle is love—the gift of oneself, the perfect fulfillment of everything the Law contains, the accomplishment of the work of God who is Love.

Although it is appropriate to point out the important sections of the epistle, it should not be merely summarized. It is the first great treatise of theology that appeared in the Church, integrating valuable elements from the Old Testament, linking itself to the Prophets, setting down a comprehensive view of the Revelation which was fulfilled in Christ. In it, the doctrine of grace is definitively fixed. Every Christian knows in speaking of grace Paul reaches the core of his own story and of his mission, and that he does so with a logic and an eloquence that is always overwhelming, and with a profundity that the meditation of the Church will never exhaust.

Because of the debate on "faith and works," the Letter to the Romans has often been compared with the Letter of St. James. Whatever may be said of the comparison, it is quite possible that they were composed at nearly the same time. Some exegetes think, in fact, that James wrote his letter shortly before his death; others, whom it is very tempting to follow, hold for an earlier date, for example, 49-50 A.D.[5] If this is true, James' letter, which, by the tone of the preaching, is, a little treatise on "wisdom," and which is as

[5] There is also reason to believe that this writing is a complex composition, made up of several fragments or of texts worked over some time after the date of James's death.

truly Jewish as it is perfectly Christian, would be the very first Christian writing (cf. p. 332). It serves remarkably as a sequel to the latest of the canonical books, which we saw before, the Book of Wisdom (cf. p. 243), and a very happy link between the Old and the New Testaments.

What is known of James is not startling. He speaks as one who preached in the synagogues, which many Judaeo-Christians certainly still frequented, but in the way that one should speak to the faithful of Christ among the people. The relationships between the epistle and the sacred books, especially the psalms and the wisdom writings, are many, and the manner in which the author expresses himself is profoundly Hebrew in character If, from a literary point of view, the text is well written (one of the best in the New Testament), using an elegant Greek which is both lively and meticulous, perhaps it is because James, who was addressing Christians of the Diaspora, entrusted the pen to a good Hellenist among his disciples, through whom the personality of the bishop of Jerusalem can be perfectly felt. Written in the form of counsels and of maxims, employing religious and moral examples on the themes of ordeals, of true piety, of poverty and riches, of faith and works, of the use of the tongue, of wisdom, of brotherly understanding, his preaching is astonishingly close to that of the Lord. No doubt it is a unique approach to the thought and words of Jesus, with a clear echo of the catechesis in its ancient and popular form. The most striking note is the predilection of this "brother of the Lord" for the humble and the indigent. The Letter of James is one of the jewels of the biblical literature of the "poor."

The Letter to the Romans is dated 57-58 A.D. Four years later, enriched by many experiences and trials, Paul was a prisoner at Rome (cf. p. 305). During his captivity, which was no doubt lenient but which prevented him from going out to preach, the Apostle made, as it were, a long retreat. Again, he deepened his concepts on the mystery of Christ and of the Church, and evangelized his communities of the Near East through messages of an exceptional doctrinal maturity. We possess three letters written by him at this time.

One of them is only a short note: the Letter to Philemon. The letter is a simple Christian statement concerning a domestic matter, but it is perfectly delightful and very enlightening.

A much more important letter is the one Paul addressed to a

group whom he did not know directly. They were the inhabitants of the city of Colossae (in western Asia Minor, 125 miles from the coast), who had received Christ through a disciple of Paul's. The recipients of the Letter to the Colossians subscribed to a Christianity that was somewhat equivocal, for it was in the course of passing through a critical phase. They were undergoing the influence of a Judaism which, although it adhered strictly to the ritual precepts, seems to have been tinted by a nebulous mysticism and by notions originating from the pagan religions surrounding them concerning celestial hierarchies. The situation gave Paul an opportunity to expound the mystery of Christ in all its transcendance and in its fullness, that is, the absolute supremacy and universality of his dominion. Taking them far beyond their confused musings, the Apostle led the Colossians to contemplate Christ, who is before all creation and is its unique Head, the Redeemer of the whole world, Head of the Church which is his Body, the Christ through whom divinity fulfills all things.[6] This doctrine is the foundation of the important counsels, the strict advice, and the various recommendations the Apostle gives in the second part of the letter on "life in Christ."

Paul had not, however, said everything. Just as, after having given the Galatians who were about to go astray the vigorous help of his call to return to the Gospel, he had taken up his theme again and developed it in the Letter to the Romans, so also, having revealed to the Colossians during their crisis the splendor of the whole Christ, he felt the need of expressing his reflections still more fully.

He addresses the Letter to the Ephesians to the whole Church. More a treatise than a letter it does not seem to have been addressed to any precise community. Rather, it is a kind of encyclical addressed to a group of communities, written about the time of the letter to the Colossians. Besides using the same expressions and liturgical style as the Letter to the Colossians, it also uses the same themes, expanding them further. In addition, it contains certain major thoughts from the Letter to the Romans. The resulting "pastoral letter" is *the* great synthesis of Pauline theology. In it, one finds important assertions concerning Christ, the Wisdom of God, and the

[6] To designate this completeness, this fullness, Paul uses a term of Stoic origin, the *pleroma*. In the Letter to the Colossians the word *ecclesia* appears for the first time, not in the sense of a particular community or assembly, but in a collective and theological sense.

"recapitulation" of everything in him; the Church, Body and Spouse of Christ, appears in it in all her personal and living reality. Paul insists also on the mystery of the unity of all men, whoever they may be. All are freely redeemed and reconciled in Christ and in his Church, which is built up as a living thing. Each has his own place in the Church and each plays his own part in a new life, growing in sanctity. The developments of thoughts like these cannot be summarized; they should be known by heart.

Apostolic action had made Paul sensitive to the various aspects of the life of Christ in individual Christians and in the communities. His preaching returns again and again to the theme of sovereign Charity. In the calm of his enforced retreat, the Apostle had not only deepened and unified his thought, but he had acquired perspective, so to speak. He contemplated in Christ, with a penetration never to be surpassed, the whole divine Plan of salvation and the Mystery of the Church.

The collection of Pauline writings contains a group of three letters currently called the "Pastoral Letters" because of the part played in them by the pastors of the Church. They are also closely connected to one another in style and in every detail. Paul certainly sent them at the same period of his life. In his Second Letter to Timothy, he is still a prisoner, but this does not give certainty that it belongs to the years 61-63 A.D. No documentary evidence exists for the years following (cf. p. 306). It may, however, be correct to place the First Letter to Timothy (the well-loved and faithful disciple of Paul's early apostolic years, the companion of his long journeys and great foundations, of trials and captivity) and the Letter to Titus (another disciple of long standing, a man of character and good breeding, who could be relied upon) at the time of the apostle's fourth journey in the Near East. They were sent, perhaps, from Macedonia about 64-65 A.D. The Second Letter to Timothy may have been written at Rome at the time of Paul's last arrest, shortly before his death in 67 A.D.

The letters, then, were addressed not to communities, but to men who were charged with them. For this reason, they are strewn with frequent personal remarks. Their tone is still militant; Paul fought to the end. In them, he is still denouncing a somewhat hybrid Judaism just as he had done in his Letter to the Colossians (Timothy and Titus were both in authority over churches in Asia Minor).

Differences in both form and content are not lacking when these letters are compared with the other writings of Paul. The differences, however, can be explained by the differences of the persons to whom the letters are addressed, the purpose of each letter, and Paul's circumstancs. Furthermore, he undoubtedly wrote only through the intermediary of a secretary. It is quite easy, moreover, to show that not only is there a general agreement among the letters, but also there are exact connections and relationships with the theology of Paul as it is known elsewhere. The practical recommendations which, in the Apostle's usual manner, end these letters are based on firmly established doctrine. With what piety the Christian communities must have guarded these last testimonies of a prodigious career!

Even before the pastoral letters, undoubtedly around 63-64 A.D., before its author died a martyr (cf. p. 306), the only certain document written by the head of the Twelve and of the Church, is the First Letter of St. Peter. Its literary qualities cannot be praised; the first missionary of Christianity was not a stylist. He was a man of the people and of the working world. Like James, he was also one of the "poor," and his letter reflects their humble and courageous spirit. Peter, however, was equally a true Israelite; his soul was haunted by the Sacred History and filled with the Holy Scriptures. He addressed himself to Christians who had come from Judaism and who remained deeply attached to the Tradition of Israel. He not only quotes with ease Deutero-Isaias, the psalms, and the proverbs to them, but also makes allusions, with the greatest naturalness in the world, to the whole Old Testament, thinking as a Christian in the Hebrew values! [7] The letter is simply one of encouragement, but it continually draws on the most fundamental tenets of the theology of the apostolic era, affording a good idea of what the catechesis and the ministry of exhortation may have been in the Christian communities of the time. Peter seems to have made use of the letter of James and also of the early ones written by Paul (the Letter to the Romans and the Letter to the Ephesians, which had just been written), although their influence on his letter is rather general. Peter's aims were more practical and more modest than Paul's. The time of trials for the Christians had begun and persecution had begun to

[7] In I Pet. 1:13-2:12, for example, the militant and holy life of the baptized person is described more by constant allusions than by quotations, using the words of Exodus.

make itself felt. Their father in Christ told them urgently but kindly that, although they were saved by the Blood of Jesus, they ought to persevere firmly in faith and hope, never ceasing to sanctify their present life.

A more impressive writing from a pen that has remained anonymous, and undoubtedly set down at a later date, would also serve as a magnificent testimony to what would subsequently be called the harmony of the two Testaments.

The Letter to the Hebrews, placed traditionally with the work of Paul, which is justified by its doctrinal connections with his writings and its practical ideas, is not, however, by Paul himself. This can easily be seen, both from the literary form, which is perfect ("Hellenissimus," Origen was to call it, in a Greek even better than that of Luke), and by its content, which is centered on a theme not unknown to Paul, but one which he never treated as such. The letter, then, is attributed to a disciple of the Apostle; perhaps the writer was a priest from Jerusalem who had been converted to Christianity, or a Christian of sacerdotal origin, who had acquired a Greek culture of the very finest kind. Such a conjecture, however, merely adds one more hypothesis to too many others which are also uncertain. An unknown author, then, wrote to unknown recipients. It is evident only that the letter is addressed to some Judaeo-Christians who were threatened by tribulations and persecutions, and whose faith, moreover, was in danger because they compared their precarious position with the splendors experienced in the framework of the ancient Laws of Israelite worship. Since the Temple of Jerusalem was certainly still standing (otherwise, the letter would have seized upon the fact as an argument marvelously suited to its purpose) and since, in addition, it is impossible to date this letter any earlier, it is usually placed about the year 66 A.D., just before the "Jewish War" or at its beginning.

The Letter to the Hebrews is a "word of exhortation" (Heb. 13:22), so that this vast doctrinal thesis is continually supported by fervent and energetic recommendations; or rather, it is a discourse which, in order to strengthen faith and increase courage, develops powerfully a major aspect of the theology involved in Christian living. As far as the author is concerned, a penetrating contemplation of the Christian Mystery and practical decisions in the life of the baptized condition one another intimately.

A man who does not know the inspired literature of Israel will not know how to read these pages, all of which are written with the ancient Bible in mind. The People of God is on the march: the march of the Exodus, of the desert, of the entrance into the Holy Land. The march is processional and liturgical, because it leads to the Sanctuary of God. There, a high priest exercises the sacrificial Priesthood, especially in the solemn rite of Expiation, so that the People of God may be "holy." Let all of this be transposed, after the announcement of the Gospel, to the Church, to the level of the reality of the new People of God; Christ the eternal Son of God and the Redeemer-Man is at the center of the sacral Mystery of this New Covenant. In the admirable continuity of the Plan of God throughout the biblical Revelation, his role is seen, as the "End," as definition and accomplishment, as the height and fullness of Christ Jesus, in whom God had finished "speaking" and has said everything (cf. Heb. 1:1-2). The Letter to the Hebrews is a Christology read into the Old Testament, a Christian exegesis of the Torah, the illustration of the "concordance" of the prophetic Word and the Word Incarnate, Christ being the Truth of the Old Dispensation, its "meaning," its significance. Because of the needs of its readers (and perhaps because of the origin of its author), the letter chooses, in the personality and the role of Christ the Mediator, to dwell on his sacerdotal character and sacrifical office. Hence, the letter, whose intention was to be an encouraging homily, is also in fact a magnificent treatise on the Messianic Priesthood of Christ, his supreme pontificate, and his holy mediation before God in the Sanctuary of Heaven.

The erudite development of the theme, which is entirely Semitic in structure and method, proceeds by carefully prepared waves, partly overlapping one another, to produce a whole whose splendor is unequalled in all other biblical literature.

If James had earlier held, in the name of Christ, the pen of the ancient wise men of Israel, if Paul had relived the anxieties of an Isaias or of a Jeremias while witnessing the historic drama of the Chosen People, the anonymous disciple of the universal Apostle, who wrote the Letter to the Hebrews, recognized the Lord and Savior Jesus Christ in the Levitical heart of the Torah. He completed the theology of the Redemption by the Sacrifice of Jesus with the words of the great inspired Tradition. And his message is what he intended it to be: an encouragement for Christians on the march toward their Lord, from Sinai to the new Jerusalem, in the valiant and confident movement of hope.

[THREE]

THE GOSPELS [1] | The "evangelical tradition" (cf. p. 324) received its written and definitive form in the Gospels called the synoptic Gospels. The name is applied to them because their parallelism and their many close resemblances permit these three Gospels to give a "comprehensive view."

Although the works cannot be given definite dates, they appeared in the years extending from 60 A.D. to 70 A.D. If this is so, their respective dates of composition are not very far apart. The elements which they share in common, and which become apparent on comparative study (cf. pp. 325-26), seem to indicate the order of their appearance. The Gospel of St. Mark must have been composed first; then came the present text of St. Matthew; and finally Luke published his work, that is, the book dedicated to "Theophilus," which includes the Gospel of St. Luke and the Acts of the Apostles.

The Gospel according to St. Mark is the work of one of the first disciples of the Twelve. A companion of Paul at the beginning of Paul's missions (cf. Acts 12:12, 25; 13:5, 13; 15:37-39) and during the time of his captivity (cf. Philem. 24; Col. 4:10; II Tim. 4:11), Mark was also particularly attached to Peter from the time they both were in Jerusalem until the end of Peter's life at Rome (cf. I Peter 5:13; Eusebius, *Hist. eccl.*, 3, 15, 39). The evangelist derived his missionary and universalist spirit, which is so noticeable in his book, from both Peter and Paul. Writing at Rome, he addressed his work to readers who had come mostly from paganism (this accounts for the explanations of the kind given by Mark in 7:3-4).

[1] In accordance with our intention of keeping to general ideas in this volume, we will not give a bibliography on the Gospels. A presentation of the Gospels may be found in most of the lives of Jesus, cited on page 287, and in the book of Lucien Cerfaux, p. 321. Osty has added brief and excellent introductions to his translations of the New Testament. Comparison of the Gospels and their study in general will be greatly facilitated by using the very original *Concordance of the Synoptic Gospels* by Léon-Dufour (Desclée and Co., 1956).

A work more free from artifice cannot be found. Its simplicity, its direct and unpolished character, give it a charm which was scarcely appreciated in the past (Matthew was preferred to it) but to which our times are very sensitive. From a literary point of view, St. Mark's Gospel is poor and imperfect. It lacks vocabulary and repeats endlessly the same formulas (for example, "and at once," "again"); Mark equally is lacking in resources from the point of view of syntax, expressing himself quite simply in the kind of Greek spoken by a Semite (the simple coordination of propositions with "and . . . and," which is found, for example, 15 times in succession in Mark 4:3-8). He exhibits a clumsy naïveté in constructing a narrative (cf., for example, Mark 1:16; 2:15; 3:22-30; 5:27-28, 42-43, and the corrections supplied by Matthew and Luke). He uses the simplest methods of presentation, recounting different episodes in series of identical formulas and in a stylized way that are absolutely alike (compare Mark 1:25-27 and 4:39-41; 7:32-36 and 8:22-26; 11:1-6 and 14:13-16).

Nevertheless, the defects and asperities do not prevent the Gospel of St. Mark from being extremely striking. If it lacks style, it still has the pleasantness and picturesqueness of simplicity, a primitive flavor and complete spontaneity, a vitality and freshness. Its realism is extremely evocative. It produces such an impression of "having seen" and "having felt" that it seems like direct testimony. The fact is, however, that the testimony is the witness of Peter himself, whom Mark had heard many times, and whose words he collected and transcribed candidly, never hiding the weaknesses of the chief of the apostles (cf. Mark 8:32-33; 10:28; 14:29-31, 37, 66-72). He shows the same probity even when he treats of the apostles' lack of understanding (cf. Mark 6:52; 8:17, 21; 9:32; 10:32, 37, 41; 14:50), or of words which seem to create a difficulty (cf. Mark 3:21; 6:3, 5-6; 8:12; 10:18; 13:52).

The book is solidly constructed with regard to main outlines. The general scheme follows the original apostolic catechesis (cf. Acts 10:37-42), but Mark has been selective in his work. He has often summarized, and sometimes very briefly, the discourses of Jesus, and has even left out some of the discourses, notably the "Sermon on the Mount." On the other hand, even though he includes fewer narratives than the other evangelists, in most cases he is clearly the most detailed of the narrators (compare Mark 5:1-42 with

Matt. 9:18-34 and Luke 8:26-46; Mark 6:30-44 with Matt. 14:13-21 and Luke 9:10-17; Mark 9:14-29 with Matt. 17:14-21 and Luke 9:37-43).

The plan of the book divides the matter into three unequal parts: the ministry of Jesus in Galilee (cf. Mark 1:14-8:26); his journey to Judea (cf. Mark 8:27-10:52); and his last days at Jerusalem (cf. Mark 11-16). During the course of the account, the personality of the "Son of Man" is progressively revealed. At the same time, the meaning of his destiny, the necessity of his passion, and the value of his death gradually become apparent. As a parallel, the faith of the disciples who have attached themselves to Jesus and the hostility of those who oppose him grow. The fact of Christ is thus shown in all its drama: the Messias who sows the benefits of his word and his miracles, but who does not save men except in the humiliation and in the suffering of total sacrifice. The Gospel of St. Mark is a living commentary on the words of Jesus: "The Son of Man also has not come to be served but to serve, and to give his life as a ransom for many" (Mark 10:45).

Did the Apostle Matthew himself translate into Greek the Gospel he had composed in his native tongue about the year 50 A.D.? He may have done so, but the book which now bears his name is not simply a translation. The Gospel according to St. Matthew reproduces in substance the work written by this former taxcollector (cf. Matt. 9:9-13). It retains its Semitic flavor and Palestinian character; no doubt it has also preserved the general arrangement of its prototype; and it is still addressed to Judaeo-Christian readers. The translation, however, is acquainted with the Gospel of St. Mark and borrows much from it, at the same time correcting it, either out of literary concern, or in order to bring about a greater moderation in the descriptions. It benefits also from other sources. One of these was perhaps a collection that had already been compiled, and from which Luke may also have drawn material. The Gospel of St. Matthew is the most complete and the richest, especially with regard to the words of Jesus, which the evangelist presents in ample discourses.

Faithful to his sources, but not a slave to them, Matthew has composed a personal work. He writes in the Greek used by the Semites; his language is neither particularly beautiful nor brilliant, but it is correct, precise, and carefully set down. His style is simple, sober, serious, and rather solemn, creating a profoundly religious impression. The use of parallelism in his propositions, after the Hebrew manner, which both the Rabbis and Jesus employed (cf. p. 290), often is in evidence (cf. Matt. 7:1-14, 24-27). Furthermore, the intellectual and logical character of Matthew's Gospel appears in the general distribution of the matter, and also in certain attempts at a numerical systematization. Thus, for example, the beatitudes in Chapter 5, the maledictions in Chapter 23, the seven parables in Chapter 13, and the ten miracles of Chapters 8-9 are intentional groupings.

The general structure of the book is a beautifully and skillfully constructed edifice; its balance and its clarity have earned for the Gospel of Matthew a high pedagogical value. The book contains seven parts: a kind of prologue concerning the childhood of Jesus (cf. Matt. 1-2); five small books, each containing a narrative section and a collection of discourses (cf. Matt. 5-25); and finally the account of the passion and the resurrection (cf. Matt. 26-28). The five central sections are made up in the following way: (1) the important announcement—preparation (cf. Matt. 3-4) and the Sermon on the Mount (cf. 5-7); (2) the apostolic ministry—ten miracles (cf. Matt. 8-9) and missionary instructions (cf. Matt. 10); (3) the mystery of the Kingdom—the difficulties (cf. Matt. 11-12) and the seven parables (cf. Matt. 13); (4) the Church of Christ—Jesus a new Moses (cf. Matt. 14-17) and the rule of the new Community (Matt. 18); (5) salvation and judgment—the journey toward the redeeming Sacrifice (cf. Matt. 19-23) and the eschatological discourse (cf. Matt. 24-25). It is evident that the narratives prepare for the discourses. In order to accomplish such a presentation, the evangelist has taken liberties with the chronological order. He has placed together narrative elements which have some relationship with one another or which clarify the declarations of Jesus, grouping them according to similarities of theme or of situation.

The message of Matthew is "to fulfill all justice" (cf. Matt. 3:15), that is, to realize salvation (cf. *WG*, pp. 207-8) by the institution of the Kingdom which begins with the coming of Jesus. Using his great faith as a true Israelite in the whole Law, and underlining exact references to the Scriptures ("that what was written in—might be accomplished"), Matthew stresses to the Christians who were born Jews, the ones to whom his Gospel was addressed, the fact that the Advent of Jesus was the perfect achievement postulated by the Old Testament (cf. Matt. 5:17-18). The tragedy, however, is that the Chosen People, in the person of their elite and in their leaders, refused the Messias and caused his death. Although a scandal and a mystery, their reaction had been foretold, and it cannot thwart the redemption of the world. For the defection of the "children of the Kingdom," that is, of the Judaism contemporary with Jesus,[2] is compensated for by the great number of non-Israelites "come from the East and West" (Matt. 8:11-12), into a "Church" (Matthew is the only evangelist to designate the Church by name; (cf. Matt. 16: 18:17), whose institution he recounts better than the others.

A "Scribe instructed in the kingdom of heaven," Matthew "is like a householder who brings forth from his storeroom things new and old" (Matt. 13:52). His Gospel, the most Israelite of all, is as universal as Christianity itself can be. He comments on Christ by using the sacred texts of Tradition, but he sees this Tradition on the march, and he shows the value of every innovation proposed in the Christian message. The mighty and dynamic balance of St. Matthew's Gospel, and its richness of content, have caused it to be placed at the beginning of the New Testament[3] and to be used more than any other Gospel. This was true as early as the end of the first century in the Church.

The third canonical Gospel and the book of the Acts of the Apostles are one single work, written for the "excellent Theophilus" (cf. Luke 1:3; Acts 1:1). Since the first part parallels the other two Gospels, it has been separated from the second part, although the author undoubtedly saw in the whole only a single "gospel." The reader discovers the presence of the author in the book of Acts, halfway through the narration of Paul's second journey (cf. Acts 16: 10). From this time on, the discreet "we's" indicate that Luke accompanied the Apostle and that the "dear physician" scarcely left him afterwards (cf. Col. 4:14; Philem. 24; II Tim. 4:11). The disciple had the same missionary duty as his master: to address all men, whoever they might be. Therefore, he made himself a Jew to the

[2] It must not be forgotten that Christianity, in its beginnings, came entirely from Israel. Matthew knows it, being a Jew himself, like the rest of the Twelve.

[3] Magnificently begun with the "Genealogy of Jesus Christ, son of David, son of Abraham" (with its table of three times 14 names, 14 being the sum of the letters in David's name, counted in the Hebrew manner).

Jews (cf. I Cor. 9:20) by his astonishing knowledge of the Bible, and a Greek to the Greeks by the literary quality of his work and the "goodness and kindness" (Titus 3:4) of his message.

Although he was a writer of only average cultivation, his work is valued high among the literature of his time, because he himself was endowed with tact and was a highly agreeable person. The Gospel according to St. Luke is written in excellent language. He used the tongue of the Hellenistic period, naturally, without either aesthetic pretentions or an attempt to popularize. His style is sober and measured, refined and delicate. He corrects the Gospel of St. Mark with discreet care. In the narratives that are proper to him, he shows himself to be an incomparable storyteller (everyone knows the scenes of the annunciation and the nativity, the miracle at Naim, the story of the sinful woman in Simon's house, and that of the disciples at Emmaus; with regard to the parables, which only Luke tells, the parable of the "Good Samaritan" or of the "Prodigal Son" cannot be forgotten). He has, in addition, an uncommon aptitude for imitation: his Prologue is composed in the style of the secular writers of his day. His first two chapters might be right out of the Old Testament and are marked with its simple note of the sacred. He readily gives a Hebrew coloring to his text (for example, by using the formula, "and it came to pass," which is found only three times in Mark and six times in Matthew, but thirty-six times in Luke and seventeen times in the Acts) and certain passages are strewn with Semitic expressions (cf. Luke 13:10-17). He is, moreover, so impregnated with the Greek Bible that his "Septuagintism" and his desire to become "a sacred writer" are spoken of.

St. Luke's most important source for his Gospel is the Gospel of St. Mark, which he uses as a basis of documentation and of organization. He follows its development, but freely, and its text, which he improves. Also, he is acquainted with the Gospel of St. Matthew, under its more ancient form, the two having many passages in common. But Luke also collected information in other ways: the supplementary source already discussed when the documentation of Matthew was presented; certain "attempts" at the preparation of a Gospel, which have not been preserved (cf. Luke 1:1-2); and information which he was able to acquire himself. Among the elements that are proper to Luke alone, the following can be cited in particular: Luke 1:1-3:4; 6:20-8:3; 9:51-18:14 (the great "Lucan section"); 19:1-27, 39-44; 23:7-12; 24:13-35.

Autonomous sections or "little books" can be detected in Luke's work, but he has not tied himself down to a systematic order; he does not force the evangelical tradition into a pre-established framework; rather, he retains his flexibility as a narrator. He tries to present the words of Jesus in their psychological and natural context and attempts to give the flavor of their episodic and fragmentary character. He intends to be a historian; he has a real competence in the field and gives good proof of it.[4] Above all, he is an evangelist, that is, a catechist and missionary; hence, his work is primarily a presentation of the Christian Message. One of the most original characteristics of his presentation is the journey of Jesus toward Jerusalem: he is on the way to the Holy City for a long time (cf. Luke 9:51; 13:22; 17:11; 18:31; 19:11, 28, 41); in addition, the Temple is at the beginning and the end of the Gospel (Luke 1:8-10; 24:53). In the Acts, Jerusalem is still the pole, but of an inverse movement, the point from which one sets out (according to the program of Acts 1:8).

Among the other special characteristics of the evangelical presentation of Luke can be mentioned the atmosphere of kindness and of joy it contains throughout, the meeting with many fine feminine types he speaks of, the frequent happy songs of praise to the glory of God, the emphasis laid on the importance of prayer, and the major place given to the activity of the Holy Spirit (as in the Acts). Undoubtedly, however, the most evident characteristic of Luke's work is the fact that he, more than anyone else, stresses the divine goodness and mercy. He does not soften the seriousness and the rigorousness of Christ's demands. On certain points, such as poverty, he is exceptionally clear. Nevertheless, he is the evangelist par excellence of the pity and the tenderness of God, of the pardon and the reconciliation preached by Jesus. His message, which in no way weakens the force of the Master's preaching, but

[4] "He is, in short, to the great Greek or Latin historians what a good provincial teacher is to a professor at the Sorbonne: he knows the good methods, but does not always apply them with the breadth of view desirable" (Trocmé, *The Book of Acts and History* [P.U.F., 1957], p. 98).

which is marked by moderation and prudence, although not as incisive or as dramatic as the works of his precedessors and friends, has a charm calculated to win the hearts of men to Christ and to make the Word of salvation sink into them.

The literary qualities, the patterns of thought, the goodness of heart, and the apostolic notions of Luke, Paul's Hellenistic disciple, a lover of good language but also wholly penetrated by the Septuagint, are found again in the second part of his Gospel, the book of the Acts of the Apostles. In it, he intends to give a quick survey of the progress of evangelical preaching in the eastern Mediterranean region during the thirty years that followed the ascension of the Lord.

Certainly, however, he had also another object in mind: he desired to present Paul as an apostle on a par with the Twelve, to narrate the missionary work of the one in whom was incarnated the apostolate outside of Israel, and, no less important, to defend him against those who accused him of treason with regard to Judaism.

Any attempt to make comparisons with the Acts is impossible, because the book has no parallel (it has, however, certain relationships, not deliberately intended and for this reason very valuable, with the letters of Paul, the most notable instance being that of Acts 11 and 15 and Gal. 2). Furthermore, no one knows its sources. Consequently, a work of this kind, so obviously complex cannot be studied without the help of literary criticism. Many problems have arisen, not all of which are resolved. They force the scholar to use wise judgment and a certain prudence (which does not mean distrust) in regard to this fine and honest work.

The fundamental documentation is especially difficult to establish in the first part of the work (Chapters 1-12 or 1-15). The first part is composed of narratives containing discourses which alternate with small general pictures of the life of the Christian groups in Jerusalem. The history is constructed in such a way that a sense of the rapid development of the youthful Christianity can be felt. Events are considerably simplified; they are recounted in representative scenes and in obviously "idealized" summaries. Many events, and no doubt the least favorable (cf. for example Gal. 2:11-21), are passed over in silence. A kind of heroic narrative results, one which readily overlooks the shadows, and which is reminiscent of, differences being allowed for, the Book of Joshua (cf. pp. 68-69). This first section is centered on Jerusalem and is dominated by the figure of Peter.

The second part (Acts 13-28) is oriented toward the entire world and follows Paul in his missionary expeditions. The account this time is usually first hand, for Luke himself took part in the events described (cf. Luke 16:10-17; 20:5-15; 21:1-18; 27:1-28:16—the "we" sections," as they are called by the critics), or else he received his information from eyewitnesses. Thus, he wrote a kind of journal or report of the missions. The book could not have been given a better ending, from the point of view of Luke's Gospel: arrived at Rome, Paul is shown "preaching the Kingdom of God and teaching about the Lord Jesus Christ with all boldness and unhindered" (Acts 28:31).

Throughout the book, discourses are distributed according to the method used by the ancient historians. They are certainly based on authentic tradition, even though Luke did construct them according to accepted literary modes. They have, then, a real documentary value because of the knowledge they provide concerning the beginning of apostolic preaching. Luke's probity is also proved by the fact that he has left the words of Peter in their original theological clumsiness, their highly Jewish tenor, and, so to speak in their archaicism. With regard to the discourse of Paul, on the other hand, although some of his ideas known from other sources (fortunately!) are found in them, it is clear that the evangelist has not in any way drawn on his master's letters, to the extent of seeming to be ignorant of them.

Luke, then, has succeeded in making a presentation of Christian origins which is precious to the historian. He desired primarily, however, to write a true gospel, one that would be harmonious and attractive in form, and one that would present events in a pleasing light. The history he tells is manifestly the work of the Holy Spirit. No other book of the New Testament is so filled with his interventions; it is truly the "acts of the Spirit." Furthermore, the universality of such a message need not be stated: Luke's work is a marvelous preface to the history of the Church on the march, carrying the gospel to the whole world. Scarcely any other writing is more refreshing or more encouraging.

[FOUR]

JOHN AND THE END OF THE APOSTOLIC ERA

The history recounted by the Acts of the Apostles ends with the year 62 A.D. Only fragmentary information is available concerning Christianity during the last third of the century in which the "apostolic era" came to a close. This period was the era of the Twelve Apostles, some of whom were already dead, and of their immediate disciples. Certainly the Church continued to develop and to spread during the course of this period. Indeed, it spread not only among the people of the lower classes (among whom it began its original development, in conformity with its very mission), but also among the highest social circles, and even in the court of the emperor.[1]

The Christians were no longer confused with the Jews, as was the case in the time of Claudius (cf. p. 254). Evidence that the two groups were considered distinct was the persecution decreed by Nero, who was trying to find a way to put the people on the wrong scent in regard to the causes of the burning of Rome in 64 A.D. (cf. p. 255). Tacitus says of Nero's decree: "Neither the gifts of the prince nor the sacrifices offered to the gods effaced the ignominious suspicion that the burning had been ordered. Thus, in order to suppress this rumor, Nero substituted others for the guilty, inflicting most refined tortures on those people detested for their crimes whom the populace called Christians. He from whom they derived this name, Christ, had been executed by the procurator Pontius Pilate under the reign of Tiberius. Suppressed for a while, the detestable superstition broke out again, not only in Judea, where it originated, but even in Rome, where everything evil and shameful that exists comes together and is concentrated" (*Annals*, 15:45). The martyrs are thought to have numbered in the hundreds.

The horror of this the first persecution made an enoromus impression on the Christians. They had, however, not failed in loyalty toward the state, according to the doctrine of Jesus and his apostles. Indeed, recently Paul had appealed to Caesar against his Jewish

[1] This was the case with Flavia Domitilla, a niece of Domitian, and her husband, Flavius Clemens.

detractors at Jerusalem. He had justified and recommended submission to the authorities, giving the best reasons (cf. Rom. 13:1-7); Peter had done the same (cf. I Peter 2:13-17). Nevertheless, since the state wished to be master even in the religious domain, it had learned to distrust the religious autonomy of the Jews, even though the Jews had been shown favor at first. Hence, before long the authorities sensed the same sort of autonomy among the Christians. Having been classed as "public enemies," the Christians realized the threat to their lives and the fact that they were liable to be condemned as "Christians" (cf. I Peter 4:16; cf. John 15:20; 16:2). In Nero, they saw the "Antichrist." Even after his death, the ignoble and dreadful tyrant continued to haunt their dreams and enjoyed a strange, popular survival in the legend of "Nero redivivus."

The Jewish War (cf. pp. 308-13) was an occasion of sadness for the Christians. Even though it fulfilled some of the words of their Master, still the evocation of the terrible events was tragic for all. It provided, however, a new opportunity for them to be known as distinct from the Jews, and from that time on the distinction was definitive. In fact, the true separation between the Church and Judaism dates from the catastrophe of 70 A.D. Until then, the pluralism of Judaism had permitted movements as diverse as those of the Pharisees, the Sadducees, the Essenes, and the Zealots; its tolerance toward the Judaeo-Christians was, therefore, not exceptional. The various movements within Judaism, however, had caused its ruin at the very time when its prosyletism (never before attempted) was about to win the world for it. After the great disaster, then, the Jewish community realized that it could rebuild itself only by unifying its doctrine and uniting its members. The doctrine accepted was the teachings of the Pharisees, to the exclusion of other and divergent tendencies. Obviously the question of admitting the Christians never arose again.

By this very fact, the Church was confirmed in her consciousness of her autonomy. The "catholic" theology of Paul, often contested during the life of the Apostle, became the common doctrine, and his letters enjoyed a wider and wider diffusion among the communities. The universality of the Church was no longer brought into question. Naturally, the relationships between Jews and Christians did not become any easier. In Judaism is found a desire to ignore Jesus and his disciples. The Christians, on their part, did not always refrain from showing distrust, if not animosity, toward the Jews. Nevertheless, positive reactions and controversies between Jews and Christians did not begin until the following century. In addition, conversions of Jews to Christianity continued.

The break between the two communities did not imply the abandonment by the Christians of the Israelite tradition. The Church held onto the conviction that it was remaining in that living and divinely led tradition when it opened its doors to non-Jews also. It always believed that it was not destroying the Law, but fulfilling it. Having recognized the Messias and having received the mission of making him known to the world, knowing that the Redemption had taken place and that the "last days" had begun, it had the absolute certainty that it was "the people God had purchased for himself" (Isa. 43:21; I Peter 2:9).

Christian literature at the end of the first century is the clearest manifestation of the fidelity to the Plan that God had been following since Abraham and Moses. Like the letters of St. James and St. Peter, these writings refer to the Old Testament in a way that is both spontaneous and constant, both simple and profound. They show that the Christians were perfectly aware of living the history of the Covenant and of Salvation, which had been inaugurated by the pledge of the Fathers.

Like the Letter of St. James, the Letter of St. Jude was written by a relative of Jesus (cf. Matt. 13:55). He was not one of the Twelve, although he must have lived in their company and been associated with their apostolate. The letter may have been written before 70 A.D., but it is much more probable that it dates from ten or twenty years later.

A short piece containing only twenty-five verses, and addressed to Judaeo-Christians, the letter vehemently denounces both serious offenses in the moral order and doctrinal aberrations (especially with regard to the celestial hierarchies). The same dangers are also evident in the pastoral letters and in the "letters to the churches" in the Apocalypse; they foreshadow the gnosticism of the second century. Allusions to these incipient heresies do not make an understanding of the letter easy. The difficulty is further increased by Jude's references to apocalyptic writings that were known and in circulation at that time, notably the Assumption of Moses and the Book of Enoch (cf. pp. 233-34). Nevertheless, the letter is not merely a witness to the vitality of early Christianity; it is also valuable today because of its admonitions, teachings, and exhortations.

The second chapter of the Second Letter of St. Peter, is so similar to the text of Jude that it must have been inspired by Jude's letter, for it undoubtedly was written a little later. The fact that the letter is attributed to the chief of the apostles should not surprise us. Biblical literary customs of the time authorized the procedure. Attributing the letter to Peter might mean that it did not intend to teach anything that had not been transmitted by the apostles or that was not indeed related to the preaching of Peter. The theory has also been advanced that it is a letter from Peter himself, reworked and rewritten later by a disciple.

Like Jude, but almost more forcefully and more emphatically, the author condemns false and deceitful spirits, men of dissolute morals, and those who fall back into error or into misconduct after their conversion. He speaks, of the "Day of the Lord" in terms of upheavals and of the destruction of the impious, after the style of the apocalyptic writers; his eschatology recalls the teaching of the synoptics and of Paul; some of the descriptive elements he uses will be found again in the Apocalypse of St. John.

From the viewpoint of biblical tradition, the Second Letter of St. Peter is valuable for two reasons: for one thing, it not only testifies to the faith, common among the believers, in the divine origin of the Holy Scriptures, but also to reflection on that doctrine (cf. II Pet. 1:20-21; cf. *WG*, pp. 51-52); for another thing, there is an interesting statement concerning St. Paul's letters, which were practically "canonized" already (cf. II Peter 3:15-16).

According to tradition,[2] the Apostle John, one of the most illustrious among the Twelve and a missionary who traveled with Peter in the early days of the Church, survived Peter and Paul by more than thirty years, dying at the beginning of Trajan's reign (cf. p. 257). During the latter period of his life, having become a kind of patriarch of the churches of Asia Minor, with Ephesus, apparently, as their principal center, he wrote the fourth Gospel, three letters,

[2] Represented by Irenaeus of Lyon, Clement of Alexandria, Tertullian, and the Canon of Muratori. One cannot, however, ignore another tradition, less certain of course, which would lead one to believe in John's martyrdom before the end of the century; in which case his work would have been finished and published by his disciples.

and the Apocalypse. His personality, like Paul's, was to have a great effect on the first Christians as well as on the destiny of the Church. He did not, however, resemble Paul. His life was certainly not as adventurous and his genius, although no less brilliant, manifested itself in a very different way.

The order in which his writings appeared is not known precisely. Probably the Apocalypse was composed first; the third letter is undoubtedly earlier than the other two and earlier than his Gospel. Nevertheless, because of the uncertainty that persists and also because the Gospel is the oldest with regard to content, we shall follow the order of these writings as they appear in the traditional Canon.

The Gospel according to St. John, like the other three, proclaims Jesus as Messias and Son of God, and is proposed for belief, thereby giving "life" (John 20:31). It differs considerably, however, from the work of Mark, Matthew, and Luke.

From the literary point of view, two points must be made. The language is mediocre; St. John wrote in the Greek of a Semite, using a very limited vocabulary and an entirely Hebraic syntax, which consists essentially in the constant use of paratoxis and a simplicity greater than any other writing in the New Testament. Nevertheless, unpolished though his style may be, dull, monotonous, and poor in resources, it has a secret and extraordinary power. Not only does it bespeak the naturalness and spontaneity of a witness much like Mark, but also it is filled with a rhythm, a power, a grandeur, an accent on the sacred that are most unique. The "Johannine" style is so extraordinary and so intrinsic to the message that it remains perceptible even in translation. Undoubtedly, this is one of the finest examples of a language whose quality and energy proceed not from art but from the personality of the author and from the vitality that dwells in him.

A comprehensive plan is not evident in St. John's Gospel, except insofar as the life of Jesus is followed according to the outline dictated by evangelical tradition: the preaching of the Baptist; the preaching and actions of Jesus; the passion and resurrection. A progressive and dramatic unfolding of events is strongly felt. A parallel with the synoptics, however, cannot be established. Perhaps the difficulty of finding an order in the fourth Gospel comes from the fact that it was written at various times and that the texts are testimonies of different periods, which include the first preaching of the apostle, the elaboration of his doctrine at a later date by a more experienced Church, his own further meditation, and perhaps even a revision made by some of his disciples.

These facts give assurance that the message of John is a faithful "testimony" (John 21:24); John seems to have fully intended his Gospel to be his own testimony about Christ. If, knowing the synoptics, he took their work into consideration, and if he supplied concrete evidence of great value—for example, the chronological and topographical setting of the life of Jesus—he nevertheless did something more than merely supply complementary documentation. John's Gospel is a personal and original work.

The small number of episodes he relates may surprise the reader at first. Obviously, they have been chosen on purpose. Each of the approximately two dozen events (apart from the account of the passion) recalled in connection with the words of Jesus (sometimes with a commentary by the evangelist), constitutes a "sign"; the reality signified by these signs is both the history of Jesus—actions he performed or words he spoke—and the history of salvation in Christian life. Like Nicodemus, each baptized person "is born from on high," that is, is a new creature of God (cf. John 3); like the Samaritan woman, every believer drinks "from a fountion of water, springing up unto life everlasting" (cf. John 4 and 7); as in the case of the paralytic of Bezatha and of Lazarus, "the son also gives life to whom he will" (John 5 and 11); as on the shore of the lake, Jesus always gives the "Bread of life" (John 6); as in the case of the man born blind, he is for every man the "Light" (John 8-9). For this reason, then, John places these episodes together, since they refer especially to the sacraments of baptism and the Eucharist. The clearest examples are obviously John 3 and 6; but study quickly reveals the many symbolisms contained in the Gospel.

In order to provide his testimony with a setting within the tradition of the Church, John connects it profoundly to the whole of biblical Revelation. The references to the Old Testament—Pentateuch, Psalter, Prophets, Wisdom Writings—both explicit and implicit, are constant. Matthew dealt in quotations, John reaches down to the underground water line, or more exactly to the inner current of the inspired tradition. His method is a delight, a marvel, and will be encountered again in the Apocalypse. It enables us to see in Johannine literature the most fitting, complete, and happy conclusion to this historical and literary inquiry.

Because of its form, words, and style, as well as its ideas, the fourth Gospel is related especially to the Wisdom Writings. From them it derives its vocabulary ("light," "life," "way," "fidelity," and "love"), its antitheses (for example, light-darkness, life-death, truth-falsehood, love-hate, joy-sadness [3]) and the parallelism of its short propositions, which are as incisive as the *meshalim*. John's theology of the divine "Word" proceeds from the entire body of Scripture, but he uses the latest line of approach as represented by Proverbs, the Wisdom of ben Sirach, the Psalms, and the Wisdom of Solomon. It reaches its culmination in the astonishing "prologue" (John 1:1-18), in which Jesus is presented as the "(divine) Word made flesh."

John reflects particularly on Jesus' statements concerning the "mission" of the Holy Spirit in the Church. A rare doctrine, the doctrine concerning the "Paraclete" is thus proposed (cf. John 7:39; 14:15-19, 25-26; 15:26; 16:7-15), admirably completing the revelation concerning the Spirit of power and of life, the creator and regenerator, who sets the boundaries of biblical tradition (cf. *WG*, p. 222). The Church, too, had already had enough experience during the lifetime of the apostle to have become aware of the action of the promised Holy Spirit (cf. John 2:22; 7:39; 12:16, 33; 20:9).

John is also the evangelist of the "agape," the love-gift, and of the "knowledge" which is its revealing and fruitful experience: the love of the Father for his son, in spite of which he gives his son for men; the love of Jesus who gives himself to men; the love of men for God, in Christ; the love of men for one another. We need only reread chapters 13 to 17 to find texts both simple and overwhelming on the mystery of charity-knowledge-communion-life, and on the mystery of Christians in Christ. To love is to "keep the commandments," and to keep the commandments is to "live." Again the same terms used at the Covenant, the same words spoken by the Prophets of "charity," Osee and Jeremias, and found in Deuteronomy and Leviticus, are repeated by John.

[3] Comparisons can be made, in this connection, between John and the Qumran texts; but it must not be forgotten that these were equally heirs of the Old Testament. These antitheses are also to be found in the work of St. Paul.

John was able to present the great realities and the major themes of Christian existence—faith, the Incarnation, the Spirit, the sacraments, the Church, charity, "eternal" life—in a manner so simple and at the same time so mysterious that the study of his Gospel, more enriching than any other, never seems to be more than an outline. Hence, although much can be gained from it, the reader is never sure of having assimilated its message sufficiently.

Christian experience, faith and charity, fidelity and vigilance, are expressed again in the First Letter of St. John. He uses sentences that are clear, forceful, simple, and as insistent as the waves, the cadence of their Semitic rhythm bordering on poetry and giving a suggestion of what is inexpressible in a mystery. To be "born of God," to live "in communion" with God and with one another, "to walk and to dwell in the light," to "do truth," "to remain in love"—these are the many distinguishing expressions of the best Christian speech.

Charity is militant. John, who knew the ambiguity of the human heart, also knew the "world" that is not of God, from which man must guard himself (cf. I John 2:15-17; 3:2, 13; 4:5; 5:19). He denounces the enemies and corrupters of the faith, who dwell in the very heart of the community of the faithful: the false prophets; the children of the devil; the "antichrists" (cf. I John 2:18, 22; 3:8-10; 4:1, 3); those who harm the churches of Asia (cf. Apoc. 2-3), and who completely destroy the whole Christian revelation by denying the Incarnation of Jesus (cf. I John 2:22-23; 4:3; 5:10-12). Therefore, a man must take care, but without fear (cf. I John 4:17-18): when sin is resisted and forgiven (I John 1:7; 2:2, 12; 3:5), the Christian is a conqueror (cf. I John 2:14; 4:4; 5:4-5). This is the message of the Apocalypse.

In St. John's first letter, the Covenant, which was both the means and the end of the Plan of God in history, is given its final formulation: "God is love . . . love comes from God and whosoever loves is born of God. . . . If God has so loved us, we ought also to love one another" (cf. I John 4:7-8, 11).

The Second Letter of St. John is very short and is dedicated to a community. It uses the same ideas and expressions as the first: to love one another, which is "the commandment"; guard yourselves against being seduced by the "antichrists," who profess that "Jesus was not incarnate."

The purpose of the Third Letter of St. John is more specific: it contains words of encouragement for an excellent disciple of the apostle's, Caius, and for another good missionary, Demetrius; then it reproaches a certain Diotrephes, perhaps the head of the community, whose conduct is a cause for sorrow. In the Third Letter a brief but vital and suggestive glimpse of the life of a church can be seen.

The aged apostle, therefore, carried in his heart, as had St. Paul before him, concern for his communities and for the whole Church. On no side was the situation encouraging. It seemed that since the reign of Nero the world had entered a gloomy phase of history. There was economic crisis and a considerable increase in the cost of living, an epidemic in 65 A.D. which claimed thirty thousand victims, civil wars, insecurity because of the Parthians, the terrible putting down of the revolt in Judea, earthquakes in Anatolia, the destruction of Herculaneum and Pompeii by Visuvius in 79 A.D., the second burning of Rome in 80 A.D., followed by a plague that was still ravaging the capital (these are the facts to which allusion is made in Apoc. 6:2-8; 8:7-12; 9:3-10; 12:7, 13, 17). In addition, the Christians were still suffering from the terrors caused by the persecution of Nero (Apoc. 6:9-11; 11:7-10).

Perhaps many of them believed, as Christians of Thessalonica had (cf. pp. 332-33), that the Coming of Christ would soon take place. But history continued to move, accompanied by misfortunes, uncertainties, and dangers. Paganism, more powerful than ever, was destructive and brutal; the Church, a minority, was subject to humiliation (cf. Apoc. 12). Worse still, however, was the new demand made by the state in the time of Domitian: the cult of the emperor was made obligatory under pain of death; men were forced to give to Caesar what belonged to God alone. The anti-God was diabolical power incarnate (the beast of Apoc. 13:1-9), who had at his disposal propaganda, coercion, and magic (the second beast: Apoc. 13:11-18; 16:13; 19:20; 20:10). His seat was at Rome, the capital of wealth, of great international commerce, and of luxury, as well as of idolatry, blasphemy, and every form of prostitution; Rome was the city "drunk with the blood of the martyrs of Jesus" (Apoc. 17:1-18; 18:11-19).

Was there still room for hope?

In the style of the great Prophets, but also using the fascinating colors of an apocalyptic writer, John proceeds to consider all the facts of contemporary history in order to show their meaning. He interprets them to the Christians in the light of the victorious Christ, to whom God has given the government of the universe, the control of history, and the care of his people. "In the world you will have affliction. But take courage, I have overcome the world," Jesus had said (John 16:33). Such was the message of the "Revelation" or Apocalypse of John, one of the most extraordinary writings in world literature, and the most magnificent conclusion possible to biblical Revelation.

The work can be dated from the end of the reign of Domitian, about 90-95 A.D. Addressed as a kind of encyclical letter to the churches of the Roman province of Asia, it was also addressed to the whole Church.[4]

The language of the Apocalypse, a Greek more Hebrew than the Greek of the Septuagint and as poor as it is careless, has always been disconcerting because of its oddities and its lack of correctness. Comparison with the Gospel and the Letters of St. John suggest the theory that it was written down by a secretary who did no more than hold the pen. For, although the writer was not an artist, his inspiration was powerful enough to create a masterpiece. A sumptuous, dizzying masterpiece. Images abound in it, to the extent of overburdening it; not only are they piled on top of one another, but their very number seems to be a means of attracting attention (cf., for example, Apoc. 11:7-10). In spite of this, the Apocalypse is a fine piece of work, written with firm broad strokes and in powerful pictures. It is filled with emotion and has infinite prophetic lyricism.

Because of the constant symbolism of the language, at first sight the book seems terribly enigmatic and disconcerting. In reality, however, the matter expressed comes almost solely from the Scriptures. The Apocalypse is, therefore, the crossroads of all the books

[4] Perhaps the book is the result of combining two writings that were at first distinct: the letter or letters to the Churches (cf. Apoc. 2-3) and the Apocalypse properly speaking. Some think, in addition, that this was the result of the fusion of two apocalypses, which were originally separate and composed at different dates. If the work were as complex as this, it would contain elements that may be earlier than the year 70 A.D., and others from twenty-five years later. It is difficult to decide. It seems, however, that the reasons postulating the unity of the composition are stronger.

of the Bible.[5] The Apocalypse is a kind of test for the reader; it shows him where he is in his knowledge of the Bible and provides him with a stimulus for studying it. The mysterious prophecy of John becomes amazingly more simple as the reader accustoms himself to the symbols running through the Scriptures, to the language of the Prophets (especially Isaias, Ezechiel, Daniel, Zacharias, and Joel), and to the trend of biblical eschatology.

The Prophets had often announced the "Day of Yahweh," the Coming of the Lord at times of crisis in history, or during plagues and other calamities. They foretold the loosing of hostile forces, and also their sudden defeat and the advent of an era of peace and of happiness for the People of God. John picks up this theme, adding to it the new concept of Christ who has come (cf. Apoc. 1:4), who alone has been given the power to open the sealed book of history (cf. Apoc. 5). The last of the Prophets evokes and interprets known events, similar to those that are to come. He sees in these misfortunes not only the punishments of God and the exhortations to conversion, but also the salvation which is effected for the elect of God. The tribulations (cf. Apoc. 6; 8-9; 15-16), which should lead men to repent (cf. Apoc. 9:20-21; 16:9-11), are a prelude to the destruction of the satanic powers that oppose Christ (cf. Apoc. 17-18; 20). At the same time, the people who have been bought by the Blood of Jesus grow, reign and sing to the Lord (cf. Apoc. 7; 15). The Church is on trial, but is divinely protected (cf. Apoc. 12) and advances toward its perfect state, its definitive union with its Lord (cf. Apoc. 21-22).

The vision of John is in the present. Christ is in the midst of the communities; he "walks" in the Church (Apoc. 1:13, 20; 2:1); the Christians form a "priestly kingdom" and reign "on earth" (Apoc. 1:6; 5:10); together they attack the "beast" and he is crushed—the Church suffers and triumphs. In "the things that are" are the "things that are to come hereafter" (Apoc. 1:19). The Kingdom of God is already here and it is to come; it is being formed—this is certain. To his disciples who were rejoicing at having cast out demons, Jesus said: "I was watching Satan fall as lightning from heaven. Behold, I have given you power . . . over all the might

[5] Each of its verses contains one or more allusions to the sacred books. From 500 to 1000 biblical references can be counted in its 406 verses.

of the enemy; and nothing shall hurt you" (Luke 10:18-19). He said also: "The hour has come for the Son of Man to be glorified. . . . Now is the judgment of the world; now will the prince of the world be cast out" (John 12:23, 31). John taught the same thing: "Antichrist . . . now is already in the world. . . . You are of God . . . and have overcome him" (I John 4:3-4).

The last two chapters of the Apocalypse bring the book to a magnificent close. In terms which are simultaneously those of Genesis and Exodus, of Isaias and Ezechiel, of Osee and the Canticle of Canticles, of the First Letter to the Corinthians and the Letter to the Ephesians, John describes the marriage of Christ to the Church, and the fulfillment of the whole Plan of God in history. A New Jerusalem is born, a new heaven, a new earth, a new people!

The Apocalypse is thus the Gospel of the "last days," the book of the great calm after the terrible storm, the message of unfailing faith in a victorious Christ and in the firm hope of Christians.

The last page of the Apocalypse closes the Book of the Scriptures with a song concerning the divine Covenant, which has been the Bible's essential, constant, and vital subject. The song, in the form of a dialogue, is turned toward the future but is forever present. The Lord, already present, still announces his imminent coming: "It is true, I come quickly!" And the Church waits for him and calls him: "Amen! Come, Lord Jesus!" (Apoc. 22:20). The dialogue, which has been responsible for the biblical tradition, will continue; it will go on in history, directing history toward its fulfillment in Charity.

INDEX

A

Aaron, 205
  mutiny of, 104
Abdias, Book of, 188
Abiathar, 144 (n. 3)
Abimelech, 76 (n. 1)
Abraham, 4, 6, 10 (n. 15), 13 (n. 5), 14, 42, 44, 46, 48, 96, 99, 101, 103-4, 235 (n. 6), 337-38, 349 (n. 3), 356
Absalom, 80
Accko, plain of, 33
Achab, king of Israel, 92, 96 (n. 9), 97
Achaeans, the, 3
Achaemenians, the, 155-56, 181
Achaia, 303, 307
Achaz, king of Juda, 112, 113 (n. 8), 114, 135
Achior, the Ammonite, 240
Actium, 257
Acts of the Apostles, the, 296 (n. 1), 300, 314 (n. 1), 345, 349-54
Adadinari III, 108 (n. 2)
Adam, 206, 235 (n. 6)
  life of, and Eve, 234
Adonis, 23, 251
Aegea, 68
Aegean Sea, 304
Aelia Capitolina, 313
Aeschylus, 187
Agape, the, 360
Aggadoth, 283
Aggeus, 175, 179 (n. 1), 182
  Book of, 182
Agrippina, 253-54
Agrippina the younger, 254-55
Ahias, 118
Ahikar, 200-201 (n. 9)
Ahmosis, 14, 49
Ahriman, *see* Angro-Mainyush
Ahura-Mazda, 155-56, 190 (n. 5)
Akhetaton, 50 (n. 2)
Akhnaton, 49-50
Akiba ben Joseph, 270
Akkad, 3-4
Akkadians, 2
Albinus, 309
Alcimus, 225
Alexander Balas, 225
Alexander Jannaeus, 227-28, 235 (n. 7), 267
Alexander the Great, 188, 211-12, 214, 216-17, 235 (n. 7), 251
Alexandra, 228, 258, 269
Alexandria, 161, 211, 213, 217-18, 242, 298, 303
  antisemitism at, 263-64
  Jews of, 241, 260, 310
Aleyin, 22
Amalekites, 68
Amasias, king of Juda, 98
Amasis, 153
Amenemhats, the, 13
Amenophis II or III, 56
Amenophis IV, 50
Ammon, 57
Ammonites, 68, 79
Amon, 50, 51 (n. 5), 93-94, 136
Amon-Ra, 16
Amorites, 6, 41 (n. 1), 107
Amos, the Prophet, 61 (n. 10), 83 (n. 13), 85, 108 (n. 1), 109, 111, 113, 116, 118, 124, 144, 198, 234
Amri, king of Israel, 92
Anatolia, 362
Anatoth, 144 (n. 3)

Anaw, anawim, 185-86, 210, 279
Anawah, 186 (n. 7), 203
Anaxagoras, 187
Anaximander, 154
Anaximenes, 154
Angro-Mainyush, 156
Anna, 278
Annas, 260, 287
Annius Rufus, 260
"Anointed One," 122
Anthological style, 196, 198
Anthropomorphism, 102 (n. 3)
Antichrist, 355, 361, 365
Antigonus, 216, 229
Antioch, 216, 257, 298, 329
  the Church at, 299-300, 302, 304
  of Pisidia, 300
Antiochians, 217
Antioch-on-the-Orontes, 213
Antiochus III, the Great, 222
Antiochus IV Epiphanes, 223-25, 230, 235 (n. 7), 238
Antiochus V, 225
Antiochus VI, 226
Antiochus VII, 226
Antipater, 228-29, 257
Antisemitism, 263-64
Antonia, the, 311
Antonines, the, 250, 256-57
Antonius Pius, 313
Antony, 229, 257
Anzan, 157
Aphrodite, 251
  Temple of, 313
Apocalypse, 233 (n. 1)
Apocalypse of St. John, 166 (n. 10), 189 (n. 3), 233, 356-59, 361, 363-65
Apocalyptic literature, 166, 183, 189, 198, 233-39, 242, 264, 276, 285, 313, 333, 356-57, 363
  characters in, 235 (nn. 6-7)
  fundamental theme of, 237
  style of, 234-37
  symbols in, 235 (n. 10), 236
Apocrypha, 235 (n. 8)
Apollonius, 225
Apollos, 303
Apologetics, literature of, 241-42, 264
Apophis, 27 (n. 22)
Apostles, the, 321
  preaching of, 322-23
Apries, Pharaoh, 149, 153
Aqabah, Gulf of, 84 (n. 16), 126 (n. 5)
Arabah, 65, 188 (n. 2)
Arabia, 81, 112
  Nabatean, 228, 267, 299
Arabs, 192 (n. 6), 259
  Nabatean, 259
  Nabayot, 188 (n. 2)
Aram, 194
Aramaic, 194, 201 (n. 11), 206 (n. 3), 212-13, 217, 283, 290, 324-25
Arameans, 6 (n. 9), 41 (n. 1), 51, 79, 91, 108, 132
Arbela, 211
Archelaus, 259-60, 275
Aretas IV, 259
Aristobulus, 215, 227
Aristobulus II, 228-29
Aristotle, 187, 214
Ark of the Covenant, 72, 79, 100 (n. 2)
Armenia, 225
Arnon, the, 35
Artaxerxes, 187, 190-91
Artaxerxes II, 188, 211
Artaxerxes III, 211
Arwad, 3
Asarhaddon, 131-32
Asia, 155, 157, 303, 361, 363
Asia Minor, 95, 132, 134, 154, 157, 187, 222, 262, 280 (n. 2), 300, 302, 304, 307, 336-37, 340-41, 357
"Asmodeus," the, 156 (n. 5)
Asphaltite Lake, the, 35
Assur, 114, 131, 134
Assurbanipal, 132-33
Assuretililani, 133
Assurnasirpal, 92
Assuruballit, 134
Assyria, 51, 91-92, 94, 108, 110, 112-13, 135, 145, 161, 194, 216
  history of, in seventh century B.C., 131-34
  terror of the Near East, 93
Assyrians, 2, 49, 51, 67, 95, 133-34
Astarte, 39, 97 (n. 13)
Astyages, 157

Aswan, 160
Atargatis, 251
Athalia, queen of Juda, 92, 96 (n. 9), 98
Athens, 154, 187-88, 213, 248, 303, 329
Aton, 49, 51 (n. 5)
Atonement, Feast of the, 280
Attic dialect, 212-13
Attica, 154
Attis, 251
Atum, the Air, 22
Augustus, 221, 227 (n. 5), 246, 250-51, 253, 257-60
Avaris, 14
Azarias (Ozias), king of Juda, 108

B

Baal, 23-24, 39 (n. 24), 41 (n. 30), 72 (n. 15), 97 (n. 13), 119, 141
Baalism, 83, 96, 98, 102, 105
Babylon, 4, 51, 67, 131-33, 135, 147-49, 150, 157-58, 161-62, 167, 171-72, 177 (n. 9), 189, 191-92, 211, 221, 283
Babylonia, 1, 5, 84 (n. 17), 114, 159, 179, 190, 209, 216
Babylonian Chronicles, 133 (n. 4)
Babylonians, 2, 49, 95, 134-35, 162
Bacchides, 225
Bagoar, 205
Balaam, 104
Balthazar, *see* Belsharusur
"Bank of Murashu and Son," 162 (n. 4)
Baptism, 296-97, 314, 338, 359
Bar-Koseba, 257, 313
Barnabas, 299-300
Baruch, 118 (n. 5), 147, 220
  Apocalypse (Greek) of, 234
  Apocalypse (Syriac) of, 234
Beatitudes, the, 348
Beersheba, 45
Beirut, *see* Beruta
Bel, 238
Belsharusur, 157-58
Benedictions, the, 280
Ben-Hadad II, 92
Benjamin, 78, 79 (n. 7)
ben Sirach, 51 (n. 5), 219-20, 244, 268, 281
  Wisdom of, the, 218, 219 (n. 6), 360
Berith, the, 47, 60
Beroea, 303
Beruta (Beirut), 3
Bethel, 45, 57, 83, 100, 109
Bethulia, 240 (n. 13)
Bezatha, paralytic of, 359
Bible, the, 117, 138, 156 (n. 5), 159 (n. 1), 164, 171, 192, 197 (n. 5), 202, 279, 283, 331, 344, 350, 364-65
  canon of, 236, 240, 312, 358
  Greek, 218, 240, 350
  Semitic temperament and heredity of, 32
Bishops, 320; *see also* Presbyters
"Blessing of Jacob," 75
"Book of Comfort of Israel," 167, 169; *see also* Deutero-Isaias
"Book of the Just," 75
"Book of the Law of Moses," 192
Book of the War of the Sons of Light and the Sons of Darkness, 234
"Book of the Wars of the Lord," 75
Boule, the, 246
Britain, 256
Britannicus, 254-55
British Isles, 245
British Museum, 93 (n. 2), 133 (n. 5)
Bucolics, Fourth Book of the, 242 (n. 15)
Buddha, 155
Buddhism, 155
"Burning bush," 58 (n. 1)
Byblos, 3
Byzantium, 154

C

Cades, 64, 176
Caesar, 229, 305, 354, 362
Caesarea, 260, 267, 298, 305, 309-10, 325 (n. 4)
Caesars, the, 250
Caiaphas, 260, 287
Caius, 362
Caligula, 250, 254, 256, 259-61, 265

Cambyses, 158, 181
Canaan, 33-41
geography of, 33-37
Israelite occupation of, 67-71, 140
language of, 38-39
people of, 37-38
the promised land, 65
religion of, 39-41
Canaanites, 3, 13, 38-39, 41, 67, 71, 76, 107, 135
Canticle of Canticles, 51 (n. 5), 199, 201-2, 281, 365
"Canticle of Debora," 75
Canticle to charity, 315
Capri, 254
Carchemish, 134-35, 146 (n. 6), 147
Carmel, 33-34, 97 (n. 13), 98 (n. 16), 142 (n. 12)
Carthage, 95, 221
Caspian Sea, 133
Cassander, 216
Catechesis, 320, 324, 326, 339, 342, 346
Catiline, conspiracy of, 229
Cato, 221
Cedron, the, 79 (n. 7), 114 (n. 13)
Cephren, 13
Cestius Gallus, 310
Chaeronea, 211
Chalcis, 310
Charisms, 319
Cheops, 13
Chief priests, the, 265
China, 155
Chosen People, the, 60, 78-79, 129, 168-69, 198, 231, 240, 284, 306, 344, 349; *see also* People of God
Christianity, 241, 253-54, 270, 277-79, 298, 301, 303 (n. 8), 304, 307, 315-16, 319, 333, 337, 340, 342-43, 349, 352, 354, 357
Christians, the, 264 (n. 5), 296-300, 304-7, 309, 314-19, 323, 332, 334-35, 339, 341-44, 354-56, 358, 360-65
Gentile, 301
love of first, 318
prayer of, 316-17
Chronicler, the, 206-7
Chronicles, Book of, *see* Paralipomenon, Books of
Church, the, 293, 295-307, 314, 318-20, 327-30, 333, 337-42, 344, 348-49, 353, 360-61, 364-65
at Antioch, 299-300, 302
in the apostolic era, 354-65
of Jerusalem, 299, 301, 304-5, 337
Cicero, 154 (n. 2), 249, 280 (n. 2)
Cilicia, 302
Cimbrians, the, 221
Circumcision, 48, 224, 227, 263, 300-302, 313, 336
Citizen, the, 246-47
Claudius, 250, 254-55, 261, 354
Clement of Alexandria, 357 (n. 2)
Cleopatra, 229, 257
Clisthenes, 154
Cnossos, 4
Coele-Syria, 216, 224
Colossae, 304-5, 340
Colossians, the, 340
Letter to, 340-41
Commandment, a new, 292
Commandments, the, 139, 360
Communities, Christian, 318-20, 323, 332, 334-37, 339-42, 355, 362, 364
ministries of, 320
Community, Jewish, 263, 265-78, 312, 355
Essenes in, 274-77
Scribes, Pharisees, and Sadducees in, 268-74, 277
the poor in, 277-78
Zealots in, 271-72
Confucius, 155
Conversion, 314-16, 364
of Jews, 315-16, 356
of non-Jews, 316
Coponius, 260
Corbulon, 255
Corinth, 303-4, 318-19, 329, 332, 334-37
community of, 334-35
Congress of, 187
letters to Christians of, 303
Corinthians, 318, 335
First Epistle to the, 335, 365
Second Epistle to the, 335-36
Cornelius, 298

Covenant, the, 60-62, 64, 72, 96, 110 (n. 6), 121, 138-40, 144, 168, 177, 190-91, 193, 207, 225, 284, 301, 315, 356, 360-61, 365
  Book of, 137
  interchange of love, 60, 139
  new, 164, 276, 320, 344
    community of the, 226
Covenant Code, the, 74, 104, 174
Covenants, 47-48
Crassus, 221, 229
Crete, 3
Crimea, the, 134
Croesus, 154, 157
Crucifixion, the, 294-95
Cumanus, 309
Cuneiform writing, 2 (n. 3), 19, 50 (n. 2), 133 (n. 6), 194
Cuspius Fadus, 261, 309
Cyaxaras, 134
Cybele, 251
Cyclades, 3
Cynics, the, 214
Cyprus, 3, 298, 300
Cyrenaica, 307, 313
Cyrus, 153, 157-59, 167, 179, 181-82, 187 (n. 1), 194

D

Dacians, the, 256
Damascus, 81, 91-92, 96 (n. 8), 110, 112, 188, 226, 274-75, 298-99, 301
Dan, 83
Daniel, 118 (n. 5), 162 (n. 5), 210 (n. 7), 235 (n. 6), 237, 364
  Book of, 233, 236-39, 240-41, 292
Danites, 84 (n. 16)
Danube, the, 181
Darash, 200
Darius, 181-82, 186, 188, 194, 243
Darius III, 211
David, King, 78-80, 85, 88-89, 92, 122, 129, 141, 192 (n. 7), 199, 206-7, 230, 276, 288
  creator of Israelite State, 79
  initiator of the Psalter, 87
  Memoirs of, 86, 140
  second lawgiver after Moses, 207
  Son of, 112, 349 (n. 3)
Deacons, 319-20
Dead Sea, the, 34-35, 65, 97 (n. 15), 188 (n. 2), 201 (n. 11), 226 (n. 4), 275, 287-88
Dead Sea Scrolls, 274
Decalogue, 58 (n. 3), 64, 104, 284
Decapolis, 267
Dedication, Feast of, 280
Delta, the, 57, 68, 93, 132-33, 161, 212
Deluge, the, 11
Demetrius, missionary, 362
Demetrius Poliorcetes, 216
Demetrius II, 226
Demetrius III, 228
Derbe, 300
Deuterocanonical Books, 218
Deutero-Isaias, 155, 164, 167-70, 175, 182-83, 189, 196, 201, 342
  "suffering Servant" of, 294
"Deuteronomic," 55 (n. 19), 68, 70 (n. 11), 87 (n. 7), 98 (n. 16), 113 (n. 10), 128, 137-38, 141, 143, 177, 200, 206
Deuteronomy, Book of, 58 (n. 3), 63, 125 (n. 1), 138-40, 142-44, 149, 170, 174, 185, 190, 202, 206, 207 (n. 5), 360
  reveals love of God for his people, 139
  style of, 138
Deutero-Zacharias, 198
Diadochi, 216
Dialogue, 62
Diana, temple of, 303
Diaspora, the, 179, 208-10, 217, 220, 232, 241, 262, 264-65, 281, 298, 300, 312-13, 339
Didascali, 268
Dionysus, 251
Diotrephes, 362
Divination, 6, 9, 29-30
"Doctor of Justice," the, 276
Doctors of the Law, 265, 293; *see also* Scribes
Domitian, 250, 256-57, 354 (n. 1), 362-63
Dorians, 4, 68
"Doublets," 62 (n. 11), 107
Draco, 154

Dragon, the, 238
Dravidians, 3
Drusilla, 254
Dummuzi or Tammuz, 23

E

"E" texts, 99-100, 105; *see also* "Elohist" texts
"Earthly Paradise," the, 101
Ebionism, 307
Ecbatana, 211
Ecclesia, the, 246, 293, 340 (n. 6)
Ecclesiastes, Book of, 203-4, 219 (n. 6)
Ecclesiasticus, Book of, 199, 219
Edom, 57, 167, 188
Edomites, 43 (n. 6), 68, 126 (n. 5), 159, 188, 192 (n. 6)
Egypt, 3, 12, 42, 56, 84 (n. 17), 93-94, 103-4, 108, 110, 112, 132, 146-48, 151, 158, 160, 172, 176, 181, 187, 190, 209, 211, 216-17, 221, 223-24, 229, 231, 241, 243, 248-49, 251, 257, 262, 274, 307
  Alexandrine, 215
  Ancient Empire of, 12-13
  "archaic period" of, 12, 62
  art and architecture of, 15
  literature of, 17-18, 51
  Middle Empire of, 13-14
  New Empire of, 49, 67
  religion of, 16-17
Egyptianism, 88
Egyptians, the, 241, 316
El, 39 (nn. 21-22)
Elam, 132
El-Amarna, 56
Elath, 126 (n. 5)
Elders, 209, 265
  Council of, 222
Elea, 154
Eleazar, 311
Elephantine, Island of, 160-61
Elias, 83 (n. 13), 85, 87, 96-98, 118, 140, 142 (n. 12)
  Geste of, and Eliseus, 141
Eliezer, 118
Eliseus, 85, 87, 97-98, 118, 140
  Geste of Elias and, 141
Elizabeth, 278
Elohim, 99, 107
"Elohist," the, 99-100, 103-5, 121
  what we owe to, 103-4
"Elohist" texts, 52 (n. 9), 55 (n. 19), 100-101, 106, 125, 137, 172 (n. 4), 177, 200; *see also* "E" texts
"El-Shaddai," 46
El-Yam, 24
Emmanuel, 112
  Book of, 113 (n. 8)
Emmaus, 350
Emperor, cult of the, 246, 249-50, 362
Enoch, Book of, 233, 235 (n. 7), 237, 356
  Book of the Secrets of, 234
Enuma Elish, 10-11, 20 (n. 3), 24 (n. 16), 30 (n. 40), 133 (n. 6)
Ephebes, the, 247
Ephesians, Letter to the, 340-42, 365
Ephesus, 154, 303-5, 307, 329, 334-36, 357
Ephraim, 34, 56 (n. 19), 72, 79 (n. 7), 82
Ephraimites, 111
Epicureanism, 248
Epicureans, the, 214
"Epimanes," 223
Er-Raha, 58 (n. 1)
Eschatology, 197, 237, 240, 273, 285, 357, 364
Esdras, 162 (n. 5), 189 (n. 4), 190-93, 195, 235 (n. 6), 242
  Book of, 176 (n. 8), 179 (n. 1), 180 (n. 2), 192, 205, 206 (n. 3), 239
  Fourth Book of, 234, 235 (n. 7), 243
  Memoirs of, and of Nehemias, 192
  second founder of Judaism, 191
  Third Book of, 242-43
Esdrelon, 34
Essenes, the, 97 (n. 15), 233, 274-77, 279, 288, 292, 316, 355
  a Jewish religious order, 275-76
  doctrine of, 276
Esther, 210 (n. 7)
  Book of, 239-41
"Ethiopian dynasty," 132

Etruscans, the, 95, 153, 221
Eucharist, the, 318, 335, 359
Euphrates, the, 134, 161
Euripides, 187
Europe, 304
Eusebius, 325 (n. 4)
Euxine Sea, 154, 181
Eve, 235 (n. 6)
  Life of Adam and, 234
Exile, the, 101, 116, 123-24, 137-38, 142, 148, 160, 167, 169-71, 175, 185, 193, 200, 234, 283
  Israel in, 161-65
  Prophet of, 149, 169
  return from, 179-80
Exodus, the, 48, 55, 57, 58 (n. 2), 59, 82, 99, 264 (n. 6), 344
  new, 168, 175
Exodus, Book of, 52-53, 55, 62 (n. 11), 63, 101, 172, 174-76, 342 (n. 7), 365
  chronology of, 56-57
Ezechias, King, 94, 113 (n. 8), 114, 125-26, 129, 135-36, 141, 207
Ezechiel, 124, 149, 155, 164-67, 170, 173, 175-77, 183, 189-90, 198, 201, 207 (n. 5), 235 (n. 6), 236 (n. 11), 238, 240, 271, 279, 364-65
  Book of, 165, 174
    apocryphal, 234
  Levitism of, 182
  Torah of, 165

F

Feasts, Jewish, 280-81
Felix, 305, 309
Festus, 305, 309
Flavia Domitilla, 354 (n. 1)
Flavius Clemens, 354 (n. 1)
Flavius Josephus, 234 (n. 4), 274
Flood, the, 101, 102 (n. 6), 177
Forty Years, the, 65

G

Gabaon, 72
Gad, 118
Galatia, 336
Galatians, the, 302, 340
  Epistle to, 336-37
Galba, 255
Galgal, 69, 97 (n. 15)
Galileans, the, 268
Galilee, 34, 225, 228-29, 259, 267-68, 287, 289, 292, 294, 298, 310, 323, 347
  of the Gentiles, 262
  Lower, 288
  Upper, 228
Gallio, Proconsul, 303 (n. 8)
Garizim, 227
Gaul, 229, 307
Gaulonitis, 267
Gauls, the, 221
Gaza, 64 (n. 16), 112
Geb, the Earth, 22
Gedeon, 71 (n. 12), 73 (n. 18), 76 (n. 1)
Gehenna, the, 79 (n. 7)
Gelboe, 78
Genealogies, 176, 180, 192 (n. 6), 206, 349 (n. 3)
Genesis, Book of, 11, 42, 43 (n. 6), 44, 52, 101-2, 172, 176, 201, 205, 365
Genii, the, 249
Gennesareth, Lake of, 34, 36, 266, 289
Gentiles, the, 163, 285, 300-301, 337
  Apostle of, 302, 322
  Court of, 280
  gospel to, 301, 329
Germanicus, 253-54
Germans, the, 253
Germany, 255-57
Gerousia, the, 246
Gessius Florus, 310
Ghettoes, 262
Ghor, the 35-36, 42, 69 (n. 9)
Gibborim, the, 73 (n. 20)
Gihon, 114 (n. 13)
Gilgal, 72
Gilgamesh, 11, 20 (n. 5), 23, 102 (n. 6), 133 (n. 6)
Gizeh, 13 (n. 5)
"God-fearing," the, 263
Godolias, 150
"God-with-us," 122; *see also* Emmanuel

Gola, the, 164, 170-71, 190
Golden age, the, 237
Golden Calf, 104
Golgotha, 313
Good Samaritan, the, 350
Gorgias, 225
Gospel, the, 237 (n. 12), 270, 288, 295, 297-98, 302-3, 306-7, 317, 319-23, 326-27, 331, 335-36, 340, 344, 353, 365
  canonical, 324, 327-28, 349
  synoptic, 322, 324-26, 345-53
Goym, the, 264
Gracchi, the, 221
Grace, doctrine of, 338
Graeco-Roman world, 245-53, 257, 263, 303, 313
Grammate, 209 (n. 6), 268
Granicus, 211
"Great Mother," 251
Greece, 153-54, 187-88, 212, 215, 222, 229, 237, 242, 255, 304, 337; *see also* Hellas
Greek language, 212-14, 217-18, 231-32, 245, 297, 312, 325-26, 330, 339, 343, 346-47, 358, 363
"Greek miracle," 187
Greeks, the, 133, 187, 211-12, 214, 242, 316, 350
  colonial effort of, 95
Gudea, 4
Guti, 4
Gyges, 154

H

Habacuc, the Prophet, 146-47, 203
Habirou, the, 56
Hadad, 22
Hadrian, 257, 313
Halakhoth, 283
Hallel, the, 196
Hammurabi, 4-5
  Code of, 10 (n. 15)
Hanani, 118
Hananos, 309
Haran, 42, 134
Hasideans, the, 220, 222, 225, 227, 269, 273
Hasmon, 225 (n. 2)
Hasmoneans, the, 225, 230, 232, 239, 269, 272
Hassidim, 279
Hatshepsut, Queen, 49, 56
Hebrew language, 39, 84-85, 98, 124, 185, 193-94, 201 (n. 11), 203, 206 (n. 3), 217-18, 282
  "neo-Hebrew," 85 (n. 2)
  "palaeo-Hebrew," 85 (n. 2)
  sacred language of Israel, 194
Hebrews, the, 41, 51-52, 55-56, 58 (n. 1), 70, 84 (n. 16), 140, 171 (n. 1), 172, 208, 242
  Letter to, 343-45
Hebron, 42 (n. 3), 45, 64 (n. 16), 188
Helcias, 138
Heli of Silo, 144 (n. 3)
Heliodorus, 222-23
Hellas, 94-95, 187; *see also* Greece
Hellenism, 213, 215, 220, 224, 231-32, 245, 248, 269, 334
"Hellenists," 297-98, 319-20
Hellenization, 212, 215-16, 222, 245, 267
Hellenophiles, the, 227
Hellenophobia, 227
Henoch, 235 (n. 6)
Heraclitus, 154
Herculaneum, 362
Herihor, 93
Herod Agrippa I, 259, 261, 299, 309-10
  Agrippa II, 310
Herod Antipas, 259, 287
Herod Philip, 259
Herod the Great, 227 (n. 5), 229-30, 235 (n. 7), 257-59, 261, 267, 271-72, 275, 280
  seven sons of, 258 (n. 2)
Herodias, 259
Herodotus, 122 (n. 10), 187, 239
Hierapolis, 304, 325 (n. 4)
Hieroglyphics, 14-15, 19
High priests, the, 272, 294, 305, 310, 344
Hillels, the, 270
History of forms, 327
History of Salvation, 322, 338, 356, 359
Hittites, 5, 38, 49, 51

Holda, 118, 143 (n. 1)
Holy Spirit, the, 297, 314-15, 319-20, 322, 333, 335, 351, 353, 360-61; *see also* Spirit of God
Honestiores, the, 248
Horeb, 107
Horites, 5, 38 (n. 18)
Horus, 22
Humbaba, 23
Humiliores, the, 248
Hyksos, the, 14, 43, 49, 56
Hyperbolic language, 27-28, 120 (n. 8)
Hyrcanus, John, 226-27, 267
Hyrcanus II, 228-29, 230, 257

I

Iconium, 300
Idumea, 188, 225-26, 228, 259, 261
Idumeans, the, 267
Incarnation, the, 361
India, 155, 158, 181
Indies, the, 245
Indus, the, 211
"Instructions of Amenemhat," 17
Ionic dialect, 213
Iran, 181
Iranians, the, 155
Iranism, 276
Irenaeus of Lyon, 357 (n. 2)
Isaac, 101
Isaias, the Prophet, 85, 109 (n. 4), 111-16, 118 (n. 5), 124, 132, 135, 136 (n. 2), 144, 166-67, 183, 201-2, 235 (n. 6), 344, 364-65; *see also* Deutero-Isaias, Trito-Isaias
  Apocalpyse of, 189
  ascension of, 234
Ishmaelites, 43 (n. 6)
Ishtar, 39 (n. 25), 131, 158
Isis, 251
Ismael, 150
Ismael ben Elisee, 270
Israel, 26, 41 (n. 30), 44-46, 48, 51, 56 (n. 19), 58-60, 63, 85 (n. 3), 88, 97, 102 (n. 4), 107, 115-17, 121, 123, 127-28, 135, 139-40, 142, 156, 163, 169, 170, 171 (n. 1), 173, 175-77, 179, 182, 184, 189, 191, 194, 196-97, 199, 200-202, 205-8, 210, 217-20, 232, 235, 239, 241-42, 244, 253, 268, 272-73, 277, 287-88, 290-91, 295, 300, 308, 312, 315-18, 330, 338, 349 (n. 2), 352
  a missionary, 217, 274
  exilic, 155, 161-65, 168
  in the Roman Empire, 257-66
  literature of, 84-88, 344
  songs of, 128-29
  the faith of, 278-86, 289, 296-97
  traditions of, 99
Israel, kingdom of, 82, 83 (n. 13), 89, 91-92, 98, 110-11, 125, 126 (n. 4), 140
  Annals of, 141
Israelites, 55, 57, 64, 76, 119, 125, 140, 150, 162-63, 171 (n. 1), 172, 179, 190, 192 (n. 6), 208-10, 215, 222, 232, 239-42, 262, 267, 280, 306, 308, 316
  dangers for, in Canaan, 71-72
"Israilou," 57
Issus, 211
Isthmic Games, 303
Italian peninsula, 95
Italy, 153, 229, 255-56, 307
Iturea, 267, 287

J

"J" texts, 99-100, 105; *see also* "Yahwist" texts
Jabbok, the, 35
Jacob, 42, 44, 48, 101, 107, 235 (n. 6)
Jacobites, 53, 57
Jaffa, 33
Jainism, Hindu, 155
James, head of Church of Jerusalem, 299, 301, 305, 307, 309, 315, 319, 339, 342, 344
  Letter of, 332 (n. 4), 338-39, 342, 356
James, son of Zebedee, 299
Jamnia, 312
  Synod of, 281, 312
Jason, high priest, 224
Jason, writer, 231

Jebusites, 79 (n. 7)
Jehu, king of Israel, 98, 118, 141
Jephtha, 73 (n. 18)
Jeremias, the Prophet, 124, 129, 136, 139, 143-51, 159, 162, 164, 167, 169-70, 185, 198, 201, 220-21, 344, 360
  Book of, 147 (n. 8), 150, 202
  Book of Consolation of, 145
  Lamentations of, 160, 170
  sorrows of, 144-46
Jericho, 35-36, 56, 69, 71, 266
Jeroboam, 82, 141
  "sin of," 83 (n. 13)
Jeroboam II, king of Israel, 108-9, 199
Jerusalem, 34, 79, 82, 83 (n. 13), 92, 100, 125-27, 129, 131, 136, 144, 146, 159-61, 167-68, 170, 176, 180, 182, 188, 190-91, 193, 195-96, 198, 201, 205, 209-10, 222, 224, 229, 241, 255-57, 260, 262, 265, 267-68, 276, 281, 289, 294, 298-301, 304-7, 313, 316, 319, 324-25, 329, 343, 345, 347, 351-53, 355
  clergy of, 79, 83-84
  destruction of, 235 (n. 7), 273, 308-12
  fall of, 141, 149-50
  functionaries in, 84
  liturgy of, 79, 83-84
  the Church of, 299, 301, 304-5
  the new, 184, 345, 365
Jesus Christ, 270-71, 274, 277-78, 287-98, 300-301, 303, 305-7, 314-23, 327, 329-30, 332-41, 343-44, 346-49, 351-56, 358-65
  crucifixion of, 294-95
  disciples of, 292-96, 299
  genealogy of, 349 (n. 3)
  miracles of, 289, 294, 323
  opponents of, 293-94
  preaching of, 288-92, 294, 358
  resurrection of, 295, 297, 314, 317, 321, 323, 348, 358
Jewish War, the, 275, 308-12, 343, 355
Jews, the, 171 (n. 1), 179, 191, 193, 201, 209-10, 214, 216-18, 223-24, 226, 238-39, 255-57, 258-67, 269, 273, 276, 278, 284-85, 291, 296-300, 302, 304-13, 336-37, 350, 354-56
  belief of, concerning God, 279-80
  conversion of, 315-16
  differences among, 267-68
  in Rome, 253-54
  privileges conceded to, 265
Jezebel, 96 (n. 9), 97
Jezrael, plain of, 34, 36, 71
Jina, 155
Joachaz, king of Israel, 98
Joachaz, son of Josias, 146
Joakin, 148-49
Joaqim, king of Juda, 146-48
Joas, king of Israel, 98
Joas, king of Juda, 98
Joatham, 75, 116
Job, 199, 202-3, 204 (n. 12), 219
  Book of, 196, 202-4
Joel, 197-98, 236, 240, 364
Johanan ben Zakkai, 270, 312
Johannine style, 358
John, Apostle and evangelist, 288, 307, 315-16, 323, 328, 357-65
  First Letter of St., 361
  Gospel of St., 357-61, 363
  Second Letter of St., 361
  Third Letter of St., 358, 362
John de Giscala, 310-11
John the Baptist, 97 (n. 15), 259, 277, 289, 314
  preaching of, 287-88, 323, 358
Jonas, 198 (n. 6)
  Book of, 198-99
Jonathan, 225-26, 227 (n. 6)
Joram, king of Israel, 98
Joram, king of Juda, 92, 96 (n. 9), 98
Jordan, the, 34-35, 42, 69 (n. 7), 97 (n. 15), 287, 311
Josaphat, king of Juda, 92
Joseph, 278
Joseph, son of Jacob, 14, 42, 44, 103-4
Josephus, 308, 310
Joshua, 55-57, 67, 69, 99, 180, 182, 230
  Book of, 38 (n. 19), 68, 70, 74, 121, 140, 353
Josias, king of Juda, 129, 134, 136-37,

Josias, king of Juda (*continued*) 141-42, 145-46, 148-49, 174, 207
Jotapata, 310
Jubilees, Book of, 233
Juda, 78, 79 (n. 7), 82, 83 (n. 13), 159-60, 180, 207, 225
Juda, kingdom of, 82, 89, 91-92, 98, 100, 113, 125, 126 (n. 4), 131 (n. 1), 135, 139-40, 146, 147 (n. 8), 161, 206
  Annals of, 141
Judaeo-Christians, the, 298-99, 304, 307, 326, 339, 347-48, 355-56
  Greek, 298
Judaeo-Hellenic teachings, 215
Judah, tribe of, 72
Judaism, 166, 170, 171 (n. 1), 189, 194-95, 204-5, 207, 216-17, 223, 242, 244, 253, 255, 260-64, 267-68, 271, 276, 278-79, 282-83, 295-98, 304, 307, 312-13, 315-16, 337, 340-42, 349, 352, 355
  converts to, 263
  Egyptian, 242
  Esdras, second founder of, 191
Judas, 224-25
Jude, 356-57
  Letter of St., 356-57
Judea, 34, 109, 188, 194, 204-5, 208, 210, 216, 222-24, 226, 228-29, 232, 255, 257, 259, 261-62, 265, 267, 271, 287, 298-300, 306-7, 309-10, 312, 318, 347, 354, 362
Judeans, 111, 144, 148, 159-60, 180, 188, 191, 226-27
Judges, 56, 73-74, 76, 86, 99, 199, 201, 230
  Book of, 70, 74, 121, 141, 199 (n. 7)
Judgment, 238
Judith, Book of, 239-41
Jupiter, 251
  Temple of, 312-13
Juvenal, 250

K

Kandalanu, 132-33
Karkar, 92
Karnak, 13 (n. 4)
Kassites, 5
Kerygma, 320
Ketubim, the, 199 (n. 7)
Khamsin, 36
Khorsabad, 113 (n. 9), 133 (n. 7)
Kingdom of God, the, 237, 270, 277, 288, 290-92, 321, 323, 364
Kings, Books of, 83 (n. 13), 87, 96 (n. 7), 97, 118, 121, 126, 141, 206, 207 (n. 5)
Kingu, 20
Koine, the, 213, 217

L

Lachish, 57, 188
Lagash, 4, 47 (n. 6)
Laodicea, 304
Lao-Tse, 155
Lares, the, 249
Latinization, 215
Latins, the, 95
Law, the, 208-9, 222, 226-27, 239-40, 269-71, 273-75, 291, 293, 297, 300, 302, 312, 315, 331, 338, 356
Lawyers, 126-27, 222, 268
Lazarus, 359
Lebanon, 34, 310
Lepidus, 229
Letter of Aristeus, 218 (n. 5), 242
Levi, 207
  Testament of, 233
Levites, 63, 73, 192, 207, 272-73
Leviticus, Book of, 63, 142, 172, 174-75, 360
  Torah of, 176
Light of the Gentiles, 122
Ligurians, the, 95
Literalism, 282
Liturgy, 129, 163, 169, 195, 209, 281
  Christian, 317
  Jewish, 196
Luke, 288, 302, 324-26, 343, 345-47, 349-53
  Gospel of St., 345, 350-53, 358
Luxor, 13 (n. 4)
Lycaonia, 300, 302
Lydda, 312
Lydia, 154, 158
Lysias, 225

Lysimachus, 216
Lystra, 300

M

Macedonia, 188, 211, 216, 221, 302, 304, 307, 332, 335-36, 341
Machabees, the, 224-25, 230, 262, 273
  Books of, 225 (n. 3), 230-32, 239
  First Book of, 230-31, 241
  Fourth Book of, 243
  Second Book of, 231-32, 241
  teachings on the dead, 232
  Third Book of, 241
Macpela, 42 (n. 3)
Madianites, 68
Magi, the, 156, 172 (n. 2)
Magic, 6, 9, 30, 362
Magnesium, 222
Mahavira, *see* Jina
Malachias, 175, 189-90
Malta, 305
Manahem, 110
Manasses, 94, 132 (n. 2), 135, 138, 142
Marathon, 187
Marcellus, 260
Marcus Ambivius, 260
Marduk, 5, 10-11, 20, 23, 158
Mariamne, 230, 257-58
Mark, 324-26, 345-46
  Gospel of St., 345-47, 350, 358
Marseilles, 154
Martyrs, the, 223, 354, 362
Marullus, 260
Mary, mother of Jesus, 278, 288, 294, 296
Mary, mutiny of, 104
"mashiah," 89
Massada, 310, 312
Mattathias, 224, 226, 230
Matthew, 324-26, 346-49, 359
  Aramaic, 325-26, 347
  canonical, 326
  Gospel of St., 345-50, 358
Mauretania, 245
"Maxims of Ptahotep," 17
Mazdaism, 155-56, 159
Medes, the, 133-34, 157
  Wars of the, and Persians, 181, 187
Media, 113, 157, 201
Mediterranean, the, 217, 261, 298, 352
Megarians, the, 154
Megiddo, 134, 146
Memphis, 12-13, 50 (n. 2), 132
Menelaus, 224
Menes, 12
Meradach-Baladan, 114, 131
Meshalim, 127, 184, 196, 219, 290, 360
Mesopotamia, 8, 51, 194, 221, 262, 313
  Lower, 5, 158, 161-62, 168
  Upper, 5, 188
Mesopotamians, ancient, 1-11
  art of, 6
  governmental system of, 6-7
  literature of, 9-11
  religion of, 7-9
  sciences of, 6
Messalina, 254
Messianic Kingdom, 238
Messianism, 89, 122, 156 (n. 5), 240, 273, 285, 309
Messias, the, 89, 112, 113 (n. 8), 115, 236, 292, 294-96, 300, 313, 322, 347, 349, 356, 358
  days of, 285
  Jewish notions of, 285
Michas, 71 (n. 12)
Micheas, the Prophet, 111, 114, 116, 118, 124 (n. 12)
Middle-Euphrates, 134
Midrash, midrashim, 200, 207, 283
Midrashic literature, 237-39, 244
Milesians, the, 154
Miletus, 154, 304
Minephtha, 57
Minoans, 4
Minos, 3
Miracles, 289, 294, 296-97, 321, 347-48
Mishna, the, 283
Mithridates, 228
Mizpa, city of, 150
Mizpah, sanctuary of, 72
Moab, 57, 65, 176
Moabites, 68, 79
Monarchy, Israelite idea of, 88-89
Monotheism, 59, 156, 159

Morality, Jewish, 284, 291, 315
Moses, 52 (n. 7), 53-56, 58 (n. 1), 60, 61 (n. 10), 62-65, 87, 104, 117 (n. 3), 121, 137-38, 140, 149, 164, 172, 177, 191, 223, 235 (n. 6), 276, 300, 322, 348, 356
Apocalypse of, 233-34
Assumption of, 234, 356
Canticle of, 170
lawgiver, 62
Mediator of the Covenant, 65
Mot, 22
Mount Athos, 187
Mt. Hermon, 34
Mount of Olives, 34 (n. 6)
Muratori, Canon of, 357 (n. 2)
Mycenean civilization, 4
Mycerinos, 13
"Mysteries," Eastern, 251-53
Mystical Body, doctrine of the, 330, 340-41
Myths, Oriental, 22-26

N

Nabateans, the, 188 (n. 2)
Nabonidus, 157-58, 166
Nabopolassar, 133-34
Nabu, 158
Nabucodonosor, 134-35, 147-50, 157, 180, 240 (n. 13)
successors of, 157
Nabuzardan, 150
Nahum, the Prophet, 131-32, 145-46
Naim, 350
Names, doctrine of, 30-31
Narmer, 12
Nathan, 89, 113 (n. 8), 118, 122, 196 (n. 3)
Nazarene, the, 296
Nazareth, 288, 299
Nazirites, the, 73
Near East, 209, 212-17, 226, 228-29, 238, 245, 249-50, 252-53, 256-57, 259, 262-63, 303, 306, 330, 337, 339, 341
Nechao, 134, 146, 148
Nefer-Rohu, 18
Negeb, 188
Nehemias, 162 (n. 5), 176 (n. 8), 179 (n. 1), 191-93, 195, 205, 242, 272
Book of, 192, 205, 239
Memoirs of Esdras and of, 192
Nero, 250, 254-56, 306, 309-11, 354-55, 362
Nerva, 257
New Testament, 277, 281, 306, 332, 339, 349, 353, 358
Nicanor, 225
Nicodemus, 359
Nile, the, 12, 132, 160
Nineve, 113 (n. 9), 131-34, 136, 145, 198 (n. 6)
Ninevites, the, 199
Nippur, 162 (n. 4)
Nirvana, 155
Noah, 235 (n. 6)
Nob, 72
Nomadism, 44, 81
Nubia, 13-14, 132
Nubians, the, 160
Numbers, Book of, 62 (n. 11), 63, 65, 101, 104, 172, 175-76, 205
Numbers, symbolism of, 31
Numidia, 221
Nut, the Sky, 22

O

Ochozias, king of Israel, 98
Ochozias, king of Juda, 98
Octavius, 229, 245, 257
Old Testament, 243, 333, 338-39, 342, 344, 349-50, 356, 359, 360 (n. 3)
Onias III, 224
Ophel, 79 (n. 7)
Oriental views on: the activity of men, 28; the nature of man, 28-29; the universe, 27-28
Origen, 343
Ormazd, *see* Ahura-Mazda
Orphism, 251
Oscae, the, 95
Osee, King, 112-13
Osee, the Prophet, 61 (n. 9), 83 (n. 13), 108 (n. 1), 110-11, 113, 116, 124, 139, 144-45, 201, 360, 365
Osiris, 16, 22, 251
Otho, 255

Othoniel, 71 (n. 11)
Ozias, *see* Azarias

P

"P" texts, 172 (nn. 3-4), 173 (n. 5), 206-7
Paideia, the, 247
Palestine, 1 (n. 2), 14, 19, 33 (n. 1), 34-38, 42, 50, 52, 57, 68 (n. 2), 92-93, 95, 104, 134-35, 140, 148, 165, 179, 180, 188, 194, 204, 208, 211, 213, 216, 218, 221, 228-29, 231-32, 241, 256-58, 260-62, 264, 267, 274, 281, 283, 306, 310, 313, 325-26, 337
  a farming community, 266
  in the prophetic era, 108-15
  religious center of the Jews, 261
Palestinians, the, 267, 322
Pamphylia, 300
Panion, 222
Papias, 325 (n. 4)
Papyrus of Leyde, hymn from, 17 (n. 12)
Parables, the, 290, 348, 350
Paraclete, the, 360
Paralipomenon, Books of, 79 (n. 8), 180 (n. 2), 192, 205-8
Parallelism, 345, 348, 360
Parmenides, 154
Parousia, the, 333
Parthians, the, 229, 255, 362
Pasch, the, 176, 183, 280, 311
"Passage of the Red Sea," 55
Passover, 54
Patriarchs, the, 99, 200-201, 207, 235
  history of, 41-45, 58 (n. 2)
  religion of, 45-48
Paul, St., 146, 286, 296 (n. 1), 299-307, 316-20, 326-27, 328-45, 352-54, 357-58, 360 (n. 3), 362
  first theologian of the Church, 329-30, 338, 340, 342, 355
  journeys of, 299-300, 302-6, 328, 349
  letters of, 314 (n. 1), 315, 322, 328, 330-42, 352-53, 355, 357
    pastoral, 340-42
Paul, St. (*continued*)
  literary genius of, 330-31
  mission of, 329, 338
  personality of, 328-29
"Pelishti," 68
Pella, 213, 307
Peloponnesian War, 188
Peloponnesus, 4
Pelusium, 229
Penates, the, 249
Pentateuch, the, 10 (n. 15), 63, 74-75, 105, 107, 177-78, 227 (n. 5), 359
  Greek, 218
Pentecost, 280, 321
People of God, 59-60, 76, 80, 88, 99, 102, 105, 115-16, 121-22, 125, 127, 129, 136, 141, 164-66, 171, 174-75, 183, 195, 199-200, 207, 220, 231, 239, 270, 273, 279, 282, 284, 301, 308, 327, 344, 364; *see also* Chosen People, the
  soul of, revealed in psalms, 196
Pepi I, 13
Perea, 228, 259, 267, 311
Perge, 300
Pericles, 187
Persecution of Christians, 257, 342
  first great, under Nero, 255, 306, 354, 362
  of Jerusalem, 261
  under Domitian, 256-57
Persepolis, 211
Persia, 211, 239
Persian Empire, 209
Persians, the, 155, 157, 180, 187-88, 211, 239
  Wars of the Medes and, 181, 187
Peter, St., 296-99, 301-2, 306, 315, 319, 326, 342-43, 345-46, 353, 355-57
  First Letter of, 342-43
  preaching of, 322, 324-25
  Second Letter of, 357
Petra, 188 (n. 2)
Petronius, 261
Pharisaism, 269-70
Pharisees, the, 227-28, 240, 258, 261, 266, 279, 286, 291, 293, 296, 308, 310, 312, 316, 355

Pharisees, the (*continued*)
in Jewish community, 268-75, 277
Pharsalus, 229
Phasael, 229
Phidias, 187
Philemon, Letter to, 339
Philip, 259, 287
Philip II, 188, 211
Philippi, 302, 336
Philippians, the, 336
Epistle to, 336
Philistia, 225
Philistines, 67, 74, 76, 78, 79 (n. 6), 159
Philo, 215, 234 (n. 4), 242, 274
Philosophy, 154, 214-15
Phocaeans, the, 154
Phoenicia, 92, 95, 135
Phoenicians, 3, 84 (n. 16), 154
Phrygia, 216, 249
Pisistrates, 154
Piso, 253
"Plagues" of Egypt, 54
Plataea, 187
Plato, 187, 242
Plebeian Revolutions, the, 221
Pleroma, the, 340 (n. 6)
Pliny, 234 (n. 4), 257, 274
Pluto, 251
Pogroms, 264
Polis, 213
Polycletus, 187
Polytheism, 135, 155, 168
Pompeii, 362
Pompey, 221, 228-29, 240
Pontius Pilate, procurator, 260, 265, 287, 294, 354
Pontus, 221, 228
Poor, the, 185-86, 196, 197 (n. 4), 203, 208, 223, 277-78, 288, 295, 307, 334, 339, 342
Poppaea, 255
Presbyters, 320; *see also* Bishops
Priesthood, 176, 205, 219, 272-73, 275-76, 312, 344
Priests, 62, 72, 76, 127, 136-37, 142, 161-62, 165, 169, 172-75, 195, 205, 207 (n. 5), 209, 222, 224-25, 227 (n. 6), 268, 272, 275, 296, 310-11, 343
Priests (*continued*)
percentage of, in Jewish population, 272 (n. 4)
"Prince of Peace," 122
Procurator, 260-61, 271, 287, 294, 305, 309
Prodigal Son, the, 350
Promised Land, 69 (n. 8)
Joshua introduced Israel into, 69
Prophetism, 117-19, 122, 124
Prophets, 77, 80 (n. 10), 84, 93, 108-25, 127, 136-37, 142-43, 149, 160-64, 167, 171-73, 177, 179, 182, 185, 193-94, 197, 200, 202, 206, 208, 232, 234-35, 284, 289-90, 301, 305, 338, 359-60, 362, 364
Earlier, 96 (n. 7), 140, 206, 218, 230
false, 119, 361
literature of, 123-24
sons of, 97 (n. 15), 117
spokesmen of God, 119
the Twelve (minor), 198
vision of history of, 121-23
Writing, 118, 218
Proselytes, 217, 263
"Proto-Deuteronomy," the, 138
Proverbs, Book of, 87-88, 126-28, 170, 184-85, 196, 202, 204, 219, 342, 360
Psalms, the, 86, 89, 127 (n. 7), 129, 163, 169-70, 186, 195-97, 202, 204, 207, 220, 278, 280, 317, 339, 342, 360
Jeremian, 148
literature of the Poor of Yahweh, 196
Psalter, 195-96, 359
Psammeticus, 133-34, 160
Psammeticus II, 149
Pseudepigrapha, 235 (n. 8)
Ptolemais, 213
Ptolemies, the, 222-23
Ptolemy, 216
Ptolemy II, 217-18
Ptolemy V, 222
Punic Wars, the, 221
Purim, Feast of, 280
Pyrrhonists, the, 214

Pythagoras, 154, 242
Pythagorism, 276

Q

Qinah, 170
Qiriathyarim, 72
Qoheleth, *see* Ecclesiastes, Book of
Qumran, 201 (n. 11), 226 (n. 4), 234, 274-77, 279, 311, 316, 360 (n. 3)

R

Ra, 16, 27 (n. 22)
Rabbi, 269, 279-80, 282, 290, 312-13, 329-30, 348
Rabbinical literature, 282-84
Rains, the, in Palestine, 36 (n. 13)
Rameses, 57
Rameses II, 50-51
Rameses III, 68, 93
Rameses XII, 93
Rasin, 112
Ras-Safsafé, 58 (n. 1)
Razon, 81
Rechabites, 97 (n. 15), 120 (n. 6), 148
Redemption, 323, 330, 344, 356
Red Sea, 69 (n. 7)
"Remnant," the, 109 (n. 4), 115, 122, 137, 140, 161, 185
Resisters, the, 223
Resurrection of the body, 286, 335
Revelation, 48, 62 (n. 12), 76, 103, 151, 218, 263, 273, 282, 291, 302, 322, 330, 338, 344, 359, 361, 363
  Judaeo-Christian, 60
  of Sinai, 58, 61, 62 (n. 12), 110 (n. 6), 121, 242
Rhodes, 213
Roboam, 82, 94
Roman Empire, the, 245-57, 302
  army of, 246
  city of, 246-47
  Eastern cults in, 251-53
  education in, 247-48
  emperor worship in, 249-50
  Israel in, 257-66
  religion of, 264-65
Roman Empire, the (*continued*)
  slavery in, 247
  total number of Jews in, 262
Romans, the, 222, 225-26, 229, 231, 247-49, 256, 261, 271-73, 275, 307-8, 311, 316
  Letter to, 332 (n. 3), 337-40, 342
  religion of, 249
Rome, 95, 153, 221-22, 226, 228-29, 237, 245, 247-49, 257-60, 264-65, 278, 298, 303-6, 308-9, 312-13, 325-26, 329, 337, 339, 341, 345, 353-54, 362
  antisemitism at, 263-64
  burning of, 255, 354, 362
  governmental history of, in 1st century, 253-57
Ruth, Book of, 199

S

Sabbath, the, 192, 224, 263, 265, 270 (n. 3), 280-81, 313, 317, 323
"Sacerdotal," 52 (n. 9), 55 (n. 19), 87 (n. 7), 101, 107, 142, 166, 171, 173, 176-78, 183, 200, 206; *see also* "P" texts
  circle, 172
  writers, 73, 177
Sacerdotal Code, the, 172-73, 190, 192
Sacred Books, 163, 209, 218, 224, 269, 339
Sacred History, 103, 196, 220, 230, 342
Sacrifice, 281, 311-12, 335, 344, 348
  of the Canaanites, 40-41
Sadducees, the, 227-28, 265-66, 286, 293, 296, 355
  in Jewish community, 268, 273-74
Sadoc, 176 (n. 7), 205, 225, 227 (n. 6), 276
Sadocites, 206, 224-25
Sakhyamuni, *see* Buddha
Salamis, 187
Salmanasar I, 51
Salmanasar III, 92
Salmanasar V, 113
Salome, 259
Salt Sea, the, 35

Samaria, 34, 56 (n. 19), 82-83, 92, 100, 109, 112-13, 116, 125-26, 159, 162, 188, 205, 209, 227, 259, 261, 298
Samaritans, 159, 182, 191, 192 (n. 6), 227, 267
Samaritan woman, 359
Samnites, the, 221
Samos, 154
Samson, 71 (n. 13), 73 (n. 18), 74 (n. 24)
Samuel, 73 (n. 18), 76-77, 86, 118
 Books of, 86, 121, 141, 206
Sanhedrin, the, 222, 265-66, 294, 298
Saoshyant, 156
Sardanapal, 134 (n. 10)
Sardis, 154, 158
Sargon, the Elder, 4
Sargon II, 113
Satan, 364
Saul, King, 77-78, 86, 117, 141
Savior, the, 115, 122, 169, 285, 323, 344
Scribate, 2
Scribes, 84, 125-28, 161-62, 172, 184, 194, 209, 222, 225, 265, 283, 291, 312, 349
 characteristics of, 127-28
 in Jewish community, 268-69, 273
Scriptures, Sacred, 193-94, 200, 207-8, 217-18, 227 (n. 5), 238, 244, 276-77, 281-84, 288-89, 291, 297, 315, 317, 322, 342, 348, 357, 360, 363-65
 canon of, 233, 281-82
 Hebrew collection of, 232
Scythians, the, 134, 158
Sebaste, 227 (n. 5)
Sectaries, the, 234
Sedaqa, 227 (n. 6)
Sedecias, king of Juda, 149-50
Seianus, 254
Sela, 188 (n. 2)
Seleucia-on-the-Tigris, 213
Seleucids, the, 213, 216, 222, 225, 238, 264 (n. 5), 273
Seleucus, 216
Seleucus IV, 222-23
Semeias, 118
Semites, 1-3, 14, 21, 25 (n. 18), 37, 346-47, 358
Sennacherib, 114, 131
Septuagint, 218, 232, 317, 331, 352, 363
Septuagintism, 350
Serabit-el-Hadim, 56
Serapis, 251
Sermon on the Mount, 291, 346, 348
Seron, 225
Sesostrises, the, 13-14
Set I, 50
Seth, 22
Seven, the, 298, 319
Shabataka, 94
Shalom, 81 (n. 11)
Shamash, 23
Shamashumukim, 132
Shammais, the, 270
Sharon, plain of, 33
Shehonk I, 94
Sheol, 167, 198 (n. 6), 285
Shephelah, the, 33, 67, 79, 228
Shiloh, 72, 100 (n. 2)
Sibyl, 242
 Fifth Book of the, 234
 Fourth Book of the, 234
Sibylline Oracles, Third Book of the, 233, 235 (n. 7)
Sicarii, the, 272, 308-10
Sichem, 42, 45, 48 (n. 16), 69, 72 (n. 15), 92 (n. 1)
 Covenant with Yahweh at, 69-70
Siculi, the, 95
Sidon, 3, 96 (n. 9), 112
Siloe, 79 (n. 7), 114 (n. 13)
Simeon, 278
Simon, 226, 230
Simon bar Giora, 310-11
Sin, 158
Sinai, 48, 52, 55, 57, 58 (n. 2), 59-60, 62, 99, 102-4, 107, 138, 172, 176, 279, 345
Sinsharishkun, 133-34
Sinshumulishir, 133
Sion, 79, 209
Siracid, the, 218, 220; *see also* ben Sirach
Sisara, 71
Slavery, 247, 284

Slaves, 247, 250-51, 307, 313, 334
Smyrna, 304
Socrates, 187
Solomon, King, 77, 80-84, 87-89, 100 (n. 1), 126, 199
  Acts of, 141
  Chronicle of, 87, 140
  Psalms of, 240-41
  religious crisis in time of, 81-82
  social crisis in time of, 81
  Wisdom of, 243, 360
  works of, 81
Solon, 154
Song of Degrees, 196
"Song of the Vineyard," 111 (n. 7)
Songs of Ascent, 196
"Songs of the Servant of Yahweh," 169
Son of God, 294, 344, 358
"Son of Man," 237-38, 292, 347, 365
Sopher, 163 (n. 8), 209 (n. 6)
Sopherim, 268
Sophocles, 187
Sophonias, 136-37, 143 (n. 1), 185, 198, 234, 235 (n. 6)
  Apocalypse of, 234
Spain, 221, 229, 255, 304, 307, 337
Sparta, 94-95, 154, 187-88, 226
Spirit of God, 164, 208, 220, 270, 279, 282, 295, 307, 315, 327, 334, 338; *see also* Holy Spirit, the
Stephen, 298-99
Stoicism, 248
Stoics, the, 214, 248
Strategi, 229
Succoth (feast of Tabernacles), 63 (n. 13)
Suetonius, 254
Sulla, 221
Sulpicius Quirinus, 271
Sumer, 3-4, 19
Sumerians, 2-4
  language of, 2
  religion of, 2
Sun, the, 251
Sunday, 317
Susa, 157, 211
Susanna, 238
Synagogues, 209, 219 (n. 6), 263, 265, 281, 300, 312, 317, 320, 339
Synoptic problem, the, 324-26
Synoptics, the, 357-59
Syria, 67, 81, 91-92, 135, 209, 211, 216, 221, 228-29, 248, 253, 255, 259-62, 274, 302, 307, 310, 337
Syrians, the, 225
Syria-Palestine, 159
Syro-Ephraimite War, 112

T

Tabernacle, the, 175
Tabernacles, feast of, 180, 280; *see also* Succoth
Tacitus, 354
Taharqa, 94, 132
Talmud, the, 283
Tammuz, *see* Dummuzi
Taoism, 155
Tarbis, 134
Targum, the, 283
Tarquins, the, 153
Tarsus, 299
Tartary, Chinese, 158
Tell-el-Amarna, 50 (n. 2)
Temple of Jerusalem, the, 79 (n. 7), 80 (n. 10), 82-83, 111, 125, 129, 137, 142 (n. 12), 143, 145, 147, 150, 160-61, 164, 173, 175, 177, 190, 192, 194-95, 206-7, 209, 223-25, 227-28, 231, 256, 258, 261, 265, 267, 273, 296, 298, 305-6, 310, 313, 317, 343, 351
  destruction of, 311-12
  manifestation of faith of Israel in, 280-81
  rebuilding of, 179-83, 196 (n. 3)
Tentamon, 132
Tequoa, 109
Terah, 42
Tertullian, 357 (n. 2)
Testament of the Twelve Patriarchs, 233, 237 (n. 12)
Thales, 154
Thebes, 12-14, 16, 50, 93-94, 132, 188
Themistocles, 187
Theophany, 28, 58 (n. 1)
  the great, 104
Theophilus, 345, 349

Thessalonians, First Epistle to the, 332-33
Thessalonians, Second Epistle to the, 333
Thessalonica, 302-3, 332, 362
Thinis, 12
Thrace, 181, 216, 251
Thucydides, 187
Thutmosis III, 49, 56
Tiamat, 23
Tiberius, 250, 253-54, 259-60, 287, 354
Tiberius Alexander, 261, 309
Tiglath-Pileser I, 92
Tiglath-Pileser III, 108 (n. 2), 110, 112-13
Tigris, the, 131, 161
Timothy, 302, 319, 341
  First Letter to, 341-42
  Second Letter to, 341-42
Tirza, 92 (n. 1)
Titus, 235 (n. 7), 255-56, 311
Titus, disciple of St. Paul, 301, 319, 341
  Letter to, 341-42
Tobias, 199
  Book of, 156 (n. 5), 200-201, 210 (n. 8)
Torah, 44 (n. 9), 61, 138, 150, 176, 193
Torah, the, 30 (n. 38), 61, 62 (n. 12), 63, 87, 121, 125, 140, 142-43, 149, 171-73, 177, 183, 189, 190-92, 194, 208-9, 220, 227, 263, 266, 268-69, 273-74, 300, 313, 315, 344
  book of, 137
  new, 173-74
  of Holiness, 174
  of Sacrifices, 174
  of the Pure and of the Impure, 174
Toroth, 62, 72, 101, 103-4, 138, 205
Tosephta, the, 283
Tower of Babel, 101
Trachonitis, 287
Tradition, 269, 273, 282-83, 291, 293, 306, 312, 342, 344, 349, 353, 356-57, 359-60, 365
  evangelical, 321, 323-26, 345, 351, 358
Trajan, 257, 313, 357
Transeuphrates, Province of, 180, 188
Transjordania, 225, 228, 259, 266, 307
Trito-Isaias, 182-84, 196, 201
Trojan War, 68 (n. 3)
Turkestan, 158
Tutankhamon, 50 (n. 4)
Twelve Apostles, the, 296-99, 302, 306, 319-20, 342, 345, 349 (n. 2), 352, 354, 356-57
Twelve tribes, the, 72
Tyre, 3, 81, 95, 112-13, 154, 165, 211
Tyropaeum, the, 79 (n. 7)

U

Ugarit, 3, 19
Umbrians, the, 95, 221
Ur, 4-5, 42
Urarteans, 112

V

Valerius Flaccus, 280 (n. 2)
Valerius Gratus, 260
Venus, 39 (n. 25), 303
Vespasian, 250, 255-56, 310-12
Vesuvius, 362
Virgil, 242 (n. 15)
Vitellius, 255-56, 259
Vulgate, the, 243

W

"Warnings of the Sage Ipouver," 18
War of Judas Machabeus, 237
Wisdom, Book of, 243-44, 339
"Wisdom for Ka Gemni," 17
"Wisdom for Merikara," 17
"Wisdom of Ani," 17
Wise Men, the, 208, 210, 284-86, 290, 301, 305, 323, 344
Witnesses, 314, 319, 321, 326-27
Word, the, 297, 314, 319-22, 327, 344, 352, 360
Words, power of, 31

X

Xerxes, 187, 189

Y

Yahweh, 41 (n. 30), 43 (n. 4), 51 (n. 5), 59-62, 64, 70, 72, 77, 82-83, 96, 99, 107, 109-10, 116, 118, 125, 135, 141, 143-44, 158-60, 163-65, 173, 175-77, 179, 183-84, 189, 192, 195-96, 198-99, 201-2, 207 (n. 4), 209, 217, 223-24, 264, 281, 312-13, 315
    Day of, 136, 140, 151, 190, 197, 234, 364
    Servant of, 122, 147, 169
    Spirit of, 111
    the divine name, 59
    the one God, 59
Yahweh Sabaoth, 71, 208
Yahwism, 63, 73, 80 (n. 10), 81, 88, 98, 102, 117, 137, 156, 160, 163, 168, 180, 253, 315
"Yahwist," the, 99-105, 121
    fragments due to, 101
"Yahwist" texts, 52 (n. 9), 55 (n. 19), 100-101, 105-6, 125, 137, 172 (n. 4), 177, 200, 202; *see also* "J" texts
Yarmuq, the, 35
YHWH, 59 (n. 5)

Z

Zacharias, 118, 175, 179 (n. 1), 182-83, 198, 236, 364; *see also* Deutero-Zacharias
Zachary, 278, 287
Zagreus, 251
Zarathustra, 155, 159
Zealots, the, 271-72, 292, 308-9, 312, 316, 355
Zebedee, 299
Zeno, 154
Ziggurat, 9 (n. 14), 15 (n. 9)
Zoroaster, *see* Zarathustra
Zorobabel, 180, 182, 196 (n. 3)